REMEMBER THE DAYS
HISTORY FOR JUNIOR READERS

BOOK TWO:
MEDIEVAL DAYS

SECOND EDITION

by Rob and Julia Nalle

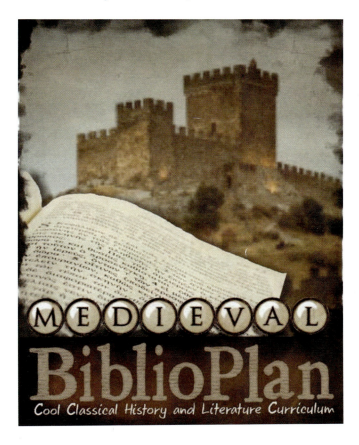

"Remember the days of old; consider the generations long past. Ask your father and he will tell you; your elders, and they will explain to you."

— *Deuteronomy 32:7*

"I remember the days of long ago; I meditate on all your works and consider what your hands have done. I spread out my hands to you; I thirst for you like a parched land."

— *Psalm 143:5-6*

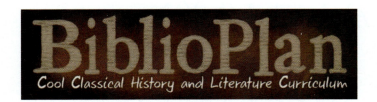

Copyright Policy

Please visit www.biblioplan.net to see how we may best serve your family, homeschool cooperative or Christian school. Or email contactus@biblioplan.net.

Welcome to BiblioPlan!

BiblioPlan is a classical history curriculum that covers World History, U.S. History, Church History, Geography and more, starting at Creation and continuing through modern times. Our program is divided into four years of study.

➢ **Year One, Ancients** covers Ancient and Biblical History from Creation to the Fall of Rome, with World Geography

➢ **Year Two, Medieval** covers World and Church History from the Fall of Rome to the Renaissance, with World Geography

➢ **Year Three, Early Modern** covers U.S., World and Church History from 1600 – 1850, with U.S. Geography

➢ **Year Four, Modern** covers U.S. and World History from 1850 – 2000, with Missionary Highlights and U.S. Geography

Remember the Days is BiblioPlan's four-volume textbook for grades K – 6. Each volume is divided into 34 weeks for a 34-week school year. The easiest way to follow our program is as follows:

1. Cover one chapter each week, spreading the material over three days.

   a. Grades K – 2: Read to your students, feeling free to paraphrase or skip whatever you choose.

   b. Grades 2 – 6: Younger students may need help reading; while older students may read independently. Either way, we recommend reading and discussing alongside your students to help them get the most out of every lesson.

2. Either throughout the week or at week's end, work on your assignments. All assignments for grades K – 2 come from a supplement called **Cool History for Littles**. History assignments for grades 2 – 6 come from a supplement called **Cool History for Middles**. Geography assignments for grades 2 – 6 come from a supplement called **Hands-On Maps for Middles**. All supplements are sold separately. Use your judgment to decide how much help your students need on any assignment.

Textbooks, Cool Histories and Hands-On Maps are only part of all that BiblioPlan has to offer! Another key resource is the **Family Guide**, which provides outside reading resources to go with each week's lessons. The Family Guide also offers writing assignments, video options and more.

Besides all these, BiblioPlan also offers:

❖ **Craft Books**: arts, crafts and activities to go with each week's lesson

❖ **Timelines**: flowcharts for students to assemble, filled with cutouts of important historical figures

❖ **Notebooking**: fun projects that help students research and record history and geography

❖ **Coloring Books**: simple sketches from history for younger students to color

To learn more, please visit our website: www.biblioplan.net. Or email: contactus@biblioplan.net.

We dedicate this book to Rob's mother, Sharon Fry Nalle.

The fear of the Lord is the beginning of knowledge,
but fools despise wisdom and instruction.
Listen, my son, to your father's instruction
and do not forsake your mother's teaching.
They are a garland to grace your head
and a chain to adorn your neck.

— Proverbs 1:7-9

Table of Contents

PROLOGUE: What Was the Medieval Era?

The **medieval era** was the 1,000-year period between the Fall of Rome and the **Renaissance**. This same period is also called the **Middle Ages**. Medieval times started in the 400s, and ended in the 1400s.

For most of Europe, the medieval era can be divided into three shorter parts. The first part was the **Dark Ages**, which lasted from the 400s to the 1000s.

There are two reasons for the name "dark." The first has to do with learning. The ancient Greeks and Romans were well-known for their great learning. But when the Dark Ages came, a lot of that learning was forgotten for a while— at least in Western Europe.

Why? Because the **barbarians** who conquered Rome couldn't read or write— which put higher learning out of their reach. Wherever the barbarians conquered, higher learning disappeared for a while. Doctors forgot how to heal; engineers forgot how to build great buildings; and sculptors forgot how to carve fine art.

All this forgetfulness led to the second reason for the name "dark." Since most barbarians couldn't write, they couldn't record stories for historians to read. Without more stories, much of their history will always be unknown— or "dark."

Thanks to the Dark Ages, the word "medieval" has two meanings. "Medieval" usually means "belonging to the Middle Ages." But it can also mean "ignorant" or "backward." Right or wrong, modern people often think of medieval people as dimwits— backward fools who were so blinded by old superstitions that they couldn't see the truth.

One example of backward medieval thinking was the strange practice of **trying animals in court**. In modern times, most people believe that animals act mainly on instinct— which means that they can't make **moral** decisions like people can. Medieval judges believed otherwise. From time to time, medieval judges hauled animals into court and put them on trial— accusing them of theft, assault and even murder.

> **Morals** are rules about right and wrong.

ERAS OF HISTORY

Ancient Era
Creation – Fall of Rome (476 AD)

Medieval Era
Dark Ages: 400s – 1000s
High Middle Ages: 1000s – 1300s
Late Middle Ages: 1300s – 1400s

Renaissance
1400s – 1600s

Early Modern Era
1600 – 1850

Modern Era
1850 – 2000s

The name **barbarian** comes from the Greek word *barbaros*, meaning "babbling." The ancient Greeks called anyone who didn't speak Greek a barbarian, or babbler. The Romans used the same word.

In other words, "barbarian" wasn't a proper name for anyone. Instead, it was an insulting nickname for outsiders— uncivilized people from outside the Greek and Roman empires.

Medieval freemen and serfs working on their lord's castle

The strangest things about these trials were the punishments. At least one court hanged a pig to death for murder. Other courts tried to punish rats for eating grain, or swarms of insects for gobbling crops in the field. They announced that the swarm must have been possessed by a demon, and then called on God to smite the demon!

An accused pig on trial for its life in 1494

††††††††††††††††††††††††††††

The second part of the medieval era was the **High Middle Ages**, which lasted from the 1000s to the 1300s. The High Middle Ages were the glorious days of castles, knights and knights' tournaments. Alas, they were also the ugly days of the **Crusades**— long, horrible wars between Christians and Muslims.

The third part of the medieval era was the **Late Middle Ages**, which lasted from the 1300s to the 1400s. The Late Middle Ages were some of the worst times in all history— deadly days of war and crisis.

The worst war of the Late Middle Ages was a long struggle for the throne of France. The **Hundred Years' War** started in 1337, when the King of England decided he should be King of France as well. Despite its name, the Hundred Years' War actually lasted well over 100 years— all the way to 1453. Imagine being at war for more than a century!

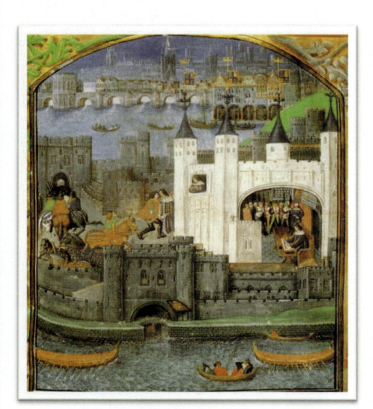

The Tower of London, started by William the Conqueror soon after he conquered England in 1066

Around 1430, it looked like England might win— bringing all France under the Crown of England. What stopped England from winning was the Christian faith of a French teenager: an inspiring peasant girl called **Joan of Arc**.

The worst crisis of the Late Middle Ages was an epidemic called the **Black Death**. Early in the Hundred Years' War, a disease called bubonic plague killed astonishing numbers of people. When the plague had run its course, somewhere between one-third and six-tenths of all the people in Europe lay dead.

After reading all this, you might be afraid that studying the medieval era will be depressing. But take heart, for it can also be fascinating. If you ever find yourself getting depressed, then just count your blessings— and thank the Lord that you weren't born in the Late Middle Ages!

What Has Gone Before

The first known civilizations all grew up around one of four rivers. In the fertile valleys around these rivers, mighty kings built the first known empires.

One was the Nile River, which flows through Egypt. The first King of all Egypt, Menes, lived around 3,000 BC. The buildings and art left behind by the ancient Egyptians are some of the most amazing objects in all the world. Historians may never discover all the mysteries hidden in that enormous tomb, the Great Pyramid of Giza. Nor may they ever understand all the thoughts and feelings that went into that incredible sculpture, the Great Sphinx.

A second river was the Tigris-Euphrates, which flows through Iraq. The land between the Tigris and Euphrates was called *Mesopotamia*, which means "between the rivers." The first great King of Mesopotamia, Sargon, lived around 2,300 BC. Like the Hebrew hero Moses, Sargon started as a baby in a reed basket floating down a river. From this humble beginning, Sargon somehow became the mightiest king the world had yet seen.

The Great Sphinx of Giza, Egypt

Bronze head believed to represent Sargon

A third was the Yellow River, which flows through China. The first King of all China was Yu the Great, who founded the Xia **dynasty** around 2,200 BC. Before Yu came along, the Yellow River was terribly unpredictable— almost always either too high or too low. Yu built dams to hold the river back in wet years, and canals to spread its water around in dry years.

A fourth was the Indus River, which flows through India and Pakistan. The first known people of India, the Harappans, were even more mysterious than most ancient peoples. The most mysterious thing about them was how they vanished. The Harappans seemed to be doing fine until about 1750 BC, when they suddenly disappeared!

> A **dynasty** is a line of rulers who all come from the same family.

††

Compared to the Harappans, the ancient Greeks aren't mysterious at all. The first known Greek people were the Minoans, who appeared on the island of Crete around 1800 BC. Other Greek peoples

~~~ 9 ~~~

followed, building cities all around the Aegean Sea and beyond.

The main reason the Greeks aren't mysterious is because they wrote so much. Almost anything that could be written, the Greeks wrote— from plays to law, history, science and more. They wrote so well that people still study their work, even in modern times.

The Parthenon standing on the Acropolis of Athens, Greece

All that Greek writing might have been forgotten, though, if the Persians had had their way. Persia lay on the far side of the Ancient Near East, in what is now called Iran. Around 550 BC, a Persian genius called **Cyrus the Great** built the biggest empire the world had yet seen. The **Persian Empire** stretched all the way from Egypt to western India, and from the Black Sea to the Arabian Sea. In 480 BC, Cyrus' descendant **Xerxes I** led a huge army into Greece— hoping to make Greece part of his empire too.

Xerxes might have gotten his wish, if not for one of the best-known battles of all time: The **Battle of Thermopylae**. Thermopylae was a mountain pass on the road to southern Greece. That summer, at least 100,000 Persians pushed toward that mountain pass. The Greeks rode out to stop them— with only about 7,000 troops. The Greeks were outnumbered by at least fourteen to one, perhaps a lot more. Yet somehow, they kept the Persians out of Thermopylae for two solid days.

On the third day, the Greeks were betrayed. A traitor showed the Persians how to go around Thermopylae, so that they could attack the Greeks from behind. At this, most of the Greeks retreated— but not all of them. About 1,400 stayed behind at Thermopylae, led by a hard core of 300 Spartan Greeks. The famous **300** fought to the bitter end, sacrificing their lives for their countrymen. Although the Persians finally broke through, the 300 stopped them long enough to save Greece.

✝✝✝

A hundred and fifty years later, it was the Greeks who set out to conquer the world. Starting in 334 BC, a young **Macedonian** called **Alexander the Great** conquered the whole Persian Empire. He even went beyond Persia, pushing deep into India. For a few short years, most of the known world belonged to the **Macedonian Empire** of Alexander the Great.

> **Macedonia** lay in northern Greece.

If Alexander had survived, then who knows how long his empire might have stood? Of course, Alexander didn't survive. He was just 32 years old in 323 BC, when he fell sick and died— possibly because someone poisoned him. Poison or no, Alexander's generals wound up splitting his empire— causing its power to fade.

As Greek power faded, another power arose to take the Greeks' place.

Alexander the Great doing battle with the Persians

CHAPTER 1:

The Western World after the Fall of Rome

The Roman Empire

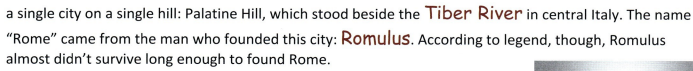

The Roman Empire was one of the biggest, most powerful empires of all time. The matchless might of Rome left deep marks on everything it touched, from language and culture to law and government. All Western countries, and even some Eastern ones, still bear those marks today.

Of course, Rome wasn't always an empire. It started out as a single city on a single hill: Palatine Hill, which stood beside the Tiber River in central Italy. The name "Rome" came from the man who founded this city: Romulus. According to legend, though, Romulus almost didn't survive long enough to found Rome.

The Founding of Rome (753 BC)

The story of Romulus starts with a king called Numitor, who ruled a small kingdom along the Tiber. Numitor had several sons, but only one daughter: a princess called Rhea.

Unfortunately, Numitor also had a jealous brother called Amulius. Numitor was just getting settled on his throne when Amulius drove him off it. To save himself, Numitor had to run away— leaving Rhea and her brothers behind. Amulius' first act as king was to murder all of Rhea's brothers, so that none of them could ever claim his throne!

Fortunately for Rome, Amulius didn't kill Rhea. For Rhea was only a girl; and in those days, no girl could ever rule an Italian kingdom. The only way Rhea could hurt Amulius was by having a son, who might try to claim the throne as Numitor's grandson. To keep that from happening, Amulius sent Rhea to live in a women's temple— where she would never meet any men!

A little later, Amulius got a nasty surprise. Despite living in a temple, Rhea somehow had not one son, but two: a set of twins called Romulus and Remus!

The moment Amulius found out, he sent a servant to kill the twins. Fortunately for Rome, the servant couldn't bring himself to kill such beautiful children. Instead, he set the twins in a basket and abandoned them on the banks of the Tiber.

Left in the wild to fend for themselves, most infants surely would have died. But these were no ordinary infants. According to legend, the Tiber picked up the basket and carried it downstream, where it snagged on a gnarled root of a fig tree. There they were rescued by a wild she-wolf, who fed the twins milk while a woodpecker carried them food. This went on until a shepherd called Faustulus found the twins, adopted them and raised them as his own. This special beginning marked the Romans as a special people with a special destiny— according to legend, at least.

Romulus and Remus drinking milk from a she-wolf

Over the centuries, the Romans lived under three main types of government. Rome was a kingdom from 753 – 509 BC; a republic from 509 – 27 BC; and an empire from 27 BC – 476 AD.

A **kingdom** is a country ruled by a monarch— that is, a king or queen. Rome had seven kings over the years, starting with Romulus and ending with a tyrant called Tarquin the Proud.

A **republic** is a country governed by representatives who are elected by the people. After overthrowing Tarquin the Proud, the last thing free Romans wanted was another tyrant. So they built a government that left no room for tyrants: a republican government. The modern-day United States is a republic, and so are many other free countries around the world.

An **empire** is a big country or group of countries, all ruled by one all-powerful emperor. Around 50 BC, a popular Roman called Julius Caesar made his people forget how bad tyrants could be. It was in Caesar's day that Rome started its fall from the freedom of a republic to the tyranny of an empire.

"The Shepherd Faustulus Bringing Romulus and Remus to His Wife" by artist Nicolas Mignard

Most tales of early Rome read more like legend than history. Any tales written by eyewitnesses were all burned by Rome's enemies long ago. The tales that remain are mostly half-remembered legends of men like **Cincinnatus**— mighty heroes whose deeds represent the highest ideals of the Roman republic.

Cincinnatus was born into the wealthier class of Romans, the patrician class, around 519 BC. As a young man, Cincinnatus quickly became one of Rome's favorite soldier-politicians. His popularity pushed him steadily upward through the ranks of government— all the way to **consul** in 460 BC.

Alas for Cincinnatus, one of his sons got into serious trouble with the law; and that trouble led to a costly fine. To raise the money for the fine, Cincinnatus had to sell almost everything he owned. The only thing he kept was a small plot of farmland. When his time as consul was over, Cincinnatus had to tend his small farm with his own hands— just like a peasant.

The **consuls** headed Rome's government and commanded its armies, much like presidents do in the United States.

"Cincinnatus Leaves the Plow for the Roman Dictatorship" by Juan Antonio Ribera

Cincinnatus was doing just that— tending his farm— when some senators dropped by to make an unusual request. Soon after Cincinnatus left office, Rome found itself in terrible danger. An enemy had trapped a Roman army in a mountain pass and was threatening to destroy it. Not even the best Roman generals knew what to do— until someone thought to call on Cincinnatus.

All agreed that Cincinnatus was the one man in Rome with enough skill and courage to rescue those trapped soldiers. But even Cincinnatus would have to act fast— which meant that he would need a great deal of power.

Desperate to save Rome, the Senate offered Cincinnatus all the power Rome had to give. The senators who came calling at Cincinnatus' farm that day offered to make him **Dictator** of Rome— a supreme general with the power to command every Roman citizen. The only limit on Cincinnatus' power was time. Cincinnatus was to lay down his power after six months; for no Roman wanted another tyrant like Tarquin the Proud!

> A **dictator** was a supreme general with the power to command any Roman citizen to do anything at all.

In his first act as dictator, Cincinnatus commanded every able-bodied man in Rome to be ready to march by the end of the next day. Equipped with this new army and a bold, clever strategy, Cincinnatus soon crushed Rome's enemies and rescued that trapped Roman army.

What happened next proved that Cincinnatus was more than just a great soldier. He was also a great Roman citizen! When the fighting was over, Cincinnatus could have used his powers as dictator to grow rich again— could have taken back all the property he'd sold to pay his son's fine.

Fortunately for Rome, Cincinnatus was a strong believer in republican government. He knew that if a dictator ever seized power in Rome, then the Roman people might lose their freedom forever. And so, for the good of Rome, Cincinnatus humbly laid down his power and went back to his tiny farm— just sixteen days after the Senate made him dictator!

It was in laying down his power that Cincinnatus became a Roman legend. Some men spend their whole lives fighting for power; and once they have it, they never want to lay it down. But Cincinnatus wasn't seeking power when the crisis arose. Instead, power sought Cincinnatus— not because he was high-born, but

Symbols of Roman Power

The **fasces** was a cylinder-shaped bundle of wooden rods, all bound around an ax with the head sticking out one side. Roman leaders used fasces as symbols of power. The bundled rods stood for the strength that came from the unity of the Roman people; while the stood for Rome's power over life and death.

A **toga** was a long woolen dress robe worn by Roman men, usually over a tunic. Togas were so bulky and inconvenient as to be utterly useless for physical labor. The only Romans who wore them were the ones who didn't need to labor— like consuls, senators and rich businessmen. Poor Romans and slaves almost never wore togas.

Roman women wore a different type of dress robe called a **stola**.

Statue of a toga-wearing Cincinnatus handing over the fasces, an important symbol of Roman power

because he was the best man for the job! Then when his task was over, Cincinnatus traded his dictator's toga for the simple garb of a humble farmer— setting the needs of Rome far above his own needs.

Sad to say, few Romans cared much about the needs of two kinds of people: women and slaves. Roman men treated their wives like property, not like free people. As for slaves, the Romans owned them by the hundreds of thousands— using them mercilessly for all sorts of hard labor. Slaves mined countless tons of copper, iron, silver and gold ores; quarried countless blocks of stone for buildings; raised countless crops to feed hungry Romans; and pulled oars on countless ships. Many did these things under miserable conditions— with no pay, and with little hope of ever being free again.

A Roman Warrior's Equipment

The **galea** was a Roman battle helmet designed to protect as much of the head and neck as possible. Galeae were made of cast bronze with iron trim, and often had colorful crests made of horse hair or feathers.

The **pugio** was a small dagger that served as both weapon and general-purpose knife. Wealthier warriors carried ornate pugios decorated with carvings and even gems; while poorer warriors carried plain ones.

The **gladius** was a short double-edged stabbing sword, about 18-22 inches long. A heavy round ball at the end of the handle helped balance the blade, making the gladius easier to handle.

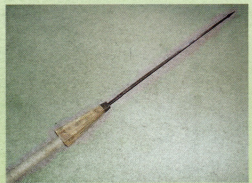

The **pilum** was a light javelin, or throwing spear, about seven feet long. Roman soldiers often threw their javelins just before they drew their swords, hoping to knock out as many enemies as possible before closing in for hand-to-hand combat.

The **scutum** was a rectangular shield that was curved to fit around a warrior's body, covering him from shoulder to knee. Warriors standing side by side could interlock their shields to create a strong protective wall.

As long as Rome produced selfless heroes like Cincinnatus, republican government stayed strong in Rome. It was only later, when greedy Romans started caring more for themselves than they did for Rome, that the republic gave way to an empire. Rome traced its sad path from free republic to tyrannical empire through three rulers: Julius Caesar, Caesar Augustus and Tiberius.

Julius Caesar was a smart soldier-politician who won the Roman people's admiration in two ways: through glorious victories on the battlefield, and through generous gifts to poor Romans. In Caesar's day, mobs of idle Romans wandered the streets of Rome— depending on the government for their daily bread. Caesar took advantage of these greedy mobs, feeding their hunger with expensive public parties.

Julius Caesar
(100 BC - 44 BC)

In 49 BC, a rival called Pompey tried to stand in Caesar's way. In the process of defeating Pompey, Caesar claimed the same title that the Senate had once given Cincinnatus: "Dictator of Rome."

Unlike Cincinnatus, Caesar had no intention of laying down his power. He was well on his way to becoming the first Emperor of Rome— until the Ides of March, 44 BC, when a group of senators murdered him.

The abbreviation **SPQR** stood for *Senatus Populusque Romanus*, Latin for "The Senate and People of Rome." Appearing on public buildings, battle standards and the like, the "SPQR" logo reminded everyone that the power of Rome sprang from two sources: the free citizens of Rome, and their representatives in the Senate.

Now that Caesar was out of the way, several ambitious men fought to take his place. One was **Octavius Caesar**, Julius Caesar's nephew and adopted son. Another was one of Julius Caesar's most trusted generals— a brave Roman called **Marc Antony**.

Marc Antony hoped to defeat Octavius by joining forces with Cleopatra, Queen of Egypt. Alas for Antony, his hopes turned to ash when Octavius defeated him at the famous Battle of Actium. Both Antony and Cleopatra committed suicide, leaving Octavius to conquer Egypt.

Octavius used the riches of Egypt to transform Rome— rebuilding it from sagging city of dirty brick into a proud one of gleaming marble. The more money he spent to benefit Rome, the more honors the Roman Senate heaped upon him. One of those honors was the title he carried into history: *Augustus*, meaning "Honored One."

Caesar Augustus
(63 BC - 14 AD)

Despite his lofty title, **Caesar Augustus** was always careful to avoid the title "emperor." He preferred another title the Senate gave him: *Princeps*, meaning "First Citizen." By insisting that he was only a citizen, not an emperor, Caesar Augustus fooled the Roman people into believing that their country was still a republic.

The **Circus Maximus** was a public racetrack that stood near the Roman Coliseum. The Romans used their Coliseum for gladiator fights, executions and other big public events; but they used the Circus Maximus mainly for horse-drawn chariot races. The Circus Maximus may have held as many as 150,000 spectators on race days.

Model of ancient Rome with the Circus Maximus in the foreground and the Coliseum in the background

The Roman diet was heavy on three basic foods: grains, grapes and olives. Romans ate their beloved olives whole; used them in relishes and spices; and pressed them into olive oil, which they used to cook or dress other foods.

If the rise of Caesar Augustus didn't mark the end of the Roman Republic, then the rise of Tiberius certainly did. Just before Caesar Augustus died, he handed down the office of First Citizen to his step-son Tiberius. If Rome had still been a republic, then Tiberius would have had to win an election. Instead, power passed directly from father to son— which meant that the Roman people had forgotten the ideals of Cincinnatus, trading the freedom of a republic for the tyranny of an empire.

This is not to say that the end of the republic meant the end of Roman prosperity— quite the opposite! The reign of Caesar Augustus was the beginning of the *Pax Romana*— a "Roman Peace" that lasted more than two hundred years. The Roman Empire was never larger, nor its power and wealth ever greater, than during the *Pax Romana*.

This went on until around 180 AD, when Rome's fortunes finally started to fade. After the *Pax Romana*, problems plagued Rome

The Fall of the Western Roman Empire (476 AD)

on all sides. One problem was that each time an emperor died, his former generals fought over his throne. These fights weakened Rome's defenses, leaving it open to attack.

To better defend his vast empire, an emperor called Diocletian tried splitting it in two— forming a **Western Roman Empire** and an **Eastern Roman Empire**. Diocletian hoped that two emperors would be stronger than one, since each would have less territory to defend. Unfortunately, splitting the empire created new problems— including high new taxes to pay for two expensive governments.

The worst problem of all came from outsiders called barbarians. Around 400 AD, huge numbers of barbarians started pouring across Rome's old boundaries— the Rhine and Danube Rivers. As mighty as the Romans were, even they couldn't fight off so many barbarians all at once!

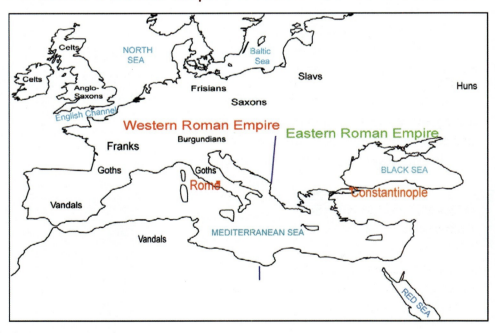

The fall of the Western Roman Empire came in stages. A barbarian people called the Visigoths **sacked** Rome for the first time in 410 AD. The next big threat came from Attila the Hun, who nearly sacked Rome in 452. The Vandals succeeded where Attila had failed, sacking Rome in 455. The last Emperor of the Western Roman Empire finally fell in 476. Oddly enough, this last emperor was named Romulus!

To **sack** a city is to ravage it— to attack its people, loot its treasure and destroy its buildings.

As for the Eastern Roman Empire, it survived for another 1,000 years— but under a different name. The capital of the Eastern Roman Empire lay far to the east, in a Greek-speaking city called Constantinople (now Istanbul, Turkey). The Greek culture of Constantinople was quite different from the Latin culture of Rome. Because of this, and because Constantinople had once been called *Byzantion*, the Eastern Roman Empire is called the Byzantine Empire.

The Early Christian Church

The whole history of the early church happened in Roman times. Jesus Christ was born to the Virgin Mary around 6 – 0 BC, when Caesar Augustus was emperor. Roman soldiers crucified Christ around 30 – 33 AD, when Tiberius was emperor. After Christ rose from the dead and ascended into heaven, His apostles set out to spread His gospel all over the known world— most of which was controlled by Rome.

The gospel couldn't have come at a better time. When Christ's apostles set out to "make disciples of all nations," as the Bible says in Matthew 28:19, the road-loving Romans had already built convenient roads all over their huge empire. Also, the law and order of the *Pax Romana* was just beginning— which made traveling those roads far safer. These two advantages, the *Pax Romana* and the Roman roads, were extremely helpful to the first Christian missionaries.

Of course, any help the Romans gave the early church was purely unintentional. The Roman Empire didn't want to help Christians— no, it wanted to destroy them! Christian-hating emperors like Nero, Trajan and Decius tortured and murdered countless Christians.

Persecutions of Early Christians

One such tortured Christian was Ignatius of Antioch, bishop of Antioch, Syria. Ignatius probably studied under the Apostle John, who of course was a close friend of Jesus. When John died, Ignatius was one of the last men alive who had studied under someone who had studied under Jesus Himself. Knowing how other Christians looked up to him, Ignatius felt a duty to speak out loudly about his faith.

The Romans loved to make examples of loud-speaking Christians. They had learned that if they silenced one Christian leader, then the rest would usually fall silent too. This is what Emperor Trajan had in mind around 110 AD, when he ordered the 70-year-old Ignatius of Antioch arrested and hauled off to Rome for trial!

"The Ascension" by Rembrandt

But Ignatius refused to fall silent. On his way to Rome, he wrote inspiring letters to churches all over the empire— encouraging them to keep the faith. Ignatius was not afraid to die, he said. No, he welcomed death; for it was only by dying that Christians could get to heaven! Since Christ Himself had died on the cross, Ignatius was not surprised that Christ's followers should have to die for their faith too. In fact, he considered it a high honor to be chosen to die for Christ. To the struggling young church at Rome, Ignatius wrote:

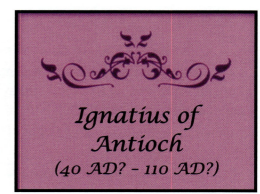

Ignatius of Antioch
(40 AD? - 110 AD?)

> "I would rather die and come to Jesus Christ than be king over the entire earth… Let me be food for the wild beasts, for they are my way to God."

Emperor Trajan was happy to grant Ignatius' wish. The old saint was just one of many Christians who were fed to hungry lions at the Roman Coliseum.

Just as the Bible says in James 1:3, the testing of Christians' faith produced endurance. Despite many such horrible persecutions as the one Ignatius suffered, the early church continued to grow.

Ignatius of Antioch being attacked by lions in the Roman Coliseum

The more the early church grew, the more church officers it needed. The Book of Acts says that at first, the apostles directed everything themselves. Then, as the church started to grow, the apostles chose seven deacons to help them (Acts 6:1-6). Later, the Apostle Paul chose elders— also called presbyters— to manage the new churches he started (Acts 14:23).

Bishops and Popes

Later still, Paul set trusted disciples like Timothy and Titus in charge of several churches each. Timothy, Titus and Ignatius were all early **bishops**— overseers who managed many Christian churches.

At first, no one bishop was more powerful than any other. Over time, though, the bishop of Rome grew more powerful than the rest— probably because Rome itself was so powerful. As the most powerful bishop in the whole Christian world, the bishop of Rome took on a new title: *Papa*, or Father. English speakers know the Bishop of Rome as the **Pope**.

A **bishop** was an overseer who managed all Christian churches in a certain area.

According to Catholic tradition, the **Apostle Peter** was the first pope. The special authority of Peter comes from these words of Christ in Matthew 16:18-19:

> "And I tell you that you are Peter, and on this rock I will build my church, and the gates of Hades will not overcome it. I will give you the keys of the kingdom of heaven; whatever you bind on earth will be bound in heaven, and whatever you loose on earth will be loosed in heaven."

Tradition also says that when Peter died, he handed down his power to the next pope in line, who in turn handed it down to the next. Even today, each new pope inherits power from the pope before him— in an unbroken line that stretches all the way back to Peter. Catholics call this handing-down of power **Apostolic Succession**.

Symbols of the Pope

The popes of medieval times used **papal coats of arms** as symbols of authority. Each pope designed his own special coat of arms. Many papal coats of arms included the two keys from Matthew 16:18-19. One key represented the power to "bind" sin, while the other represented the power to "loose" sin.

Coat of arms of Leo X, the pope who reigned during the early years of the Protestant Reformation. Pope Leo's arms included both the Keys of St. Peter and the Papal Tiara.

On special occasions, medieval popes also wore the **Papal Tiara**— a fantastically expensive crown with three gem-studded tiers. However, later popes felt that such a rich ornament was too extravagant for a servant of Christ. After all, Christ had been the son of a poor carpenter. No pope has worn the papal tiara since 1965, when Pope Paul VI laid it down on the altar of St. Peter's Basilica in Rome.

Part of every bishop's job was keeping the Christian faith pure. From the very beginning, false teachers called **heretics** tried to lead Christians astray. As defenders of Christ's church, bishops tried to stop **heresies** before they could spread.

> A **heretic** is someone who spreads false teachings about Christ. Such teachings are called **heresies**.

The First Heresies

The first big heresy was called **Gnosticism**. The word "Gnostic" comes from the Greek word *gnosis*, meaning "knowledge." The Gnostics taught that people could only be saved through certain special knowledge— mysterious secrets that only Gnostics knew. One Gnostic secret was that the spirit world was good, but the physical world was evil.

The trouble started when Gnostics tried to blend this secret with Christianity. Gnostic Christians asked, "How could a spirit as good as Christ's possibly live inside an evil physical body?" The answer, they said, was that he couldn't. Since Christ was too good for the physical world, his body couldn't have been real. Instead, Gnostics said, Christ's body must have been an **illusion**.

> An **illusion** is something that appears to be real, but really isn't. The Gnostics believed that Christ's physical body was only an illusion.

The bishops of the early church answered these Gnostic heretics with one of the most important statements of faith ever written: The Apostles' Creed. In modern English, the Apostles' Creed reads:

"I believe in God the Father, Almighty Maker of Heaven and Earth.

"And in Jesus Christ His only begotten Son, our Lord, who was conceived by the Holy Spirit, born of the Virgin Mary, suffered under Pontius Pilate, was crucified, dead and buried. He descended into hell. On the third day, He arose from the dead. He ascended into heaven, and sits at the right hand of God the Father Almighty, from whence He will come to judge the quick [living] and the dead.

"I believe in the Holy Spirit, the holy catholic [universal] church, the communion of the saints, the forgiveness of sins, the resurrection of the body, and the life everlasting."

By insisting that Christ was born and died, the Apostles' Creed dismissed the idea that Christ's body wasn't real. Unlike the Gnostics, the bishops of the early church insisted that Christ was really a man— but also really God, both at the same time.

Constantine the Great

When the Apostles' Creed first appeared, probably around 150 AD, most Romans still hated Christians. Almost no one would have believed that Rome would have a Christian emperor one day!

Believe it or not, that day came in the early 300s— when a Christian called Constantine claimed the throne of the Roman Empire.

Before the 300s, Constantine stood with one foot in the Roman world and the other in the Christian world. His father Constantius started as a Roman general, and ended as Emperor of Rome. His mother Helena may have started as a lowly Christian stable-maid. While Constantius raised his son to be an emperor, Helena raised him to be a Christian.

Constantine's moment of decision came in 312 AD, just before the most important battle of his life: The Battle of the Milvian Bridge. It is said that on the night before this battle, Constantine received a vision of heavenly angels— telling him to paint a new symbol on his soldiers' shields. That symbol was the Chi-Rho, which combined the first two letters in the Greek word for "Christ." With Christ's help, Constantine went on to beat an army twice the size of his!

Constantine the Great (272 - 337)

"Apparition of the Cross to Constantine" by artist Jacopo Vignali

A Chi-Rho, the symbol from Constantine's vision

The following year was a banner year for Christians. Before now, Christianity was still mostly illegal in Rome. All that changed in 313, when Constantine announced a new law called the Edict of Milan. The emperor's edict made it legal for all Romans to worship any god they liked— even Christ. After nearly three hundred years of persecution, Christians all over the Roman Empire were finally free to come out of hiding!

Even so, Constantine was careful about Christianity. He was lying on his deathbed when he finally let a priest baptize him.

Helena
(250? – 330?)

Before he died, though, Constantine sent his mother **Helena** to the Holy Land. Helena used Roman money to build two of the best-known churches in the world: The Church of the Holy Sepulcher, which stands on Calvary Hill in Jerusalem; and the Church of the Nativity, which stands in Bethlehem.

Legend says that in digging the foundations for the Church of the Holy Sepulcher, Helena discovered three wooden crosses— one belonging to Christ, and two belonging to the criminals who were crucified on either side of Christ (Luke 23:33). To find out which was the True Cross of Christ, Helena asked a deathly ill woman to touch all three. Nothing happened when the woman touched the first two. When she touched the third, though, the power of Christ miraculously healed her.

Seven Continents, Five Oceans

A **continent** is a vast body of land, far bigger than an island. Planet Earth has seven continents: **Africa**, **Antarctica**, **Asia**, **Australia**, **Europe**, **North America** and **South America**. Together, these continents cover about three-tenths (30%) of Earth's total surface. The other seven-tenths (70%) is covered with water.

The biggest continent, Asia, is home to about six-tenths (60%) of the world's people. More than half of these live in the two most populated countries on Earth: China and India. China comes in first, with about 1.4 billion people. India comes in second, with about 1.3 billion. As of 2018, Planet Earth has a total of about 7.6 billion people.

The fifth-biggest continent, Antarctica, is so unbearably cold that no one lives there full-time! However, as many as several hundred scientists may be living in science stations on Antarctica at any one time.

〰〰〰〰〰〰〰〰〰〰〰〰〰〰〰〰〰

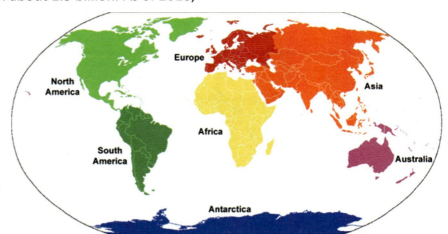

An **ocean** is a vast body of water, far bigger than a sea. By most people's count, Planet Earth has five oceans: the **Arctic** Ocean, the **Atlantic** Ocean, the **Indian** Ocean, the **Pacific** Ocean and the **Southern** Ocean. Since each ocean blends into the next, one could also say that

Planet Earth really has only one ocean: the **World Ocean**. Either way, oceans cover about seven-tenths (70%) of Earth's surface.

The biggest ocean, the Pacific, dwarfs all the rest. With an area of more than 60 million square miles, the Pacific is almost twice as big as the second-biggest ocean: the Atlantic. A Pacific crossing from San Francisco, California to Tokyo, Japan is well over 5,000 miles. An Atlantic crossing from Newfoundland, Canada to Ireland is only about 2,000.

The British Isles

The **British Isles** are big islands off the northwest coast of mainland Europe. Two of the British Isles are far bigger than all the rest. The biggest, **Great Britain**, lies just across the English Channel from France, and just across the North Sea from Belgium and the Netherlands. The second biggest, **Ireland**, lies west of Great Britain— just across the Irish Sea.

How big are the British Isles? Great Britain is the ninth-biggest island in the world— just a bit smaller than Honshu, the biggest island in Japan. At about 81,000 square miles, Great Britain is not quite as big as the fifteenth-biggest U.S. state: Kansas. Ireland isn't half so big. At about 32,000 square miles, Ireland is a bit bigger than the fortieth-biggest U.S. state: South Carolina.

In modern times, Great Britain is home to three countries: **England**, **Scotland** and **Wales**. Ireland has two: **Northern Ireland** and the **Republic of Ireland**. Four of these five countries belong to a union called the **United Kingdom of Great Britain and Northern Ireland**. The fifth, the Republic of Ireland, is independent of all the rest.

In ancient times, different peoples used different names for different parts of the British Isles. For example, **Britannia** was the Roman name for southern Great Britain. The Romans conquered Britannia around 50 AD, and ruled it for most of the next 400 years.

Caledonia was the Roman name for northern Great Britain— the part the Romans never conquered.

Dover Castle in Dover, Kent, England

The Celtic People

Before the Romans came, the British Isles belonged to an ancient people called the **Celts**. Celts lived in many parts of Europe, not just the British Isles. They brushed up against many ancient peoples over the centuries, including Greeks and Romans.

The triskelion, a favorite symbol of the Celts

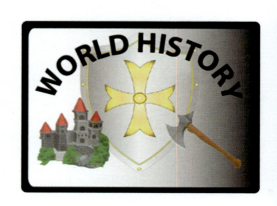

A Celtic warrior in blue war paint

Unlike the Greeks and the Romans, the Celts never pulled themselves together into one big empire. They were always split into tribes, each led by a warrior chieftain or petty king. Every Celtic tribe was unique, with a special name and story all its own. Every tribe was also independent— except when they banded together to fight a common foe, like the Roman Empire.

As a tribal people, the Celts built no great cities or towering structures. But they did make clever pottery, jewelry, tools and weapons. They even made a kind of armor that was good enough for the Romans to borrow: chain mail.

Chain mail was a metal fabric made by weaving together rings of bronze or iron. Celtic blacksmiths probably forged their first chain mail sometime after 300 BC. Their Roman neighbors admired chain mail so much that they copied it, spreading this Celtic invention around the world.

An ancient hauberk on display at a museum in France

Since chain mail was almost as flexible as cloth, blacksmiths could weave it into armor for any part of the body. The most common mail piece was a long shirt called a **hauberk**. But there were also chain mail helmets, scarves, aprons, leggings, socks and gloves. Even in the 1300s, when the first plate armor came along, chain mail was still popular. For chain mail was cheaper, lighter and far more flexible than any plate armor.

Celtic families often lived in one-room buildings called roundhouses. The Celts probably built their roundhouse walls by mixing mud with straw, and then spreading thick layers of this mixture over a frame of sticks. Roundhouse roofs were cone-shaped, and probably covered with **thatch.**

Thatch is a roof covering made of bundled straw or reeds, all bound to the roof frame in thick layers.

With all that thick mud and thatch, most families probably needed only small fires in the centers of their roundhouses to keep them warm. Unlike Native American tepees, roundhouses probably didn't have smoke holes in their roofs. If they had, then any sudden draft might have drawn the flames up into the thatch— setting fire to the roof! Instead, the Celts probably just let smoke seep out of their smoky roundhouses through tiny gaps in the thatch.

Modern-day reconstruction of a Celtic roundhouse

The leaders of the Celtic religion were mysterious priests called **druids**. Much of what the druids believed and taught is now forgotten— for the Celts had no written language, which means that they never wrote down their scriptures and rituals. Even so, historians know part of what the Celts believed. For example:

Two druids, one with a crown of mistletoe

➤ Like many ancient peoples, the Celts were **polytheists**— people who believed in many gods. Celtic gods and goddesses often appeared in threes; for the number three was special to the Celts.

> **Polytheists** believe in many gods, not just one.

➤ The Celts were tree-lovers— great admirers of the strength and long life found in trees. Druids taught that certain trees and plants were sacred, especially oak and **mistletoe**. Some druidic rituals could only happen in sacred tree groves.

➤ The Celts believed in **reincarnation**— the idea that the dead are reborn into new bodies.

> **Reincarnation** is the belief that when people die, their souls move into new bodies and live on.

This last belief was especially important to warriors; for it gave them great courage. If a warrior truly believed in reincarnation, then he had no reason to fear dying in battle— for he felt sure that his soul would not die, but would simply move into a different body.

Courage was part of what made **Celtic warriors** so fearsome. They fought like madmen— holding nothing back, throwing their whole bodies into every blow. Another part was their size, which was a lot bigger than the average Roman's. Celtic warriors were legendary for their great height and strength.

> The blue pigment for the Celts' war paint may have come from a flowering plant called **woad**.

Yet another part of what made Celtic warriors so fearsome was their looks. Some of them went into battle wearing only two items: a little bit of armor, and a lot of **blue** war paint. The Celts may have worn blue because they believed that it helped them channel power from their gods. On the other hand, they may have worn it for a simpler reason: because their gruesome blue faces terrified their enemies!

The druids played an important part in war. Some of them taught that if the Celts wanted their gods' help to win a battle, then they must offer sacrifices before that battle. According to the Romans, some evil druids did the unthinkable: sacrificing live human beings to their gods!

A Celtic shield

A helmet worn in Celtic ceremonies

The Roman Empire in Britannia

The more the Roman Empire grew, the more the Celts shrank. Each time the Romans conquered new land in Europe, the beaten Celts had to retreat farther from Rome. By Julius Caesar's day, they were down to just two lands: **Gaul** and the British Isles.

Caesar was determined to take those lands too. He was working on Gaul in 55 BC, when he first sailed over to Great Britain. Why go to Britain, when what he wanted was Gaul? Because war is never simple. Each time Caesar conquered new ground in Gaul, more Celts fled to Great Britain. But they didn't stay in Britain. Instead, they often sailed back to Gaul for revenge! This is what Caesar was doing in 55 BC— trying to stop the Celts' revenge attacks.

> **Gaul** was an ancient name for what is now France.

Almost 100 years passed before the Romans invaded Great Britain again. This time, though, the Romans came to stay. In 43 AD, Emperor Claudius sent four whole **legions** of Roman soldiers into Britain— as many as 40,000 troops! Although the Celts fought as fiercely as always, their simple tribes were no match for the mighty Roman Empire. In 50 AD, the Romans finally conquered southern Great Britain— the part they called Britannia.

One of the many Celts the Romans faced was a warrior chief called Caratacus. Caratacus tried **guerrilla** tactics against the Romans. In other words, he and his men leapt out of hiding, struck quickly and then disappeared before the Romans could strike back.

As long as Caratacus stuck to guerilla tactics, he did well. In 50 AD, though, Caratacus tried to tackle a big Roman army head-on. The result was a disaster called the Battle of Caer Caradoc. After losing this battle, Caratacus tried to flee— only to be betrayed by a friend and handed over to the Romans in chains.

> A **legion** was a Roman army unit with anywhere from 5,000 to 10,000 troops.
>
> **Guerrilla** is Spanish for "little war."
>
> **Barbarian** was a Greek and Roman word for uncivilized people from outside their empires.

As a proud Roman, Emperor Claudius thought he knew just what to do with a **barbarian** like Caratacus. He would haul Caratacus to the Roman Forum, where he would hold a crowd-pleasing victory parade to show off his beaten foe. Then he would execute him for daring to defy Rome. Roman hearts would swell with pride as Claudius proved, once again, that Rome was unstoppable.

But Caratacus turned out to be no ordinary barbarian. Unlike others the Romans had conquered, Caratacus was well-educated and well-spoken. Instead of cowering before the emperor, Caratacus defended himself in a proud speech. He asked, "Why on Earth should it be a crime to defy Rome? For who on Earth would willingly become a slave?"

Claudius was so impressed by Caratacus' thoughtfulness that he decided to spare his life. But he didn't send him home; for he didn't want him leading any more rebellions. The great Celt spent the rest of his days in Rome— part prisoner, and part a guest of the emperor.

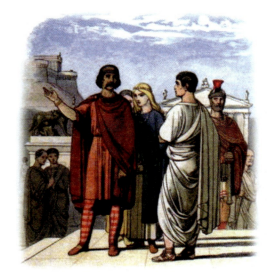

Caratacus touring Rome after his release

Meanwhile, the Roman Empire was turning out to be less unstoppable than Claudius thought. After conquering Britannia, the Romans tried to conquer northern Great Britain as well— the part they called Caledonia. Each time they tried, though, a fierce Celtic people called the Picts drove them back. The Picts also raided Roman outposts in Britannia, making off with horses, supplies and more. They were like a thorn in the Romans' paw, constantly nagging at them.

After seventy-plus years of trouble with the Picts, an emperor called Hadrian thought of a new way to protect Britannia: by walling them out. If Hadrian's Wall was going to work, then it would need several virtues:

➢ First, it would need to stretch all the way across Great Britain. Even at its narrowest point, the big island was still about 75 miles wide— which meant that Hadrian's Wall would have to be about 75 miles long.

➢ Second, it would need to be high, thick and strong. The finished wall was built mostly of stone, and stood about 15 feet high and 8 feet thick.

➢ Third, it would need soldiers and forts to guard it— for without them, the Picts could simply climb the wall when no one was looking. The finished wall included at least one fort at every milepost. Sixteen of these were big, impressive forts— complete with strong gates, barracks for troops and barns for horses.

A surviving section of Hadrian's Wall just south of Scotland

For most of the next 300 years, Hadrian's Wall marked the northernmost border of the whole Roman Empire. Try as they might, the Romans could never hold anything north of Hadrian's Wall for long.

By the early 400s, the Picts weren't the only ones who were giving the Romans trouble. As we read in Chapter 1, barbarian tribes invaded the Western Roman Empire from all sides at once. The only way to fight off these barbarians was to call Roman troops home— starting with the ones in far-off provinces like Britannia.

Despite the extra troops, the Visigoths sacked Rome itself in 410. This disaster sent the Romans into a panic. Desperate to save itself, the dying Roman Empire called its last armies home from Britannia. Great Britain was on its own again, for the first time in almost 400 years.

The Roman Retreat from Britannia (410 AD)

The British Dark Age

A lot can change in 400 years. When the Romans first invaded Britannia, the Celts fought like madmen to keep them out. But when the Romans left, the Celts' descendants mourned to see them go.

Why did they mourn to see their conquerors go? Because the Romans were more than just conquerors. They were also great teachers! The people of Britannia had learned a lot from the Romans in four hundred years. Roman ways had made them happier, healthier and more comfortable than ever before.

In fact, Roman ways had changed their lives so much that they no longer saw themselves as Celts. Instead, they saw themselves as **Romanized Britons**— a new people who were proud of their Roman learning.

The Romanized Britons wanted to do what the Romans had done: to defend their civilization against the barbarians beyond Hadrian's Wall. Unfortunately, the barbarians outnumbered the Britons— just as they outnumbered Romans all over the empire! If the Britons were going to fight off the barbarians, then they would need more troops.

To get those troops, British kings started hiring **mercenaries**— paid soldiers from outside Britain. Oddly enough, these mercenaries would turn out to be a bigger problem than the barbarians they were hired to fight!

> A **mercenary** is a soldier who will fight for anyone who can afford to pay him.

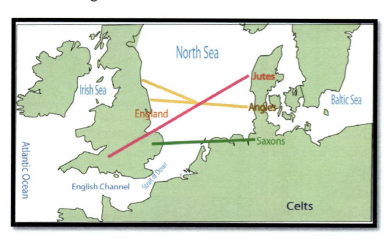

The first to hire mercenaries was probably a British king called **Vortigern**. When barbarians threatened his kingdom, Vortigern hired a people called the **Saxons** for help. Vortigern's Saxons came from across the North Sea, probably near what is now Denmark.

Vortigern paid the Saxons in two ways: with money, and with land. The first Saxon land in Britain was a southeastern one called Kent.

Other British kings invited other mercenaries to other parts of Britannia. A people called the **Angles** came mainly to the east, north of Saxon territory. A people called the **Jutes** came mainly to the southwest, west of Saxon territory. The Jutes blended with the Saxons, leaving two main tribes of foreigners in Britain: Angles and Saxons.

The Angles and Saxons soon discovered that they liked Britain very much. They poured into Britain by the thousands, demanding more money and more land. If the Britons didn't pay, then the Angles and Saxons simply took what they wanted— driving the poor Britons out of their homes. In time, the Angles and Saxons took over most of southern Britain!

> The Angles grew so powerful in southern Britain that the country took on a new name. What had once been Roman Britannia now became "Angle-land," or simply **England**."

Like the barbarians who conquered Rome, the Anglo-Saxons who conquered southern Britain could neither read nor write— which meant few written records. Without written records, historians can only guess at what happened after the Anglo-Saxons took over. In taking over southern Britain, the Anglo-Saxons brought on a **British Dark Age**— a time when British history goes mostly dark.

> The **British Dark Age** was a time when the bright light of Roman learning went dark in Britain. Few historical records survive from the British Dark Age.

Wherever history leaves a gap, legend rushes in to fill it. The gap of the British Dark Age is filled mostly with the **legend of King Arthur**.

If Arthur ever really lived at all, then he was probably a British king from the early 500s. According to legend, Arthur led the Britons to a great victory over their worst enemies: the

The Angles and Saxons divided southern Britain into seven kingdoms. Historians call these seven kingdoms the **Heptarchy**— a combination of "hepto," meaning "seven," and "archy," meaning "rule." The seven Anglo-Saxon kingdoms of the Heptarchy were (1) East Anglia, (2) Essex, (3) Kent, (4) Mercia, (5) Northumbria, (6) Wessex and (7) Sussex.

Saxons. Arthur's victory bought a short time of peace and prosperity— a golden age when the heroic Arthur and his beautiful wife Guinevere reigned from their new castle at Camelot, aided by virtuous knights like Lancelot, Gawain and Galahad.

Like so many good things, the golden age of Arthur ended in treachery. For years, Arthur never knew that he had a son named Mordred— born to a woman he met before he married Guinevere. After Mordred grew up, he did the unthinkable: he turned traitor, joining forces with the Saxons to attack his father. Arthur and Mordred killed each other in battle; the Saxons took over the country; and Britain descended into its Dark Age.

These basic ideas of Arthur's story are easy enough to believe. Unfortunately, the story also contains magical details that are impossible to believe! For example, Mordred's mother Morgan le Fay was said to be an enchantress who cast a magical spell on Arthur. Arthur's wise old helper, Merlin, was said to be a powerful wizard. Arthur's sword, Excalibur, was said to be sharp enough to cut through steel, and bright enough to blind Arthur's enemies. Excalibur's sheath was said to be more magical yet— blessed with the incredible power to save the one who wore it from being wounded.

With so much magic mixed into Arthur's story, it is hard to know how much of it is real— or even if Arthur himself was real. Serious historians tend to see Arthur as more entertaining legend than real history.

Another tale that mixed magic with history was the **legend of the Holy Grail**. The real Holy Grail was the cup that Jesus used to serve the wine of the Last Supper— the first Holy Communion (Matthew 26:27-28). What happened to the real Holy

Arthur of Britain woven into a tapestry

Grail, no one knows. But according to legend, the long-lost Holy Grail wound up in Britannia— perhaps because **Magnus Maximus** carried it there.

After defeating the Saxons, Arthur and his Knights of the Round Table needed a new mission to keep their hearts loyal and their fighting skills sharp. The quest to find the long-lost Holy Grail became that mission. The legends say that a few of Arthur's knights caught glimpses of the Holy Grail; but none of them ever managed to bring it back to Camelot.

Magnus Maximus was a soldier-turned-Roman-emperor who once commanded troops in Britannia. Maximus was also a devoted Christian, which may explain why legend has him carrying the Holy Grail to Britannia.

As junior emperor over part of the Western Roman Empire, Maximus ruled for just a few years before two senior emperors joined forces to crush him. These emperors hated Maximus so much that merely executing him wasn't enough to satisfy them. Instead, they added the *damnatio memorae*— a dreaded punishment that made it a crime for any Roman even to speak Maximus' name, or to remember him in any way.

ꑍꑍꑍꑍꑍꑍꑍꑍꑍꑍꑍꑍꑍꑍꑍꑍꑍꑍꑍꑍꑍꑍꑍꑍꑍꑍꑍꑍꑍꑍꑍ

If the Angles and Saxons had no written language when they conquered Britannia, then when did they learn to write? The answer may lie in a long poem titled *Beowulf*.

Beowulf is the oldest surviving long poem written in Old English, the language of the Angles. Exactly how old *Beowulf* is, no one knows for sure. Saxon storytellers may have recited *Beowulf* aloud for many years before someone finally wrote it down.

Like the tales of King Arthur, *Beowulf* mixes magic with legend. Beowulf is a mighty Anglo-Saxon warrior who tackles three monsters too terrible to be real. The first is a hideous man-eater called Grendel, who kills many warriors before Beowulf finally tears off his arm. Next comes Grendel's furious mother, bent on revenge. Fifty years after he kills Grendel's mother, a much older Beowulf tackles a huge, fire-breathing dragon. This last monster turns out to be Beowulf's undoing. Although he manages to kill the dragon, he soon dies of his battle wounds.

What makes *Beowulf* so important is that it is the only work from the British Dark Age that hasn't been lost. As such, it gives the modern world a rare glimpse into the world of that time and place.

Beowulf fighting the dragon

The **Celtic knot** is a form of art that first appeared in the British Isles around 400 AD, when the Roman army was starting to head back to Rome. The basic pattern of the Celtic knot is a woven cord that appears to have no beginning and no end. British artists used Celtic knots in all sorts of places— drawing them in books, weaving them into fabric and carving them onto monuments. Art scholars have identified eight basic Celtic knot patterns, along with several variations.

At first, the endless pattern of the Celtic knot may have represented the druids' teachings about endless reincarnation. Later, British Christians used Celtic knots to decorate beautiful books called illuminated manuscripts. One well-known example of the Celtic knot appears on the Celtic cross.

Celtic cross

The Arian Controversy

In Chapter 1, we read about the first big **heresy** that troubled the early church: Gnosticism. This chapter tells of the next big heresy: the **Arian Controversy**. The name "Arian" comes from **Arius**, an Egyptian priest who asked a troubling question: Was Jesus Christ really God, or was He only a special human being?

Ever since Christ was born, people have found it hard to believe that He was really the Son of God. Even the people who knew Him best, His own disciples, needed time to understand who He was. The disciples' confusion shows in Mark 4:41, after Jesus calms a wild storm on a lake. In awe at what the Lord has done, the disciples turn to one another and ask: "Who is this? Even the wind and the waves obey him!"

All that confusion went away after Jesus rose from the dead. That very day, Jesus opened the Scriptures to his disciples on the road to Emmaus— explaining who He was, why He had to die on the cross, and what His resurrection meant (Luke 24:13-32). After hearing from the risen Jesus, the disciples finally understood that He was the Son of God.

Centuries later, Arius offered a new way of thinking about Jesus. Arius came from Alexandria, Egypt— one of the leading cities of the early church. Around 315 AD, Arius started teaching that Christ was part of God's creation— not part of God Himself. He believed that God created Christ first, and then Christ helped God create everything else. In other words, Arius said, "There was a time when the Son [Christ] was not."

The problem with Arius' teaching was that it went against these words from John 1:1-3:

Arius arguing about Christ

"In the beginning was the Word [Christ], and the Word was with God, and the Word was God. He was with God in the beginning. Through him all things were made; without him nothing was made that has been made."

In other words, Arius went against a very important Christian belief: that Christ the Son is God, just as God the Father is God. If what Arius said was true, then Christ the Son would be lower than God the Father— which would mean that Christ wasn't really God.

Arius' main opponent was another priest from Alexandria: a brilliant Bible scholar called **Athanasius**. Unlike

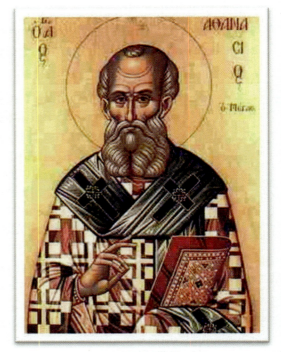

Icon of Athanasius

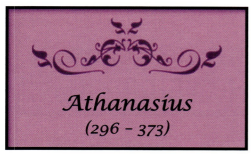

Athanasius
(296 – 373)

Arius, Athanasius was absolutely convinced that Christ was God. Why? Because God alone has the power to forgive sin. If Christ were not God, Athanasius wondered, then how would Christ's sacrifice on the cross save sinners from their sin? "Jesus that I know as my Redeemer," Athanasius said, "cannot be less than God."

The contest between Arius and Athanasius came to a head in 325 AD. In that year, Emperor Constantine summoned church leaders from all around the Roman Empire to Nicaea— a city not far from Constantinople. When they got there, he gave them an important job to do: finding an answer to the Arian Controversy.

After a month of arguing, the Council of Nicaea finally declared that Athanasius was right, and Arius wrong. Christ the Son is not lower than God the Father, as Arius wrongly said. Instead, true Christians are to believe in the Holy Trinity:

God the Father, God the Son and God the Holy Spirit. All three persons of the Holy Trinity are equally God.

This does not mean that Christians worship three gods! Instead, each person of the Trinity represents one of three ways in which God has revealed Himself to man. God the Father revealed Himself by creating everything we see. God the Son revealed Himself by being born as a man, by bearing the penalty for man's sin, and by rising from the dead. God the Holy Spirit revealed Himself as the Lord and Giver of life, and by speaking through the prophets. The Council Nicaea wrote all this down in an important new statement of faith called the Nicene Creed.

The Arian Controversy didn't end at the Council of Nicaea. Poor Athanasius often had to defend his ideas, and sometimes lost. Over the years, Athanasius' enemies managed to kick him out of Alexandria no fewer than five times! No matter what happened, Athanasius never stopped insisting that Christ was both God and man— fully divine and fully human, both at the same time. The persistent Athanasius is now honored as a "doctor of the Catholic Church"— one of the greatest Christian thinkers of all time.

Athanasius is also remembered as a father of the canon of Scripture. He was among the first to collect the twenty-seven books of the New Testament, and to insist that these books alone were inspired by God.

Emperor Constantine and his bishops at the Council of Nicaea, with the condemned Arius under their feet

CHAPTER 3

The Christian Church in the Early Middle Ages

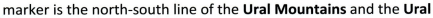

Europe

Europe is the sixth-biggest continent, smaller than all others except Australia. But this is a bit misleading. For Europe also shares a long border with the biggest continent: Asia. Some people call it all one continent, naming it **Eurasia**.

Because no ocean separates Europe from Asia, mapmakers use other markers to separate them. The first marker is the north-south line of the **Ural Mountains** and the **Ural River**. Europe lies west of this line, and Asia east. The other marker is the east-west line of the **Caspian Sea**, the **Caucasus Mountains** and the **Black Sea**. Europe lies north of this line, and Asia south.

Three big peninsulas jut off the southern edge of Europe. The western one is the **Iberian Peninsula**, home to Spain and Portugal. The center one is the **Italian Peninsula**, home to the Republic of Italy. The eastern one is the **Balkan Peninsula**, home to Greece, Bulgaria and more.

The giant peninsula that juts off northern Europe is called **Fenno-Scandia**. The Scandinavian countries of Norway and Sweden stand on Fenno-Scandia. So does Finland, as well as part of Russia.

Relics

The Bible tells of miracles that happened when people touched certain objects. The first example comes from the Old Testament, which says in 2 Kings 13:21: "Once while some Israelites were burying a man, suddenly they saw a band of raiders; so they threw the man's body into **Elisha**'s tomb. When the body touched Elisha's bones, the man came to life and stood up on his feet."

Elisha was the heir of Elijah, a great prophet from Old Testament times.

Another example comes from the New Testament, which says in Acts 19:11-12: "God did extraordinary miracles through Paul, so that even handkerchiefs and aprons that had touched him were taken to the sick, and their illnesses were cured, and the evil spirits left them."

Special objects like Elisha's bones and Paul's handkerchiefs are called **relics**. A relic can be anything connected to someone from Christian history, either Christ Himself or one of the old saints. It might be something a saint owned, something a saint touched, or even the bones of a saint.

With miracles like these, it isn't hard to understand why early Christians were fascinated with relics. Some would travel any distance, and pay any price, for their chance to see a miracle!

In modern times, though, most Christians are more doubtful about relics. By now, most relics have changed hands so many times that it's hard to know for sure if they ever really belonged to a saint. Who can say that at some unguarded moment over the centuries, some greedy soul didn't steal the real relics— leaving false ones in their places?

Even so, the Catholic Church still preserves many relics. Some are supposed to be pieces of wood from the True Cross— the cross upon which Roman soldiers crucified Jesus. Others are supposed to be iron from the spikes that held Jesus on the

Well-known Relics

cross. There are also the sword of St. Peter, which the Apostle Peter used to slice off the ear of the high priest's servant in John 18:10; the Spear of Longinus, which a Roman soldier used to pierce Jesus' side in John 19:34; and many, many others.

The **Shroud of Turin** is a linen burial cloth that is supposed to bear an image of Jesus' face. Some people believe that the face was burned onto the shroud by the same mighty power that raised Jesus from the dead. Others believe the shroud is a hoax— a clever fake painted by some medieval artist.

An altered photo of the Shroud of Turin

Reliquaries are special containers made to show and preserve relics. A reliquary may be a glass-sided display case like the one at left, which is supposed to hold the chains Roman soldiers used to bind St. Peter. One may also be a church-shaped casket like the one at right, which is supposed to hold remains of Archbishop Thomas Becket (Chapter 13).

The Monastic Movement

The first Christians almost never worshipped in church buildings. Instead, they worshipped in house churches. These were small groups that met quietly in believers' homes, hiding from the prying eyes of Christian-hating Romans.

Some early Christians also dug secret chambers called catacombs, hidden in and around cities like Rome and Naples. Most

House churches were small groups of Christians who met in believers' homes.

Catacombs were secret underground chambers built by early Christians, mainly to bury their dead.

catacombs started as burial places for Christian dead. For the Romans usually burned their dead; while Christians preferred to bury their dead, in hope of the resurrection. A few catacombs also held special rooms for church services.

All that changed when **Constantine** came along. As we read in Chapter 1, Constantine was the first Christian Emperor of Rome. Under the approving nod of Constantine, Christianity moved from forbidden to fashionable. The emperor donated public lands to churches, and even spent public money to build the first Christian cathedrals. No longer did Roman Christians have to hide in catacombs!

Grave niches in the walls of a catacomb beneath Rome, photo courtesy Dnalor 01

Alas, Constantine's help came with a price. Before Constantine, most churches were poor. The few churches that did have extra money rarely spent it on buildings; for they had no buildings. Instead, they used extra money to help hurting church members, or to benefit the poor.

After Constantine, though, churches found all kinds of new uses for money. For the first time, churches could spend money on big buildings and rich possessions. Misguided churches started paying more attention to worldly treasures than they did to their own people.

Some Christians weren't comfortable with all these riches. They feared that the richer Christians grew, the less they followed Christ. For Christ was never rich in worldly treasures. He taught his disciples to be "rich toward God"— to store up treasures in heaven, as He said in Matthew 6:19-21:

> "Do not store up for yourselves treasures on earth, where moths and vermin destroy, and where thieves break in and steal. But store up for yourselves treasures in heaven, where moths and vermin do not destroy, and where thieves do not break in and steal. For where your treasure is, there your heart will be also."

One of the first Christians who felt this way was an Egyptian called **Anthony of Thebes**. The future Saint Anthony was born into a rich Christian family from **Thebes**, one of Egypt's ancient capitals. He was just eighteen years old when his father died, leaving him enough money to stay rich all his life.

Most young men would

Anthony of Thebes
(251? – 356?)

Thebes stood across the Nile River from the famous Valley of the Kings, where the ancient Egyptians buried so many pharaohs.

have done just that: stayed rich. But Anthony was one of those rare Christians who really took Jesus' words to heart. Instead of keeping his family fortune, Anthony followed the advice Jesus gave the rich young man in Mark 10:21-22:

> "Jesus looked at him and loved him. 'One thing you lack,' he said. 'Go, sell everything you have and give to the poor, and you will have treasure in heaven. Then come, follow me.' At this the man's face fell. He went away sad, because he had great wealth."

Unlike the rich young man from Mark, Anthony really did sell all his father's property and give to the poor— holding back only enough to care for his sister. He then moved out to the deserts of Egypt, where he took up an extremely hard lifestyle: the self-denying life of an **ascetic**.

Why the desert? Because Anthony wanted to put the material world out of his mind, so that he could focus on the spiritual world. Anything that reminded him of his old life was a distraction— something that might come between him and God.

The things Anthony gave up for Christ were the very things other men wanted most. For example, he gave up women— for fear that if he married, then he might love his wife more than he loved God. He also gave up big meals— for fear that if his stomach was too full, then he might forget to thank God for daily bread. Anthony sometimes ate only once every three or four days!

Denying oneself isn't easy, especially if one has once been rich. Many times over the years, Anthony was tempted to leave his harsh desert and go back to the comfort of city life. Medieval artists painted several pictures of Anthony in his desert home, steadfastly battling the demons of temptation.

No matter what demons he faced, Anthony never gave in. True to his promises, he stayed in his desert home for the rest of his life— which lasted 105 years! In resisting temptation so long and so well, Anthony won a reputation as one of the holiest Christians who ever lived.

Anthony of Thebes being tempted by demons

As Anthony's reputation grew, others followed him into the desert— trying to live lives as holy as his. In time, special Christians like Anthony and his followers got a special name: **monks**.

A monk is a devoted believer who pulls away from the world he can see, so that he can focus on the world he can't see— the invisible spiritual world of God. The female version is called a **nun**. Both monks and nuns use spiritual **disciplines** to draw closer to God— things like prayer, fasting, studying the Bible and serving others.

Some monks built little communities for themselves— places where they could live together, work together, and help each other fight off temptation. These were the first **monasteries**. The nun's version of the monastery was usually called a **convent**. But there were other names for both, including priory, cloister, abbey and more.

Every monk or nun who joined a monastery or convent vowed to live by special rules. Although some rules were stricter than others, nearly all required at least three common vows:

- **The Vow of Poverty**: Monks and nuns promised to give up all worldly possessions, holding back next to nothing for themselves. Some owned nothing but a bowl to hold their bit of food.
- **The Vow of Chastity**: Monks and nuns promised never to marry, and never to be involved with the opposite sex.
- **The Vow of Obedience**: Monks and nuns promised to do whatever their leaders ordered.

Early monks worked hard to support themselves. Most monasteries sewed all their own clothes, and grew as much of their own food as they could. Most also made trade goods— valuable items to sell, so that they could buy things they couldn't make for themselves. Some monasteries made wine, beer or baked goods; others cloth or shoes; still others furniture.

Older monasteries often had several buildings, all arranged around a central court. Of course, each monastery had its church or chapel. Each also had a dormitory filled with cells— tiny bedrooms for the monks. Many also had schools and/or hospitals. There might also be a library for the monastery's precious books, as well as a **scriptorium** for copying books.

St. Catherine's Monastery at the foot of Mount Sinai, Egypt, built in the 500s

Some monasteries surrounded themselves with walls, which served two purposes. First, they protected the monks. Second, they shielded the monks from the temptations of the outside world.

Part of every **abbot**'s job was making sure that his monks kept their vows. Some abbots allowed their monks to eat only once per day in winter, and twice in summer. They ate in silence, not talking and laughing like schoolboys. Eating too much, talking too much and laughing too much were all signs that monks no longer felt sorry for their sins— which meant that they were no longer grateful for Christ's sacrifice.

A **scriptorium** was a room in which special monks called **scribes** copied out books by hand.

Abbot was one name for the leader of an abbey, or monastery.

Early monks never let themselves get too comfortable. For example, they often wore hair shirts beneath their **habits**, or outer robes. A hair shirt was a scratchy shirt woven from the roughest goat hair, to make it as uncomfortable as possible. The constant discomfort of hair shirts was a constant reminder of Christ's sufferings.

To set themselves apart from other men, some monks cut their hair in a special style called the **tonsure**. Tonsured monks shaved the tops of their heads, but kept a ring of unshaven hair around the top.

In addition to their **habits**, some nuns wore a white headdress called a **wimple**.

Early monks also slept as little as possible; for sleep was also too comfortable. Such luxuries as soft beds and comfortable chairs were unthinkable. Many slept on the hard floor in their hair shirts and habits, ready to rise for prayer at a moment's notice.

Some medieval monasteries followed a daily schedule called the **canonical hours**, which set aside certain times for prayer and worship. These monasteries called all monks to prayer seven times each day. The idea for the canonical hours may have come from King David, who wrote in Psalm 119:164: "Seven times a day I praise you for your righteous laws."

More Giants of the Early Church

The future **Saint Jerome** was born into a wealthy family from a part of the Roman Empire called Dalmatia, just across the Adriatic Sea from Italy. Wanting the best education for his son, Jerome's father sent him to school in Rome.

Jerome
(340? – 420)

Young Jerome was an excellent student— when he wasn't wasting his time, as most rich young men did. Although Jerome called himself a Christian, he rarely studied the Bible. Instead, he studied what most Roman schools taught: the classics of Greek literature. He spent his days reading great Greek authors like Homer and Plato, and his nights partying.

Years later, Jerome was suffering through a serious illness— when out of nowhere, the Lord sent him a life-changing vision. Just what Jerome saw, no one now knows for sure. It is said that he saw himself in the afterlife, being punished for wasting his time on Greek classics. Whatever Jerome saw, this vision was the end of his classical studies. As soon as he recovered, he focused his whole attention on his new life's work— becoming a great Christian **scholar**.

A **scholar** is someone who studies a subject deeply, learning all there is to know about it.

Jerome went on to become one of the greatest Christian scholars ever. His friend Augustine of Hippo paid him this highest of compliments: "What Jerome is ignorant of, no mortal has ever known." Even so, Jerome was in his forties before he finally found the best use for all that scholarship.

Before Jerome's time, there was no complete translation of the Bible in Latin. Instead, there were several incomplete translations— all in different styles of Latin, done at different times over the years.

The Vulgate

That started to change in 382, when the pope asked Jerome to translate the four gospels into good Latin. Now Jerome understood why he had spent all those years studying Greek! Since Matthew, Mark, Luke and John all wrote mostly in Greek, the Greek expert Jerome was the perfect choice to translate their work. After finishing this first assignment, Jerome went on to translate the rest of the Greek New Testament into Latin.

Translating the Old Testament would turn out to be much harder. For the Old Testament authors wrote in Hebrew, which

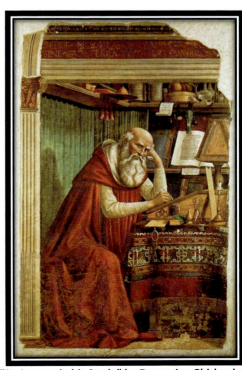

"St. Jerome in his Study" by Domenico Ghirlandaio

Jerome didn't know as well as he knew Greek. Jerome's solution was to spend years studying Hebrew, with help from a Jewish-born man who was now a Christian. Then he spent more years finishing an enormous task: translating all thirty-nine books of the Hebrew Old Testament into Latin!

The outcome of Jerome's long years of work was one of the most important books of all time: a complete Latin Bible called the **Vulgate**. Its name comes from *versio vulgata*— Latin for "the version commonly used."

To say that Jerome's Vulgate was "commonly used" is a huge understatement. From the next 1,000 years, the Vulgate was the only version of the Bible that most people in the West ever saw or heard. No matter what their native language, Western priests always read the Bible in the Latin of the Vulgate.

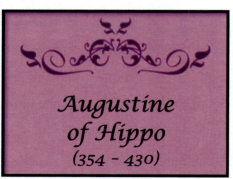

Monica of Hippo
(331 – 387)

ௐௐௐௐௐௐௐௐௐௐௐௐௐௐௐௐௐௐௐௐௐௐௐௐௐௐௐௐௐௐௐௐௐௐௐ

The future **Saint Monica** started as a Christian mother from Hippo, a port in North Africa (now Annaba, Algeria). Like all Christian mothers, Monica wanted all her children safe in the arms of Christ. Alas, Monica's eldest son resisted Christ. The worst day of Monica's life came when her eldest son rejected Christ altogether, and instead took up a strange religion called Manichaeism.

In fear for her son's life, Monica cried to her bishop— begging him to do something, anything, to save her son. Touched to the heart by Monica's tears, the bishop told her that she must never stop praying for her son. For he promised her, "the child of those tears shall never perish." At the time, Monica had no idea that she was praying for a future saint!

Monica's eldest son, **Augustine of Hippo**, wasn't saintly at all— at least, not as a young man. Despite all Monica's pleading, Augustine drank too much, gambled too much and partied too much. Worst of all, Augustine had a child with a woman who wasn't his wife. Although it pained Augustine to disappoint his mother, he loved his wicked lifestyle too much to give it up.

Augustine of Hippo (354 – 430)

This went on until Augustine was 32 years old, when a devoted Christian named Alypius stopped by to share some scriptures from Paul's letter to the Romans. In his head, Augustine knew that everything Paul said was right; but in his heart, he still didn't feel ready to give his life to Christ. Anguished to the point of tears, Augustine walked away— mostly so that Alypius wouldn't see him crying.

As Augustine walked along his tortured way, he heard a childish voice coming from a nearby house— or at least, he thought he heard a childish voice. The child seemed to be chanting, "Take up and read, take up and read." Augustine searched his memory for some childhood song or game that used these words, but couldn't think of one.

Augustine of Hippo with his beloved mother Monica

Finally, Augustine understood what he was supposed to "take up and read": The Bible! Running back to Alypius, Augustine seized the Book of Romans, opened it and read the first words that met his eyes.

Just as Anthony of Thebes found his life verses in Mark 10:21-22, so Augustine found his life verses in Romans 13:13-14. These verses begin, "Let us behave properly as in the day, not in carousing and drunkenness…" From the moment he read them, Augustine knew that the Lord was calling him to give up his life of sin and serve the Church. Other than Alypius, the first person to hear the good news of Augustine's conversion was his faithful mother Monica— who had never stopped praying for her son.

Augustine went on to become one of the best servants the Church ever had. He is best remembered for two important Christian ideas: (1) **original sin** and (2) **total depravity**.

According to Augustine, the original sin happened when Adam and Eve deliberately disobeyed God in the Garden of Eden— as we read in Genesis 3. As parents of the whole human race, Adam and Eve handed down sin to all their children. This means that everyone is born "totally depraved"— completely sinful, and completely unable to turn toward God without Christ's help.

> **Original sin** means that all human beings are born under the sin of Adam and Eve.
>
> **Total depravity** means that all human beings are completely sinful, and completely unable to turn toward God without Christ's help.

Original sin helps explain why God the Father had to send His Son Jesus Christ. Out of all people who ever lived on earth, only Christ wasn't born into original sin. Why? Because Christ was born of God, not of Adam. Christ went on to live the only perfect, sinless life ever. This is why only Christ can help people turn away from their sin, and turn toward God.

The Pelagian Controversy

A preacher called **Pelagius** disagreed with Augustine. Like Anthony of Thebes, Pelagius was a monk who denied himself every day— turning away from sin every day. He thought, "If I can turn away from sin, then why can't others do the same?" In other words, Pelagius didn't believe that people are born into original sin. Instead, he believed that people choose to sin— which means that if they try hard enough, then they can also choose not to sin.

The problem was that if Pelagius was right, then Augustine was wrong about original sin— which meant that people could turn toward God on their own, without Christ's help!

Just as the Council of Nicaea met to answer Arius (Chapter 2), so the **Council of Carthage** met to answer Pelagius. In 418, the Council of Carthage decided that Augustine was right, and Pelagius wrong. True Christians were to believe what Augustine taught: that all people are born into original sin, and need Jesus Christ to save them from their sin. As for Pelagius, the Council declared him a heretic.

Christian Missionaries in the British Isles

When the Roman army left the British Isles, it left behind many Christians there— including, if the legend is true, King Arthur and his knights (Chapter 2). But Christianity wasn't the only religion in the British Isles. The Celtic religion of the druids had not yet died out; and the invading Anglo-Saxons brought in religions of their own.

None of those other religions lasted. Within three hundred years after the Romans left, almost everyone in the British Isles called himself a Christian! This huge change was partly the work of three great missionaries: Saint Patrick, Saint Columba and Saint Augustine of Canterbury.

Patrick of Ireland
(? – 493)

The future **Saint Patrick** was born to Christian parents in a Christian part of Scotland. Patrick was still a teenager when Celtic raiders kidnapped him and carried him off to Ireland. There Patrick became what no Christian boy ever dreamed of being: a slave to a druid, a priest of the Celtic religion.

At first, young Patrick hated his master's savage religion. Later, though, Patrick's hatred turned to pity for the Irish people. His time among the Irish helped him understand why the Celts lived like savages: because they had never heard of the mercy and salvation that God offered in Jesus Christ!

After six years in Ireland, Patrick suddenly received a vision— telling him that a ship was waiting to take him back to Scotland. Certain that his vision was true, Patrick slipped away from his druid master and headed for a port on the east coast. The fact that this port lay 200 miles away, all of it on foot, didn't stop him. Upon reaching the coast, the tired Patrick boarded his waiting ship and sailed home to Scotland.

After all he'd been through, Patrick expected to find peace and safety in Scotland. Instead, he received another vision. This time, poor Irishmen appeared to Patrick— begging him to come and "walk among us once more." Forgetting all the dangers that Christians faced in Celtic Ireland, Patrick sailed back to share the gospel with the Irish people he had grown to love.

Patrick spent the rest of his life in Ireland— arguing with druids, sharing the gospel and baptizing new Christians. As the one missionary who did more to bring Christianity to Ireland than any other, Saint Patrick became the **patron saint** of Ireland.

> A **patron saint** is a saint who is special to a certain place or person.

The name of Patrick is also tied to three well-known Irish legends. The first says that as Patrick sat on a hilltop, trying to fast and pray, snakes attacked him. Patrick answered by asking God to banish all snakes from Ireland— which explains why there are no wild snakes in Ireland, even now.

A second legend says that Patrick used the **shamrock** to represent the Holy Trinity. The shamrock is a three-leafed clover found all over Ireland. Patrick said that just as the shamrock is one plant with three leaves, so God is one God in three persons: God the Father, God the Son and God the Holy Spirit.

Yet another legend tells how Patrick drew the first **Celtic cross** (Chapter 2). One day as Patrick was preaching to some Celts, they showed him a standing stone engraved with a circle— probably a monument to some Celtic moon goddess. Patrick answered by drawing a cross through the circle, and then filling his cross with a Celtic knot. As Patrick saw it, the endless Celtic knot represented the endless love of God.

Stained glass of Saint Patrick holding a shamrock

Columba of Iona
(521 – 597)

Saint Columba

did what Patrick did, only in reverse: instead of being born in Scotland and ministering in Ireland, Columba was born in Ireland and ministered in Scotland.

Columba making the sign of the cross at the gates of Inverness

It all started in 563, when Columba moved from Ireland to the island of **Iona**. Iona is one of the Inner Hebrides, which lie off the northwest coast of Scotland. There Columba built a new monastery, which he used to train Scottish ministers. From his base at Iona, Columba sent ministers all over Scotland— planting churches wherever they went.

But there was one city where Columba's ministers weren't welcome— a place called Inverness, near the northern end of the famous Loch Ness. Inverness was the home of Brude, a stubborn Pictish king who wanted nothing to do with Christianity. When Brude heard that Columba was on his way to Inverness, he barred his gates.

Columba was having none of it. As he drew near to Inverness, he drew the sign of the cross in the air— at which the bars flew back, and the gates swung wide open! Awed by Columba's miracle, Brude changed his mind about Christianity. Columba went on to baptize all Inverness.

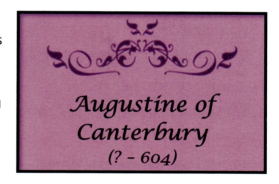

Augustine of Canterbury
(? – 604)

Around 595 AD, a powerful pope called Gregory the Great decided to send a missionary to Great Britain. Sharing the gospel was only part of this missionary's task. The other part was to establish the Church of Rome's authority over Britain. Gregory wanted all British Christians to know that he was their holy father, and that they must obey him. The man he chose to tell the British this was another Augustine— not Augustine of Hippo, but the future **Saint Augustine of Canterbury**.

At first, Augustine didn't think much of the pope's choice. For Augustine was a monk, not a missionary. He had expected to serve out his life in a safe monastery, not risk his neck in a barbarian backwater like Britain. He had heard how savage the Anglo-Saxons were, and how many ships sank while crossing the treacherous English Channel.

In fact, Augustine was so upset about the pope's choice that he almost didn't go. Halfway to Britain, a frightened Augustine announced that the savage Anglo-Saxons simply weren't ready for civilization—and started to turn back! Before he did, though, Pope Gregory wrote another letter— ordering him on to Britain.

Canterbury Cathedral, seat of the Archbishop of Canterbury

After landing in southeastern England, Augustine set up his church capital at a place called Canterbury, Kent. Pope Gregory appointed Augustine as the first **Archbishop of Canterbury**— the overseer of all bishops in southeastern England. Ever since then, the Archbishop of Canterbury has been one of the top two or three church officers in all England.

Augustine of Canterbury went on to convert many Saxons to Christianity— including the first Christian Anglo-Saxon king ever, Ethelbert of Kent.

Christ on His throne in an illustration from the Book of Kells

〰〰〰〰〰〰〰〰〰〰〰〰〰〰〰〰〰〰〰〰〰〰〰〰〰〰〰〰

Before about 1450, when Johannes Gutenberg invented the printing press, all books had to be copied by hand. Some monks spent their whole lives in dreary scriptoriums, copying out books word-for-word.

The Book of Kells

Not all books were plain words, though. To make their books more pleasing to the eye, some monks added fancy initials to start every page— or even every paragraph. The best books also had hand-painted illustrations by the monastery's best artists. Any hand-copied, hand-illustrated book from medieval times is called an **illuminated manuscript**.

"Writing is excessive drudgery. It crooks your back, it dims your sight, it twists your stomach and your sides."

"As the harbor is welcome to the sailor, so is the last line to the scribe."

— Scribes' comments found in the margins of two medieval manuscripts

To **illuminate** something is to shed light on it.

The best example of an illuminated manuscript is the famous **Book of Kells**. The Book of Kells is a copy of the four gospels made by the monks of Iona around 700 – 800 AD— probably in honor of Saint Columba. Stunning art marks almost every page of the Book of Kells, making it a precious treasure.

Around 800 AD, a band of fierce Vikings raided Iona— scattering frightened monks in all directions. One of those monks probably carried the precious Book of Kells to the monastery at Kells, Ireland, which is how the book got its name.

Kells turned out to be no safer than Iona had been. Around 1,000 AD, some unknown thief stole the book— to get the gold and gems on its cover. After ripping off the cover, the thief hid the rest under some damp sod, where monks later found it. The Book of Kells is still missing its cover, and still has water damage from its time under the sod.

A hand-drawn initial letter from the Book of Kells, complete with Celtic knot

The Black Sea

The Black Sea is a big body of water on the border between Europe and Asia. Like the Mediterranean, the Black Sea is an inland sea— one that is almost completely surrounded by land.

To reach the Black Sea from the Mediterranean, ships must first sail through the **Aegean Sea**. If the Mediterranean Sea is shaped like a duck, then the Aegean is the duck's right wing. From there, ships must sail on through three narrow bodies of water: (1) the **Dardanelles** strait, (2) the **Sea of Marmara** and (3) the **Bosporus** strait.

At the southern end of the Bosporus stands a very old, very important city. Different peoples have called this city by different names over the centuries. The ancient Greeks called it **Byzantion**, and the ancient Latins **Byzantium**. The Romans renamed it **Constantinople**— after Constantine, their first Christian emperor. It was the Turks who gave it the name everyone uses today: **Istanbul**.

What made Constantinople so important was its location. Since the Bosporus was so narrow, Constantinople acted like a gatehouse between the Black Sea and the Mediterranean Sea.

Whoever ruled Constantinople had the power to decide who could trade in the Black Sea and who couldn't.

Besides its great location, Constantinople was also blessed with a great natural harbor called the **Golden Horn**. The calm, deep waters of the Golden Horn made Constantinople the perfect place to load and unload trade ships.

Just west of the Black Sea stands a section of Europe called the **Balkan Peninsula**, or simply the **Balkans**. The Balkan Peninsula is the easternmost of three big peninsulas that jut off the southern edge of Europe; the other two are the Italian Peninsula in the center and the Iberian Peninsula in the west. In medieval times, Constantinople and the Balkans were the heart of the **Byzantine Empire**.

The Balkan Peninsula

The Byzantine Empire

The story of the Byzantine Empire starts with a Roman emperor. In 285 AD, Emperor Diocletian split the Roman Empire in two— hoping that two big empires would be easier to run than one huge one. Starting then, there were usually two Roman Empires: one in the west, and another in the east. The **Western Roman Empire** usually had its capital at Rome; while the **Eastern Roman Empire** always had its capital at Constantinople.

We've read how the Roman Empire fell. It happened in 476 AD, when Emperor Romulus surrendered to the Ostrogoths. But it was only the Western Roman Empire that fell in 476. The Eastern Roman Empire lived on for almost 1,000 years— all the way to 1453, when the Ottoman Empire finally broke into Constantinople (Chapter 20).

This was a bit of a problem for historians. On the one hand, the Eastern Roman Empire lived on long after the Fall of Rome. On the other hand, this empire was far different from the old Roman Empire!

Why? Because the East was so different from the West. One difference was that most easterners spoke Greek— not Latin, as the Romans did. They had different stories, and looked back to different heroes. Other differences showed up in the Christian church. By the late 400s, the Greek churches of the East were growing apart from the Latin churches of the West.

Because the Eastern Roman Empire was so different, historians settled on a new name for it. They called it the Byzantine Empire— after *Byzantion*, the old Greek name for Constantinople.

Of course, the people of the Byzantine Empire didn't know about this name change— because it hadn't happened yet! In their minds, the Byzantine Empire was still the Eastern Roman Empire. The greatest Byzantine emperor, **Justinian I**, didn't see the Fall of Rome as a historic milestone. Instead, he saw it as a setback— a bump on the road toward rebuilding the great Roman Empire.

Emperor Justinian I (483? – 565)

A **commoner** is someone born into a family with no royal or noble blood.

Unlike most emperors, Justinian wasn't born into a royal family. He was born a **commoner** by the name of Flavius. But Flavius had two big advantages in life. One was that his uncle, whose name was Justin, was the best general in the Byzantine army. The other was that Justin had no sons.

General Justin's big chance came in 518, when an old emperor died. Since this emperor also had no sons, there was an election to decide who would take his place. As the best general in the empire, Justin easily won!

Now that Justin was emperor, he needed an heir to take his place when he was gone. To get one, he adopted his nephew Flavius. Along with the adoption came a new name: "Justinian," meaning "son of Justin."

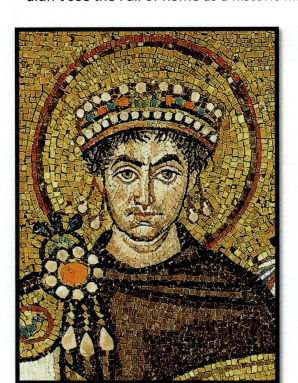

Mosaic of Justinian I from the Basilica of San Vitale in Ravenna, Italy

Justinian's future wife, **Theodora**, was born far lower than he. Her father was in a business that most Byzantines looked down on: the entertainment business. He worked as an animal handler, training bears to amuse crowds between chariot races. Young Theodora worked in the same business, acting in naughty plays. Given how Byzantines felt about entertainers, it seemed unlikely that Theodora would ever be anything but an actress.

A trip to Egypt changed all that. When Theodora was about sixteen years old, she moved from Constantinople to Alexandria, Egypt— where she became a Christian. As a young woman learning strong Christian morals, Theodora couldn't act in naughty plays anymore! Instead, she took up an even lowlier profession— becoming a wool-spinner.

Justinian was still a young man when he somehow crossed paths with this lowly wool-spinner, and fell in love with her. He longed to marry Theodora; but unfortunately, an old law said that nobles couldn't marry entertainers— even if they weren't entertainers anymore. Justinian begged and begged Justin to get rid of that old law. For a long time, though, Justin refused— partly because his wife looked down on Theodora.

Then the young couple caught a break. After his wife died, Justin finally repealed that old law! Justinian and Theodora were married in 525. Justin died two years later, leaving Justinian to take his place. With that, Theodora finished her incredible rise— all the way from wool-spinner to Empress of the Byzantine Empire!

Empress Theodora

The first thing Justinian did as emperor was to fix his laws. Before his day, the Byzantine Empire was a confusing collection of conquered peoples— each with its own laws. Justinian wanted to bring all his people under one set of laws— one righteous system that would be the same all over his empire. Historians call this system the **Justinian Code**.

The Justinian Code came in four main parts. First came the Codex, which contained the laws themselves. Next came the Digests, which explained the thinking behind the laws. Third came the Institutes, which were textbooks for law students. The fourth part, the Novels, presented new laws written after the Codex.

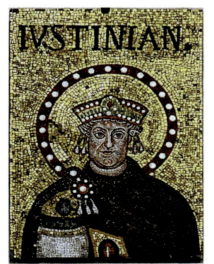

Mosaic of an older Justinian

One important goal of the Justinian Code was to make the Byzantine Empire more Christian. The

very first law said that all good citizens must be faithful Christians. So it was that in Justinian's day, Roman law came full circle. Early Roman emperors had made it illegal to be a Christian. Now Justinian made it illegal to be anything but a Christian!

Bringing law and order isn't easy, especially for people who aren't used to them. Early in Justinian's reign, his obsession with law almost ruined him!

The trouble started over a chariot race, of all things. Fast, dangerous chariot racing was as popular in Constantinople as it had been Rome. The city's main racing arena, the Hippodrome, held up to 100,000 fans. They all screamed for one of four teams: the Greens, the Blues, the Whites or the Reds. Justinian and Theodora were Blues fans; but the Greens were also popular.

Mosaic of a chariot race winner

After an especially important chariot race, a fight broke out between Blues fans and Greens fans. When the fight was over, several people lay dead!

Most racing fans saw these deaths as accidents— unfortunate, but understandable after such a big race. Justinian saw them differently. As a strong believer in law and order, Justinian insisted on arresting the killers— both Blue and Green— and sentencing them to death!

The next big racing event at the Hippodrome fell on January 13, 532. From the start of the first race, both Greens and Blues chanted at Justinian— warning him not to put his prisoners to death. The longer Justinian didn't answer, the angrier the chanters grew.

At race's end, the chanters demanded that Justinian release his prisoners. When Justinian refused, they started to riot! This was the start of the Nika Riots— deadly riots that threatened to tear Justinian off his throne. The rioters set huge fires, destroying some of the best buildings in Constantinople.

As that awful week wore on, Justinian learned that his enemies in the Hippodrome had elected a new emperor to take his place. At this, Justinian decided that his reign was probably over— and that he had better get out of Constantinople while he still could!

> The **Nika Riots** of 532 were named for the cries of the rioters, who shouted "Nika"— Greek for "Conquer!"

This is when Theodora proved her worth. When the empress heard that Justinian was planning to run away, she stopped him, saying: "Those who have worn the crown should never survive its loss. Never will I see the day when I am not saluted as empress. Royalty makes a fine burial shroud." In other words, Theodora would rather die young as an empress than live on as a disgraced commoner. Taking courage from Theodora, Justinian decided to either save his throne or die trying!

Justinian's plan took advantage of the hatred between Greens and Blues. Six days into the Nika Riots, Justinian sent a loyal friend called Narses into the Hippodrome. At Narses' belt hung a purse bulging with gold. Heading straight for the Blues, Narses reminded them that Justinian had always been a loyal Blue. He also reminded them that the man they had chosen to replace Justinian was as Green as Green could be. Each time Narses spoke, a bit of gold passed from his purse to a Blue leader's purse.

Whether it was the reminders or the gold, Justinian's plan worked. After a bit of thought, the Blues walked out of the Hippodrome— much to the astonishment of the Greens. With the Blues out of the way, Justinian's best troops came crashing in on the rioters who remained— killing them by the thousands. Instead of weakening Justinian, the Nika Riots ended up strengthening him.

Justinian I Coin

One of the buildings destroyed by the Nika Riots was an old cathedral called the **Hagia Sophia**.

The Hagia Sophia

Actually, this was the second Hagia Sophia to be destroyed. Another riot had destroyed the first Hagia Sophia long ago, back in the time of John Chrysostom (below).

After the Nika Riots, the empire had to rebuild the Hagia Sophia a second time. Justinian vowed to make his new Hagia Sophia the grandest church ever built— grander, even, than Solomon's Temple in Jerusalem.

Outside the Hagia Sophia

Five years later, Justinian delivered on his vow. The third Hagia Sophia is without a doubt one of the grandest buildings ever built! The most fantastic part was its domed roof. The immense dome measured 102 feet across the base, and soared to an incredible 180 feet high at its peak. Forty arched windows ringed the base of the dome, filling the church with warm, glowing light. The effect was so stunning that the human eye could hardly take it all in.

Another fantastic part of the Hagia Sophia was all the **mosaic** art inside. The Byzantines were expert mosaic artists; and the mosaics in the Hagia Sophia were some of their best. They filled whole fields of their mosaics with *tesserae* cut from real gold, silver and precious stones. The warm glow from the Hagia Sophia's high windows made these mosaics even more stunning.

A **mosaic** is a work of art made of many small tiles, all cemented onto a wall, floor or ceiling. Mosaic tiles are called **tesserae**.

As the grandest cathedral in all the East, the Hagia Sophia became a symbol of Eastern Christianity. The **Patriarch of Constantinople**, leader of all Eastern churches, made his headquarters at the Hagia Sophia.

After putting down the Nika Riots, Justinian turned to the biggest task of his reign: rebuilding the Roman Empire. He wanted to take back all the lands that had been lost when the barbarians conquered the Western Roman Empire. To make that happen, Justinian turned to his favorite general: a Byzantine hero called **Belisarius**.

The first place Belisarius tackled was North Africa. His enemies there were the **Vandals**— the same Vandals who had sacked Rome back in 455. Since then, the Vandals had moved down to North Africa. The Vandals' capital, Carthage, is now part of Tunis, Tunisia.

Inside the Hagia Sophia, looking up at the dome

The big showdown between Belisarius and the Vandals came at a place called **Ad Decimum**. This was nothing but a milepost on the road to Carthage, ten miles south of the city.

Things looked bad for Belisarius at first. The Vandals brought 15,000 troops to the **Battle of Ad Decimum**— about twice as many as Belisarius brought! Early in the battle, the huge number of Vandals forced Belisarius to retreat.

> **Ad Decimum** is Latin for "at the tenth."

But then fortunes reversed. As the Vandals moved forward, their king came across the body of his beloved brother— who had just been killed in battle. The sight sent King Hilderic into a fit of grief, making him forget all about his army. Without Hilderic to lead it, the Vandal army collapsed— leaving Belisarius on top! With this great victory, Justinian won back the part of North Africa that had been lost at the Fall of Rome.

ᔕᔕᔕᔕᔕᔕᔕᔕᔕᔕᔕᔕᔕᔕᔕ

The next place Belisarius tackled was his most important: Italy. His enemies there were the **Ostrogoths**— the same Ostrogoths who had collapsed the Western Roman Empire back in 476. If Justinian could recapture Italy from the Ostrogoths, then he would truly restore the lost glory of the Roman Empire!

Mosaic with Mary and Jesus at center, Emperor Constantine on the right and Emperor Justinian on the left. Constantine offers Jesus the walled city of Constantinople, while Justinian offers the Hagia Sophia.

Belisarius' work in Italy was slow but steady. He took back Sicily, the big island off the toe of the boot, in 535. The next year saw Belisarius moving up the Italian Peninsula, taking back Naples and Rome. By 540, Belisarius held all Italy!

Although no one knew it yet, the Byzantine Empire was now as big as it would ever be. Thanks to Belisarius, Justinian took back much of what the Roman Empire had lost. But he never took back the rest. Far-off provinces like Gaul, Britannia and Hispania were never to be his.

ᔕᔕᔕᔕᔕᔕᔕᔕᔕᔕᔕᔕᔕᔕ

Just when everything was going so well for Justinian, tragedy struck. In the middle years of his reign, a killer disease swept through the Byzantine

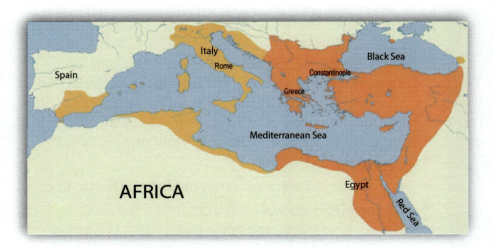

The Byzantine Empire under Justinian. Red marks the empire at the beginning of Justinian's reign. Red and orange together mark the empire at the height of Justinian's reign.

Empire. The horrible **Plague of Justinian** was about to undo almost everything the great emperor had done.

The Plague of Justinian was probably an outbreak of an awful disease called **bubonic plague**. The

A **plague** is a very contagious, very deadly disease that can kill many people in a short time.
Bubonic Plague is a dreadful disease named for **buboes**— ugly swellings that appear on its victims' skin.

germs that cause bubonic plague live in fleas, which live in the coats of rats and mice. The problem with rats and mice is that they love to eat grain from barns and granaries. Every time a flea-bitten rat took a bite of grain, it left behind plague germs. After that, catching the plague was easy: All one had to do was carry home a sack of flour.

The Plague of Justinian struck Egypt in 541. Since the Egyptians sold grain all around the Mediterranean Sea, the plague spread quickly from there. It reached Constantinople in 542 – 543, just a couple of years after Belisarius took back Italy.

Unfortunately, Byzantine doctors knew nothing of germs— which meant that they had no

Plague victims receiving a blessing

way to fight bubonic plague. On its worst days in Constantinople, the Plague of Justinian may have killed an astonishing 5,000 people per day— or even twice that many! Young or old, rich or poor made no difference to the cruel plague; it killed them all. With so many people dying at once, a sadder time is hard to imagine. Before it was over, it may have killed about one-third of all the people in the empire— as many as 100 million!

Another thing the plague killed was the Byzantine army. After the Plague of Justinian, the empire was too weak to defend all the ground it had taken back.

The year 565 was another bad one for the Byzantines; for both Belisarius and Justinian died that year. Between the Plague of Justinian and the loss of these two heroes, the Byzantine Empire was sure to be in big trouble the next time an enemy attacked.

The attack in Italy came from a people called the **Lombards**. The Lombards were yet another barbarian tribe from the north, much like the Vandals and the Ostrogoths. Three years after Justinian died, the Lombards swept down into northern Italy. The Plague of Justinian had weakened the Byzantine army

For centuries, any man who wanted to call himself "King of Italy" had to wear a symbolic crown called the **Iron Crown of Lombardy**. Although this crown is made mostly of gold and gems, it also has an iron ring inside. Legend says that the iron for this ring came from the spikes Roman soldiers used to nail Jesus to the cross.

so much that the Lombards ran right over it. The Byzantines retreated, leaving the Lombards to settle into their new home.

The Lombards would rule northern Italy for most of the next two hundred years. Part of northern Italy is still called **Lombardy**, after the Lombards who took it from the Byzantine Empire.

The Lombards were just one of many threats the Byzantines faced after Justinian died. Over on the Balkan Peninsula, a people called the Slavs swept down from the north. The Persians were always a threat in the east. The 600s brought the worst threat of all: the Islamic Empire, founded by the prophet Muhammad in Arabia. See Chapter 5 for more on the Islamic Empire.

Like the Roman Empire before it, the Byzantine Empire struggled to survive against so many threats. One thing that helped it survive as long as it did was a mighty weapon called **Greek Fire**.

Greek Fire was a sticky fuel that the Byzantines hurled at all kinds of targets, from ships to chariots and supply wagons. Wherever it struck, Greek Fire blazed hotter than a torch. Hot fires like these spread quickly, and are hard to put out.

Greek Fire

Byzantine marines hurling Greek Fire at their enemies

Greek Fire was especially deadly to enemy ships. Besides the fuel itself, the Byzantines also invented a ship-mounted flamethrower that could spray Greek Fire from afar. Fires that hot were impossible to ignore; for any ship that burned near the water line was sure to sink. Once a ship was burning with Greek Fire, its crew was too busy fighting the fire to fight the Byzantines!

Mighty though it was, Greek Fire wasn't enough to save the Greeks forever. The Byzantine Empire grew and shrank many times after Justinian; but it shrank more than it grew.

Heroes of the Eastern Church

The Christians of the West sometimes forget that Christianity started in the East. Some of the greatest heroes of the early church came from the Eastern Roman Empire— famous names like Saint Nicholas and John Chrysostom.

The original **Saint Nicholas** was a real bishop from a real place called Myra. Myra stood in the Eastern Roman Empire, near what is now Demre, Turkey. Although **Nikolaos of Myra** was quite real, most stories from his life read more like legend than real history.

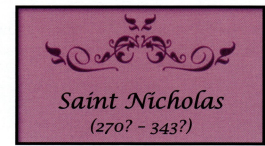

Saint Nicholas
(270? – 343?)

According to legend, Nicholas loved to give secret gifts to the poor. He was always handing out coins, small purses or other treasures when no one was looking. Nicholas was particularly anxious about one family he knew: a poor father with three daughters. The father couldn't afford to pay his daughters' **dowries**— the price of marrying them off. Without dowries, his daughters might never find husbands. And without husbands, his daughters would never find happiness— not in those days.

Fortunately, Nicholas had plenty of money to pay the girls' dowries. Unfortunately, their father was too proud to take Nicholas' money. So instead of paying the dowries in public, Nicholas paid them in secret. The night before the eldest daughter was old enough to marry, Nicholas quietly tossed a purse through her window! He did the same for the second daughter when her time came along.

> A **dowry** was the money and property a bride brought into her marriage, given to the groom by the father or brother who gave away the bride.

St. Nicholas passing money through a window

The third daughter was different. By the time this daughter grew old enough to marry, her proud father had caught on— and was waiting at the window. Instead of tossing the purse through the window, Nicholas had to toss it down the chimney. As it happened, the third daughter had just hung her stockings over the fire to dry— so that instead of falling into the fire, Nicholas' purse fell into her stocking!

Nicholas' story spread around the world, changing a bit with each telling. The name "Saint Nicholas" changed to "Sinterklaas," which eventually became "Santa Claus." The round-bellied, white-bearded Santa Claus that everyone knows now was created by a cartoonist called Thomas Nast, who first drew Santa that way in 1863.

The name John Chrysostom was really more a title than a name. Greek-speakers called John *chrysostom*, or "golden-mouthed," because he was one of the greatest preachers who ever lived!

Before he was a preacher, John was a brilliant young student from Antioch, Syria. Like the young St. Jerome, the young John Chrysostom couldn't decide: should he study Greek classics, or the Bible? He was about twenty-five years old when he finally settled on the Bible. To help his studies, John became a monk— giving up worldly comforts so that he could focus on God alone (Chapter 3).

But John Chrysostom was no ordinary monk. Most monks allowed themselves at least a few small comforts— enough to be sure they stayed healthy. As for John, he was so strict with himself that he wouldn't even sit down. He spent week after week, month

John Chrysostom
(344? - 407?)

John Chrysostom

after month on his feet, studying Scripture constantly. He slept hardly at all, and ate as little as he possibly could.

This hard lifestyle turned out to be more than John's poor body could stand. A few years as a monk ruined his health, forcing him to move back to Antioch and become a preacher.

Even so, John never forgot his time as a monk. Back in Antioch, John preached that all Christians should live more like monks. He warned that true Christians cared nothing for riches, but instead gave away everything they had to help the poor. He based his sermons on Bible verses like Matthew 25:44-45, which reads:

> "They also will answer, 'Lord, when did we see you hungry or thirsty or a stranger or needing clothes or sick or in prison, and did not help you?' He will reply, 'Truly I tell you, whatever you did not do for one of the least of these, you did not do for me.'"

The more John preached, the greater his reputation grew. By 397, John's reputation was so great that the Eastern church offered him its highest office: Archbishop of Constantinople.

The problem was, the rich Byzantines who called John to Constantinople had no idea what he preached in his sermons. All they knew was that John Chrysostom was the best preacher in the East. Since Constantinople was the capital of the East, they felt that Constantinople deserved the best preacher— no matter what he preached. So when John showed up, preaching that rich Christians should sacrifice themselves for the poor, he was headed for trouble.

It wasn't long before John Chrysostom was the most hated man in Constantinople— among the rich, that is. Not even John's fellow preachers wanted to sacrifice themselves for the poor. The rich wanted to even less; for Constantinople was one of the richest cities in the world, full of exquisite luxuries.

John was especially hard on the emperor's wife, Empress Eudoxia. He blasted the empress for spending fortunes on clothes and jewelry for herself, while spending not a penny to help the poor.

Empress Eudoxia would turn out to be John's worst enemy. By 403, she was so angry with him that she ordered the Church to **banish** him from Constantinople. But the poor people of Constantinople wouldn't hear of it. They loved John Chrysostom so much that when they heard of his banishment, they started to riot! This was the riot that destroyed the first Hagia Sophia cathedral, as we read above. The second Hagia Sophia, of course, was destroyed by the Nika Riots.

To calm the rioting, Eudoxia ordered John back for a second chance. Most preachers would have taken this chance— but not John Chrysostom! Instead, John criticized Eudoxia even more harshly. She wound up banishing him again— this time farther away. He was on his way to his second exile when his ruined health finally failed, and the great champion of the poor died.

To **banish** someone is to send him or her out of the country, into exile.

John Chrysostom being driven into exile

The Monophysite Controversy

When Christianity was a few hundred years old, the churches of the East, West and South started to grow apart from one another. One of the first big arguments between the three started with an Egyptian idea called **monophysitism**.

Most Christians believe that Jesus Christ has two natures: the divine nature of God, and the human nature of mankind. Around 400 AD, though, some Egyptian Christians decided that Christ couldn't possibly have a human nature. Why? Because human nature was just too sinful for a holy God.

In thinking this through, these Egyptians decided that Christ must have only one nature: His divine nature. When the Son of God came down to Earth as a man, His divine nature must have absorbed His human nature— much like a sponge absorbs water. This is what **monophysite** means: "one nature."

The Council of Chalcedon (451)

An idea that big needed a church council to decide. Just as the Council of Nicaea met to answer Arius (Chapter 2), and the Council of Carthage met to answer Pelagius (Chapter 3), so the **Council of Chalcedon** met to answer the monophysite question.

Basically, the Council of Chalcedon decided that monophysitism was wrong. Just as Athanasius said to Arius, Christ must be both divine and human— fully God and fully man, both at the same time. If the Egyptians were right, then Christ couldn't be fully man. And if Christ wasn't fully man, then He couldn't have suffered the same temptations as man— which meant that He couldn't have conquered sin.

Nothing the Council of Chalcedon said or wrote could change the Egyptians' minds. Instead of agreeing with the Council, the Christians of Egypt decided to split off from all others. This was the start of a new church in Egypt: the **Coptic Orthodox Church**.

> The name **Coptic** comes from a Greek name for the people of Egypt.

The split between Coptic Christians and others has never healed. Even today, the Coptic Orthodox Church is still separate from both the Roman Catholic Church and the Eastern Orthodox Church.

> Empress Theodora, wife to Emperor Justinian I, was a **monophysite** Christian. She learned monophysitism during her fateful trip to Egypt (above).

The symbol of the **Coptic Orthodox Church** is called the Coptic Cross. The Copts may have developed this special cross from the ankh, an ancient Egyptian hieroglyph that represented eternal life.

> The Byzantines played a board game that was much like modern-day backgammon: **Tabula**. One difference between Tabula and backgammon is that tabula players rolled three dice, while backgammon players roll only two.

The Arabian and Sinai Peninsulas

The **Arabian Peninsula** is a big, boot-shaped peninsula in West Asia. If the Italian Peninsula looks like a ladies' dress boot, then the Arabian Peninsula looks more like a men's work boot.

Arabia lies just across the **Red Sea** from Africa. Southeast of Arabia lies the **Arabian Sea**, which opens into the Indian Ocean. Northeast of Arabia lie the **Persian Gulf** and the **Gulf of Oman**.

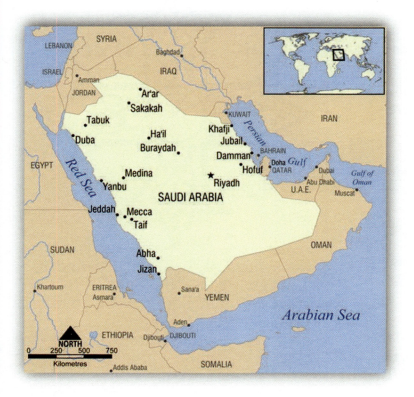

Just west of Arabia lies a much smaller peninsula called the **Sinai**. The Sinai is an almost-triangle with bodies of water on all three legs. The **Mediterranean Sea** lies to the north; the **Gulf of Suez** to the southwest; and the **Gulf of Aqaba** to the southeast.

The distance between the Mediterranean Sea and the Gulf of Suez is only about 100 miles. Yet for most of human history, ships had no way to cross those 100 miles. Instead, they had to sail all the way around Africa— a voyage thousands of miles long!

> A **canal** is a manmade waterway.

All that changed in 1869, when French engineers finished a fantastic project called the **Suez Canal**. After ten years of digging, they finally finished a waterway between two ports: **Port Said** on the Mediterranean Sea, and **Port Suez** on the Gulf of Suez. Before the Suez Canal, to sail from the Mediterranean Sea to the Arabian Sea was a dangerous journey of many weeks. That same sail now takes less than one day!

The Sinai is mostly desert. For most of human history, the only people who lived there were wandering nomads. One of these wanderers was **Moses**, who led the Hebrews through the Sinai after their Exodus from Egypt.

Arabia is mostly desert too. However, the side of Arabia along the Red Sea gets more rainfall than the rest. This greener part of Arabia is where the prophet **Muhammad** started one of the biggest religions in the world: Islam.

Moses was a Hebrew, and Muhammad an Arab. Yet they both looked back to the same ancestor: **Father Abraham**.

The Rise of Islam

For someone who is famous for being a father, Abraham got off to a late start. In Genesis 15, we read how he complained to God about having no children. Although Abraham was grateful for all God had given him, none of it meant anything— for he had no children to inherit it when he was gone.

Abraham's wife **Sarah** felt the same way. By the time Sarah reached her seventies, she was so desperate for children that she did something drastic. She gave Abraham her slave as a wife, hoping to have children through her. Sarah's slave, an Egyptian woman called **Hagar**, soon gave Abraham his first child: a boy called **Ishmael**.

From the moment Ishmael was born, Hagar was cruel to Sarah— mocking her poor mistress for having no sons. The longer this went on, the more Sarah hated Hagar; and the more she prayed for a son of her own.

Ishmael was about thirteen years old when God finally answered Sarah's prayers. By now, Sarah was ninety years old— well past the age when most women have children. Yet it was Sarah who gave Abraham her second child: a boy called **Isaac**!

The birth of Isaac set up a contest between him and Ishmael. Both mothers wanted to know: Would Isaac inherit Abraham's great wealth, or would Ishmael? On the one hand, Ishmael was the older son. On the other hand, Ishmael had been born to a lowly slave woman; while Isaac was born to Abraham's true wife, Sarah.

The moment of decision came when Isaac was **weaned**. In ancient times, a lot of children died as babies— before they were weaned. The fact that Isaac didn't die meant that he would probably live a long life. To celebrate that life, a grateful Abraham threw a weaning feast.

> A **weaned** child is one who is old enough to eat solid food instead of his mother's milk.

In the middle of the feast, Sarah happened to see Ishmael making fun of Isaac. The sight brought years of rage against Hagar flooding into Sarah's heart. She went straight to Abraham, ordering him to "… get rid of that slave woman and her son, for that woman's son will never share in the inheritance with my son Isaac" (Genesis 21:10).

As a good father who loved both his sons, Abraham hated to send Ishmael away. But when Abraham prayed about it, God told him to do as Sarah asked. He promised to make Ishmael the father of a nation, just as He would make Isaac the father of a nation. Trusting God to take care of it all, Abraham sent Hagar and Ishmael off into the desert alone— giving them nothing but some food and a skin of water.

Hagar and Ishmael waiting in the wilderness

When the water in the skin ran out, Hagar felt sure that Ishmael would die. Just then, though, an angel appeared to Hagar— reminding her of God's promise to Ishmael. The next moment, God opened Hagar's eyes to something she had missed before: a well full of sweet water! Instead of dying in the desert that day, Ishmael thrived. He went on to become the father of a great people: the **Arabs**, who made their home in Arabia.

The well that God showed Hagar is very important to Arabs, and so is the place where she found it. They call it the **Zamzam Well**, and believe that it is the same well that still stands in **Mecca**, Arabia.

Arab **tradition** is full of stories about Ishmael. According to Arab tradition, Abraham didn't just send Ishmael into the desert and then never see him again. Instead, Abraham visited Ishmael from time to time— like the good father he was.

One day, Abraham showed up at Ishmael's tent with a strange story. Long ago, Abraham said, God wanted Adam and Eve to build an **altar**— a holy place to worship their holy God. To mark the spot for the first altar, God sent a sign from heaven: a special stone that Arabs call the **Black Stone**.

> A **tradition** is a story or belief that is handed down from one generation to the next.
>
> An **altar** is a special place for worship.

Centuries later, Adam and Eve's altar was washed away by the Great Flood of Noah (Genesis 6 – 8). Now God had appeared to Abraham in a vision, telling him to rebuild it. This was why Abraham came to see Ishmael that day: because he wanted his help to rebuild the altar. The new altar, which Arabs call the **Kaaba**, was to stand in what is now Mecca— just a few yards from the Zamzam Well.

Of course, the Great Flood had washed away the Black Stone too. But as father and son worked together on the Kaaba, an angel brought the long-lost Black Stone to lay in its eastern corner.

The Black Stone is still part of the Kaaba today. These three holy objects— the Black Stone, the Kaaba and the Zamzam Well— mark Mecca as the holiest city in the Arab world.

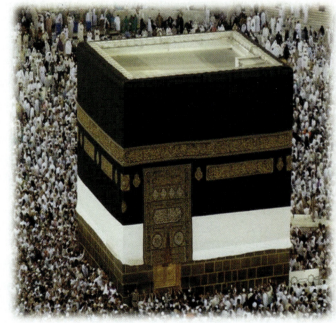

The Kaaba as it appears today, covered with a tapestry called the *kiswah*. This Kaaba is only a copy of the first Kaaba, which collapsed long ago.

Muhammad (570 - 632)

Mecca is also holy to Arabs for another reason: because the prophet **Muhammad** was born there. Before Muhammad's day, most Arabs were **polytheists**— people who believed in many gods. The Kaaba was full of idols, all carved to represent different gods. When Muhammad came into his own, he would tear all those idols out— making most Arabs **monotheists**.

> **Polytheists** believe in many gods. **Monotheists** believe in just one god.

All that came later, though. The young Muhammad got off to a rough start. His father died before he was even born. His mother died when he was just six years old, leaving him to be raised by an uncle. This uncle taught Muhammad to earn his living the way many Arabs did: as a traveling trader.

The entrance to the Cave of Hira, which stands about two miles outside Mecca

Even so, Muhammad was always deeply interested in religion. In studying his people's gods, he learned that some Arabs believed in an especially mighty one: a great god called **Allah**. When Muhammad reached his 30s, he started spending more time alone— so that he could **meditate** on this Allah. To avoid distractions while he was meditating, Muhammad holed up in a private spot called the **Cave of Hira**.

> To **meditate** on something is to think deeply about it.

While Muhammad was meditating, something unexpected happened. Tradition says that one day in 610, the archangel **Gabriel** appeared to Muhammad in the Cave of Hira— bringing him a vision straight from Allah! This was just the first of many visions Muhammad received, telling him who Allah was and how he wanted to be worshipped.

At first, these visions seemed so strange that even Muhammad himself didn't believe them— fearing that Gabriel might really be a demon. In time, though, Muhammad started sharing his visions with other Arabs around Mecca.

The first thing Muhammad shared was that the Arabs' old way of worship was all wrong. The many gods that most Arabs worshipped were all false, he said. Instead, all must worship the one true god— almighty Allah. Furthermore, Allah hates everyone who worships false gods!

Muhammad called his new religion **Islam**, and his followers **Muslims**. Both names came from *salema*— Arabic for "surrender," "submission" or "peace." Both mean that the way to make peace with Allah is to surrender to Allah's will.

At first, only a few Meccans believed Muhammad. The city leaders treated the first Muslims horribly, trying to stamp out Muhammad's religion before it could take hold.

After several hard years in Mecca, Muhammad tried a new city. In 622, Muhammad led his followers about 200

Muhammad himself laid the first stones for this oldest mosque in the world: the Quba Mosque, built at Medina just after the Hegira. The high towers, called *minarets*, are for calling faithful Muslims to prayer five times each day.

The Hegira (622)

miles to the north— on a famous journey called the **Hegira**. Islam's new home was a place called Yathrib, which soon changed its name to **Medina**.

Medina turned out to be much more welcoming than Mecca had been. Muhammad won followers so quickly that he soon ruled Medina. Soon after that, Muhammad ruled all the Arab tribes around Medina. The government he set up was a **theocracy**— the kind run by religious leaders.

> **Hegira** is Arabic for "migration" or "journey."
>
> The Hegira is so important to Muslims that they base their calendar on it. The Islamic calendar marks its years not as "BC" or "AD," but as "BH" or "AH"— "Before Hegira" or "After Hegira."

As Islam spread beyond Medina, Muhammad's followers ran into trouble back in Mecca. The Meccans who had driven the Muslims out had also taken the Muslims' property; and the Muslims wanted it back.

Since Muhammad wasn't ready to attack Mecca, his followers settled for the next best thing: robbing traders on their way to and from Mecca. Muhammad himself led more than two dozen raids against Meccan traders. Each raid brought more wealth and power for the Muslims.

Eight years after the Hegira, Muhammad finally felt wealthy and powerful enough to take Mecca itself. In January 630, Muhammad led a big army down to Mecca and captured it. So it was that Mecca, the holiest of all Arab cities, joined the Islamic Empire.

One of the first things Muhammad did as master of Mecca was to destroy every old idol in the Kaaba. From then on, the Kaaba was for worshiping Allah alone!

From Medina to Mecca and beyond, Islam spread like wildfire. By the time Muhammad died in 632, the **Islamic Empire** ruled the whole Arabian Peninsula!

> **A theocracy is** a government in which religious leaders control everything— not only religion, but also the military, the police and everything else.
>
> The **Islamic Empire** was a theocracy that ruled the whole Muslim world.

The Five Pillars of Islam

The Islamic faith rests on the five "pillars," or basic beliefs. The first pillar of Islam is **Shahada**— Arabic for "faith" or "creed." All good Muslims know this creed well, and repeat it often: "There is no god but Allah, and Muhammad is his prophet."

The second pillar of Islam is **Salah**— Arabic for "prayer." Five times each day, Muslims must drop whatever they may be doing, turn toward Mecca and pray. The story of how five was chosen is an interesting one.

Muslim tradition says that just before the Hegira, the archangel Gabriel set Muhammad on a winged horse and flew him off to a holy place. The chosen spot was probably the **Temple Mount** in Jerusalem, where Solomon's Temple had once stood. From there, Muhammad flew on up to heaven— where he met Allah himself.

This trip to heaven is called the **Night Journey**; and it is one of the most important stories in Islam. It was on the Night Journey that Muhammad learned the details of Islam— not only what Muslims were to believe, but also how they were to live.

Tradition says that at first, Allah expected Muslims to pray fifty times each day! But then Muhammad begged Allah to change his mind— protesting that fifty was too many. At this, Allah mercifully reduced it from fifty to five. Since then, prayer leaders called **muezzins** have called all Muslims to prayer five times each day.

> The **Temple Mount** is a big, level space atop a hill in east Jerusalem. Its name comes from the Hebrew Temple, which stood there until the Romans destroyed it in 70 AD.
>
> When Muslims conquered Jerusalem, they built a shrine on the Temple Mount in honor of the Night Journey. It is called the Dome of the Rock, after a special rock that forms part of its floor: The Foundation Stone. It is said that this stone was the first part of the world created by God. It is also said that God made Adam out of dust from around the Foundation Stone.

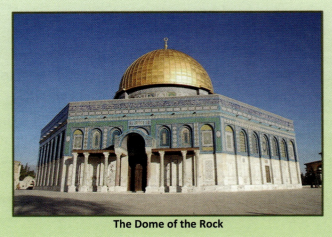

The Dome of the Rock

Another story explains why Muslims turn toward Mecca when they pray. Early in his reign, Muhammad followed some Jewish traditions— hoping that the Jews might accept Islam someday. After all, both Jews and Muslims believed in one God! One Jewish tradition Muhammad followed was turning toward Jerusalem when he prayed.

Later, though, Muhammad grew disgusted with the Jews. They kept insisting that their promised Messiah must come from the family of King David, which meant that they would never follow anyone from the family of Ishmael. When Muhammad realized this, he stopped turning toward Jerusalem— turning toward Mecca instead.

The third pillar of Islam is **Zakat**— Arabic for "giving." Muslims must give freely to the poor, never hoarding their wealth.

The fourth pillar of Islam is **Sawm**— Arabic for "fasting." Most Muslim fasting happens during the ninth month of the Islamic calendar, a special month called **Ramadan**. Muslims honor Ramadan as the holy month when Allah sent his first visions to Muhammad.

Faithful Muslims celebrate Ramadan in several ways. One way is to read or listen to the whole Quran (below). Another way, especially in Egypt, is to hang special Ramadan lanterns.

But the most important way to celebrate Ramadan is by fasting. Good Muslims fast all through Ramadan, every day from sunup to sundown. In the strictest Islamic countries, only small children, pregnant women, nursing mothers and the sick may eat during the day. Relief comes after sundown, when everyone breaks his fast with a meal.

The fifth pillar of Islam is **Hajj**— Arabic for "**pilgrimage**." At least once in their lifetimes, all able-bodied Muslims must take a pilgrimage to their holiest city: Mecca. The point of this pilgrimage is to remember and honor the origins of their faith.

A **pilgrimage** is a religious journey.

A **hajji** is a Muslim pilgrim on the **Hajj** to Mecca.

The last month of the Islamic year is called Dhu al-Hijjah. Near the middle of that month, Muslims from all over the world go to Mecca on the great pilgrimage called the Hajj. The five days of the Hajj are filled with rituals to remind **Hajjis** how their faith began.

Khamsa amulets are hand-shaped good-luck tokens used all over the Middle East and North Africa, especially in Morocco. Their name comes from the Arabic word for "five," meaning the five fingers of the hand.

Both Muslims and Jews use khamsa amulets. Muslim khamsa may represent the hand of Fatima, daughter to the prophet Muhammad. The five fingers may represent the Five Pillars of Islam. Jewish khamsa may represent the hand of Miriam, sister to Moses. The five fingers may represent the five books of the Torah: Genesis, Exodus, Leviticus, Numbers and Deuteronomy.

One ritual has all the Hajjis walking around the Kaaba counterclockwise seven times. If they can come close enough through the surging crowd, then they may touch or kiss the Black Stone on each pass. If not, then they may simply point to the stone as they pass.

〰〰〰〰〰〰〰〰〰〰〰〰〰〰〰〰〰〰〰〰

Muslim tradition says that Muhammad's visions were very powerful— so powerful that he could always recite them word-for-word, exactly as he received them from the archangel Gabriel.

The Quran

Muhammad often recited his visions when he preached. The beauty of his words was a big reason why Islam grew as fast as it did.

The problem was, Muhammad never wrote his visions down. When he died in 632, the Muslim world was in danger of losing the very foundation of its faith: the words of its only prophet, Muhammad.

To keep that from happening, Muhammad's followers quickly wrote down all his sermons from memory. They collected them all in a book called the Quran— Arabic for "he recited." According to Muslim tradition, Muhammad's followers remembered his sermons so well that the Quran recites his visions word-for-word— exactly as Allah spoke them to Muhammad through the archangel Gabriel.

More Muslim Beliefs

➢ Muslims believe that if they want to go to paradise when they die, then they must first please Allah on Earth. One way to please Allah is to show constant devotion to him. Another way is to lead a righteous life under Islamic law.

➢ Anything that is forbidden under Islamic law is called *haram*; while anything approved is called *halal*. Among many other things, pork, alcohol and gambling are all *haram*.

➢ *Jihad* is an Arabic word for "struggle." A Muslim *jihad* may be a spiritual struggle; or it may be an armed struggle against the unbelieving enemies of Islam, whom Muslims call **infidels**.

A very old Quran on display in a museum

The Arabian Nights

One Thousand and One Nights, also called *The Arabian Nights*, is a collection of old folk tales from Arabia, Persia and other Middle Eastern countries. Some of the best-known stories in the world come from *The Arabian Nights*— including "Sinbad the Sailor," "Aladdin and the Wonderful Lamp" and "Ali Baba and the Forty Thieves."

All these stories come wrapped inside a special story called a frame story. The frame story of *The Arabian Nights* tells of an Arabian kingdom with a terrible problem. Its king, whose name is **Shahryar**, believes that no woman can be trusted!

One Thousand and One Nights

The story starts with Shahryar getting married for the first time. Soon after the wedding, Shahryar is horrified to learn that his wife has been carrying on with another man. Naturally, Shahryar executes his wife for her terrible crime.

Then he goes a step farther. Wounded by his wife's faithlessness, Shahryar bitterly declares that no woman on Earth can ever be faithful to her husband!

Despite his bitterness, Shahryar still wants a new wife. He asks his top adviser, his **vizier**, to find him one— which the vizier soon does. After one night with this new wife, Shahryar takes a simple step to make sure that she can never be unfaithful to him: he kills her!

This tragic story plays out again and again: Shahryar marries a new bride one night, and then kills her the next morning. Before long, the vizier starts to have trouble finding new brides!

The answer to the vizier's trouble turns out to be his own daughter— a clever girl called **Scheherazade**. With her father's permission, Scheherazade becomes Shahryar's next bride.

"Scheherazade and Sultan Shahryar" by artist Ferdinand Keller

After the wedding, Scheherazade offers to tell Shahryar a bedtime story. When Shahryar agrees, Scheherazade starts telling him the first tale of *The Arabian Nights*. But Scherezade doesn't finish her tale. Instead, just when her tale reaches its climax— its most exciting moment, when Shahryar is dying to know what happens next— Scheherazade suddenly refuses to say another word! If the king wants to hear the end of her story, Scheherazade says, then he will just have to let her live until tomorrow night. Fighting his distrust of women, Shahryar agrees to let Scheherazade live— just until tomorrow night, when he can hear the end of her fascinating tale.

The next night, Scheherazade finishes her story as promised. But she doesn't stop there. Instead, she moves on to the second tale of *The Arabian Nights*— which Shahryar finds just as fascinating as the first! Night after night, Scheherazade finishes her tale from the night before, and then starts a fresh new tale that leaves the king in agonized suspense.

After 1,001 nights, or nearly three years, Scheherazade finally runs out of tales to fascinate her husband. By this time, though, the two have been married long enough to have children together; and Shahryar has learned to trust women again.

The Iconoclastic Controversy

Islamic law says that Muslims must never worship **idols**. The law is so strict that Muslim artists steer clear of anything that even looks like an idol. They almost never make images of people or animals, for fear that someone might mistake them for idols. Most of all, Muslim artists never make images of Muhammad— for fear that if they did, then misguided Muslims might worship Muhammad instead of Allah.

The Eastern Orthodox Church feels very differently about images. Many Orthodox churches are full of special images called **icons**. They cover the floor, the ceiling and everything in between, flooding the eye with inspiring images. Some icons picture Jesus or a saint; while others picture scenes from the Bible or the lives of saints. But Orthodox churches weren't always this way.

An **idol** is an image of a false god.

An **icon** is an image that Eastern Christians use for worship and prayer. Icons come in many types, from painted pictures to carven sculptures, tiled mosaics and more.

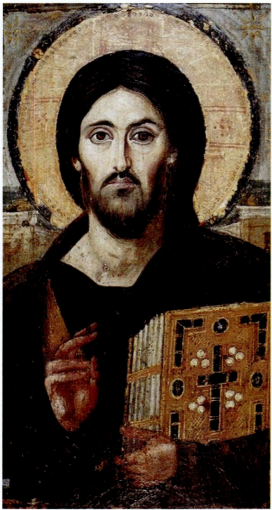

A painted icon of Jesus from St. Catherine's
Monastery on Mt. Sinai, Egypt

A mosaic icon of Jesus from the Hagia Sophia in Constantinople

An *iconostasis*, or wall of icons, from the front of an Eastern church

The story starts around 700 AD, when a big argument broke out between two kinds of Eastern Christians: those who loved icons, and those who hated them. Those who loved icons were called **iconophiles**. Iconophiles used icons to remember people from the Bible, just as mourners used pictures to remember lost loved ones. Over time, gazing at icons became a beloved tradition— much like singing hymns or reading Scripture in church.

Those who hated icons were called **iconoclasts**. The iconoclasts saw icons the same way Muslims saw them: as idols. Iconoclasts accused iconophiles of worshiping idols, when they should be worshiping Christ!

> An **iconophile** is someone who loves to use icons in worship. An **iconoclast** is someone wants to tear down all icons.

Not so, said the iconophiles. For in their eyes, icons and idols were two very different things. An idol was an image of a false god— something that wasn't real. An icon, on the other hand, was an image of a real person from church history— someone whom all Christians should honor. Iconophiles said it was unfair to accuse them of worshiping idols, when what they were really doing was gazing at icons.

The bitter argument between iconoclasts and iconophiles dragged on for about 120 years, off and on. Every so often, a band of iconoclasts would attack an iconophile church— fighting to tear down or plaster over its icons. The iconophiles would fight back, trying to defend their icons.

The end came at an important church meeting called the **Synod of Constantinople**, held in 843. The synod announced that the iconophiles were right— that it was perfectly alright for Christians to use icons in worship. However, the synod added this important bit of advice: that Christians should only **venerate** icons, not worship them. To venerate an icon is to honor the holy person pictured in that icon, which is fine. To worship an icon is wrong; for true Christians are to worship Christ alone.

Pope Gregory the Great

Long before the Iconoclastic Controversy hit the churches of the East, a strong pope called **Gregory the Great** brought big changes to the churches of the West.

The future Pope Gregory was born to a Roman senator and his wife around 540 AD. The years of Gregory's youth were the same years when the Byzantine Empire took back Italy, as we read in Chapter 4. But then came the Plague of Justinian, which weakened the Byzantine Empire. After Gregory grew up, the Lombards took northern Italy from the Byzantines— as we also read in Chapter 4.

Gregory the Great
(540? – 604)

The Lombards would turn out to be the biggest problem of Gregory's life. He spent six years in Constantinople, begging the Byzantines to send more armies against the Lombards. When begging failed, Gregory returned to Rome— where the Church elected him pope in 590.

Pope Gregory did things no pope before him had ever done. Most churchmen would never think of raising an army; for they saw themselves as spiritual leaders, not military ones. Gregory saw himself differently. Since the Roman government was too weak to deal with the Lombards, Gregory dealt with them himself— as if he were Governor of Rome, and not just the head bishop of the Church of Rome. Strange as it sounds, Gregory even raised armies to keep the Lombards out of Rome!

Gregory also changed how Christians lived and worshiped. For example, Gregory taught that the Vow of Chastity shouldn't apply only to monks (Chapter 3). Instead, he said, it should apply to all priests. It is partly because of Gregory that Catholic priests never marry, even today.

Other examples came in church worship. Gregory started a school for church musicians, and may have inspired a new style of church music called the **Gregorian Chant**.

Besides all that, Gregory was also a missionary pope. It was he who sent Augustine of Canterbury to the Anglo-Saxons of southern Britain, as we read in Chapter 3.

Pope Gregory I

France is the biggest country in Western Europe. Strong natural barriers protect France on most sides:

➤ To the northwest lies the stormy **English Channel**, which divides France from **England**.

➤ To the west lies the huge **Bay of Biscay**, which opens onto the Atlantic Ocean.

➤ To the southwest stand the **Pyrenees**, the big mountains that divide France from **Spain**.

➤ To the south lies the **Mediterranean Sea**. The French enjoy a long, lovely coastline on the Mediterranean.

➤ To the southeast and east stand the biggest mountains in all Europe: the **Alps**, which divide France from **Italy**, **Switzerland** and **Germany**.

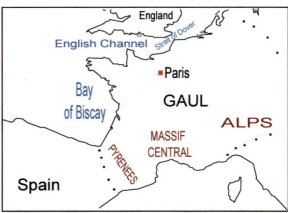

France's barriers to the northeast are not as strong. Between the Alps and the North Sea, the land descends from high mountains to low, marshy plains full of creeks and rivers.

The biggest river in this part of Europe is also one of the most beautiful rivers in the world: the famous **Rhine River**. The name "Rhine" comes from the Celtic word *renos,* which means "raging flow." Rising in the Swiss Alps, the Rhine rages mostly northward on its way to the North Sea.

The Rhine has always been important for shipping. In medieval times, nobles started demanding a toll from every trader who used their river. To collect these tolls, they built strong, beautiful castles all along the Rhine. One such castle stands near a famous rock called the **Lorelei**.

The Lorelei is an arm of rock that juts into the Rhine near Koblenz, Germany. Its name comes from a poor girl who went mad when the man she loved chose to marry someone else. In a fit of grief, Lorelei hurled herself from the top of the great rock— dashing herself to pieces on the hidden rocks below.

A view of Katz Castle on the Rhine River, with the Lorelei in the background

According to legend, the power of Lorelei's grief changed her into a siren— much like the Sirens of Greek mythology. As Lorelei sings her mournful song, she lures sailors onto the hidden rocks near the base of the Lorelei— where they shipwreck on the same rocks that killed the poor girl!

The Roman name for what is now France was **Gaul**.

Roman Gaul

The story of Roman Gaul is a lot like the story of Roman Britannia, which we covered in Chapter 2. Like Britannia, Gaul belonged to the Celts before the Romans came. Like Britannia, Gaul was swallowed by the huge Roman Empire as it grew northward. And like Britannia, Gaul fell to the barbarians as the dying Roman Empire shrank back to the south.

The man who swallowed Gaul for Rome was the most famous Roman of all: **Julius Caesar**. The wars Caesar fought for Gaul are called the **Gallic Wars**. They happened just before Caesar defeated Pompey, making himself Dictator of Rome. But Caesar never would have made it that far, if a Celt called **Vercingetorix** had had his way.

The Gallic Wars (58 - 51 BC)

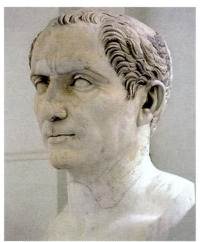

Bust of Julius Caesar

Vercingetorix was a skilled general from a Celtic tribe in south central Gaul. Like Caratacus of Britannia, whom we met in Chapter 2, Vercingetorix tried to pull all Celtic tribes together— knowing that this was their only hope of fighting off the Romans.

The big showdown came in 52 BC, when Caesar trapped Vercingetorix inside a hilltop fort at a place called **Alesia**. With the Roman army surrounding the fort, Vercingetorix had only one hope left: his Celtic friends outside the fort. If his friends hit Caesar from behind, then Vercingetorix might be able to break through and escape.

It almost worked. One of the darkest days of Caesar's whole life came at the **Battle of Alesia**, when Vercingetorix and his friends both hit the Romans at once— Vercingetorix from inside Alesia, and his friends from outside.

The only way Caesar could fight off both enemies was by doing something smart generals rarely did: splitting his army. He left most of his army to deal with Vercingetorix. Meanwhile, Caesar personally led a bold cavalry charge against Vercingetorix's friends. The sight of 6,000 Romans thundering toward them scared the Celts so much that they scattered, leaving Vercingetorix all alone. He surrendered to Caesar the next day.

Vercingetorix surrendering to Julius Caesar

Bronze sculpture of Vercingetorix

In beating Vercingetorix, Caesar also beat the last organized Celtic army in Gaul. After the Battle of Alesia, most of the Celts in Gaul stopped resisting the Romans. The Gallic Wars were over, leaving mighty Rome in charge of all Gaul.

The Roman government divided Gaul into **provinces**, each run by a **provincial** governor. Along with Roman government came Roman law, Roman learning and the Roman way of life. In time, the Celts' descendants in Gaul became "Romanized"— just as the Celts' descendants in Britain became Romanized.

> A **province** was a section of the Roman Empire governed by a **provincial** governor.

The Persecution at Lyon (177 AD)

Like other Romans of their day, the Romans of Gaul hated Christians. One of the worst-ever Roman persecutions of Christians happened at a city called Lyon, Gaul in 177 AD. A total of forty-eight innocent Christians died at Lyon that year, including one poor girl whose sufferings are too painful too imagine.

Blandina was a slave girl who was arrested for **cannibalism**, of all crimes. The Romans often accused Christians of cannibalism, for a strange reason: because when Jesus led the first Holy Communion, He spoke of eating His flesh and drinking His blood (Matthew 26:26-28).

> **Cannibalism** is the terrible crime of eating human flesh.

Blandina
Died 177 AD

As always, the Romans tortured the Christians before killing them— trying to turn them against each other. Knowing what terrible tortures awaited them, the Christians of Lyon did their best to encourage each other. They promised never to deny their faith in Christ, no matter what the Romans might do to them. For to deny Christ was to discourage other Christians. There was also the warning in Matthew 10:32-33, where Jesus says:

> "Whoever acknowledges me before others, I will also acknowledge before my Father in heaven. But whoever disowns me before others, I will disown before my Father in heaven."

Since Blandina was only a poor slave girl, and rather frail, her friends feared that she might deny Christ at the first sign of torture. Instead, Blandina held up longer than anyone. Despite the worst the Romans could do, Blandina never denied her faith in Christ!

When they couldn't destroy Blandina's faith, the Romans finally destroyed Blandina's body. Her torturers wrapped her in a net and tossed her under the feet of raging bulls.

Blandina netted and thrown to raging bulls

The terrible persecution at Lyon happened near the end of the *Pax Romana*— the 200-year-long "Roman Peace," which we covered in Chapter 1. After the *Pax Romana*, the once-mighty Roman Empire started to weaken. The Romans' weakness left openings for their worst enemies: the outsiders whom they liked to call "barbarians."

The strongest outsiders in Gaul were a group called the **Franks**. The Frankish tribes came from east of the Rhine River, in what are now the Netherlands and northwestern Germany. Although the meaning of the Franks' name is uncertain, it may have come from a word that meant "fierce." The fierce Franks moved west of the Rhine around 275 AD, starting in what is now Belgium.

Barbarians in Gaul

A second set of strong outsiders was a group called the **Alemanni**. The name *Alemmani* may mean "all men," which may mean that the Alemanni were made up of many different tribes. They came from what are now Switzerland and southwestern Germany. As the Romans grew weaker, the Alemanni started moving into eastern Gaul.

A third set of strong outsiders was a group called the **Burgundians**. The Burgundians seem to have come all the way from **Scandinavia**. They showed up in Gaul in 411, when a king called **Gundahar** moved west of the Rhine.

Scandinavia lies in far northern Europe, beyond the Baltic Sea.

Gundahar lasted until 437, when he was defeated by a Roman general called **Flavius Aetius**. Even so, the Burgundians were still a dangerous force in Gaul— but not the most dangerous. The most dangerous force in Gaul was a people called the **Huns**.

The Burgundian King **Gundahar** is a character in the **Ring Cycle**, a set of operas by the German composer Richard Wagner.

The Huns were fierce warriors from somewhere in East Asia. Almost everything the Huns did, they did on horseback. Hunnic warriors fought on horseback, held meetings on horseback, ate on horseback, and sometimes even slept on horseback. According to one Roman historian, the Huns were so used to horses that they seemed to feel a bit dizzy when they stepped down. This is one reason why historians know so little about the Huns: because they were always on the move, never settling in one place for very long.

This unusual way of life was part of what made the Huns so dangerous. Unlike the Franks, the Huns didn't come to Gaul looking for new homes. Instead, they came looking for new people to **plunder**! The Huns were like a plague of locusts. They came flooding into an area, swallowed up everything in sight and then moved on.

To **plunder** is to steal in wartime.

Huns in battle

Whenever the Huns moved into a new place, their first step was to raid a few cities and towns— killing men, women and children alike. After everyone nearby was thoroughly terrified, the Huns offered them two options:

They could either give the Huns a lot of money and goods, or else get ready for a fight. Faced with a choice between paying **tribute** or fighting the Huns, most cities and towns chose to pay!

The most dangerous Hun of all was also the most famous: **Attila the Hun**, who was born around 405. Attila and his brother Bleda inherited the Hunnic Empire from their uncle, who died in 434. Thirteen years later, Bleda died too— maybe of natural causes, or maybe because Attila murdered him. Either way, Bleda's death left Attila on top.

Attila the Hun

At the time, the Huns lived mainly in the East— just north of the Eastern Roman Empire. That changed in 450, when an unusual letter drew Attila's attention from East to West. The letter came from the older sister of a Western Roman Emperor called **Valentinian III**: a troubled woman called **Honoria**.

Honoria suffered from two big troubles. The first was that she liked to flirt with men, a fault that deeply embarrassed her emperor brother. To stop the embarrassment, Valentinian sent Honoria to a nunnery while he tried to find a husband for her.

Honoria's second trouble was the husband her brother found for her. To keep Honoria out of trouble, Valentinian arranged for her to marry a rather dull member of the Roman senate. The fun-loving Honoria wanted nothing to do with this dull senator; but her brother insisted.

With nowhere else to turn, Honoria turned to someone with the power to frighten her emperor brother. In 450, Honoria wrote a pleading letter to Attila the Hun, of all people— asking him to marry her! As a token that her letter was sincere, Honoria sent her engagement ring along with it.

"Attila and his Hordes Overrun Italy" by artist Eugene Delacroix

To Valentinian's horror, Attila took Honoria's foolish offer seriously— saying that he wanted to marry Honoria. But he wouldn't marry her for nothing. Like many husbands in those days, Attila demanded a bride price called a **dowry**. The dowry Attila wanted for Honoria was a rather large one: half the Western Roman Empire!

Naturally, Valentinian refused to pay such a ridiculous dowry. The emperor's refusal was all the excuse Attila needed. In 451, Attila led a huge Hun army into the Western Roman Empire. His first target was Roman Gaul, where he immediately started burning cities and killing innocents.

To defend Gaul, Valentinian sent **Flavius Aetius**— the same Roman general who had defeated Gundahar back in 437. Needing troops to fight Attila, Flavius called on the only ones he could find: the so-called "barbarians" who were living in Gaul. Many of the barbarians who came to Flavius' aid were Franks.

The big showdown between Flavius and Attila came in northeastern Gaul. To the amazement of all, the Romans won the **Battle of the Catalaunian Plains**! Just why Attila lost this battle, when he had never lost before, no one knows. It may be that Attila's long trip from the east had worn out too many horses, forcing the horse-loving Huns to fight as slightly-dizzy foot soldiers. Whatever the reason, this stunning defeat sent Attila retreating to the east.

A year later, though, Attila was back. This time, his target was Rome itself. Although Attila didn't capture Rome in 452, he did lay waste of northern Italy— just as he laid waste of eastern Gaul the year before. Attila's merciless attacks in Italy and Gaul mark him as the most terrifying barbarian in Roman memory.

Huns versus Romans, Franks and others at the Battle of the Catalaunian Plains

These attacks continued until 453, when Attila the Hun suddenly died. Just how he died, no one now knows for sure. Some say that one of his many wives stuck a knife between his ribs!

The Rise of the Franks

Besides the big defeat of Attila the Hun, the Battle of the Catalaunian Plains was also famous for another reason: because it helped the Franks become the most powerful people in Gaul.

Before the 500s, there was no one great king of all the Franks. Instead there were several, each with his own small territory. Because the Franks had no written language yet, historians know very little about these early Frankish kings.

One of the first Frankish kings that historians do know about was one the Romans

The fleur-de-lis, a lily that became a symbol of France

called **Merovius**. The first great Frankish dynasty, the

Merovingian dynasty, is named for Merovius. The Merovingians are also called the **long-haired kings**, for a simple reason: because none of them ever cut his hair or beard.

Merovius was like the Frankish version of King Arthur: an honored king who was part history and part legend. Judging from the dates when he lived, though, Merovius may have been the general who helped Flavius Aetius beat Attila the Hun at Catalaunian Plains.

> A **dynasty** is a line of rulers who all come from the same family.

The story of the Merovingian kings becomes a bit clearer after Merovius. Merovius' grandson **Clovis** was the first to rule all Frankish tribes, instead of just some of them.

Like his Frankish ancestors before him, Clovis started out as a **pagan** idol-worshiper. But Clovis didn't stay pagan. Instead, he became a Christian— partly because of his Christian wife, a Burgundian princess called **Clotilda**.

> A **pagan** is a non-Christian who worships idols.

The Conversion of Clovis

From the moment she married Clovis, Clotilda hated his pagan idols. She was always reminding her husband that his so-called "gods" were mere images carved from chunks of wood or stone, making them no more god-like than a tree or rock (Isaiah 44:9-20). The God whom Clovis ought to worship, Clotilda said, was the One who had created all things by the power of His Word. As a believing pagan, Clovis answered that it was his gods who had created all things— not Clotilda's God.

What changed Clovis' mind was an important battle between the Franks and the Alemanni. Midway through the **Battle of Tolbiac**, fought in 496, Clovis started to fear that his gods had abandoned him. Desperate to save his army, Clovis prayed this promise to Jesus Christ: that if Christ would give Clovis the victory, then Clovis would believe in Christ and be baptized.

According to a medieval historian called Gregory of Tours, Clovis' prayer had hardly left his lips when the Alemanni suddenly turned and fled the battlefield! True to his word, Clovis became a Christian soon after Tolbiac— which meant that he had to be baptized.

Clovis calling on Christ for aid at the Battle of Tolbiac

The **baptism of Clovis** was one of the most memorable scenes in all Frankish history. Legend tells that during the baptism, a white dove brought a bottle of holy oil down from above. This sign from heaven marked Clovis as special— the one man whom God had chosen to lead all the Franks.

Since the King of the Franks was becoming a Christian, all loyal Franks wanted to become Christians too. Altogether, priests baptized some 30,000 Franks that day! Just as the conversion of Constantine helped make Christianity the religion of Rome, so the conversion of Clovis helped make Christianity the religion of Gaul.

After the baptism, Clovis built an even bigger kingdom. It covered almost all of what is now France— which explains why modern-day France is named for Clovis' tribe, the Franks.

Besides long hair and Christianity, the Merovingian dynasty is also remembered for the strange set of laws it followed: the Salic Laws. Two laws set the Salic Laws apart from most other law codes. The first said that no woman could inherit property. When a Frankish king died, his kingdom always went to a male relative— never to a daughter. What the Franks liked about this was that no Frankish kingdom ever went to a daughter's husband— which meant that foreign kings couldn't take over Frankish lands just by marrying Frankish princesses!

The second unusual Salic law said that when a Frankish king died, his sons divided his lands between them. Most everywhere else, the whole kingdom passed to the eldest son. In France, though, every son received a share— which meant that if a Frankish king had more than one son, then his kingdom would be broken into pieces as soon as he died.

This second law was bad news for the huge kingdom Clovis built (above). When Clovis died in 511, the Frankish Empire fell apart— split between the four sons who outlived him!

Two Frankish Saints

The baptism of Clovis might never have happened without a churchman who lived about 150 years before Clovis: Martin of Tours. The name "Tours" comes from the city of Tours, Gaul, where Martin became a bishop in 372.

The bishop's robes came later, though. The future Saint Martin was born around 315, when Emperor Constantine ruled the Roman Empire. Thanks to Constantine, more and more Romans were turning Christian every day. Young Martin longed to study this new faith; but alas, his father wouldn't let him— insisting that he join the Roman army instead. Martin's army unit was sent to Gaul.

As Martin's unit was riding up to a city one cold day, he happened to see a near-naked beggar freezing beside the road. Even though Martin hadn't been baptized yet, he understood that Christians were supposed to care for the poor. Unsheathing his sword, he sliced his warm officer's cloak in two— giving one half to the beggar, and keeping the rest for himself.

That night, Martin dreamed that he saw Christ admiring the beggar's half of his cloak— saying, "Look at this cloak Martin gave Me!" Martin already understood what Christ said in Matthew 25:40: that "whatever you did for one of the least of these brothers and sisters of mine, you did for me."

The simple act of caring for a penniless beggar was so unusual in Martin's day that he became a Christian hero of Gaul. Like Christ Himself, Martin was legendary for his humility and self-sacrifice.

Martin of Tours
(316 – 400)

The future St. Martin of Tours as a Roman soldier, giving half of his cloak to a beggar

After leaving the army, Martin went on to plant churches all over Gaul. Without Martin's churches, King Clovis' wife Clotilda might not have been a Christian— which means that the Baptism of Clovis might never have happened!

Genevieve
(422 – 512)

✝✝✝✝✝✝✝✝✝✝✝✝✝✝✝

Genevieve was a Frankish nun who was living in Paris in 451. As we read above, that was the year when Attila the Hun raged through eastern Gaul— sacking city after city. Most Parisians were so terrified of Attila that they were ready to flee the city.

Genevieve was braver. Instead of fleeing, Genevieve told the people of Paris to fast, pray and trust in God. It seemed to work; for when the time came, Attila decided to bypass Paris— sacking another city instead. This is partly why Genevieve became a **patron saint** of Paris: because she saved Paris from Attila the Hun.

A **patron saint** is a saint who is a special friend to a certain person or place.

Every year on Good Friday, the Friday before Easter, all the church bells in France suddenly fall silent. When children ask why, their parents tell them that French church bells only seem like regular bells. What they really are, parents say, is *cloche volants*— "flying bells."

According to French legend, *cloche volants* gather the sorrows of all who mourn Jesus' crucifixion. When Good Friday comes, the flying bells carry these sorrows off to the center of power in the Catholic Church: Rome. Then comes Easter morning— when Jesus rises from the dead, erasing all sorrow. At this, the flying bells go back to their French bell towers and ring out in celebration.

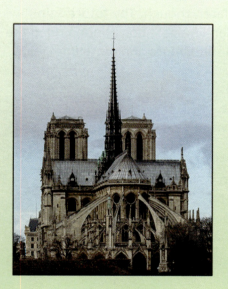

One of the best-known cathedrals in all the world stands on an island in Paris. The *Ile de la Cite* parts the Seine River, the big river that flows through Paris. This is the home of the big cathedral called *Notre Dame de Paris*— French for "Our Lady of Paris."

Among other things, Notre Dame is famous for its many gargoyles. A gargoyle is a gruesome statue that doubles as a spout to carry rainwater away from a building's foundation.

The stone bridge that connects the west end of the *Ile de la Cite* to the mainland is called *Pont Neuf*— French for "New Bridge." Oddly enough, the *Pont Neuf* was finished in 1607— which makes the "New Bridge" the oldest bridge in modern-day Paris!

Gargoyles on a corner of Notre Dame

Gargoyle atop Notre Dame

The *Pont Neuf*, or "New Bridge"

CHAPTER 7:

The Islamic Empire; The Carolingian Empire

Chapter 5 told of the Islamic Empire built by Muslims in the Middle East. Chapter 6 told of the Christian empire built by the Franks in Gaul. This chapter tells how these two empires fought a great battle, and what that battle meant for the Christian world.

The Islamic Empire

For its first ten years, Islam knew only one leader: the prophet Muhammad. Starting with the **Hegira** in 622, Muhammad guided every decision Muslims made. Unfortunately, Muhammad left one important decision unmade: Who would lead the empire when he was gone?

Just ten years after the Hegira, Muhammad fell sick and died— leaving no clear leader to take his place. Muslims probably would have followed their prophet's sons, if he had had any. Alas, Muhammad's wives had given him no sons— only daughters. Since no good Muslim would follow a woman, Muslims needed another way to choose the next leader of Islam.

Some Muslims felt that Allah had already chosen their next leader. In their minds, the right man for the job was the one Muhammad named in one of his sermons: Ali ibn Abi Talib, a.k.a. Ali. Ali was Muhammad's son-in-law, the husband of his daughter Fatima. Ali was also Muhammad's first cousin, his close friend, and a great Muslim leader. Besides all that, Ali may have been the only person ever born in the Kaaba (Chapter 5).

Other Muslims wanted to elect their next leader. Soon after Muhammad died, Muslim leaders held an emergency meeting at Mecca. Since Ali was still in Medina burying Muhammad, he wasn't in Mecca when these leaders elected someone else. The man they chose was Muhammad's father-in-law: Abu Bakr.

If Ali had wanted to fight for Muhammad's place, then many Muslims would have fought beside him. Instead, Ali graciously let Abu Bakr take Muhammad's place. Abu Bakr became the first caliph, or successor of Muhammad— the first to lead the Islamic Empire after the death of the prophet.

> Islam started in 622, when the prophet Muhammad led his followers on the **Hegira**— a journey from Mecca to Medina.

Muhammad receiving a vision from the archangel Gabriel

> **Caliph** is Arabic for "successor." A successor is one who takes a leader's place after the leader is gone.
>
> A **caliph** was a successor of Muhammad, someone who led the Islamic Empire after the prophet died.

Thanks to the graciousness of Ali, most Muslims accepted Abu Bakr. For the moment, everyone agreed that Abu had been Allah's choice— not man's choice.

The same was true of the three caliphs who came after Abu. Most Muslims accepted them as Allah's choices, for two main reasons. First, all four had been close friends of Muhammad. Second, none of the four inherited the job of caliph. Instead, all four were elected by Muslim leaders. For now, most Muslims agreed that this was the best way to know the will of Allah.

To mark their approval, most Muslims call these first four caliphs *rashidun*— Arabic for "rightly guided." The government that these four caliphs led is called

the **Rashidun Caliphate**.

The Rashidun caliphs accomplished a lot for Islam. First, they collected all Muhammad's visions and wrote them down— putting together the first complete **Quran** (Chapter 5).

Second, they spread Islam like wildfire. By the time the last Rashidun caliph died in 661, Islam ruled the whole Middle East— from Arabia and Egypt to Palestine, Syria, Persia and beyond.

One stunning result was that the birthplace of Christianity turned Muslim. By the mid-600s, the entire Holy Land was Muslim. So were some of the biggest cities of the early church, like Alexandria and Antioch!

Wherever Muslims conquered, they tried hard to convert their new subjects to Islam. Some converted easily; while others were more stubborn. Some Jews and Christians insisted on keeping their faith— even when Muslims threatened to kill them.

> A **caliphate** was an Islamic government set up by a caliph or a dynasty of caliphs.
>
> The **Rashidun Caliphate** ruled the Islamic Empire from 632 - 661.

Green shows the Islamic Empire in the time of the last Rashidun caliph

Just how many of these stubborn faithful the Islamic Empire killed, no one now knows. It certainly killed many, and sold many others into slavery. But Muslims didn't always kill the stubborn faithful. For Muhammad had a certain amount of respect for Jews and Christians— the ones he called **People of the Book**.

The "book" Muhammad was talking about was the Bible. Although Muhammad didn't exactly believe in the Jewish Bible or the Christian Bible, he did accept parts of them as true. Because he respected the Bible, he also respected Jews and Christians who believed in the Bible. Thanks to Muhammad's respect for People of the Book, Muslims sometimes allowed Christians and Jews to stay Christians and Jews.

A Muslim slave trading caravan

On the other hand, Islamic law made it clear that Jews and Christians were lower than Muslims— **infidels** who were not to be trusted. Some Islamic laws said that non-Muslims couldn't serve in the army or the police. Others said that non-Muslims couldn't own weapons, nor even ride horses.

Still other Islamic laws set up the *jizya*— a special tax that only non-Muslims had to pay. The *jizya* served two purposes. First, it paid for army and police. Since non-Muslims couldn't serve in the army or the police, Muslims made them pay extra for protection. Second, the *jizya* helped convince stubborn non-Muslims to convert to Islam. For if they gave in and became Muslims, then they wouldn't have to pay the tax!

> An **infidel** is someone who is unfaithful or unbelieving.
>
> The *jizya* was a special tax paid by non-Muslims who lived in the Islamic Empire.

In conquering the whole Middle East, the Rashidun caliphs made a whole lot of enemies for themselves. Some of those enemies took murderous revenge. Of the four caliphs after Muhammad, only the first died of old age. The second and third caliphs were both murdered by their enemies— Persians and Egyptians who were furious with them for taking over their countries.

The fourth caliph was the one many Muslims had wanted from the start: Ali, Muhammad's cousin and son-in-law (above). Unfortunately, there were also many Muslims who didn't want Ali as caliph. The rise of Ali started the first civil war between Muslims— an ugly fight called the First Fitna.

Ali was in his fifth year as caliph when the end came. He was on his knees praying when a fellow Muslim slipped up behind him and cut him with a poison-tipped blade. He died two days later.

The end of Ali set up a contest between two possible caliphs. One was Ali's son Hasan. The other was the Islamic Governor of Syria— a man named Muawiyah, who led an Arab clan called the Umayya.

The Dome of the Treasury from the Umayyad Mosque in Damascus, Syria

To stop the First Fitna (civil war), Hasan made the same gracious choice Ali had made. He stepped aside, allowing Muawiyah to become caliph. Hasan did this on one condition: that when Muawiyah died, either Hasan himself or some other member of Muhammad's family would be caliph.

Once Muawiyah became caliph, though, he forgot all about Hasan's condition. When Muawiyah died, his throne didn't go to a member of Muhammad's family. Instead, it went to Muawiyah's son. Muawiyah's clan, the Umayya, became the first Muslim **dynasty**— the first family to hand down the throne from father to son.

With that, the Rashidun Caliphate was over. The Umayya clan started the second Islamic caliphate: the Umayyad Caliphate.

> A **dynasty** is a line of rulers who all come from the same family.
>
> The **Umayyad Caliphate** ruled the Islamic Empire from 661 - 750.

Some Muslims accepted the Umayyads as the will of Allah; but others never did. These other Muslims believed that handing down the throne from father to son was wrong— for it meant that men were choosing the next caliph, instead of Allah choosing.

The argument over caliphs helped start a big split in Islam. Starting in Umayyad times, there were two main kinds of Muslims: Sunni and Shia.

➤ The larger group, the **Sunni**, followed the Umayyad caliphs. The name "Sunni" comes from *sunnah*, the religious ways of Muhammad.

➤ The smaller group, the **Shia**, refused to follow the Umayyad caliphs. Instead, the Shia followed special leaders called **imams**. The First Imam was Ali, cousin and son-in-law to Muhammad. This is what the name "Shia" means: "Follower of Ali."

Despite the bitter split between Sunni and Shia, Islam grew just as fast under the Umayyad Caliphate as it had before. To the east, Islam spread as far as western India. To the west, Islam spread across North Africa— all the way over to Morocco.

What came next set the Christian world on edge. In 711, Islam jumped across the Strait of Gibraltar— threatening the Christian countries of Western Europe!

꧁꧁꧁꧁꧁꧁꧁꧁꧁꧁꧁꧁

The **Strait of Gibraltar** is a narrow waterway that connects the Mediterranean Sea to the Atlantic Ocean. South of the strait lies Morocco, and north of the strait lies Spain. At its narrowest point, the Strait of Gibraltar is only about eight miles wide. On clear days, a person on the shore of Morocco can easily see the shore of Spain— even without binoculars.

At the eastern entrance to the strait, on the Spanish side, stands one of the best-known landmarks in the world: the **Rock of Gibraltar**. With its peak rising 1,400 feet above sea level, this huge chunk of limestone is

The Twelfth Imam

An **imam** is a Muslim spiritual leader. Both Sunni Muslims and Shia Muslims follow imams. However, Sunni imams are quite different from Shia ones.

The Sunni have many imams. Almost all Sunni mosques have at least one imam to teach the faithful, and to lead prayers five times each day.

Shia imams are much rarer. To the Shia, an imam is a perfectly righteous Muslim and a great leader. Allah sends these perfect leaders as examples to other Muslims, to show how he expects the faithful to live.

The biggest branch of Shia is a group that outsiders call the **Twelvers**. Twelvers believe that there have been just twelve imams in all history. The First Imam was the one we've already met: Ali, cousin and son-in-law to Muhammad.

The **Twelfth Imam** is particularly special to Twelvers. His name is Muhammad al-Mahdi, and he was born to the Eleventh Imam in 869. Five years later, the Eleventh Imam was murdered— like many imams before him. After leading his father's funeral, the five-year-old Muhammad al-Mahdi simply disappeared— and hasn't been seen since!

What happened to him? Twelvers believe that Allah has hidden the Twelfth Imam for now— and that when he returns, he will bring perfect Islamic justice on Earth.

Looking across the Strait of Gibraltar from Morocco

impossible to miss. Ancient mapmakers marked the Rock of Gibraltar as one of the two **Pillars of Hercules**.

The Rock of Gibraltar is named for the Muslim general who leapt across the Strait of Gibraltar in 711: Tariq bin Ziyad. "Gibraltar" is another way of saying *Jebel Tariq*, which is Arabic for "Mountain of Tariq."

ᗡᗡᗡᗡᗡᗡᗡᗡᗡᗡᗡᗡᗡ

Tariq bin Ziyad probably came from an ancient race called the **Berbers**. The Berbers lived all along the coast of North Africa, everywhere west of Egypt. When the Islamic Empire took over North Africa, most Berbers became Muslims— some sadly, others gladly.

Tariq bin Ziyad was one of the glad Berbers. According to legend, Tariq had once been a slave. The wars that brought Islam to North Africa gave Tariq a chance to show his talent as a military man. It was because of this great talent that his master set him free. As a military Muslim, Tariq took on the task of growing the Islamic Empire.

Tariq's target was Hispania— the country we now call Spain. Like Britannia and Gaul, Hispania had been a province of the Roman Empire. When Rome fell, Hispania was home to the Visigoths— the same Visigoths who had sacked Rome back in 410 (Chapter 1). Like the Franks, the Visigoths had become Christians since then.

The trouble started one day in 711, when Tariq quietly rowed his army of Berber Muslims across the Strait of Gibraltar. They started in Morocco, and ended in Hispania.

On the way across, Tariq sensed fear in his troops. After landing near the Rock of Gibraltar, he took a bold step to quiet that fear: burning all his ships! Without ships to take them home, Tariq's men had two choices: They could either beat the Visigoths or take up swimming!

Thanks to Tariq's boldness, Hispania fell even faster than Arabia had. City after city went from Christian to Muslim. Almost all Hispania was Muslim by 718— just seven years after Tariq invaded!

The Rock of Gibraltar

After taking Hispania, the Islamic Empire looked forward to an even bigger task: taking Gaul, the land of the Franks.

The Pippinid Dynasty

Meanwhile up in Gaul, the **Salic Laws** were making it hard for the Frankish empire to grow as fast as the Islamic Empire did.

In Chapter 6, we read how the **Merovingian dynasty** pulled all Frankish tribes together— starting with Clovis, the first Christian King of the Franks. We also read how the Salic Laws undid what Clovis had done. When he died in 511, the Salic Laws divided his empire between his sons. Since Clovis had four living sons when he died, the Frankish empire split into four pieces!

The same thing happened to Clovis' son **Chlothar**. After all his brothers died, Chlothar finally pulled his father's empire together again. But when Chlothar died, the empire split again— with four pieces for four living sons.

> The **Merovingian dynasty** was the first great dynasty of Frankish kings.

Coin of Clothar I

〰〰〰〰〰〰〰〰〰〰〰〰〰〰〰〰〰〰〰〰〰〰〰〰〰〰〰〰〰〰〰〰〰〰〰〰

The years to come brought a new problem for the Merovingian dynasty. Over time, the Merovingian kings grew too lazy to run their kingdoms for themselves! To save themselves the trouble, they started falling back on their most trusted advisers—skilled organizers called **majordomos**.

Majordomo is French for "Mayor of the Palace." The first majordomos were just that: palace managers. They arranged the details of palace life for the king— making schedules, planning meetings and so on.

Later, though, the majordomos grew much more powerful. Some majordomos rose to power as **regents** for boy kings. When a king was too young to run his government on his own, his majordomo ran it for him.

The problem was that with majordomos to do everything for them, boy kings grew up lazy and soft. When these soft kings grew old enough to take charge, they didn't want

> A **regent** is a government officer who makes decisions for a king who is too young to make them on his own.

Majordomo Pippin II speaking for his boy king, Clovis III of the Merovingian dynasty

to— preferring to leave their majordomos in charge. In time, the Merovingian kings became what the Franks called **roi fainéant**: "do-nothing kings" who let their majordomos handle everything for them!

The longer this went on, the mightier the majordomos grew. By the late 600s, they saw themselves as far more than just palace managers. They were starting to see themselves as royalty!

The first to see himself this way was a majordomo called **Pippin II**, a.k.a. Pippin of Heristal. Starting in 687, Pippin claimed a royal title for himself: "Duke and Prince of the Franks." When he died in 714, he handed that royal title down to his heir— just as if he were a king. Now there were two **dynasties** at the top of the Frankish government: the Merovingian dynasty of kings, and the **Pippinid dynasty** of majordomos.

> A **dynasty** is a line of rulers who all come from the same family.

The next majordomo in line was Pippin's son **Charles Martel**. It was Charles Martel who led the Franks through their biggest test: being invaded by the Islamic Empire.

The Battle of Tours

The trouble started in 719, just eight years after Tariq bin Ziyad invaded Hispania (above). In that year, Muslims captured a bit of Mediterranean coastline on Gaul's side of the Pyrenees. Using this as a base, they launched raids into Christian Gaul— making off with treasure, slaves and more.

The biggest raid came thirteen years later. In 732, the Muslims gathered an enormous army near the coast— most of it on horseback. Pushing northwestward, this army surrounded **Bordeaux**— a rich city near the Bay of Biscay. Bordeaux soon surrendered, handing over a fortune in gold and gems.

After seizing the treasure of Bordeaux, the Muslims pushed toward another rich target: the city of **Tours**. They knew that Martin of Tours, who we met in Chapter 6, had built a big monastery there; and they also knew that his monastery must be stuffed with treasure.

What the Muslims didn't know was that Majordomo Charles Martel was nearby, and was rushing to stop them. Somewhere along the road to Tours, Martel found a wooded hill that looked like a good place to make a stand. He set his army atop this hill, and then waited for the Muslims to arrive.

In looking at the two armies before the **Battle of Tours**, most people would have said that the Muslims would win. For one thing, the Muslim army was far bigger than the Frankish army— perhaps twice as big! For another, most of the Franks were on foot; while most of the Muslims rode horses. In a test of strength between man and horse, horse usually wins!

Fortunately for the Franks, they also had advantages. Their biggest advantage may have been Charles Martel himself— for Charles was the craftiest, steadiest, most experienced general of his day. Another advantage was the battlefield— for with the Franks planted on that wooded hilltop, the Muslims had to charge uphill to attack, dodging trees as they went.

With the Franks huddled in tight ranks bristling with long spears, the Muslim horsemen couldn't find a way to break through. Against all odds, Charles Martel's Frankish foot soldiers stood up to the Muslim cavalry— maybe for hours, or maybe even for days.

The outcome of the Battle of Tours may have turned on a rumor. It is said that near the end, someone shouted that the Franks had broken into the Muslims' camp— and were stealing the treasure of Bordeaux! Hearing this, some greedy Muslims forgot about the battle. They started racing for their tents, hoping to head the Franks off.

Charles Martel and his troops surrounding the Muslim commander at the Battle of Tours

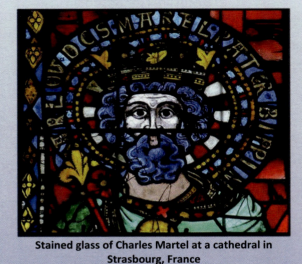

Stained glass of Charles Martel at a cathedral in Strasbourg, France

The sight of this sent other Muslims racing off too, probably thinking that their general had ordered a retreat. In the confusion of the retreat, the Franks surrounded the Muslim general and killed him!

Even then, the Franks stayed wary. It was only after sunrise the next day, when they saw the Muslims heading home, that they knew the Battle of Tours was over. The Christians had won! The Muslims would never send another army that big— which meant that Islam would never conquer Gaul the way it had conquered Hispania.

Ever since Charles Martel won the Battle of Tours, historians have wondered what might have happened if he hadn't. Martel's army was probably the strongest Christian army in the world of those days. If Martel hadn't stopped the Muslims, then it is hard to imagine that any other Christian could have stopped them. All Gaul might have fallen to Islam. And if Gaul had fallen, then the rest of Europe might have fallen too. Christianity might have died out in Europe, all because of one lost battle! Instead, Christianity survived— thanks to Charles Martel's great victory at the all-important Battle of Tours!

The Carolingian Empire

The Battle of Tours left the majordomos stronger than ever. Everyone could see that Charles Martel deserved all the glory for the Battle of Tours. As for the do-nothing Merovingian kings, they deserved no glory at all. From Charles Martel forward, the real power lay with the majordomos.

The next majordomo, Charles' son **Pippin III**, wanted to make his power more official. After putting up with a do-nothing king for several years, Pippin III sent a letter to the pope in Rome. He wanted to know:

"In regard to the kings of the Franks who no longer possess the royal power: is this state of things proper?"

The answer was just what Pippin hoped. To Pippin's delight, Pope Zachary agreed that this state of things was indeed most improper! With the pope's blessing, Pippin III got rid of his do-nothing king. The last of the Merovingian kings, young **Childeric III**, went to live in a monastery for the rest of his life.

As a sign that the Merovingian dynasty was finished, Pippin III got rid of an important symbol of Merovingian power: the king's hair. Since the time of Merovius, no Merovingian king had ever cut his hair or beard. But when Pippin sent the last Merovingian to a monastery, he also gave him a haircut. Childeric traded his long hair for a tonsure— the almost-bald hairstyle of a monk.

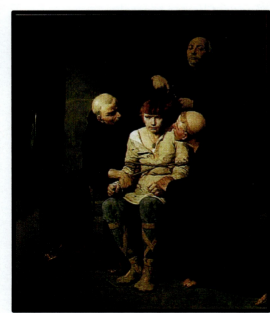

The former King Childeric III, last of the Merovingians, tied to a chair as monks forcibly cut his hair

As for Pippin III, he became the first king of a new Frankish dynasty: the **Carolingian dynasty**, which is named for Charles Martel. *Carolus* is the Latin form of "Charles."

〰〰〰〰〰〰〰〰〰〰〰〰〰〰〰〰〰〰〰〰〰〰〰〰〰〰〰〰〰〰〰〰

The deal that made Pippin III king was just one of many deals between Frankish kings and Roman popes. The next big deal started in 756, five years after Pippin became king. This one started with a letter from the pope to Pippin. The pope wanted Pippin's help with a people who had been bothering popes for a long time now: the **Lombards**.

In Chapter 4, we read how the Lombards swept down into northern Italy and took it from the Byzantines. It happened in the late 560s, soon after Justinian and Belisarius died. Then in Chapter 5, we read how Pope Gregory the Great raised armies against the Lombards— trying to keep them out of Rome.

> The **Lombards** were the barbarians who took northern Italy from the Byzantine Empire in the late 560s.

King Pippin III receiving his crown in 751

All that was over now. At the pope's request, Pippin III marched his army down to central Italy and crushed the Lombards— driving them back into northern Italy. When he finished, Pippin gave central Italy to the pope— in an incredibly rich gift called the **Donation of Pippin**.

This was the start of a brand-new country in central Italy: The **Papal States**, which were run entirely by the Church. Strange as it sounds, the popes collected taxes, hired police and even fought wars for the Papal States— just like worldly kings!

What did Pippin III get in return? Mainly, he got the pope's blessing— which was no small thing. In Christian eyes, the pope's blessing marked the King of the Franks as the rightful ruler of the whole Christian world.

Charlemagne (742? – 814)

〰〰〰〰〰〰〰〰〰〰〰〰〰〰〰〰

The king after Pippin III was the greatest king of the whole Carolingian dynasty: **Charlemagne**. Like the name Charles Martel, the name Charlemagne is part honorary title. It is short for *Charles le Magne*, which is French for "Charles the Great."

Like his father and grandfather before him, Charlemagne was a fighting king. With his sword **Joyeuse** in one hand and a cross in the other, Charlemagne built his empire in all directions at once.

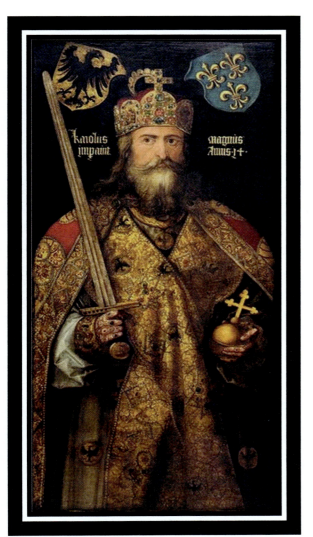

"Emperor Charles the Great" by artist Albrecht Durer. The object in his left hand is a symbol called a *globus cruciger*— Latin for "cross on a globe." It stands for the idea that Charlemagne rules the whole world with Christ's blessing.

- ➤ To the south, Charlemagne took northern Italy from the Lombards. He also drove the last of the Muslims out of Gaul, back into Hispania.

- ➤ To the north, Charlemagne conquered what are now the Netherlands and northern Germany.

- ➤ To the east, Charlemagne conquered what is now southern Germany and beyond.

The vast Carolingian Empire at its biggest

By 800 AD, Charlemagne had built one of the biggest empires the world has ever seen: the **Carolingian Empire**. It covered most of Western Europe, all of Central Europe and even part of Eastern Europe!

Wherever Charlemagne's empire spread, Christianity spread too. Sometimes, Charlemagne sent Christian missionaries to convert the people he conquered. Other times, he converted them with his sword. It is said that in 782, Charlemagne executed 4,500 Saxon rebels in a single day— partly because they didn't want to become Christians.

One of the highlights of Charlemagne's career came on Christmas Day, 800. Charlemagne was in Rome that day, taking Holy Communion at Old St. Peter's Basilica. As the great king knelt at the altar, Pope Leo III did something unexpected— setting a new crown on Charlemagne's head. That crown stood for a kingdom that had disappeared back in 476: The Western Roman Empire. In the pope's mind, Charlemagne was the emperor who finally rebuilt the Western Roman Empire!

Charlemagne receiving his crown

Poisson D'Avril, French for "Fish of April," is the French version of April Fools' Day. The tradition started in 1564, when King Charles IX officially moved the first day of the year from April 1 to January 1. Despite the new law, some backward Frenchmen still celebrated the New Year on April 1. To tease these stubborn fellows, some enlightened Frenchmen stuck paper fish to their backs!

Just why the French chose paper fish, no one now knows for sure. Whatever the reason, the French still enjoy eating chocolate fish on *Poisson D'Avril.*

CHAPTER 8

The Vikings

Scandinavia

In northernmost Europe, between the North Sea and the Baltic Sea, lies a region called Scandinavia. There are three Scandinavian countries. The first two, **Norway** and **Sweden**, stand on the huge Scandinavian Peninsula. Part of the third country, **Denmark**, stands on a much smaller peninsula: the Jutland Peninsula. The rest of Denmark stands on the Danish Islands, which lie between the two peninsulas. The biggest of the Danish Islands is called **Zealand**. The capital of Denmark, **Copenhagen**, stands on the east side of Zealand.

The climate of Scandinavia is quite different from place to place. Northern Scandinavia lies within the **Arctic Circle**, where temperatures can be unbearably cold! Most people prefer southern Scandinavia, where the cold is much more bearable. They especially like

The **Arctic Circle** is the part of the globe above 66-1/2 degrees north latitude. Within the Arctic Circle, the sun never rises for part of each winter, and never sets for part of each summer.

the coasts, where warmth from the sea keeps temperatures from dropping too low. This is one reason why the Vikings, who came from Scandinavia, were such expert seamen.

Norsemen and Vikings

The natives of Scandinavia were called Norsemen, an ancient name that means simply "north-men." Norse tribes lived all along the coasts of what are now Denmark, southern Norway and southern Sweden.

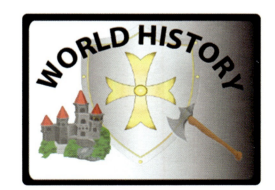

Wherever they lived, all Norsemen had two things in common. First, they all spoke an ancient language called Old Norse. Second, they all followed the ancient Norse religion— a warlike system built around warrior gods. The greatest Norse god was Odin, and the mightiest in battle was Thor.

The Norsemen's warlike religion inspired some of the deadliest warriors ever: the **Vikings**. The Vikings were Norse raiders who always struck from the sea, at least at first. Even the very name "Viking" spoke of the sea; for it probably came from an Old Norse word that meant "sea journey."

Just before 800 AD, the Vikings suddenly started raiding monasteries and villages on the coasts of northern Europe. Viking ships appeared out of nowhere, landing where no one expected them to land. The blonde warriors who strode ashore were uncommonly tall, strong and skilled. The first thing the Vikings did was to kill everyone who stood in their way. Then they stole everything of value, loaded it aboard their ships and disappeared! This was the start of the **Viking Age**— a time when Europeans lived in constant fear of raiders from the north.

> The **Viking Age** was a time when Viking warriors launched savage raids all along the coasts of northern Europe. It started around 793, and ended around 1066.

Viking Ships

Viking ships came in two main kinds: longships and knarrs. A **longship** was a long, narrow vessel built for fast raids. The smallest longships were about 60 feet long, and carried crews of 25 – 30. The biggest were up to twice as long, and carried crews of 100 or more.

Longships could be driven by sails, oars or both. Instead of simple rowing benches, Viking oarsmen sat on clever sea chests that were part seat, part storage locker.

Two special features made longships perfect for Viking raids. First, longships were symmetrical from front to back. In other words, their backs were shaped just like their fronts— which meant that if the Vikings needed to turn around quickly, then they could just turn in their seats and row the other way!

Second, longships' bottoms were almost flat— which meant that they could sail in shallow water. This feature helped the Vikings surprise their victims. Longships went where other ships couldn't, breezing along rocky coasts and up shallow rivers. Since no one had ever seen ships in these waters before, no one expected the Vikings to land there. Flat-bottomed ships could also land on any beach, with no need for docks.

Vikings landing in England

A third special feature of longships was more decorative, but no less useful for war. The Vikings often carved the **prows** of their longships to look like dragon heads! All Vikings loved dragons— partly because Norse legends were full of dragons, and partly because dragons terrified their enemies. Dragon prows were so common that longships were also called **dragon ships**. The sight of a dragon ship nosing onto a beach was enough to strike terror in any heart!

> A **prow** is the nose of a ship.

The other kind of Viking ship, the **knarr**, was a cargo hauler for supplies and trade goods. Knarrs were wider, deeper and shorter than longships. They could carry more weight than longships, but also were slower and harder to turn. With smaller crews and fewer oars than longships, knarrs depended on sails more than oars.

Round Viking shields hung on the side of a longship

Viking warriors used many different weapons, from bows and arrows to spears, swords, battleaxes and pikes. Like their Saxon neighbors to the south, the Vikings favored a special kind of straight sword called a seax.

For defense, early Vikings carried round shields; while later Vikings carried shields shaped like kites. Their armor was probably chain mail, leather or heavy cloth.

As for their helmets, most Vikings wore simple ones made of metal or leather. Contrary to popular belief, no archaeologist has ever found a Viking helmet with horns! The horned helmets Vikings wear in pictures were probably an artists' invention— a way to show the awful terror of Viking raids.

Some Vikings warriors were even more terrifying than all the rest. When a battle was about to begin, these warriors whipped themselves up into a frenzy— a mad, violent trance called the **berserkergang**. When the trance was upon them, **berserkers** fought like wild animals— with all the strength of bears, the speed of wolves and the viciousness of cornered beasts. They held nothing back, pouring their whole strength into every blow.

> In English, a person who goes crazy is said to have "**gone berserk.**"

Helmet of a Viking buried in the 900s

Viking families often lived in special homes called **longhouses**. The usual longhouse was a long, strong building with a stone foundation, walls of stone or wood and a sod roof over a wooden frame.

Living in a longhouse was quite different from living in a modern-day house. One big difference was that longhouses combined home, storehouse and barn under one roof! The family end held living space; while the barn end held animals, feed, tools and weapons. Wooden benches lined the walls of the family end. Covered with animal skins, these benches served as padded seats by day and warm beds by night. Most longhouses were also windowless. The only light came from the doors, the kitchen fire and a chimney hole in the roof.

Another difference was that one longhouse might hold four generations of a family at once— from grandparents down to parents, children and grandchildren, all living under one roof with their animals!

Modern-day reconstruction of a sod-roofed longhouse in Iceland

The Vikings expected a lot from their children. The expectations started shortly after each child was born, when Viking leaders showed up to have a look at it. If they found any problems— missing fingers, a crooked back or anything else they didn't like— then the child's parents were not allowed to feed it. The Vikings would not waste food on any child who might weaken their people, instead of strengthening them.

Healthy Viking children started working at around age five. Viking boys learned hunting, fighting, farming, shipbuilding and weapon-making. Viking girls learned mainly homemaking and farming— although some learned fighting as well.

A Viking boy of fifteen or sixteen was old enough to marry, start a family and take on all the responsibilities of an adult. Viking girls grew up even earlier, marrying at age twelve to fourteen.

Norse Mythology

Like other ancient peoples, ancient Norsemen believed in flawed gods. The gods of Norse myths were gifted with superhuman strength, wisdom and beauty. But they were also plagued with human weaknesses— things like greed, jealousy and wickedness. The flaws of their gods helped explain the flawed world they found all around them. In the end, Norsemen believed, those flaws would lead to a terrible battle that would destroy the world.

Most of what is still known about Norse mythology comes from a pair of books called the **Eddas**. Although the Eddas weren't written down until the 1200s, the stories they tell are far older than that.

The complicated universe of Norse mythology starts with nine worlds. These nine worlds are divided into three levels: three heavens, four earths and two hells. All are built around a mighty world tree called **Yggdrasil**, which is watered by three hidden wells. The highest heaven is **Asgard**, which is home to the greatest Norse god of all: mighty, far-seeing **Odin**.

Odin is the god of war, wisdom and more. Some of Odin's wisdom came from one of three wells around the world tree: the **Well of Mimir**. The price for drinking from the Well of Mimir was to gouge out an eye and sacrifice it to the well— which explains why Odin is a one-eyed god.

Odin also has other ways of seeing. First, Odin has two clever ravens who gather news for him. One is called *Huginn*, or "Thought"; and the other *Muninn*, or "Memory." Second, Odin can see everything that is happening in all nine worlds— but only when he sits on his magical silver throne, which is called *Hlidskjalf*.

Besides Odin, the god Norsemen loved most was Odin's son: mighty **Thor**. The Vikings honored Thor, god of thunder, as the strongest and most battle-ready in all Asgard.

Like Odin, Thor possesses magical objects that make him even mightier than he already is. The mightiest is *Mjolnir*— a throwing hammer so heavy

Odin seated on his throne *Hlidskjalf*, with his ravens *Muninn* and *Huginn* and his magical spear *Gungnir*

that no one in the universe can lift it, save only Thor. The best parts of Mjolnir's magic are that it never misses its target, and always returns to Thor's hand. Thor also has *Járngreipr*, a pair of iron gloves for gripping Mjolnir; and *Megingjörð*, a battle belt that doubles his strength!

Most of the trouble in the Norse universe comes from a mischievous character called Loki. Loki is a half-god, half-giant with the remarkable power to change into any shape he likes, from fly to fish to horse. At first, Loki uses his powers for simple mischief. Later, though, Loki turns to the worst kind of mischief: murder.

The human world is called Midgard. Between Midgard and Asgard stands a rainbow-colored bridge called the Bifrost. A sleepless god called Heimdal stands constant guard over the Bifrost, making sure no human comes to Asgard uninvited.

The only way most humans are ever invited to Asgard is if they die glorious deaths in battle. Half the Vikings who die this way go to a field called *Fólkvangr*, which is ruled by a goddess named Freyja. The other half go where every good warrior hopes to go when he dies: Valhalla.

Valhalla is a victory hall where great warriors get to live with Odin himself. With a roof made of shields over a frame of spears, Valhalla is a warrior's paradise. The warriors of Valhalla fight every day, testing their skills in great battles and hunts. Any warrior who dies in battle comes back to life by nightfall, when a great feast begins!

The point of all this fighting and feasting is to keep warriors fit for their last battle: a world-ending melee called the Ragnarok. On one side will fight the gods of Asgard and the warriors of Valhalla. On the other side will fight Loki and his kin, the evil giants.

When the Ragnarok comes, it will be a battle with no winners.

➤ The greatest of all warriors, Thor, will manage to kill the world serpent: *Jörmungandr*, a giant who stretches around the world. But then the world serpent's poison will lay Thor low.

For such a heavy hammer, Mjolnir was a bit short-handled. This was because when the blacksmith was forging Mjolnir, a pesky fly bit his bellows-turner on the eyelid— causing him to stop turning the bellows before Mjolnir was quite finished.

The "pesky fly" turned out to be the trouble-making, shape-shifting Loki in disguise.

A dwarf blacksmith forging *Mjolnir* while the bellows-turner and Loki look on

Thor tackling the world serpent *Jormungandr* during the Ragnarok

- A giant wolf called Fenrir will swallow Odin whole, before one of Odin's sons tears Fenrir limb from limb.
- Heimdal will manage to slay Loki, but not without being slain himself.

In the end, a great fire will rage through all the nine worlds— destroying everyone and everything. The smoldering ruins of Asgard, Midgard and the rest will sink into the sea, leaving nothing but darkness.

From Raiders to Conquerors

The Viking Age started on an island called Lindisfarne, just off the east coast of Scotland. Lindisfarne's claim to fame was its rich, important monastery. One day in 793, a band of Vikings suddenly burst into that monastery. After killing everyone who stood in their way, they stole everything they could possibly sell— including some of the monks, whom they carried off to sell into slavery.

One thing the Vikings learned from the famous Raid on Lindisfarne was that monasteries made perfect targets for their raids. For one thing, monasteries were stuffed with donated treasures. For another, most Christian monks were completely helpless in a fight!

Exactly why the Vikings attacked when they did, no one knows for sure. Some say that the Vikings had outgrown Scandinavia, and needed more room to grow. Others say that Scandinavia suddenly grew colder around this time— making it hard for the Vikings to raise enough food.

Still others say that the Vikings didn't need a special reason to go to war. They were simply a warlike people— bloodthirsty savages who liked nothing better than a good fight!

A **valkyrie** is a heavenly shield-maiden sent by Odin to watch over a battle in Midgard. Whenever a great warrior dies a glorious death in battle, a valkyrie carries him up to Asgard.

Valkyries carrying slain warriors off to Asgard

The English names for four of the seven days of the week come from Norse gods.

- ❖ **Tuesday** is named for a god called Tyr.
- ❖ **Wednesday** is named for Odin, which is sometimes pronounced Woden.
- ❖ **Thursday** is Thor's day.
- ❖ **Friday** is named for a goddess called Frigga.

Hnefatafl was a popular board game that ran much like a Viking raid. In the center of a checkered board stood a king, defended by a home army of about eight pieces. Around the edges of the board stood a Viking army twice that size. The king tried to reach safety by running for the edges of the board; while the Vikings tried to surround the king.

Hnefatafl stayed popular until a new game arrived to replace it: Chess.

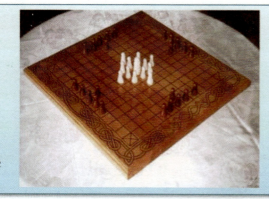

Quick raids like the one on Lindisfarne were only the beginning. As the Vikings grew more confident, they started sending bigger raiding parties— hitting targets farther inland. In time, they sent armies to conquer new lands for the Norse people.

By the 840s, Viking families were settling into new lands all over northern Europe— from Britain and France in the west all the way to Russia in the east. Wherever they settled, the incredibly tough Vikings changed the course of history.

Viking Explorers in the North Atlantic

The Vikings were more than just raiders and conquerors. They were also explorers and adventurers! While some Vikings fought for old lands in Britain and France, others searched for new lands not marked on any map.

The first new lands the Vikings discovered were the Faroe Islands, which lie about midway between Norway and Iceland. From the Faroes, they leapt over to Iceland; then farther on to Greenland; then farther yet.

The great mystery is how the Vikings managed to find all these islands! The North Atlantic is a very big place, and there are no signs pointing the way to the next island. Yet somehow, the Vikings managed to find far-off islands that no other European had ever found. They also managed to keep finding those islands, going back to them again and again— all without compasses, sextants, star charts or clocks!

The first Viking leader in Iceland was Ingólfr Arnarsson, who built a settlement there around 874. Arnarsson was the first to realize what a treasure Iceland was— a luscious land full of fish, seals, walrus and good soil. When the Vikings back home heard of Arnarsson's treasure, they couldn't move there fast enough. Just 50 – 60 years after he moved to Iceland, eager settlers had already claimed all the best farmland there.

Fifty more years passed before the Vikings moved on to their next big find. This one started with Eric Thorvaldsson, who is also called Eric the Red. Norse history offers two possible explanations for Eric's nickname. One is that he had fiery red hair. The other is that he had a fiery temper; for Eric came from a family of convicted killers!

Vikings landing in Iceland

Eric's father, Thorvald Asvaldsson, had been banished from Norway for murder or manslaughter. Forced to find a new home, Thorvald moved his family to Iceland around 960. Twenty-two years later, Eric was convicted of the same crime— and got the same punishment. He was banished for three years, forbidden to live in Iceland.

Eric made good use of those three years. It was during this time that he found and explored the Vikings' next big discovery: **Greenland**. Eric the Red built the first Viking settlement on Greenland around 986.

The name "Greenland" started as an advertising stunt. The moment his three years were over, Eric was back in Iceland looking for settlers to build a colony. To make the place sound more attractive, Eric called it "Greenland"— even though it was far less green, and far more covered with ice, than Iceland was. By this time, though, most of Iceland was already taken. Eric found plenty of Vikings ready to try their luck somewhere else.

Alas, luck was hard to find on Greenland. Of the 20 – 30 ships that sailed with Eric in 986, only 14 survived the hard journey. The ones that did survive found Greenland far less green than Eric had promised. The few colonies the Vikings built on Greenland never prospered like the ones on Iceland did. Most of Greenland was simply too cold!

One of Eric the Red's sons was to become the most famous Viking of all. Like his father, **Leif Ericsson** was a skilled seaman. His first long sea voyage was from Greenland to Norway, where he probably went to beg his king for help. If the colonies on Greenland were to survive, then they needed more help than the king had sent so far.

By this time, the King of Norway was a Christian. It was around this time that Leif became a Christian too— maybe because he wanted to please his king. Either way, the king sent at least one kind of help to Greenland. Thanks to Leif's trip, Greenland received its first Christian church!

"Leif Ericsson discovers North America" by artist Christian Krohg

This same voyage led to Leif's greatest discovery. According to one version of the story, Leif was on his way home from Norway when a heavy storm blew him off course. After the big storm blew over, Leif found himself somewhere no European had ever been: off the coast of **North America**.

After exploring this unknown coast for some time, Leif named part of it **Vinland,** or "Vine-land"— after the plentiful grape vines he found there. He also built a temporary colony there for the winter. Just where Leif built his colony, no one knows for sure; but the best guess is somewhere in Newfoundland, Canada.

The few Vikings who tried to settle in Vinland had even less luck than the ones on Greenland did. Leif's brother, Thorvald Ericsson, died with an arrow in his chest— fired by angry Native Americans whom the Vikings called Skraelings. The Skraelings were probably ancestors of the Inuit, a Native American people who still live in northern Canada.

The death of Thorvald Ericsson was the end of Vinland. Although other Vikings returned to North America for grapes and wood, none of them settled there permanently— at least, none whom anyone remembers for sure.

The more time passed, the more Vikings gave up on frozen Greenland too. By about 1400, they had all moved back to Iceland or Scandinavia. Both Greenland and North America were all but forgotten.

> Some Americans believe the Vikings made it as far west as Minnesota, which is why Minnesota's pro football team is called the Vikings!

ꖀꖀꖀꖀꖀꖀꖀꖀꖀꖀꖀꖀꖀꖀꖀꖀꖀꖀꖀꖀꖀꖀꖀꖀꖀꖀꖀꖀꖀꖀꖀꖀ

Leif Ericsson discovered North America around the year 1000, nearly 500 years before Christopher Columbus discovered the West Indies for Spain. Yet in modern times, most people know a lot more about Christopher Columbus than they do about Leif Ericsson.

Why? Because when the Vikings left North America, Leif Ericsson's colony disappeared. But Columbus' colonies thrived. The Spanish spread out all over the West Indies, Middle America and South America, building one of the richest empires ever— as we'll read in Chapter 25.

The East-West Schism

In Chapter 7, we read how Islam tore through the East— tearing down Christian churches in city after city. By the end of the Rashidun Caliphate, the Christians were down to just one great city in the East: Constantinople, capital of the Byzantine Empire. Meanwhile, Rome was still the leading Christian city in the West.

Over time, the churches of East and West grew different from one another. One difference was that Western priests spoke Latin in church, while Eastern ones spoke Greek. Greek-speakers told different stories, looking back to different heroes than Latin-speakers did. Another difference was that Eastern priests could marry, while Western ones couldn't. There were also arguments over how to worship— what to read, what to say and what to sing, as well as how to use icons and relics.

Oddly enough, one of the biggest arguments between East and West started over a single word: Filioque. *Filioque* is a Latin word that means "and from the Son." Around the year 400, some Western churches started adding *filioque* to an important statement of faith: the **Nicene Creed**, which we covered in Chapter 2. Without the *filioque*, the Nicene Creed read:

> The **Nicene Creed** is an important statement of faith that describes the three persons of the Holy Trinity: God the Father, God the Son and God the Holy Spirit (Chapter 2). This creed was first written by the Council of Nicaea in 325, and expanded by the Council of Constantinople in 381.

> "I believe… in the Holy Spirit, the Lord, the Giver of Life, who proceeds from the Father…"

With the *filioque* added, the Nicene Creed read:

> "I believe… in the Holy Spirit, the Lord, the Giver of Life, who proceeds from the Father **and from the Son…**"

The difference was small, but important. Western Christians liked the *filioque*. To them, it was another way of saying that Christ the Son was God, just as God the Father was God. This was important to Western Christians, especially after Arius tried to say that Christ was less than God (Chapter 2).

As for Eastern Christians, they hated the *filioque*. To them, it seemed to say that the Holy Spirit was less than God. Besides, adding the *filioque* was bad manners. The Nicene Creed was one of the most important statements of faith ever; and yet the West had changed it without even asking the East!

The argument over the *filioque* was only part of a much bigger argument between Rome and Constantinople. The Pope in Rome saw himself as the leader of all Christian churches, not just Western ones. The East didn't see it that way at all. Eastern churches followed a different leader: the **Patriarch of Constantinople**, whose headquarters was the great Hagia Sophia (Chapter 4).

> The **Patriarch of Constantinople** was the head of the Church in the East, just as the Pope was the head of the Church in the West.
>
> A **schism** is a church split.

The argument over which was higher, pope or patriarch, was the biggest argument of all. In time, this argument led to one of the biggest church splits ever: the **East-West Schism**, which is also called the **Great Schism**.

The real trouble started in 1054, when Pope Leo IX sent his favorite secretary to Constantinople. When he got there, **Cardinal Humbert** delivered a message to **Patriarch Michael I Cerularius**. The message was simple but strong. The cardinal told the patriarch that if he wanted to be a Christian, then he had to obey the pope— just like every other Christian in the world!

Of course, the patriarch didn't see it that way. When he tried to argue, the cardinal stormed off in a rage.

What happened next broke the last tie between the churches of East and West. That July, Cardinal Humbert marched into the Hagia Sophia and laid a **papal bull** in front of the patriarch. When the patriarch read it, he learned that the pope had just **excommunicated** him. In other words, the Patriarch of Constantinople was kicked out of his own church! By order of the pope, all Christians everywhere were to cut ties with the patriarch. Most importantly, no Christian church was to serve the patriarch Holy Communion!

> A **papal bull** is a sealed letter containing important statements or instructions from the pope.
>
> To **excommunicate** someone is to cast him out of the Church, cutting him off from Holy Communion.

Naturally, no one in the East obeyed this papal bull. Instead of excommunicating their patriarch, the churches of the East excommunicated Cardinal Humbert!

Starting then, the churches of East and West went their separate ways. Churches that followed Constantinople became **Eastern Orthodox** churches; while churches that followed Rome became **Roman Catholic** churches. The two have stayed separate ever since.

Patriarch Michael I Cerularius seated on his throne at the Hagia Sophia in Constantinople

The English Channel

The English Channel is a sea channel between Great Britain and mainland Europe. This important body of water measures about 350 miles long, and about 150 miles wide at its widest.

The widest part of the English Channel is home to two island groups that are well-known to dairy farmers. One is **Jersey**, where the first Jersey cows were bred. The other is **Guernsey**, where the first Guernsey cows were bred. Together, Jersey and Guernsey are called the Channel Islands.

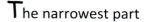

The narrowest part of the English Channel is only about twenty-one miles wide. This is the famous Strait of Dover, where most travelers go to cross from England to France and back. Beneath the Strait of Dover lies the longest undersea rail tunnel in the world: the Channel Tunnel, a.k.a. the "Chunnel." This fantastic engineering project was finished in 1994.

Two famous landmarks line the Strait of Dover. The **White Cliffs of Dover** stand on the English side, and the port of **Calais** on the French side.

The English Channel has always been one of England's best defenses. Many would-be invaders have tried to cross it over the centuries, only to fail miserably. One was King Philip II of Spain, who sent the Spanish Armada against England in 1588— as we'll read in Chapter 34. Two others were Emperor Napoleon I of France, who tried in 1805; and Fuhrer Adolf Hitler of Germany, who tried in 1940. This chapter tells of an invader who didn't fail: William the Conqueror, who started the famous Norman Conquest in 1066.

A **conquest** is a conquering.

The **Normans** were a part-Viking, part-Frankish people who lived across the English Channel from England, in a part of France called Normandy.

The **Norman Conquest** was the conquest of England by the Normans.

The **White Cliffs of Dover** are a set of chalk-white cliffs that line the English side of the Strait of Dover. They stand as a forbidding barrier against any invader who tries to cross.

A lighthouse standing atop the White Cliffs of Dover

The Vikings in France

In Chapter 7, we read how the Carolingian dynasty built a huge empire that covered most of Europe. The greatest Carolingian king was Charlemagne, who took over in 768.

Then in Chapter 8, we read how the Viking Age started: with the Raid on Lindisfarne. That notorious raid happened in 793, when Charlemagne was in his 25th year as king. In other words, the Viking Age started in the time of Charlemagne.

While Charlemagne lived, the Vikings mostly stuck to quick raids like the one on Lindisfarne. The same was true under the next emperor: **Louis the Pious**, who took over when Charlemagne died in 814. While Louis lived, the Vikings were mostly raiders— not conquerors and settlers.

The Salic Laws helped change all that. As we read in Chapter 7, Frankish law said that when a king died, his kingdom must be split between his sons. Since Louis the Pious had several sons, the Carolingian Empire split when he died. His sons were soon at war with each other, fighting over the many lands their father had left them.

An elderly Charlemagne bestowing a crown upon his son Louis the Pious

The Vikings took advantage of this. While the sons of Louis the Pious were busy fighting each other, the Vikings swept in a seized part of their empire— the part that stood just across the English Channel from England.

When everyone realized that the Vikings were there to stay, this land got a new name. They called it **Normandy**, after the "north-man" Vikings. The capital of Normandy, Rouen, stood on the Seine River— about 40 miles upriver from the coast. The Seine is the same famous river that flows through Paris, the capital of France.

When the sons of Louis the Pious finally stopped fighting each other, the Carolingian Empire split into three pieces for three sons. The western piece, which was called **West Francia**, went to a son called **Charles the Bald**. Since Normandy lay in West Francia, it was King Charles the Bald who had to deal with those awful neighbors who had just moved in: the Vikings!

Two years into Charles the Bald's reign, a Viking army sailed up the Seine River— all the way to Paris. When it got there, it quickly destroyed half of Charles' army. The rest of Charles' army ran off, leaving Paris defenseless. The Vikings spent that Easter sacking Paris— killing its people, burning its buildings and looting its treasure. Although no one knows for sure, it is said that an infamous Viking called **Ragnar Lodbrok** led this awful raid: The **First Sack of Paris**.

Viking warriors on the move

After the raid, the Vikings were in no hurry to leave. Charles the Bald was desperate to get rid of them, but couldn't find a way to fight them off. So instead, Charles paid them off. The Vikings rowed away with a fortune in gold and silver— almost three tons in all!

That was just the beginning. From 845 on, Viking armies sailed upriver almost every year— hoping for more big payoffs like the First Sack of Paris.

Obviously, Charles the Bald needed a better way to defend his kingdom. The answer, he decided, was a tough new law called the **Edict of Pistres**. Written in 864, the Edict of Pistres made it a crime to sell weapons or horses to the Vikings. It also created a fast-moving cavalry force to battle the Vikings. Before the Edict of Pistres, almost all Frankish knights fought on foot— like the ones at the Battle of Tours, which we covered in Chapter 7. After the Edict of Pistres, the Franks learned to fight from horseback.

The Edict of Pistres also brought another important change. Since Vikings always attacked upriver, the edict ordered bridges along big rivers like the Seine— but not just any bridges. Charles the Bald wanted strong stone bridges defended by tall siege towers. With bridges like that, the Franks might be able to stop the Vikings from sailing upriver every year.

Viking Coins

The first Vikings didn't understand coin money; for the ancient Norse traded only in goods, never in coin. Having no other use for the silver and gold coins they stole, early Vikings usually melted them down to make armbands, jewelry or decorations for their weapons.

After the Vikings started trading with other countries, they understood the value of coins very well! Later Viking kings minted their own coins, just like other kings around Europe.

The Edict of Pistres was twenty-one years old in 885, when Charles' bridges proved how valuable they were. That year, a Viking leader called Siegfried led a huge army up the Seine. When he reached Paris, Siegfried found the river blocked by two strong bridges with tall siege towers. No matter how hard they tried, the Vikings simply could not break past these bridges:

➢ When the Vikings tried catapulting heavy rocks at the towers, the Franks repaired them under cover of darkness.

➢ When the Vikings tried setting fire to the towers, the Franks poured down water to put the fires out.

➢ The Vikings even tried filling in the river around the towers, piling up tons of earth and rock so that they could come close enough to climb the walls. When the Vikings came too close, though, the Franks poured down hot pitch on their heads.

Scene from the Siege of Paris, 885 – 886

Even so, the Vikings kept trying. The terrible **Siege of Paris** dragged on and on, with neither side gaining any ground.

Old Charles the Bald was gone by this time. The new King of West Francia was his nephew **Charles the Fat**, who had taken over in the late 870s. The Siege of Paris was on its second year in 886, when Charles the Fat thought of a new way to get rid of the Vikings. Instead of fighting them, Charles hired them! Charles' part of the deal was to pay Siegfried a fortune in silver. Siegfried's part was to go fight for Charles in the east, leaving Paris alone. Once again, the Vikings sailed away happy— for now.

The Vikings' exit was good news in the short run, but bad news in the long run. The Franks expected their kings to fight the Vikings, not hire them. When Charles the Fat chose to hire the Vikings, his people stopped trusting him. As a result, he was the last Emperor of the Carolingian Empire. Before Charles the Fat died, the great empire of Charlemagne and his ancestors broke apart for the last time.

Another Viking who fought at the Siege of Paris was one of the most famous ever: **Rollo the Viking**. According to legend, Rollo was also one of the biggest Vikings ever— a mountain of a man, frightfully large and strong. Rollo's nickname, "Rollo the Walker," may have meant that he was too heavy to ride a horse!

**Rollo the Viking
(846? - 931?)**

Twenty-five years after the Siege of Paris, Rollo led another Viking army upriver— where he attacked Paris yet again. After failing to break into Paris, Rollo moved on to another big city: Chartres, which lay 50 miles to the southwest.

Old Charles the Fat was gone by this time. The new King of West Francia was his cousin Charles the Simple, who had taken over in 898. Fortunately for the Franks, Charles the Simple managed to beat Rollo at the Battle of Chartres.

Even so, the Franks were no closer to stopping the Viking raids that came year after year. What Charles the Simple really wanted was to tame the savage Vikings.

The answer, Charles decided, was another deal like Charles the Fat's. This new deal came in a treaty signed after the Battle of Chartres, when Rollo agreed to several things. First, Rollo would become a Christian. Second, Rollo and his people would swear loyalty to Charles the Simple. This meant defending Charles' kingdom against all attacks— including attacks from other Vikings.

In exchange, Charles officially gave Rollo what the Vikings had already stolen: Normandy. Rollo became the **Duke of Normandy**— a full member of the Frankish nobility, second in rank only to the king himself.

King Charles the Simple, whose nickname may also be translated "Charles the Straightforward"

With a few strokes from a pen, Charles the Simple did more to tame the Vikings than his ancestors had done in a century. Instead of savage Vikings, Rollo and his people slowly became the **Normans**— a French-speaking, Christian people from a fine duchy in West Francia.

The Vikings in England

Meanwhile, Great Britain was still divided. Back in Chapter 2, we read how the Angles and Saxons split southern Britain into seven kingdoms called the Heptarchy. The four biggest Anglo-Saxon kingdoms were Northumbria, Mercia, Wessex and East Anglia. Three smaller kingdoms lay along the southeast coast: Essex, Kent and Sussex. The lines between these kingdoms often blurred, as certain kings ruled more than one of them.

The Vikings attacked the Heptarchy the same way they attacked West Francia: first with raiding parties, then with invasion armies. The first big Viking army came from Denmark in 865. Since the Anglo-Saxons were Christians now, they called this terrifying force the **Great Heathen Army**. Legend tells how the Great Heathen Army crushed King Aella of Northumbria in 866— and how afterwards, the Vikings murdered Aella in the most horrifying way imaginable.

When the Great Heathen Army showed no signs of going home, the other kings of the Heptarchy realized that they were in serious trouble. What they needed was a strong leader to pull them all together, lest the Vikings pick them off one-by-one. The leader who filled that need was **King Alfred of Wessex**, who is also called **Alfred the Great**.

The future King Alfred was born in 849, the youngest son of King Aethelwulf of Wessex. With four older brothers ahead of him, Alfred seemed unlikely to inherit the throne. So instead of raising Alfred to be a king, Aethelwulf raised him to be a scholar. In a time when few Anglo-Saxons even learned to read, young Alfred learned law, Bible and much more.

AELFREDUS
MAGNUS

**Alfred the Great
(849 - 899)**

Alfred was still a young student when his brothers started dying off, one by one. Each brother's death brought Alfred a little closer to the throne. By 865, he was down to just one older brother: King Aethelred of Wessex.

As we read above, 865 was the year when the Great Heathen Army invaded. Needing a way to fight the Vikings off, Aethelred joined forces with the King of Mercia. A few years later, Aethelred was killed in battle— leaving no one but the 22-year-old Alfred to take his place.

Soon after his brother died, King Alfred signed a peace treaty with the Vikings. Like most Viking treaties, this one didn't last long. A few years later, a Viking called **Guthrum the Dane** struck deep inside Wessex— threatening to wipe Alfred out.

The low point of Alfred's reign came just after Christmas 877. After sending most of his troops home for Christmas, Alfred went to a hunting lodge for a bit of rest. He may have forgotten that the Vikings were pagans who didn't care about Christmas. Whatever the reason, Alfred was completely unprepared in January 878— when out of nowhere, Guthrum the Dane showed up at his hunting lodge. Alfred was so surprised that he barely escaped with his life!

Fortunately, Alfred knew a good place to hide. In western Wessex, not far from Bristol, lay a swampy land called Somerset Levels. Alfred spent the early months of 878 on some hidden island in these swamps, planning his next move.

Alfred in the peasant woman's cottage

According to legend, Alfred spent part of this time with a peasant family who had no idea that he was King of Wessex. One day, the woman set some meal cakes around her fire to bake. Since Alfred was sitting near the fire, she asked him to watch the cakes while she went outside for more firewood. Alas, Alfred was so lost in thought that he didn't notice the smell of burning meal cakes. When the woman returned, she gave him a good scolding— not realizing that she was scolding her king!

Those thoughtful months in Somerset Levels turned out to be time well spent. In the spring of 878, Alfred summoned every fighting man in Wessex to a meeting place called **Egbert's Stone**. After training up his army, Alfred tackled Guthrum the Dane in a huge fight called the **Battle of Edington**. This time, Alfred crushed Guthrum— leaving him no choice but to surrender!

In winning the Battle of Edington, Alfred also won the power to strike a hard bargain with Guthrum the Dane. Like Rollo the Viking, Guthrum agreed to become a Christian. He also agreed to be satisfied with the land he had already conquered, instead of constantly fighting for new land.

Since Guthrum came from Denmark, Anglo-Saxons called his part of Britain the **Danelaw**. What had once been the Heptarchy now became just two kingdoms, more or less: the Danelaw in the northeast, and Wessex in the southwest.

> The **Danelaw** was the part of Britain conquered by the Vikings— the part where Danish law ruled, rather than Anglo-Saxon law.

King Alfred's Tower

After the Battle of Edington, Alfred the Great put the education he had received as a boy to good use. Alfred was not only a great military man, but also a great king who brought fairer laws and better education to a people who had never known them before: the once-savage Anglo-Saxons.

Almost 1,000 years after Alfred, the English built a 160-foot-tall monument to him at Egbert's Stone. A plaque on **King Alfred's Tower** explains how the English feel about Alfred the Great:

"…To him we owe the origin of juries, the establishment of a militia, the creation of a naval force. Alfred, the light of a benighted age, was a philosopher and a Christian, the father of his people, the founder of the English monarchy and liberty."

Alfred reigned for twenty-eight years, from 871 – 899. In all the generations since, no other English king has ever earned the title "Great."

Although some honor Alfred the Great as the first King of all England, Alfred never claimed that title— for Alfred never conquered the Danelaw. The first true King of England was Alfred's grandson **Aethelstan**. It was Aethelstan who finally conquered the Danelaw, bringing all of what is now England under one crown for the first time. It happened in 927— the first year of the **Kingdom of England**.

Alas, the Viking Age wasn't over. For not all of Alfred the Great's descendants did as well against the Vikings as Aethelstan did. In 1013, a Danish Viking called Sweyn Forkbeard seized the throne of England from another descendant of Alfred: King Aethelred the Unready.

> The **Kingdom of England** started in 927, when King Aethelstan of Wessex finally conquered the Danelaw— bringing all of what is now England under one crown for the first time.

Starting then, the throne passed back and forth between two royal houses. One was the **House of Denmark**, which was the Viking family of Sweyn Forkbeard. The other was the **House of Wessex**, which was the English family of Alfred the Great.

To make matters even more complicated, there was also a third royal house involved. This is because two kings of England married the same woman: a princess called **Emma of Normandy**.

Emma of Normandy was a great-granddaughter to Rollo the Viking, whom we met above. When Rollo became Duke of Normandy back in 911, he started an almost-royal family called the **House of Normandy**. In marrying Emma, the kings of England gave the House of Normandy a shot at the throne of England. Emma was the knot who tied together the three houses of the Norman Conquest: the House of Denmark, the House of Wessex and the House of Normandy.

Emma of Normandy with her sons Edward and Alfred, both from her marriage to Aethelred the Unready

The Norman Conquest

To understand how Emma of Normandy tied together three royal houses, we must first look back for a moment.

Emma's first husband was King Aethelred the Unready, whom we met above. As Queen of England, she gave Aethelred two sons: **Alfred Aetheling** and **Edward the Confessor**.

Then came 1013, when Sweyn Forkbeard seized the throne from Aethelred the Unready. At this, Emma fled across the English Channel with her sons— seeking safety with her family in Normandy.

A few months later, Sweyn Forkbeard died— which meant that Aethelred could return to his throne. Just two years after that, though, Aethelred died too!

The death of Aethelred set up a contest between two sons of two past Kings of England. One was Cnut the Great, son of Sweyn Forkbeard. The other was Edmund Ironside, son of Aethelred the Unready. Edmund was an older son born to an earlier wife, not to Emma of Normandy.

Cnut the Great won, claiming the throne of England in 1016. But since Cnut was a Dane, not an Englishman, he feared that Englishmen might not trust him. To gain their trust, he married Aethelred's widow— making Emma of Normandy Queen of England again!

Two years later, Emma gave Cnut a son called **Harthacnut**. Since Harthacnut had the same mother as Alfred and Edward, he was their younger half-brother. However, Harthacnut's father was the sitting King of England— which made Harthacnut the rightful heir to the throne. Since Alfred and Edward were only sons of a dead king, they went to live with Emma's relatives in Normandy.

Poor Alfred died a horrible death in 1036, probably fighting for his father's lost throne. With Alfred gone, Edward the Confessor was the only surviving heir from the House of Wessex.

Next, Harthacnut died— just six years after becoming King of England. Some say that Harthacnut drank himself to death. However he died, young Harthacnut was childless— which meant no more heirs from the House of Denmark. The throne went to the only man alive whose father had been King of England: **Edward the Confessor**.

King Edward turned out to be just as childless as King Harthacnut. His strange nickname, "the Confessor," came from the fact that he was as religious as a monk. Edward may have even sworn a monk's vow of chastity— guaranteeing that he would stay childless!

The childlessness of Edward the Confessor was one of the main reasons for the Norman Conquest. With a childless king sitting on such a tempting throne, it is no wonder that so many people schemed to seize his throne the moment he was gone.

〰〰〰〰〰〰〰〰〰〰〰〰〰〰〰〰〰〰〰〰〰〰〰〰〰〰〰〰

After a long illness, Edward the Confessor finally died on the night of January 5, 1066. The death of the childless king set up a contest between three rivals, all eager to claim the throne.

The first rival was an English nobleman called **Harold Godwinson, Earl of Wessex**. Harold offered several reasons why the throne should be his. First, he was the richest, most powerful noble in England. Second, he was England's best, most experienced army commander.

Third, the king himself had promised Harold the throne— or so Harold said. He swore that in the last moments of his life, Edward the Confessor had come awake just long enough to name Harold Godwinson as his heir.

The second rival was **Duke William of Normandy**, who was soon to become **William the Conqueror**. One of William's claims to the throne came through his family, the House of Normandy. He was a cousin to Edward the Confessor through Edward's mother, Emma of Normandy.

William also offered a second claim. According to William, both Edward the Confessor and Harold Godwinson

Westminster Abbey is a beautiful church in a rich section of London called Westminster. Edward the Confessor started work on the first Westminster Abbey around 1042. The Westminster Abbey that stands today is a replacement church started by King Henry III in the 1200s.

Since the days of William the Conqueror, every monarch of England and Britain has received his or her crown at Westminster Abbey. The great church has become a symbol of English royalty, and of the link between God and monarch.

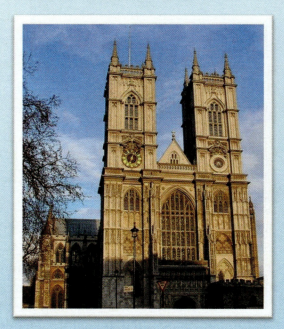

Part of Westminster Abbey

had sworn that he would be the next king of England. In fact, William said, Harold Godwinson had sworn on holy relics. By claiming the throne now, Harold was breaking a solemn vow before God!

The third rival was **King Harald III of Norway**. Harald was a Viking king whose claim to England came through the House of Denmark, the old house that had died out with Harthacnut. The Vikings felt that when Harthacnut died, the throne of England should have gone to one of his Viking relatives— not to Edward the Confessor.

With no king to choose between these rivals, the decision lay with the king's council— a group of advisers called the **Witan**. Since Harold Godwinson was the only Englishman on the list, it is not surprising that the Witan chose him! The day after Edward the Confessor died, Harold Godwinson was crowned King of England. The moment he received his crown, both of his rivals started raising armies against him.

The **Witenagemot**, also called the **Witan**, was a council that advised the King of England. *Witenagemot* is Old English for "meeting of the wise."

The first to strike was King Harald III of Norway. In September 1066, King Harald landed 300 ships in northern England— carrying about 15,000 troops. With such a big army, King Harald had no trouble seizing the surprised city of York, England on September 20.

At the time, Harold Godwinson's main army lay at his capital: London. Since York stood 175 miles north of London, and since most armies would need a long time to march that far, King Harald thought he had a long time to prepare.

He was quite wrong. Just a few days later, King Harald was stunned to see Harold Godwinson marching up to Stamford Bridge— an important bridge just east of York. The King of England had marched his army 175 miles in just four days, making an incredible 44 miles per day!

Things had never looked better for Harold Godwinson. On September 25, he crushed King Harald at the **Battle of Stamford Bridge**— killing his first rival. As it turned out, though, King Harald's loss was William of Normandy's gain.

While Harold Godwinson was busy with King Harald, William of Normandy sailed across the English Channel. With 700 or more ships, carrying about 30,000 troops, William's force was twice the size of the one Harold Godwinson had just beaten! Just three days after the Battle of Stamford Bridge, the Normans landed near a place called **Hastings**— about 50 miles southeast of London.

At the time, Godwinson was still in York— which meant that for the second time in two weeks, his army was a long way from where he needed it. Once again, Godwinson had to march his troops a long way in a short time, rushing to put his army between Hastings and London.

The Battle of Hastings (October 14, 1066)

The battle that followed was the key battle of the Norman Conquest: the famous **Battle of Hastings**. William of Normandy had three big advantages at Hastings. First, William had many archers and crossbowmen; while Harold Godwinson had few. Second, William had plenty of horse-mounted troops; while Harold had mostly foot soldiers. Third, William's army was well-rested; while Harold's army was exhausted after its long march down from York.

Even with all those disadvantages, Godwinson fought long, bravely and well. In the end, though, a Norman arrow pierced Godwinson— claiming his life. Without its leader, the English army fell apart.

In winning the Battle of Hastings, William of Normandy not only killed his last rival for the throne, but also destroyed the best army in England. The House of Wessex was at an end. The throne of England was about to pass to a new royal house: the **House of Normandy**.

Although the Normans were supposed to be civilized by 1066, they had not quite forgotten their savage Viking roots. After the Battle of Hastings, the Normans needlessly slaughtered many Englishmen. They also mutilated the remains of Harold Godwinson. As punishment for these shameful deeds, Pope Alexander II ordered the Normans to build a new church on the site of the battle. The **Battle Abbey** was dedicated to Martin of Tours, patron saint of France.

The **Bayeux Tapestry** is a long, narrow cloth embroidered with about fifty scenes from the Norman Conquest. The tapestry's name comes from Bayeux Cathedral, the church in Normandy where the tapestry has been stored for almost 1,000 years.

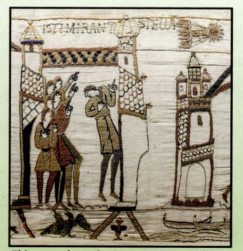

This scene from the Bayeux Tapestry shows Harold Godwinson and his advisers pointing at Halley's Comet in fear and awe

Halley's Comet is a big, bright comet that appears once every 75 – 76 years, when its long orbit around the sun carries it close enough to be seen from Earth. It so happened that 1066, the year of the Norman Conquest, was a Halley's Comet year. The comet appeared soon after Harold Godwinson claimed the throne— leading the superstitious to connect king and comet.

The Normans took the comet to mean that God was angry with Harold Godwinson for breaking his oath to William. They predicted that God would soon end Godwinson's unjust reign. In Norman eyes, that prediction came true when Godwinson died at the Battle of Hastings.

CHAPTER 10:

England after the Norman Conquest

Finishing the Norman Conquest

In Chapter 9, we read how the **Normans** invaded England. It all started in January 1066, when King Edward the Confessor died. Since Edward had no sons, his throne was up for grabs. Three men tried to grab it at once: Earl Harold Godwinson of Wessex, King Harald III of Norway and Duke William of Normandy.

The last man standing was William of Normandy, which is why he's called **William the Conqueror**. The **Norman Conquest** started on October 14, 1066— the day William killed Harold Godwinson at the famous **Battle of Hastings**.

After winning the Battle of Hastings, William marched on toward London— where he hoped to be crowned King of England. But the English didn't want a foreign king. Instead of crowning William, they quickly crowned another king from their old royal house: the House of Wessex. The new king was a fifteen-year-old cousin of Edward the Confessor called **Edgar Aetheling**. Edgar waited nervously in London, getting ready for William's coming.

Since Hastings lay south of London, William tried to enter from the south. The easiest way was to take London Bridge, which crossed the Thames River just south of the main city. Alas for William, Edgar wouldn't let him take the easy way. Hard as he tried, William simply couldn't drive Edgar's army off London Bridge.

So instead, William took the hard way. He marched far to the west, where he could cross the Thames more easily. Then he circled around, marching toward London from the northwest— where no river stood in his way.

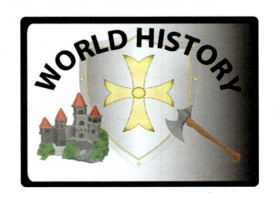

The **Normans** came from the Duchy of Normandy, France, just across the English Channel from England. They started as Viking invaders, but had become French-speaking Christians by the time of the Norman Conquest.

Without a river to help him, Edgar had little hope of holding William off. He finally surrendered, leaving William to claim the throne. The crowning happened at Westminster Abbey on Christmas Day 1066— the day William the Conqueror officially became **King William I of England**.

The Norman Conquest might have ended then and there; but it didn't. For Edgar didn't stay surrendered. Instead, he moved up to northern England and started a rebellion. The King of Scotland promised to join Edgar's rebellion. So did the King of Denmark; and so did several nobles from the north.

William the Conqueror riding a black horse in a scene from the Bayeux Tapestry

With that many allies, Edgar stood a good chance of taking back northern England. To keep that from happening, William started a **total war** called the **Harrying of the North**.

Total war was a tactic the ancient Romans knew well. They had long ago learned that the best way to beat stubborn rebels wasn't to destroy their armies. No, the best way was to destroy their homeland! Roman soldiers destroyed anything that might help the rebels in any way. In other words, they didn't just destroy food, shelter and weapons. They also destroyed the farmers who raised the food, the builders who raised the shelter and the blacksmiths who forged the weapons— along with their wives, homes and everything else.

This is what the Harrying of the North was like. Taking a page out of the Romans' book, William laid waste of northern England— killing people, burning towns and farms, destroying crops and livestock. Very few rebels survived William's attack. Even if they did survive, they had nothing to look forward to; for William had ruined their farms, leaving them no way to feed themselves. Northern England would need a long time to recover from the cruel Harrying of the North.

William's brutal tactics finally won out. The Norman Conquest wound down in 1072, six years after the Battle of Hastings. By then, William had already moved on to his next task: rewarding the **Companions of William the Conqueror**.

A **Companion of William the Conqueror** was a Norman knight who personally fought beside William at the Battle of Hastings.

The Norman Conquest was a dangerous gamble. Thousands of Normans risked their lives on it, and many of them lost. Why take that risk? Because William promised that when it was all over, he would make them all rich.

Now that the fighting was winding down, it was time to hand out the rewards. To get the rewards, William simply took land from Englishmen and gave it to his Norman friends. A few years after the Norman Conquest, almost every property in England belonged to Normans— even though there were far more Englishmen than there were Normans!

No one got more land and treasure than William's special Companions— the brave knights who fought beside him from the start. After the Norman Conquest, the Companions of William the Conqueror became the richest, most powerful nobles in all England. Even today, some of the richest families in England still trace their fortunes back to a Companion of William the Conqueror.

William the Conqueror leading his Companions into battle in a scene from the Bayeux Tapestry

At the same time, William was careful not to give his Companions too much. For he knew that even a close friend could be a danger to his king, if he grew too powerful.

William took several steps to keep that from happening. First, William gave his Companions the lowest noble rank he could. He **created** many new nobles after the Norman Conquest. But he didn't create the higher ranks, like **dukes**, **marquises**, **earls** and **viscounts**. Instead, he created mostly minor nobles called **barons**. Since **baronies** were small, barons didn't command enough men to rebel against their king.

Second, William scattered his barons' baronies. Some of the Companions had done so much that they deserved more than one barony. But William didn't give side-by-side baronies to the same baron. Instead, he gave him one in Wessex, one in Kent and maybe another in Northumbria. That way, no baron commanded too many men in any one place.

> To **create** a noble is to promote a person to a noble rank.
> - The lowest noble rank is **baron**, head of a **barony**.
> - The next noble rank is **viscount**, head of a viscountcy.
> - Next comes **earl** or count, head of an earldom or county.
> - Next comes **marquis**, head of a marquisate.
> - The highest noble rank is **duke**, head of a duchy.

Third, William insisted that baronies didn't really belong to their barons. Instead, they belonged to the king. If a baron displeased William, then he could take away his barony and give it to someone else. All these changes were part of a medieval style of government that William brought over from France: the **feudal** system.

The Feudal System

> The word "**feudal**" may come from the same root as the word "fealty," meaning "loyalty."

The **feudal system** was a kind of land ownership based on oaths of loyalty between two people. The higher person was the lord, or master; while the lower person was the vassal, or servant.

The oath between lord and vassal was partly a contract— an agreement about how the lord's land would be used. The vassal received the money from crops and livestock raised on the land. In exchange, the lord received taxes from the vassal. The vassal also sent troops for his lord's armies. In exchange, the lord promised to use those armies to protect the vassal.

The same person could be a vassal in one oath and a lord in another. For example, in the oath between king and baron, the king was lord and the baron was vassal. But then, the baron might decide to put part of his barony in the care of a knight. In that oath, the baron was lord and the knight was vassal.

The feudal oath started with a two-part ritual called a **commendation ceremony**. First came the Act of Homage, in which the vassal knelt before his lord and acknowledged him as his master. Then came the Oath of Fealty, in which the vassal swore to serve his lord faithfully and never harm him.

The lord made two promises in return. First, he promised to protect his vassal. Second, he promised to

A nobleman swearing the Oath of Fealty
to King William I of England

give his vassal whatever reward he earned. If the vassal kept his oath, then his lord would honor him. But if the vassal broke his oath, then his lord would take vengeance!

At the bottom of the feudal system stood three kinds of peasants: freemen, serfs and slaves. Some freemen were skilled tradesmen, like blacksmiths and carpenters. Others were farmers who could afford to pay the rents their lords demanded.

Serfs harvesting wheat for their lord

If a farmer couldn't afford to pay, then he became the most miserable of all medievals: a **serf**. Some became serfs because bad harvests or long winters left them too poor to feed themselves. Others became serfs because they needed a lord's protection, or because cruel lords forced them to.

Serfdom started with the harshest oath imaginable: the

> To be in **bondage** is to be a slave.
>
> A **serf** was a medieval peasant who was bound to serve his lord. Serfdom started with a harsh oath called the **oath of bondage**.

oath of bondage. The serf promised to serve his lord with all his heart— to love what his lord loved, hate what his lord hated, and always strive to please his lord. Once they swore this oath, serfs had only one advantage over slaves: they couldn't be bought and sold like property. Other than that, serfs and slaves were much alike:

➤ Like slavery, serfdom was hereditary— which meant that if a father and mother were serfs, then their children would be serfs too.

➤ Like slaves, serfs needed their lord's permission to marry.

➤ Like slaves, serfs couldn't leave their lord's land without permission. And if the land passed from one lord to another, then the serfs went with the land.

In exchange for the oath of bondage, the lord promised the serf three things: protection, a place to live, and help in times of need. Most serfs spent part of the year working the lord's land, and the rest on a small plot their lord set aside for them. Once the oath of bondage was sworn, a serf had little hope of ever becoming a freeman again.

The Beginning of the High Middle Ages

The reign of William the Conqueror marks the beginning of the **High Middle Ages**— the age of castles, knights and chivalry. William was England's first great castle-builder. Whenever he moved into a new part of England, he built at least a small castle there. Each new castle was an army base— with barracks for troops, stables for horses and storehouses for food and weapons.

Why did the Normans need so many army bases? Because the English were furious about the Norman Conquest! As hostile invaders in a foreign land, the Normans were always in danger of attack.

Each Norman castle was like a little island of safety in a big sea of trouble. If the English attacked one castle, then the Normans could usually hold out long enough for help to come from another castle.

The first kind of castle the Normans built was the simplest: a **motte and bailey**. The motte was a steep mound of earth piled up by the castle's builders. The steepness of the motte made it hard to attack what stood at its top: the keep. The keep was the safest part of the castle— a strong building with sturdy defenses.

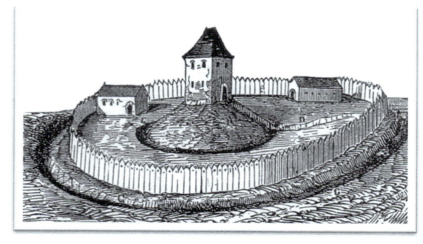

Sketch of a motte and bailey castle

The bailey was a low, level area around the motte, surrounded by strong wooden walls called palisades. Baileys were protected places for barracks, stables, blacksmith's shops and so on.

Because the Normans were in a hurry at first, they usually built their keeps out of wood. Later, they wanted to replace these wooden keeps with stone ones— for stone was not only stronger than wood, but also more fireproof. Unfortunately, mottes built from fill dirt were too soft to support the tremendous weight of stone keeps. Without a solid foundation, any stone building will first crack, and then collapse!

The answer was a type of castle called a **shell keep**. Instead of building stone keeps atop their fill-dirt mottes, the Normans added thin shells of fire-proof stone around their old wooden keeps.

Later, richer lords built a stronger type of castle: the all-stone **courtyard castle**. The simplest courtyard castles had three or four tall, strong towers bristling with defenses. Curtain walls connected the towers, finishing the defensive ring around the courtyard.

A **gatehouse** was a strong structure built to protect the gate, which was the weakest point of any castle. The best gatehouses had two gates, one at each end of a long tunnel. If an attacker managed to break through the first gate, then he still had to break through the second. Meanwhile, defenders fired at him through **arrow slits** that lined the tunnel walls.

A **portcullis** was a heavy latticework gate that slid up to open and down to close. When defenders wanted to seal an enemy inside the gatehouse, all they had to do was drop the portcullis.

A **bastion** was a structure that jutted out from a curtain wall, giving defenders a place to stand while they fired down on their attackers' flanks.

The strongest castle of all, the **concentric castle**, was protected by two sets of walls: a lower outer wall, and a higher inner wall. An attacker who managed to climb over the outer wall might find himself trapped in the deadly space between the two walls.

Bodiam Castle in East Sussex, England. This courtyard castle features towers, curtain walls and a strong gatehouse.

A **knight** was a trained fighting man who swore an oath to defend his lord. In the medieval ranking system, knights stood just below nobles— higher than gentlemen, but lower than barons. Of course, knights who served their lords well could earn noble titles. Some of William the Conqueror's men started out as knights, but wound up as noblemen.

Along with knighthood went the knight's code of conduct, which went by the

strange name of **chivalry**. Both "chivalry" and a similar word, "cavalry," started with the fact that knights rode horses. After a while, though, "chivalry" didn't mean horses anymore. Instead, it meant the way horse-mounted knights were supposed to behave.

Knights jousting in chain mail

> **Chivalry** was the knight's code of conduct.

The chivalrous knight was both mighty in battle and honorable in character. He was brave, tough, strong and skilled; but he was also courteous, well-spoken, loyal and generous. He never backed down from a fight in fear; never gave up on a task; and never stopped defending the weak. Above all, the chivalrous knight never broke an oath! He always did his duty to his God, his lord and his lady.

The importance of oaths explains how chivalrous knights could take part in an ugly total war like the Harrying of the North (above). After the Norman Conquest, William demanded the oath of fealty from every noble in England. A lot of those oaths were broken when the nobles of northern England decided to rebel. As chivalrous knights, the Normans considered it their duty to punish the oath-breaking nobles of the north.

In fact, the whole Norman Conquest was based on an oath that Harold Godwinson supposedly swore to William the Conqueror— as we read in Chapter 9. In Norman eyes, Harold broke that oath when he tried to claim the throne.

♟♟

The first **knights' tournament** probably happened in the days of William the Conqueror. Tournaments were special events that helped train knights for war. They also gave knights a way to test their skills, boost their reputations and win prizes. Later, tournaments became a kind of entertainment— something like the gladiator fights in the old Roman Coliseum.

Early tournaments were divided into two rounds. First came the *melee a cheval*— French for "battle on horseback." Teams of knights charged at

Tournament knights fighting the *Melee a Cheval*

each other with leveled lances, trying to knock their opponents off their horses. When this first charge was over, any knight who was still on his horse turned to face new opponents. The word "<u>tour</u>nament" may have come from this <u>turn</u>.

After the *melee a cheval* came the *melee a pied*— French for "battle on foot." As in a real battle, knights fought in teams.

Some knights preferred a special kind of tournament called the *pas d'armes*, or "passage of arms." The first kind of *pas d'armes* was a standing challenge to all passing knights. The challenger set up camp near some narrow spot in the road, like a bridge or a gate. Any knight who wanted to pass that spot had to fight the challenger first. If the passing knight refused, then the challenger marked him as a coward— sometimes by taking away his spurs.

The later *pas d'armes* was part of an organized tournament. In this kind, all knights nailed their coats of arms to a display called the tree of shields. To challenge another knight, one simply walked up to the tree of shields and struck that knight's coat of arms.

Some tournaments included a dangerous fight called a **jousting match**. Two horse-mounted knights galloped toward one another as fast as they dared, aiming blunt lances at each other's shields. A good strike would either drive the opponent off his horse or shatter his lance. A bad fall could lead to a concussion, broken bones or worse.

Like other tournament styles, jousting matches changed over the years. Early jousting matches didn't end when one knight unhorsed the other. The battle continued on foot, ending only when one knight struck the other senseless.

An invention called the tilt helped make later jousting matches more civilized. The tilt was a long, low fence that divided the jousting list into two lanes, one for each knight. One advantage of the tilt was that it kept knights from running into each

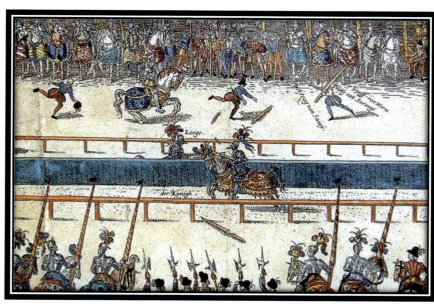

Scene from the tilt jousting tournament that killed King Henry II of France

other at full speed— which sometimes happened in the days before tilts! The tilt also made the lance strike at an angle, reducing the force of its blow.

Even with the tilt, though, jousting was still highly dangerous. In the 1500s, a long splinter from a broken lance killed a sitting King of France!

England under the House of Normandy

When he wasn't conquering countries, William the Conqueror liked to hunt. The king liked nothing better than to ride through the forest with his noble friends, shooting down wild game.

What William didn't like was sharing the forest with peasants. For hungry peasants often hunted until there was little game left for the king and his friends.

WILLIAM THE CONQUEROR

Scene from the New Forest

The solution to this problem was to set aside royal forests— private game reserves where no peasants were allowed. The first royal forest was a wood in south central England called the **New Forest**.

To make his New Forest as private as possible, William wrote a code of laws called **Forest Law**. Forest Law started by saying that all royal forests were strictly reserved for the king and his friends. No one could kill any wild animal without permission from the king. Nor could anyone harvest any plant; for plants were food for the wild game William loved.

The problem with Forest Law was that so many peasants depended on forests. Before Forest Law, England's forests had belonged to everyone. Any peasant who lived near a forest could go there to find meat, berries, firewood and more. A hard-working peasant could earn a small living selling meat or firewood from the forest. At the very least, the forest kept peasants from freezing to death.

After Forest Law, though, royal forests belonged to the king alone. Peasants had to ask the king's permission for everything— even to harvest dead wood from the forest floor!

For peasants who lived near a royal forest, Forest Law was the worst part of the Norman Conquest. The king's selfishness robbed them of their livings! With no way to replace what they had lost, many peasants had little choice but to take the oath of bondage and become serfs.

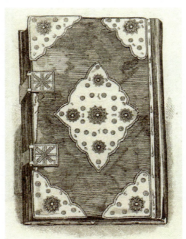

Besides being a determined hunter, William was also a determined tax collector. Near the end of his reign, he ordered a detailed inventory of every person and property in England. The king's men left no stone unturned— carefully counting every barn and mill, every plow and hoe, every ox and horse, every lord, knight, serf and child in the whole kingdom. When they finished, William's men wrote down their counts in a record called the **Domesday Book**.

William's government used the Domesday Book to decide two things. The first was how much tax the king should demand from each landowner. The second was how many troops each landowner should provide for the king.

"Domesday" is an Old English word for "Judgment Day." The name "Domesday Book" meant that all judgments in the book were final— as final as the one God will make on Judgment Day!

The decisions in the Domesday Book were final. Whatever tax was written in the Domesday Book, that was the tax one paid— or else one went to jail! This is what the Domesday Book was for: to make sure every Englishman paid every penny of tax he owed.

William's tax collectors also collected money for the church. The law required every Englishman to pay a tithe of his earnings to the church each year— in other words, one-tenth. Since most peasants had little money, they paid their tithes the only way they could: in grain or livestock. English villages built special buildings called **tithe barns** to store the mountains of grain peasants donated every year.

When William died in 1087, his lands were split between his three living sons. The oldest son, **Robert Curthose**, received William's oldest land: the Duchy of Normandy. The Kingdom of England went to William's middle son: William Rufus, who now became **King William II**. As for the youngest son, **Henry**, he received only money— for the moment.

Like his father before him, King William II was a cruel Norman who treated Englishmen more like slaves than citizens. But William II may have paid a high price for his cruelty.

It happened one fine day in August 1100, when William II was enjoying his favorite hobby: hunting in the New Forest with his noble friends. Late in the day, his friends came out of the woods with a sad story about an accident with an arrow. While flying toward a fleeing animal, the arrow glanced off a tree— turning just enough to hit the king instead. The arrow pierced William's lung, killing him!

The only problem with this sad story is that it may not be true. Since William II had so many enemies, historians have always wondered if this so-called "accident" was really no accident!

ꛉꛉꛉꛉꛉꛉꛉꛉꛉꛉꛉꛉꛉꛉꛉꛉꛉꛉꛉꛉꛉꛉꛉꛉꛉꛉꛉꛉꛉꛉꛉꛉꛉꛉ

King William II pierced by an arrow in the New Forest

When William II died, his brother Robert Curthose happened to be in the Holy Land. That was where the First Crusade was just ending, as we'll read in Chapter 12. If Robert had been home in Normandy, then he would have tried to claim his dead brother's throne. Since Robert wasn't home, his younger brother Henry stepped in!

King Henry I was cut from different cloth than his cruel father and brothers. Like Alfred the Great, who we met in Chapter 9, Henry was a younger son who had been raised to be a scholar— because no one expected younger sons to be kings. The subject Henry loved best was law. So when Henry became King of England, he tried to bring fair law to all his subjects. The English look back on Henry I as the first fair, wise king from the House of Normandy.

After beating his brother Robert Curthose at the **Battle of Tinchebray**, Henry became Duke of Normandy as well as King of England. Now Henry ruled all the lands William the Conqueror had ruled— unlike William II, who never ruled Normandy.

ꛉꛉꛉꛉꛉꛉꛉꛉꛉꛉꛉꛉꛉꛉꛉꛉꛉꛉꛉꛉꛉꛉꛉꛉꛉꛉꛉꛉꛉꛉꛉꛉꛉ

Henry's first queen gave him two children: a son called William Aetheling, and a daughter called Matilda. One evening in November 1120, the 17-year-old William set out across the English Channel aboard a brand-new boat called the White Ship. Beside the young prince rode many of his young friends, all on their way from Normandy to England. With Christmas just around the corner, the prince and his friends were in the mood to drink and celebrate.

The White Ship breaking up on a rock

The captain of the White Ship may have been drinking too. If he was, then that would explain what happened next.

The **White Ship** had a lot in common with a huge luxury liner that sank in the North Atlantic in April 1912: RMS *Titanic*. Both were brand-new ships praised for their luxury. Both carried some of the richest people of their day. And both sailed into known dangers— things their captains should have been wise enough to avoid!

When sailing out of that particular harbor, wise captains always steered south for a while. That way, they could be sure to avoid some dangerous rocks that lay hidden near the coast to the north. For some reason, the captain of the White Ship didn't follow that wise course. Instead, he steered directly to the north— where he smashed his hull wide open on a hidden rock! The White Ship sank, taking down with it the only male heir to the throne of England.

The Wreck of the White Ship

Fortunately, the king still had his daughter. When William Aetheling died, Matilda was married to a Holy Roman Emperor in Germany. Instead of Princess Matilda, she was now called **Empress Matilda**.

A few years after her brother died, Matilda's husband died too—leaving her a widow at age twenty-three. A few years after that, King Henry arranged a second marriage for his daughter. Matilda's new husband was **Geoffrey of Anjou**, who was also called **Geoffrey Plantagenet**. Geoffrey was heir to Anjou, a county south of Normandy.

Since Henry had no son to inherit his lands, he wanted Matilda to inherit them. The problem was, no self-respecting noble wanted to follow a woman. Knowing this, Henry asked all his nobles to swear double oaths to him— promising to accept Matilda as queen when Henry was gone.

The Coronation of Stephen of Blois

So far, so good. The trouble started when Henry died, and his nobles forgot all about their oaths! Instead of following Matilda, they followed her cousin **Stephen of Blois**.

Stephen was the Count of Blois, a county southeast of Normandy. He was also a grandson of William the Conqueror, just like Matilda. But unlike Matilda, Stephen was a man— which is why the nobles chose him over Matilda.

Matilda and her husband were determined to take back her lost inheritance. The rise of King Stephen started a long civil war in England and northwestern France— a terrible time that historians call the **Anarchy**.

The Anarchy dragged on for almost twenty miserable years. Mid-way through it, Matilda and her husband managed to take back Normandy. Hard as they tried, though, they never managed to take back England.

The key to ending the Anarchy was another royal death. One day in 1153, King Stephen's only son suddenly died— leaving him without an heir. Since Matilda did have an heir, the answer was simple. Stephen would stay King of England for as long as he lived. But when Stephen died, the throne would go to Matilda's son— whose name was Henry Plantagenet. It was all written down in the treaty that ended the Anarchy: the **Treaty of Wallingford**.

Thanks to this treaty, Stephen of Blois was the last King of England from the House of Normandy. When Stephen died in 1154, Matilda's son Henry became **King Henry II of England**. Since Henry's family name was Plantagenet, he was the first of a new royal house: the **House of Plantagenet**.

The Baltic Sea

The **Baltic Sea** is an inland sea in northern Europe. To reach the Baltic Sea from the Atlantic Ocean, ships must first pass into the North Sea. From there, the natural path to the Baltic lies through two straits: first the **Skagerrak**, then the **Kattegat**.

In modern times, there is also a manmade path from the North Sea to the Baltic Sea. This is the Kiel Canal, which cuts across northern Germany near the bottom of the Jutland Peninsula.

Setting aside the Skagerrak and the Kattegat, the rest of the Baltic Sea looks something like a squirrel climbing down a tree. The squirrel's big, bushy tail is the **Gulf of Bothnia**. One of the squirrel's hind legs is the **Gulf of Finland**, and the other is the **Gulf of Riga**. The squirrel's front legs are two much smaller gulfs: the **Curonian Lagoon** and the **Gulf of Gdansk**.

Ten countries line the shores of the Baltic Sea. Going clockwise from the northwest, they are **Norway**, **Sweden**, **Finland**, **Russia**, **Estonia**, **Latvia**, **Lithuania**, **Poland**, **Germany** and **Denmark**.

With so many countries lining its shores, the Baltic Sea is most important for trade. Unfortunately, the Baltic suffers from a problem that can make trade rather difficult: sea ice. Because the Baltic lies so far north, at least part of it freezes over every winter. Even in an average winter, sea ice may cover almost half of the Baltic Sea— from the northern tip of the Gulf of Bothnia all the way down to the Gulf Riga. Hard winters may freeze over even more.

Before modern times, sea ice meant closed ports. Several important ports used to close for at least part of every winter— including **Stockholm**, Sweden; **Helsinki**, Finland; **St. Petersburg**, Russia; **Tallinn**, Estonia; and **Riga**, Latvia. In modern times, ice-breaking ships keep these ports open all year— for a price.

> Lithuania, Latvia and Estonia are called the **Baltic States**.
>
> Kaliningrad is an **exclave** of Russia— in other words, a part of Russia that isn't connected to the rest.

German Beginnings

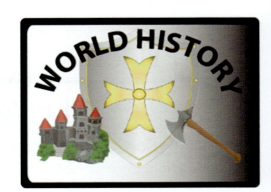

The name "Germany" comes from Roman times. We've read how the Romans conquered two far-off lands: Gaul and Britannia. After those, the Romans tried to conquer a land that was even farther off: **Germania**. The Germanic peoples lived east of the Rhine River, south of the Baltic Sea and north of the Balkans.

Alas for the Romans, they never conquered Germania. In fact, one might say that Germania conquered Rome! For the so-called "barbarians" who tore down the Western Roman Empire came mostly from Germania. The Vandals and Visigoths who sacked Rome in the 400s were Germanic peoples (Chapter 1). So were the Angles, Saxons and Jutes who took over Britannia after the Romans left (Chapter 2). So were the Franks, Alemanni and Burgundians who moved into Roman Gaul (Chapter 6). Even the Vikings were Germanic peoples.

Like most ancient peoples, the Germans started out pagan. Many of them believed in the same gods the Vikings did— Norse gods like Odin and Thor.

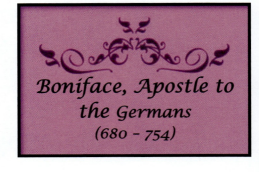

Boniface, Apostle to the Germans (680 – 754)

All that changed when the Carolingian Empire came along. As we read in Chapter 7, the name "Carolingian" came from the great Frankish general who won the Battle of Tours: Charles Martel. It was in Martel's day that the Germans got their first great missionary: **Boniface**.

Boniface moved to Germany in 718, fourteen years before the Battle of Tours. Just as Patrick was an Apostle to the Irish, and Martin of Tours an Apostle to the Gauls, so Boniface became an Apostle to the Germans.

Oddly enough, one way Boniface preached the gospel was by chopping down trees! Many Germans worshiped at special trees— perhaps because they reminded them of Yggdrasil, the world tree of Norse mythology (Chapter 8). One of their favorites was an old giant called **Donar's Oak**. Donar was a German name for every Norseman's favorite god: Thor.

Donar's special tree stood in a part of Germany called Hesse, probably near a village called Fritzlar. The Germans saw Donar's Oak as a symbol of their god's awesome might. But to Boniface, the old tree was nothing but a pagan idol. That was why Boniface decided to tackle Donar's Oak: to prove that Donar wasn't mighty, nor even real!

Boniface raising a cross beside Donar's Oak, which he has just felled

When Boniface first set his ax to Donar's Oak, some Germans were probably expecting Donar to strike him down with a bolt of lightning— or perhaps a blow from *Mjölnir*, his mighty war hammer. Of course, Donar's Oak went down just like any other tree. To add insult to **injury,** Boniface even used lumber from Donar's Oak to build a Christian church.

Besides being the Apostle to the Germans, Boniface also may have decorated the very first Christmas tree! According to legend, Boniface used a small evergreen that sprouted near the stump of Donar's Oak as a symbol of Christ. The eternal leaves of the evergreen stood for eternal life in heaven with Christ.

With help from Charles Martel's soldiers, Boniface did the same thing in many other German villages: He tore down pagan shrines, and built Christian churches instead. In 36 years of ministry, Boniface helped spread Christianity all over Germany.

The Holy Roman Empire

The Carolingian Empire was never bigger than it was in the days of Charles Martel's grandson: mighty Charlemagne, whom we covered in Chapter 7. After Charlemagne, though, the empire started to shrink. As we read in Chapter 9, Charlemagne's descendants fought among themselves— and wound up splitting his empire. As of 870, the Carolingian Empire was divided into three kingdoms:

➢ South of the Alps lay the Kingdom of Italy.

➢ West of the Rhine River lay West Francia, which would become the Kingdom of France.

➢ East of the Rhine lay East Francia, which would become the Kingdom of Germany.

The last emperor to rule all three kingdoms was Charles the Fat, whom we also met in Chapter 9. We've read how Charles the Fat tangled with the Vikings at the Siege of Paris, starting in 885. We've also read how Charles finally got rid of the Vikings: by hiring them to fight for him somewhere else. The problem was, the Franks wanted their king to beat the Vikings— not hire them! When Charles the Fat chose to hire the Vikings, he lost his people's trust. Two years later, in 888, the Carolingian Empire fell apart for the last time.

The end of the Carolingian Empire wasn't the end of the Carolingian dynasty— not yet. The King of East Francia was still a member of the Carolingian dynasty, which meant that the Germans were still ruled by a Frankish king.

Louis the Child with his father Arnulf, King of East Francia

But not for long. Soon after Charles the Fat died, the branch of the Carolingian dynasty that ruled East Francia started dying out. By 899, the family was down to its last royal: a six-year-old called **Louis the Child**. Twelve years later, Louis the Child died too— leaving no heir to take his place. The Carolingian dynasty was finished in East Francia.

Without a king to hold it together, East Francia was in danger of falling apart. At the time, the kingdom was made up of five **duchies**. Some duchies had Frankish dukes, and some had German ones. Now that the Carolingians were gone, the German dukes wanted to be free of the Franks.

A **duchy** is a land governed by a duke in the name of his king.

The dukes of East Francia elected one more Frankish king: Duke Conrad of Franconia, who became King Conrad I in 911. But Conrad had a lot of trouble with his German dukes. Seven years into his reign, Conrad fought a big battle against the Duke of Bavaria— and ended up dying of his wounds.

Before he died, though, King Conrad laid out a plan for holding his kingdom together. Conrad believed that the only way to unite the German people was to choose a German king. The right man to take his place, Conrad said, was a German duke called Henry of Saxony— who was also called **Henry the Fowler**. Conrad's choice of kings led to a strange scene in the forests of Saxony.

Duke Henry got his nickname, "the Fowler," because he liked to use falcons for hunting. According to legend, Henry happened to be working on the nets and cages he used for falconry— when out of nowhere, a crowd of nobles appeared in the middle of the forest. When Henry asked why they were there, they offered him the crown of Germany!

Naturally, Henry accepted. In 919, Duke Henry of Saxony became **King Henry I of Germany**— the first King of All the Germans who wasn't a Frank.

Like most kings of his day, Henry the Fowler was almost always at war. His worst enemies were a people called the **Magyars**. Like the Huns we met in Chapter 6, the Magyars were expert horsemen who

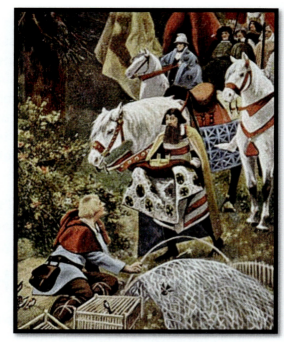

Henry the Fowler being offered the crown of East Francia while working on his falconry gear

swept in from the east— conquering everything in their paths. Also like the Huns, the Magyars demanded tribute payments from everyone they conquered.

In Henry's day, the Magyars were newcomers. They had just crossed the **Carpathian Mountains**, landing in what is now Hungary. From there, they launched deadly raids against their new neighbors to the west: Germany and Italy.

Henry had a lot of trouble with the Magyars, until he had a stroke of luck. One day in 924, Henry managed to capture the son of an important Magyar prince. With this son as his hostage, Henry was able to strike a hard bargain with the Magyars. Henry agreed to return the prince's son unharmed. In exchange, the Magyars agreed to a nine-year truce— as long as the Germans kept up their tribute.

Henry made the most of that truce. During those nine years, Henry bought horses for every knight in his kingdom. By training his knights to fight from horseback, Henry took away the Magyars' biggest advantage: their horses.

The **Carpathian Mountains** stand in Eastern Europe, arcing through Romania, western Ukraine and southern Poland. West of this arc lies the Carpathian Basin, which is where Hungary lies.

Hungary is just east of Austria, which was then part of Germany.

By the end of those nine years, Henry was ready. When the Magyars demanded another year's tribute, Henry wouldn't pay! In the battle that followed, Henry's cavalry beat the Magyars so badly that they didn't dare attack Germany again— at least, not while Henry was alive.

The Magyars crossing the Carpathian Mountains

ꙮꙮꙮꙮꙮꙮꙮꙮꙮꙮꙮꙮꙮꙮꙮꙮꙮꙮꙮꙮꙮꙮꙮꙮꙮ

After Henry the Fowler came Henry the Fowler's son: **King Otto I of Germany**. Like Charlemagne before him, Otto had big dreams of rebuilding the Roman Empire. A strange romance helped Otto claim an important part of that empire: northern Italy.

Otto's romantic tale starts with two teenaged royals who rose to the throne of Italy in 948. One was **King Lothair II of Italy**. The other was Lothair's wife, **Queen Adelaide of Italy**.

Lothair picked a bad time to grow up. In those days, most Italian nobles didn't follow the King of Italy. Instead, many followed a noble called **Berengar II**. Berengar was the Marquis of Ivrea, a land in northwest Italy.

Most people blamed Berengar for what happened to poor Lothair. Just two years into his reign, the young king suddenly died— perhaps because he was poisoned by Berengar! With Lothair out of the way, Berengar seized the throne of Italy— for himself, and for his son Adalbert.

But Berengar and Adalbert had a problem: Their blood was only noble, not royal. No member of their family had ever been a king before. If they were going to keep the throne they had just stolen, then they needed royal blood in their family. To get it, Berengar arranged for Adalbert to marry Lothair's widow: Queen Adelaide. With a royal marriage, and hopefully a royal grandson or two, the family of Berengar and Adalbert would soon be royal enough.

Berengar's plan might have worked, if not for one detail. Since Adelaide was pretty sure Berengar had murdered her husband, the last man she wanted to marry was Berengar's son! Instead of making wedding plans, Adelaide did her best to run away.

Side-by-side statues of Adelaide of Italy and her husband Otto I at a German cathedral

Alas, Berengar caught the fleeing queen and locked her up. At this point, Adelaide's life was just like something from a storybook: She was a damsel in distress, in need of a knight in shining armor to rescue her from her castle prison!

Instead of a shining knight, Adelaide got a priest. Under cover of darkness, a loyal priest called Warinus tunneled under the walls of Adelaide's prison. He scratched his way toward her night after night, until they finally escaped together. But Adelaide's adventures weren't over— for when Berengar found Adelaide's new hiding place, he quickly surrounded it.

Otto of Germany

This is where Otto of Germany comes into the story. Desperate to save herself, Adelaide hit upon a clever idea: she would write the mightiest king in Europe for help. She promised Otto that if he rescued her from Berengar, then she would marry Otto instead. That way, Otto could claim the throne of Italy through Adelaide!

Otto did just that. With Adelaide on Otto's side, most of Berengar's allies abandoned him before Otto even reached Italy. After crushing Berengar, Otto married Adelaide— making himself King of Italy as well as King of Germany!

Eleven years later, Otto received yet another title. In 962, the pope crowned Otto the first emperor of a strange government called the

Holy Roman Empire.

Despite its name, the Holy Roman Empire wasn't exactly an empire. As the French author Voltaire liked to say, every word of its name was wrong— for it was "neither Holy, nor Roman, nor an Empire."

➤ It wasn't "holy" because it was a worldly kingdom, not a spiritual one— even if the emperor did receive his crown from the pope.

➤ It wasn't "Roman" because its core was Germany, not Italy. The Holy Roman Empire grew and shrank many times over the centuries. Sometimes it included northern Italy, but sometimes it didn't.

➤ It wasn't an "empire" because the so-called "Holy Roman Emperor" wasn't as powerful as a true emperor. German noblemen had a stubborn streak. They often did what they wanted to do, not what their emperor ordered them to do!

Even so, the Holy Roman Empire lasted a long time. It didn't end until 1806, when Emperor Napoleon I of France finally tore it down.

The **Imperial Crown of the Holy Roman Empire** is an eight-sided crown made of almost pure gold, and studded with dozens of precious gems. The 12 big gems on the front of the crown may stand for Christ's twelve apostles.

One of the best-known German emperors was Holy Roman Emperor Frederick I, who reigned during the Holy Land Crusades— which we'll cover in Chapter 12. Frederick was also called Barbarossa, Italian for "red-beard," after the flowing red beard he wore. He was already an old man in 1188, when the pope asked all Christian kings to join the Third Crusade. The following year, Frederick led a big army toward the Holy Land.

Long though it was, the journey went fine— until one day, when Frederick's army started across a narrow bridge at a strong river in Asia Minor. Frederick was impatient to cross the river himself, but didn't want to make his army stop for him. To save time, he decided to swim his horse across— taking some of his knights with him.

Alas, the current turned out to be stronger than Frederick realized. The old man was washed off his horse, and wound up drowning in his own armor!

Emperor Frederick I and his knights plunging into the river

The Legend of the Sleeping Hero

An old legend says that Emperor Frederick I Barbarossa didn't really die. Instead, he is sleeping a charmed sleep in some unknown mountain cave. He will rest until his kingdom's hour of need, when he will awaken to lead his people to victory.

Barbarossa isn't the only sleeping hero of legend. King Arthur of Britain, his helper Merlin, Emperor Charlemagne and many others are also said to be sleeping heroes.

The **Rammelsberg** is a mountain in Saxony, Germany. Its name comes from a German knight called Ramm, who made an important discovery in 900.

One day while Ramm was out hunting, he tied his horse so that he could chase his prey on foot. As the horse waited for Ramm to return, it impatiently scraped its hooves through the thin turf of the mountain— revealing a glint of silver underneath. The Rammelsburg turned out to hold one of the richest silver mines in all the world!

Two Christian Heroes

The Christmas carol "Good King Wenceslaus" is based on a true story. The real Wenceslaus was a Duke of Bohemia who lived in the time of Henry the Fowler. At the time, Bohemia was a duchy of Germany.

Unlike most dukes, Duke Wenceslaus cared about the poor people of his duchy— which is why he wound up in a Christmas carol!

The carol is set on a bitterly cold day at Christmastime, when Wenceslaus and his young page are out carrying gifts to the poor. The page grows so cold that he finally complains to Wenceslaus— protesting that if he takes one more step, then he will surely freeze.

Duke Wenceslaus I of Bohemia
(907? – 935)

Wenceslaus answers his page by telling him to "walk in my footsteps." When the page does, he is stunned to find that they are quite warm! The page is feeling the love of Christ, which fills Wenceslaus' heart so full that it spills over— warming even the frigid snow beneath his feet.

ㄹㄹㄹㄹㄹㄹㄹㄹㄹㄹㄹㄹㄹㄹㄹㄹㄹㄹㄹㄹㄹㄹㄹㄹㄹㄹㄹㄹㄹㄹㄹㄹㄹㄹㄹㄹ

Elizabeth of Hungary was another kindly noble like Wenceslaus. By Elizabeth's day, Hungary was no longer an enemy of Germany. Instead, it was a Christian kingdom attached to the Holy Roman Empire. Princess Elizabeth was fourteen years old when she married a rich duke called Ludwig. Ludwig ruled Thuringia, a duchy of the Holy Roman Empire, in the name of the emperor.

A few years later, Ludwig left Elizabeth in charge of his duchy while he took a long trip. Ludwig also left older advisers to help his young wife, in case she had any tough decisions to make.

Princess Elizabeth of Hungary
(1207 – 1231)

Elizabeth of Hungary handing out bread to the poor at her castle door

While Ludwig was away, a terrible famine struck— starving the poor people of the duchy. If Elizabeth had listened to Ludwig's advisers, then she would have closed the castle gates and left the poor to starve. Instead, Elizabeth listened to the Bible— which told her that she must always help the poor. Instead of closing her gates, Elizabeth threw them wide open! She donated money from the duchy's treasury, handed out grain from the duchy's granaries, and even sold her own jewelry to raise money for a hospital.

When Ludwig returned, his advisers complained that his foolish young wife had emptied his treasury for nothing. Ludwig answered that as long as Elizabeth didn't give away his castle, he would still be far richer than most people.

Russian Beginnings

Russia is a giant country in Eastern Europe and Northern Asia. The story of Russia starts with two separate peoples: the Rus and the East Slavs.

➤ The **East Slavs** were natives of Eastern Europe. They lived mainly in what are now western Russia, Belarus and Ukraine.

➤ The **Rus** were a Viking people— Norsemen who lived along the eastern coasts of the Baltic Sea.

The East Slavs outnumbered the Rus by far. Yet in 862, a Rus leader called **Rurik the Viking** somehow became King of the East Slavs! Some say the East Slavs invited Rurik to be their king; while others say he conquered them. However he did it, Rurik was the first king of a new empire called **Kievan Rus**.

The East Slavs greeting Rurik the Viking, first king of the Rurikid dynasty

Why were the Rus so interested in Eastern Europe? The answer is mostly trade. As an eastern people, the Rus liked to shop in the best shopping center of the East: Constantinople, capital of the Byzantine Empire (Chapter 4). Constantinople sold everything! Besides common goods like grain, tools, sailcloth and rope, Constantinople also sold olive oil, wool and wine from Italy; luxurious silk and porcelain from China; rich spices from India and beyond; and even rare items from Africa.

Why didn't the Rus go to Constantinople by sea, like everyone else did? Because the sea route was too long and dangerous. The Rus preferred a route that led across Eastern Europe, mostly by river. It started at the eastern tip of the Gulf of Finland, where St. Petersburg now lies; and it ended at the Black Sea, which of course leads to Constantinople.

The biggest river along this trade route was the **Dnieper**, which flows into the Black Sea. To control the trade route, the Rus needed to control the Dnieper. To control the Dnieper, they needed to control a set of high hills that overlook the Dnieper's banks— at a place called Kiev. That was why the Rus built their capital at Kiev, and why their empire was called Kievan Rus.

Like the rest of the Vikings, the Rus started out pagan. But they didn't stay pagan. The Rus made so many trips to Constantinople that they soon picked up the religion of Constantinople.

This part of the Russian story starts with **Olga of Kiev**. Olga was queen to King Igor I, the second king after Rurik. Igor lasted until 945, when he was murdered by angry East Slavs. Since Igor's son Svyatoslav was too young to rule, Queen Olga ruled in his place.

Sometime during her seventeen-year reign, Olga took a trip to Constantinople— where she became a Christian. When she returned to Kiev, she brought along some of the first missionaries ever to preach the gospel in Kievan Rus. But missionaries were only part of making the Rus Christian. The other part was a decision made by Olga's grandson, **Vladimir the Great**.

Vladimir took over in 980, eleven years after Olga died. By this time, Kievan Rus wasn't growing as fast as before. Vladimir thought he knew why: because the old pagan religion was holding his people back. He wanted a strong new religion to get his empire back on track.

To find one, Vladimir sent advisers to countries all around him. He wanted them to study the four biggest religions in his part of the world: Islam, Judaism, Western Christianity and Eastern Christianity.

Olga of Kiev

Vladimir soon figured out that Islam was wrong for his people. For strict Muslims don't drink; and Vladimir knew that the Rus loved drinking too much to ever give it up!

After a bit of thought, Vladimir decided against Judaism too. To a fighting king like Vladimir, the fact that the Jews had been kicked out of Israel meant that God must have abandoned them. What good was Judaism, he wondered, if the Jews couldn't even defend their own homeland?

In the end, then, it came down to two choices: Western Christianity or Eastern Christianity. What made up Vladimir's mind was the beauty of Eastern churches. To Russian eyes, great cathedrals like the Hagia Sophia of Constantinople were the most beautiful places imaginable— almost like heaven on Earth. No Western church could match the Hagia Sophia in those days. Drawn in by the beauty and riches of the East, Vladimir decided to be baptized as an Eastern Christian.

Vladimir the Great deciding which religion to follow

Naturally, Vladimir expected his people to be baptized too. One day in 988, Vladimir and his priests led all their people down to the Dnieper River— where they led a historic ceremony called the **Baptism of Kiev**. Every citizen of Kiev was expected to be baptized, whether he wanted to be or not. As a sign that Kiev's pagan days were over for good, Vladimir tore down the idols he had once worshipped and tossed them into the river!

More mass baptisms followed, all over Kievan Rus. Thanks to Vladimir the Great, Kievan Rus became the second most important Christian empire in the East— behind the Byzantine Empire.

> The Baptism of Kiev was an example of a **mass baptism**, in which hundreds or thousands of people are all baptized at once.

〰〰〰〰〰〰〰〰〰〰〰〰〰〰〰〰〰〰〰〰〰

Two centuries after Vladimir the Great, Kievan Rus fell on hard times. The 1200s brought the rise of one of the biggest, most powerful empires ever: the **Mongol Empire**, which we'll cover in Chapter 19. Around 1240, the massive Mongol Empire

Khokhloma painting is a Russian way of making cheap wood look as smooth as expensive gold or glass. Khokhloma artists cover their wood with thick layers of primer made from clay, oils and powdered tin. High-temperature kilns activate the primer, making a smooth, hard surface for painting.

swallowed Kievan Rus— just as it swallowed almost everything else in the East. The Russian people would pay tribute to the Mongols for well over two hundred years.

The Mongol Empire finally faded, as all empires do. In 1480, a descendant of Rurik the Viking called **Ivan III** suddenly stopped paying tribute to the Mongols. Ivan expected a fight; but instead, the Mongols backed down. Old Rurik the Viking's dynasty was back in power!

By 1547, Ivan III's grandson was claiming a title that no Russian had ever claimed before: "Tsar of All the Russias." *Tsar* is the Russian version of "Caesar," which is another word for "emperor." Starting then, Russia was ruled not by princes or kings, but by emperors called the **tsars**. The first Tsar, Ivan IV, was also called **Ivan the Terrible**— partly because he was terribly powerful, and partly because so much of what he did was truly terrible!

Stories from the Russian Orthodox Church

Basil, Fool for Christ was a special kind of Christian called a *yurod*— Russian for "God's fool." *Yurodivy* like Basil took the Bible more literally than other Christians did. One of their favorite verses was I Corinthians 3:19, where the Apostle Paul wrote:

> "… the wisdom of this world is foolishness in God's sight."

To *yurodivy* like Basil, "wisdom of this world" meant "love of money." Worldly people store up worldly treasures, trying to enjoy life as much as they can before they die. But this is foolishness for Christians, who are to store up treasures in heaven— as we read in Matthew 6:20. That was what the *yurodivy* did. Instead of storing up worldly treasures, they gave away everything to the poor— knowing that Christ would reward them when they got to heaven. The *yurodivy* acted like fools, but fools for Christ!

Basil, Fool for Christ
(1469? – 1552?)

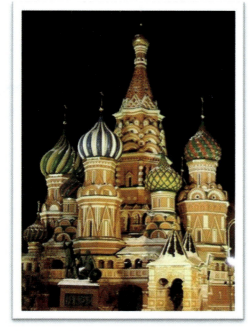

Basil the Fool was the most foolish *yurod* of all. Even in winter, Basil wandered around Moscow homeless, penniless and nearly naked. He sometimes wandered into taverns, where he begged his fellow Russians to stop drinking so much. Always he reminded people to focus on Christ. Once, he even rebuked Tsar Ivan the Terrible for not paying attention in church!

Of course, Basil the Fool made a lot of Russians uncomfortable; but he also made a lot of friends. Even a man as suspicious as Ivan the Terrible couldn't help admiring Basil. When the old saint died, the tsar personally helped carry Basil's coffin into the famous church that bears his name: **St. Basil's Cathedral**, which still stands on Red Square in Moscow.

St. Basil's Cathedral on Moscow's Red Square

Once upon a Christmas Eve, an old Russian woman carefully cleared all the spider webs from her house— making it nice and neat for the coming of the Christ child the next morning. With nowhere else to go, the poor spiders fled to a tiny hiding place in a far corner of the old woman's attic.

When the youngest spiders found that they couldn't see the Christmas tree from their hiding place, they were terribly upset. They begged and begged until finally, their parents agreed to risk a trip to the family room. After the old woman went to bed, the spiders climbed all over her Christmas tree— covering it with their ugly, dirty webs!

The Russian Spider Christmas Legend

When the Christ child came to bless the house, He of course saw the webs. He knew very well how much the old Russian woman hated spider webs! But He also loved spiders, which are after all part of God's Creation. So He stretched out His arm; and with the touch of His almighty hand, the ugly, dirty cobwebs changed into glistening strands of silver and gold.

The next morning, the old woman was delighted with how beautiful her Christmas tree had become! Every Christmas since, Russians have remembered the love of Christ by hanging two special decorations on their trees: glistening tinsel, and ornaments shaped like spiders!

Babushka was an old Russian grandmother who lived just before the birth of Christ. One night when Babushka was cleaning her house, the Three Wise Men asked her to shelter them for one night before they traveled on in search of the Christ Child. The next morning, the Wise Men invited Babushka to join them on their journey. But Babushka decided she had better stay home and finish cleaning her house.

After the Wise Men left, Babushka changed her mind, grabbed a few gifts for the Christ Child and ran out to follow them. By that time, though, the Wise Men were long gone. By worrying too much about housecleaning, poor Babushka had missed her only chance to see the Christ child!

The search continues to this day. Every year on the Eastern Orthodox Christmas, which falls on January 6th, Babushka leaves gifts in children's shoes— in hopes that when they find them, they will put on their shoes and help her find the Christ Child.

Babushka and the Christ Child

CHAPTER 12:

The Crusades; the Diaspora

The Middle East

The **Middle East** is the part of the world between the West and the East. "The West" usually means Europe and the Americas. "The East" usually means East Asia— including China, Japan, India and more. The Middle East is the meeting point between these two very different parts of the world.

Almost all of the Middle East lies in West Asia. The only exceptions are (1) Egypt, which lies in North Africa, and (2) a small piece of Turkey, which lies in Eastern Europe.

At the far west edge of Asia, a peninsula juts between the Mediterranean and Black Seas. This peninsula has two names: **Asia Minor** and **Anatolia**. Asia Minor means "lesser Asia"; while *Anatolia* comes from a Greek word that means "east" or "sunrise." In modern times, Asia Minor belongs to the Republic of Turkey.

The heart of the Middle East is what used to be the **Ancient Near East**. This is where some of the world's oldest civilizations began, along with some of the world's oldest religions.

㋡㋡㋡㋡㋡㋡㋡㋡㋡㋡㋡㋡㋡㋡㋡㋡㋡㋡㋡㋡㋡㋡

In Chapter 7, we read how the Islamic Empire tore through the Middle East— conquering everything in its path. Before then, most of the Middle East had been Christian. Now it all went Muslim, almost in the blink of eye.

Since then, almost every country of the Middle East has had an Islamic government. The only exception is the only Jewish country on Earth: Israel. During World War II (1939 – 1945), a horrible happening called the Holocaust almost wiped out the Jewish people. Two years after that war ended, the United Nations voted to let the Jews set up a new Israel— trying to give them a safe place to live. Sad to say, Israel has often been anything but safe.

One Middle Eastern city is holy to all three religions: Judaism, Christianity and Islam. That city is the capital of Israel: **Jerusalem**.

➤ Jerusalem is holy to Jews for many reasons. One is because it was the City of David, the greatest King of Israel. Another is because the Hebrew Temple, where Jews offered sacrifices to God, stood in Jerusalem. All the land God promised to Abraham in Genesis 15 is now called the **Holy Land**.

➢ Jerusalem is holy to Christians because so many important events from Christ's life happened there. Jesus was dedicated at the Temple in Jerusalem; rode into Jerusalem as a hero on the first Palm Sunday; was crucified on Jerusalem's Calvary Hill; was buried in a Jerusalem tomb; and rose from the dead at Jerusalem on the first Easter Sunday.

➢ Jerusalem is holy to Muslims partly because of the **Night Journey**, which we covered in Chapter 5. The place where the Hebrew Temple once stood is now covered by a Muslim shrine called the Dome of the Rock, which honors the Night Journey.

The longing for holy Jerusalem was one reason for some of the longest, ugliest wars ever: the Holy Land Crusades.

> The **Night Journey** was the special vision or journey that taught the prophet Muhammad how Allah wanted Muslims to worship.

Crusade is a word with many meanings. In modern times, it can mean any struggle for a moral cause. But in medieval times, it meant a holy war fought in the name of Christ. "Crusade" came from *crux*, which is Latin for "cross." A soldier who joined a crusade was said to "take the cross," which meant marking the cross on his shield and breastplate.

The Holy Land Crusades were a set of nine special holy wars ordered by the popes of the High Middle Ages. The First Crusade started in 1096, and the Ninth Crusade ended in 1272. All nine Holy Land Crusades had one main goal: to take back the Holy Land from Muslims!

The Battle of Manzikert

To understand how the Crusades got started, we must first back up a bit. In Chapter 7, we read about the first **caliphs**— the leaders who took charge of the Islamic Empire after the prophet Muhammad died. We also read about the caliph's governments, which were called caliphates. First came the Rashidun Caliphate, which took over when Muhammad died in 632. Then came the Umayyad Caliphate, which took over in 661.

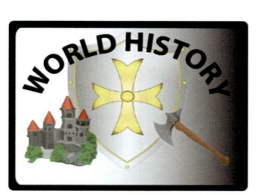

The third caliphate started in 750, when a family called Abbas overthrew the Umayyads. The Abbasid Caliphate reigned from Baghdad, which lies in what is now Iraq.

The Abbasid Caliphate turned out to be weaker than

> A **caliph** was a successor of Muhammad.
>
> A **sultan** was a governor who ruled part of the Islamic Empire in the caliph's name.
>
> An **emir** was a military leader who ruled part of the Islamic Empire in the caliph's name.

the first two. Before now, almost all Muslims had bowed to one mighty caliph. Now they didn't anymore. Instead of one Islamic Empire, there were now many Muslim kingdoms— each ruled by a **sultan** or **emir**. Some sultans had more real power than the caliphs they were supposed to obey. Just before the Crusades, the most powerful men in Islam were the sultans of the Great Seljuk Empire.

Sultan Alp Arslan of the Great Seljuk Empire

The Great Seljuk Empire started with a people called the **Seljuk Turks**. They came from northeast of Persia (Iran), between the Caspian Sea and China. That part of Asia was called <u>Turk</u>estan, after the <u>Turk</u>s who lived there. The Turks were like the Huns and the Magyars: warrior peoples who rode in from the East, demanding tribute from everyone they conquered.

In ancient times, the Turks followed a religion called **Shamanism**. In the 900s, though, they switched to the religion of their neighbor Persia: Islam. A hundred years later, the Seljuk Turks rode out of Turkestan— hoping to build a Muslim empire to their west.

> A **shaman** is a kind of Eastern monk who is supposed to be able to speak with spirits.

With a string of victories, the Turks built their empire steadily westward. Most of Persia was theirs by 1040. Then came a most important prize: Baghdad, which they captured in 1055. Since Baghdad was capital of the Abbasid Caliphate, the Sultan of the Great Seljuk Empire was now more powerful than the caliph!

At first, the Turks mostly conquered other Muslims. As they moved farther west, though, they started conquering Christians too. By 1070, they were breaking off pieces of the last Christian empire in the East: the **Byzantine Empire**, which had its capital at Constantinople.

Naturally, the Byzantines rode out to stop them. The big showdown came in 1071, when the two enemies fought the famous **Battle of Manzikert**.

> **Manzikert** was a fortress in what is now eastern Turkey. It was also called Malazgirt.

The strange thing about the Battle of Manzikert was that neither army was expecting it. The Byzantine emperor, Diogenes, was on his way to Armenia— hoped to take back some forts from the Turks. The Turkish sultan, **Alp Arslan**, was on his way to conquer the Holy Land— not from Diogenes, but from another Muslim king. Diogenes had no idea that Arslan's army was still nearby.

When Diogenes finally figured out where Arslan was, he turned to attack him. The result was one of the biggest disasters in the whole history of the Byzantine Empire. The emperor's army collapsed around him, allowing Arslan to capture Diogenes himself! According to legend, the sultan set his boot on the neck of the beaten emperor— making it perfectly clear which was master.

After the Battle of Manzikert, the Turks conquered more and more lands in Asia Minor— edging closer and closer to Constantinople. By about 1090, the only thing between Constantinople and the Turks was a thin strip of land and water. Meanwhile, the Turks seized the Holy Land too. Their empire was enormous, stretching all the way from the Mediterranean Sea in the west to Turkestan in the east.

Sultan Alp Arslan of the Great Seljuk Empire with his boot on the neck of the Byzantine emperor

The Holy Land Crusades

With nowhere else to turn for help, the Byzantines turned toward Rome. In March 1095, Emperor Alexios I Komnenos sent ambassadors to Italy with an urgent message for Pope Urban II. The emperor warned that if the pope didn't send help soon, then Constantinople might fall to the Muslims— which might mean the end of the Eastern Orthodox Church.

The timing was important. In Chapter 8, we read about the Great Schism of 1054— the one that split the Eastern Orthodox Church from the Roman Catholic Church. The Great Schism was only fifty years old in 1095, when the Byzantines asked the pope for help. If the pope could save the Byzantines, then the two churches might get back together— and under the pope's leadership.

The pope also had another reason to help. When the Great Seljuk Empire seized the Holy Land, it stopped Christians from going there! Before then, Christian pilgrims had always been able to visit the places where Jesus walked— holy cities like Jerusalem, Bethlehem and Nazareth. Now they couldn't. A victory over the Turks would re-open the Holy Land to the many Christians who wanted to go.

With that many reasons, the pope soon made up his mind. It happened at the **Council of Clermont**, which met at Clermont, France in November 1095. In a big speech before all the Christian leaders of the West, Pope Urban II announced a holy war against the Muslims. He wanted all Christian soldiers, whether rich or poor, to go and rescue the Christians of the East!

Pope Urban II announcing the First Crusade at the Council of Clermont

To reward Christians who answered his call, the pope added a special promise. According to a writer called Fulcher of Chartres, the pope said that any Christian who died fighting the Muslims would have all his sins forgiven! As the keeper of the keys of St. Peter (Matthew 16:19), the pope promised to open wide the gates of heaven for every Christian who gave his life for the **First Crusade**.

With a promise like that, the pope got a big response. Not one, but two big armies answered the pope's call to war. Each army fought part of the First Crusade. The first army fought the People's Crusade, and the second the Princes' Crusade.

The **People's Crusade** was a disaster led by a French priest called **Peter the Hermit**. After the Council of Clermont, Peter rode from city to town all over the West— calling all Christians to come and fight. Tens of thousands answered his call.

The People's Crusade (1096)

Peter the Hermit drumming up support for the First Crusade

The problem was the kind of Christians who answered. Peter's soldiers were the poorest of the poor— penniless, weaponless peasants who had no idea how to fight a war, and no business trying. The Turks destroyed Peter the Hermit's army the moment it set foot in Asia Minor.

But then everything turned around. In 1097, the year after the People's Crusade, the real soldiers of the West started showing up in the East. The knights of the **Princes' Crusade** were no unarmed, underfed peasants. Rather, they were skilled fighters with the training, experience and money it took to fight a real war. Most of them were either Normans or Franks— including a Frankish lord called **Godfrey of Bouillon**.

The Princes' Crusade (1097)

The crusaders needed almost a year to win their first great victory: the **Siege of Antioch**, Syria. In winning Antioch, the crusaders won back one of the great cities of the early church— home to famous names like Ignatius of Antioch (Chapter 1) and John Chrysostom (Chapter 4).

The problem with the Siege of Antioch was that it took too long! With both money and spirits running low after Antioch, the crusaders didn't have time for another long siege when they moved on to their most important target: Jerusalem.

Godfrey of Bouillon with other leaders of the First Crusade. Each knight who joined a crusade was said to "take the cross." Part of taking the cross was to mark breastplate and shield with the sign of the cross.

So for the **Siege of Jerusalem**, the crusaders tried something different. According to one version of the story, the crusaders marched around Jerusalem barefoot for three days— much like the ancient Israelites marched around Jericho in Joshua 6. Then they pushed **siege towers** up to the city walls, leapt into the city and started killing. Muslim or Jew, soldier or civilian, young or old made no difference; all went down under the terrible swords of the vengeful crusaders.

With Jerusalem under their belts, the soldiers of the First Crusade could honestly say they'd won! Some of them went home, where they were honored as Christian heroes. Others stayed to rule all the lands they'd won in Asia Minor and the Holy Land.

By the end of the First Crusade, the crusaders had set up four new countries called the **Crusader States**. From north to south, the four Crusader States were:

Crusaders using a siege tower to climb over Jerusalem's city walls

the County of Edessa in Asia Minor; the Principality of Antioch in Syria; the County of Tripoli in Lebanon; and most important, the Kingdom of Jerusalem.

The Second Crusade didn't go as well for the Christian side. The trouble started in 1144, almost fifty years after the First Crusade. That was when Muslims took back the northernmost Crusader State: the County of Edessa. Three years later, the knights of the Second Crusade tried to take Edessa back— and failed. The first of the four Crusader States was lost forever.

A **coat of arms** was a colorful symbol that told the achievements of a medieval knight or his noble family.

Older knights like King Arthur came from the Dark Ages, before there were coats of arms. To honor knights like these, medieval artists dreamed up special coats of arms called **attributed arms**. The attributed arms of King Arthur had three crowns, one for each of his three kingdoms: England, Wales and Scotland.

One example of an attributed arms for King Arthur

Between the Second Crusade and the Third Crusade came the rise of a great Muslim leader: mighty Saladin, Sultan of Egypt and Syria. Saladin's greatest victory was the Battle of Hattin, which started with a siege.

The Battle of Hattin (July 1187)

In the middle of the hot, dry summer of 1187, Saladin suddenly surrounded a Christian city called Tiberias. It stood on the Sea of Galilee, about 75 miles north of Jerusalem. In fear for their lives, the Christians of Tiberias sent word to King Guy of Jerusalem— begging him to bring his army.

The key to what happened next was water. Between King Guy and Tiberias lay a long stretch of near-desert ground. With thousands of thirsty troops and horses, Guy's army needed thousands of gallons of water every day— especially under a hot July sun. Yet in all this stretch of ground, there was not one working well where Guy could refill his water barrels. He would have to make do with whatever water he could carry. Fortunately, Guy thought, Tiberias was only about fifteen miles away— not too far for his army to travel in one day.

Guy might have been right, if not for Saladin's army. With Muslim troops blocking their way, Guy's army couldn't make it to Tiberias in just one day. By the end of that day, Guy's water had run out— leaving his troops thirsty and miserable.

That night, Saladin magnified Guy's misery in merciless ways. The Muslims lit fires in the dry grass, sending stinging smoke into Guy's waterless camp. The next morning, they hauled whole wagonloads of water near the camp— just out of the crusaders' reach. As the parched Christians looked on in horror, the Muslims poured out barrel after barrel of precious water on the ground! Thousands of crusaders lost their lives in the terrible battle that followed— or after the battle, when Saladin executed most of the survivors.

The Battle of Hattin was a terrible loss for the Christians. Without King Guy's army to defend the kingdom, city after city fell to Saladin. Later that year, the whole Kingdom of Jerusalem fell— handing the most important Crusader State back to the Muslims.

The **Third Crusade** was the Church's answer to Saladin. When Pope Gregory VIII heard about the disaster at Hattin, he called for a holy war to take back Jerusalem. The three mightiest kings in Europe all answered the pope's call, setting out for the Holy Land in 1189 – 1190. These were **Holy Roman Emperor Frederick I**, also called Barbarossa; **King Philip II of France**, also called Philip Augustus; and King Richard I of England, also called **Richard the Lionheart**.

Alas, Barbarossa never made it to the Holy Land. As we read in Chapter 11, the beloved old emperor drowned on his way to the Third Crusade.

Muslim leaders surrendering Acre to King Philip II of France, right, and King Richard I of England, left

The biggest, longest battle of the Third Crusade Acre happened at a Mediterranean seaport called Acre. Acre was one of many Christian cities that had fallen to Saladin after the Battle of Hattin. Starting in 1189, the Christians laid siege to Acre— hoping to take it back.

The **Siege of Acre** was almost two years old in the spring of 1191, when Philip and Richard finally showed up. With their fresh troops and fresh ideas, the two kings soon turned the tide of battle. The greatest Christian victory of the Third Crusade came in July 1191, when the crusaders finally broke into Acre.

The Christians might have won a lot more, if they hadn't quarreled with each other. The trouble started just after the Siege of Acre, when Richard insulted a German called **Leopold V, Duke of Austria**.

Duke Leopold was part of the German army that set out with Barbarossa. After Barbarossa drowned, many Germans gave up and went home. But Leopold went on to the Holy Land, getting there long before Philip and Richard did.

Since those two came so late, Leopold felt that he and his men deserved a lot of credit for winning the Siege of Acre. When the Muslims surrendered, Leopold raised his flag over Acre— right beside the flags of Philip and Richard. But when Richard saw Leopold's flag, he told his men to tear it down and throw it in the moat— saying that no mere duke had the right to fly his flag beside a king's! Enraged at this insult, Leopold gathered his troops and went home to Austria.

Flag of Austria

Then came a quarrel between Richard and Philip. Even before the Third Crusade, these two had a long history as sometimes-friends, sometimes-enemies. After the quarrel they had now, they would never be friends again. Philip went home like Leopold, leaving Richard to lead the Third Crusade by himself.

Richard the Lionheart would live to regret insulting Duke Leopold. On his way home from the Third Crusade, Richard passed through Leopold's territory— where Leopold gleefully locked him up. To get Richard home again, his mother had to pay a "king's ransom"— in other words, a huge sum of money. The total was about twice the amount England collected in taxes for a whole year!

Richard tangled with Saladin's troops many times over the next year, and often won. He might have won Jerusalem itself, if he'd tried. The problem was, the Christians had no way to hold Jerusalem once they'd taken it. Since the Muslims had them outnumbered, they would surely sweep in the moment Richard's back was turned.

Richard finally decided that the only way to get Jerusalem was by bargaining for it. In September 1192, Richard and Saladin signed a deal called the **Treaty of Jaffa**. Saladin's end of the deal was to let Christians visit Jerusalem for the next three years— but only if they left their weapons home. Richard's end was to give up and go home. Having settled affairs as best he could, Richard boarded ship for England that fall— ending the Third Crusade.

〰〰〰〰〰〰〰〰〰〰〰〰〰〰〰〰〰〰〰〰〰〰〰〰〰〰〰〰〰〰〰〰

The next crusade was the most disgraceful of all nine Holy Land Crusades. On their way to the Holy Land in 1202, the crusaders of the **Fourth Crusade** foolishly took sides in a fight between two Byzantine emperors. Instead of attacking Muslims in the Holy Land, the crusaders wound up attacking Eastern Christians in Constantinople!

〰〰〰〰〰〰〰〰〰〰〰〰〰〰〰〰〰〰〰〰〰〰〰〰〰〰〰〰〰〰〰〰

Even after three failed crusades, the crusading spirit was still strong enough to inspire many Christians back West— including children. In May 1212, legend says, a twelve-year-old French boy called Stephen of Cloyes announced that God was calling him to lead a **children's crusade**! A few months later, a twelve-year-old German boy called Nicholas of Cologne announced the same thing.

Both boys had the same idea about why the Crusades were failing: because grown-up crusaders weren't faithful enough. Instead of sending grown-ups, the boys said, the pope should children! Why? Because the pure, unquestioning faith of children was far stronger than the doubting faith of grown-ups.

On the other hand, the boys had different ideas about how to win the crusades. Stephen of Cloyes wanted to crush the Muslims with child armies; but Nicholas of Cologne wanted to win Muslim hearts by preaching the gospel.

If the legend is true, then both Stephen and Nicholas led child armies to ports along the southern coast of France. They promised their followers that when they got there, God would part the Mediterranean Sea for them— just as God had parted the Red Sea for Moses in Exodus 14!

Although Saladin and Richard were bitter enemies, the two kings treated each other with a lot of respect. When Richard's old horse died in battle, Saladin sent him a nice new Arabian horse. And when Richard had a fever, Saladin sent him fresh fruit and other hard-to-find luxuries.

Richard the Lionheart waving goodbye to the Holy Land after the Third Crusade

The Children's Crusades (1212)

Muslim artists often work in a style called **arabesque**. Since Islamic law forbids idol worship, and since pictures of people and animals look too much like idols, Muslim artists create art with no people and no animals. Arabesques include mostly vines, leaves and flowers, all woven into flowing, never-ending patterns.

Much to their disappointment, the waters didn't part. At this, some children gave up and tried to go home; while others boarded ship for the Holy Land. Some were shipwrecked, and some captured by Muslims and sold into slavery. Only a few ever made it home again.

The well-known legend of the **Pied Piper of Hamelin** may have come from the tragedy of the Children's Crusades. The Pied Piper was said to be a mysterious man in a "pied," or multi-colored, suit. The legend says that in 1284, the town of Hamelin, Germany struck a deal with the Pied Piper. The town agreed to pay the piper a lot of money. In exchange, the piper promised to get rid of Hamelin's many rats— which were a common problem in those days.

The Pied Piper held up his end of the deal. Pulling a flute from his pocket, the Pied Piper piped a tune that drew the rats to him like magic. Still piping his tune, the Pied Piper led the rats to the banks of the nearby Weser River— where they all fell in and drowned!

The townspeople should have been pleased; but instead, they were furious. As good Christians, the Germans of Hamelin hated magic. When they found out the Pied Piper was a magician, they refused to pay him— even though he had done exactly what they asked.

The Pied Piper waited for a Christian holiday to take his revenge. While all the good people of Hamelin were sitting in church, the Pied Piper used his magical pipe to lure their children out of town. 130 boys and girls disappeared into a cave, and were never seen again!

Analyzing the Crusades

As we read above, there were nine Holy Land Crusades in all. They spread out across 176 years, all the way from 1096 – 1272. Of the nine, there was only one that the crusaders could honestly say they'd won: the First Crusade.

Even that victory didn't last; for in the end, the crusaders' hard work was all undone. All four Crusader States finally fell to the Muslims. The road to the Holy Land was still often closed to Christians. And Muslims still threatened the Byzantine Empire, as we'll read in Chapter 20.

A People Set Apart

The time of the Crusades was a terrible time to be Jewish. When the Crusades began, the Jews were already scattered around the Middle East and Europe. Their scattering is so old and well-known that it has a special name: the **Jewish Diaspora**.

> A **diaspora** is a scattering of a group of people.
>
> The **Jewish Diaspora** is the scattering of the Jewish people all around the world— far away from their ancient homeland, Israel.

It started in 722, when the Assyrians conquered the Kingdom of Israel and dragged off many of its people— as we read in Year One. The Diaspora got worse in 586 BC, when the Babylonians did the same thing to the Kingdom of Judah.

The Diaspora got even worse in Roman times. The Jews hit bottom in 70 AD, when Roman soldiers tore down the last Hebrew Temple. By 135, angry Romans were kicking all Jews out of Jerusalem— thanks to a Jewish uprising called the Bar Kohkba Revolt.

Wherever they scattered, Jews held themselves apart from their non-Jewish neighbors. As children of Abraham, Jews saw themselves as God's chosen people— heirs to a special promise that God had made to them alone. Remembering this, they refused to worship their neighbors' gods, or let their children marry their neighbors' children.

Many Jews moved all the way to in Europe, where most of their neighbors were Christians. The Christians should have understood the Jews better than others; for after all, Christ Himself was a Jew. Even so, many Christians found reasons to hate Jews:

➤ Some Christians called Jews "Christ-killers"— remembering how a crowd of Jews had practically forced Pontius Pilate to crucify Jesus Christ (Matthew 27:22-25).

➤ Some Christians accused Jews of sacrificing Christian children in secret worship services. This was ridiculous— for after the Temple was destroyed, the Jews no longer sacrificed any animals, even birds. These false accusations are called **blood libel**.

> A **synagogue** is a house of worship where Jews come together to pray, worship God and learn Torah. The Jews do not sacrifice animals in their synagogues. That form of worship ended in 70 AD, when the Romans destroyed the Second Temple at Jerusalem.

➤ Some Christians resented the Jews for loaning out money at interest, the way banks do. Before the Renaissance came, the Church forbade most Christians to loan money at interest (Chapter 26). Since Jews weren't forbidden, some of them grew rich from lending money.

As so often happens, hatred turned to violence. The violence was worst when Christians were thinking most about their faith, as they were during the Crusades.

The First Crusade may have been the worst for Jews. The trouble started when the peasant mobs of the People's Crusade set out for the Holy Land. With that many angry Christians on the road, any Jew who got in their way was in big trouble. The peasants robbed and murdered many Jews— just how many, no one now knows. Whole Jewish communities died at the hands of pitiless Christians who were supposed to be doing God's will.

A mob of peasants from the People's Crusade attacking Jews at Metz, Germany

More British Isles

In Chapter 2, we read that the British Isles lie off the northwest coast of mainland Europe. Two of the British Isles are far bigger than all the rest. One is **Great Britain**, which is home to three countries: England, Scotland and Wales. The other is **Ireland**, which is home to two countries: Northern Ireland and the Republic of Ireland.

Besides these two main islands, the British Isles also include hundreds of smaller islands. Some of these belong to **archipelagos**, or groups of islands; while others stand more or less on their own.

> An **archipelago** is a group of islands.

The biggest archipelago is actually two archipelagos: the **Inner Hebrides** and the **Outer Hebrides**. Both lie off the northwest coast of Scotland. The island of **Iona**, where Columba built his famous monastery (Chapter 3), is one of the Inner Hebrides.

North of Scotland lie two well-known archipelagos: the **Orkney Islands** and the **Shetland Islands**. The Orkneys lie near the northern coast; while Shetland lies more than 100 miles off the coast. The farmers of Shetland have bred some well-known animals, including the small-but-tough Shetland pony.

One of the biggest single islands is the **Isle of Man**, which lies midway between Great Britain and Ireland. The name "Man" does not mean the human race! Instead, it may be short for a Celtic sea god called *Manannan mac Lir*. A few people on the Isle of Man still

speak an ancient Celtic language called Manx. The Isle of Man is also famous for the Manx cat, a breed without a tail. Another big single island is the **Isle of Wight**, which lies in the English Channel just off the coast of Portsmouth.

THE BRITISH ISLES

Shetland Islands

Outer Hebrides   Orkney Islands

Inner Hebrides

Scotland

Ireland   North Sea

Isle of Man

Irish Sea

Wales

England

Celtic Sea

Isles of Scilly

Isle of Wight

English Channel

The House of Plantagenet

In Chapter 10, we read about the last son of William the Conqueror to rule England: **King Henry I**. Henry was the wise but unfortunate king who lost his teenaged son, William Aetheling, in the awful Wreck of the White Ship.

After Henry lost his son, his nobles promised to follow his daughter: an ex-Holy Roman Empress called Matilda. But when Henry died, his nobles broke their promise. Instead of following Matilda, they followed a French noble called Stephen of Blois— who now became King Stephen of England.

King Henry II

Matilda and her husband, a French noble called Geoffrey Plantagenet, fought long and hard to take back her inheritance. After twenty years of fighting, they finally found a way to end it: with an agreement called the Treaty of Wallingford. The treaty said that King Stephen would keep the throne of England for as long as he lived; but that when Stephen died, Matilda's son Henry Plantagenet would take his place. Since the new king had a new family name, the old House of Normandy was finished. **King Henry II** was the first king of a new royal house: the **House of Plantagenet**.

Like William the Conqueror, Henry II ruled lands in both England and France. Through his great-grandfather William, Henry was Duke of **Normandy**. Through his father Geoffrey of Anjou, Henry was Count of **Anjou**. And through his wife Eleanor of Aquitaine, Henry became Duke of **Aquitaine**.

In fact, Henry II ruled so many lands that he was more like an emperor than a king. Historians call Henry's lands the **Angevin Empire**— after his father, the Duke of Anjou.

꠸꠸꠸꠸꠸꠸꠸꠸꠸꠸꠸꠸꠸꠸꠸꠸꠸꠸꠸꠸꠸꠸꠸꠸꠸꠸꠸꠸꠸꠸꠸꠸

Normandy was a duchy in northwestern France, just across the English Channel from Great Britain.

Anjou was a county south of Normandy.

Aquitaine was a duchy in southwestern France.

Eleanor of Aquitaine (1122 - 1204)

Henry's queen lived one of the longest, most fascinating lives of the High Middle Ages. One fascinating fact about **Eleanor of Aquitaine** is that before she was Queen of England, she was Queen of France!

Eleanor was still just a girl in August 1137, when she inherited the rich Duchy of Aquitaine from her dying father. The King of France, who was also dying, wanted the riches of Aquitaine for his son. To get them, he arranged for Eleanor to marry his son— who soon became **King Louis VII of France**.

It so happened that Eleanor and Louis weren't just husband and wife. They were also fourth cousins— a fact that would prove most important in years to come.

Like many royal marriages, the marriage between Eleanor and Louis was an unhappy one. One reason for their unhappiness was the **Second Crusade**, which fell in the middle of their married years (Chapter 12).

The first problem was that Eleanor was much too interested in the Second Crusade. In a time when women never, ever went to war, Eleanor stubbornly insisted on following Louis to the Holy Land— much to her husband's embarrassment.

Some storytellers blame Eleanor for what happened next. As the story goes, Eleanor was a finicky royal lady who insisted on traveling in style, even in a war zone. To keep Eleanor happy, Louis had to drag along a lot of ladies, servants and useless baggage— none of which belonged anywhere near a war.

King Louis VII of France marrying Eleanor of Aquitaine (left) before sailing off to fight the Second Crusade (right)

When the French army was on the move, Eleanor's slow-moving baggage train couldn't keep up. The army started to spread out— with most of it pushing ahead, and a small part staying behind to defend the queen and her ladies. Sensing weakness, the Turks attacked the thin French rear— and almost destroyed it. Eleanor's husband Louis barely escaped with his life!

Whether or not that old story is true, it is certainly true that the Second Crusade failed. The royal couple never stopped arguing about it— with Eleanor blaming Louis, and Louis blaming Eleanor.

Another reason for Louis' unhappiness was the kind of children Eleanor gave him. Like all kings, Louis wanted sons to carry on his dynasty. But Eleanor gave Louis only daughters, never sons.

Both royals were eager for a divorce. Alas for both, divorce was no simple matter in the High Middle Ages! In those days, all Christian marriages were governed by the Church; and the Church almost never allowed an outright divorce. However, the Church sometimes allowed a tricky kind of divorce called an **annulment**— which is how Eleanor and Louis finally ended their unhappy marriage.

> To **annul** a marriage is to dissolve it, making it as if the couple had never married.

After fifteen years together, Eleanor and Louis suddenly started complaining that the Church never should have let them marry in the first place. Why? Because they were fourth cousins— as we read above. Church law said that fourth cousins couldn't marry, because they were already too closely related by blood.

Of course, the Church had known all along that Eleanor and Louis were fourth cousins, and had blessed their marriage anyway! Even so, the Church accepted their thin excuse— annulling their marriage in 1152.

What happened next proved what a thin excuse it was. Just two months after the annulment, Eleanor married an even closer relative: her third cousin Henry Plantagenet, who was soon to become King Henry II of England!

Kings from the Royal House of Plantagenet

1. King Henry II
(Reigned 1154 - 1189)

2. Henry the Young King
(Co-reigned 1170 - 1183)

3. King Richard I
(Reigned 1189 - 1199)

4. King John
(Reigned 1199 - 1216)

Eleanor went on to give Henry eight children— including several of the boys Louis had wanted so badly. Three of Eleanor's boys grew up to be the next three kings from the House of Plantagenet: **Henry the Young King**, **Richard I** and **John**.

〰〰〰〰〰〰〰〰〰〰〰〰〰〰〰

King Henry II wasn't a big favorite with the English. Even so, they still honor him for one big accomplishment: bringing common law to England.

England was a mess when Henry took over. The long war between King Stephen and Empress Matilda had left the country in chaos, with lawless **mercenaries** wreaking havoc everywhere. Without good law, the courts couldn't punish these criminals fairly. For example, one town court might lock a criminal in the stocks for stealing. But another town court might cut off the thief's hand, or even put him to death!

> A **mercenary** is a hired soldier.

King Henry II and his wife Eleanor of Aquitaine

Common law changed all that. Instead of the old town courts, Henry set up new courts called **assizes**. Assize judges traveled from place to place, hearing cases all along their **circuit**.

Common law is law that is the same for everyone, everywhere.

The **assizes** were courts that traveled around England. Assize judges held court at each town or county along their **circuit,** or route.

Once the assizes decided on a fair punishment for a certain crime, all courts punished that crime the same way. For example, if one court locked thieves in the stocks, then all courts locked them in the stocks. Common law was an important step toward equal justice for all.

Oddly enough, Henry's love of law was one reason for his downfall. In 1170, the king's stubbornness about common law led to a deadly argument with an old friend of his: **Thomas Becket**.

Thomas Becket was a brilliant man who stood with one foot in the Church, and the other in the government. He started out as an aide to the Archbishop of Canterbury, head of all English churches. Years later, the archbishop recommended him as an aide to the king. In 1155, Thomas Becket became King's Chancellor to Henry II— the king's top adviser, and the officer in charge of carrying out the king's orders.

Over the next seven years, Henry II grew quite fond of Thomas Becket. With the Crusades going on, the Church was as powerful as it would ever be. King and Church were always arguing— with the king pulling the country one way, and churchmen pulling it another. In times like those, it was a big help to have a smart churchman like Thomas on the king's side.

The trouble started in 1162, when the old Archbishop of Canterbury died. Needing a new one, Henry decided to make Thomas Becket Archbishop of Canterbury. He believed that Thomas would still be on his side, even when he was head of the Church.

What Henry didn't count on was how the archbishop's job changed Thomas. As King's Chancellor, Thomas had lived almost like a king— eating rich food, wearing rich clothes, going to rich parties and so on. But as Archbishop of Canterbury, Thomas took his faith more seriously. He started wearing a hair shirt and sleeping on the hard floor, just like a monk. Now when king and Church argued, Thomas always took the Church's side!

Henry's knights cutting down Thomas Becket

What king and Church argued about most was common law. Before Henry II, any priest who stood accused of a crime was tried in a court run by the Church. The problem was, Church courts were far too easy on priests. Even if a priest was convicted of murder, the worst the Church might do was to kick him out of the priesthood. If that same priest had been convicted in the assizes, then he would have been put to death!

As a believer in common law, Henry wanted priests to be tried in the assizes— just like everyone else. But Thomas refused— saying that priests were too holy to stand trial in common courts. Henry grew so frustrated with his old friend that he finally shouted to no one in particular: "Is there no one who will rid me of this turbulent priest?"

The king may have meant what he shouted, or he may not have. Either way, some of his knights thought he meant it. Soon after Henry shouted it, four of them burst into Canterbury Cathedral— shouting, "Where is the traitor, Thomas Becket?" Becket answered, "Here am I— no traitor, but a priest of God."

Henry's knights commanded Thomas to submit to his king. When Thomas refused, the knights cut him down— right there on the altar of Canterbury Cathedral.

When the news got out, Henry pleaded innocent— swearing that he never ordered his knights to kill Thomas Becket. But it didn't matter; for his people blamed him anyway. The murder of Thomas Becket became the darkest of many stains on the reputation of King Henry II.

Ⴠ Ⴠ

Much as the English people hated Henry II, his family hated him more. Twenty years into Henry's reign, the hatred of his family led to a revolution that almost pushed him off his throne!

The trouble started in 1170, the year Thomas Becket died. That same year, Henry II made his eldest son Henry a junior king. The idea was that if anything should happen to Henry II, then no one would question his son's right to take his place— for the younger Henry would already be king.

For now, though, the older Henry didn't give the younger Henry any real jobs to do. Instead of learning kingly duties, **Henry the Young King** spent his time enjoying knights' tournaments.

The problem with tournaments was that they cost a lot of money. There were so many things to buy, from weapons and armor to party clothes, decorations, prizes, gifts and more. Most kings raised money by collecting taxes from their lands. But as junior king, young Henry didn't have any lands. He tried asking his father for lands to tax; but the older Henry wouldn't give him any.

Young Henry also had a problem with jealousy. In looking at his brothers, he couldn't help noticing that John always got everything he wanted. In fact, John even got some castles that his father had promised to young Henry!

Those castles were the last straw. In his third year as junior king, young Henry started a rebellion called the **Revolt of 1173 – 1174**— trying to overthrow his father!

Young Henry wasn't the only family member who rebelled against Henry II. Richard the Lionheart joined him, also because his father wouldn't give him lands to tax. Eleanor of Aquitaine joined the rebellion too— partly because Richard was her favorite, and partly because Henry II had been carrying on with other women.

Despite having most of his family against him, Henry II wound up crushing the rebellion. Afterward, he forgave Henry the Young King and Richard the Lionheart— but not Eleanor of Aquitaine. The aging queen spent her next sixteen years under **house arrest**.

The king had no more troubles with Henry the Young King after 1183; for that was when young Henry died. Sad to say, the king's troubles with Richard were far from over.

Like young Henry before him, Richard was terribly jealous of John. As the older son, Richard stood next in line for the throne. Yet he couldn't help worrying that his father might make John king instead! For John was the king's only loyal son— the only one who hadn't joined the Revolt of 1173 – 1174.

**Henry the Young King
(co-reigned 1170 - 1183)**

Eleanor of Aquitaine heading off to start her sixteen years under house arrest (1174 – 1189). To be under house arrest is to be a prisoner in one's own home, forbidden to go anywhere or meet anyone without permission.

Desperate to stay ahead of John, Richard rebelled against his father again. This time, Richard brought a powerful new friend to the fight: **King Philip II of France**. This was the same Philip who would soon join Richard on the Third Crusade, as we read in Chapter 12.

If Henry II had been young and well, then he probably could have beaten both Richard and Philip. By this time, though, Henry was neither young nor well. Sensing that death was near, Henry turned to meet with his son one last time.

In these last meetings of his life, Henry II learned one last horrible truth about his family. Up till now, his favorite son John had always stayed loyal to him. But in this latest revolt, John had sworn loyalty to Richard!

The news hit Henry like a death blow, sending him into a feverish sleep. Before he died, though, Henry came awake just long enough to speak this bitter curse against Richard: "God grant that I may not die until I have had my just revenge on you!"

So it was that King Henry II died the loneliest of deaths, leaving Richard to claim his throne in the ugliest of ways. Anyone who thinks that money and power are the keys to happiness must have forgotten the sad story of Henry II!

Richard the Lionheart as a crusading knight

🐍🐍🐍🐍🐍🐍🐍🐍🐍🐍🐍🐍🐍🐍🐍🐍🐍🐍🐍🐍🐍🐍🐍🐍🐍🐍🐍🐍🐍🐍🐍🐍

The year of Richard's crowning, 1189, was the same busy year when the Third Crusade started up. Richard was just settling down on his throne when he had to set out for the Holy Land.

Before he left, Richard made his mother Eleanor of Aquitaine his regent— the officer who would run his government while he was gone.

Although John had sworn to be loyal, Richard didn't quite trust his younger brother— with good reason, as it turned out!

As we read in Chapter 12, Richard was gone for a long time— not only fighting the Third Crusade, but also sitting in a German jail! While Richard was away, two rivals tried to claim his lands:

**King Richard I
(reigned 1189 - 1199)**

➢ One was Richard's old friend **King Philip II of France**. After arguing with Richard in the Holy Land, Philip came home and seized part of Normandy.

➢ The other rival was Richard's slippery brother **John**. When Richard didn't come home, John announced that his brother must have died in the Third Crusade. As a dutiful brother, John said, he had no choice but to take Richard's place!

Of course, Richard finally did make it home from the Holy Land— but only after Eleanor paid the Germans a king's ransom. He spent the rest of his life in Normandy, trying to win back what Philip had stolen from him.

To defend Normandy against Philip, Richard built a mighty castle called **Chateau Gaillard**. The two fighting kings often teased one another about this great castle. Philip bragged that he could take it from Richard "even if its walls were made of steel." Richard answered that he could hold his castle against Philip "even if its walls were made of butter." Alas, Richard never got a chance to test Chateau Gaillard.

The central keep of Chateau Gaillard castle, built by Richard the Lionheart to defend Normandy against King Philip II of France

One day in the spring of 1199, Richard was trying to break into the castle of a rebellious noble. While inspecting his army, Richard saw something that made him laugh out loud. An enemy soldier was standing on the castle wall, using a frying pan to knock crossbow bolts out of the air!

Richard laughed so hard that he didn't notice an enemy crossbowman hiding nearby. The unseen archer took Richard by surprise, burying a bolt in the king's shoulder. The deep wound got infected, sapping even Richard's great strength.

As Richard lay dying, he was tormented with guilt over the horrible things he had done to his father. Before he died, Richard asked to be buried at the feet of Henry II— so that when his eyes opened on the next life, he could immediately beg his father's forgiveness.

The true story of Richard and John gave rise to a legend that probably isn't true: **Robin Hood**. Robin is supposed to have been a noble who saved poor Englishmen from the evil King John while the good King Richard was away fighting the Third Crusade.

What the legend of Robin Hood doesn't tell is that Richard was more French than English! Like his mother, Richard spent most of his life in France, and probably didn't speak much English. When Richard thought of England at all, he thought of it as a place to collect taxes. Once when Richard was raising money for his crusade, he said this about England: "If I could have found a buyer, I would have sold London itself!"

The Magna Carta

After Richard the Lionheart, the throne passed to one of the worst kings in English history: King John. No King of England has a worse reputation than John. In the eight hundred years since John lived, there have been many English kings named Richard, Henry, William and so on. But there have been no more named John— nor will there ever be, as long as Englishmen remember the first King John!

King John (reigned 1199 - 1216)

A monk who lived in John's day condemned the hated king with this verdict:

"Foul as it is, Hell itself is defiled by the fouler presence of John."

King John of England

King John was just getting started when he tangled with two dangerous enemies. The first was one of his nephews: Arthur of Brittany, who was a son to one of John's dead older brothers. Before Richard died, young Arthur of Brittany had high hopes of inheriting the throne. When John inherited it instead, Arthur decided to take the throne by force.

The second enemy was a French noble called Hugh IX of Lusignan. Hugh was an enemy of John's own making. The year after he became king, John suddenly insisted on marrying a beautiful young woman called **Isabella of Angouleme**— even though Isabella was already promised to Hugh!

King John's beautiful wife Isabella of Angouleme

Arthur of Brittany joining forces with King Philip II of France

Naturally, Hugh was most upset with the greedy John.

In 1202, these two enemies teamed up with a third. This latest enemy was one who loved to make trouble for any King of England: Richard's old enemy, King Philip II of France. That summer, Philip attacked John from the east, while Arthur and Hugh teamed up to attack him from the south.

Arthur and Hugh made their first move at a place called Mirabeau. Mirabeau Castle was where Eleanor of Aquitaine, John's 80-year-old mother, was living when the war broke out. Like a good son, John hurried down to rescue his mother.

Arthur and Hugh had no idea John was coming. Since Mirabeau stood 100 miles from where they thought John was, they thought they had a long while to get ready for him. They were just sitting down to breakfast, expecting a pleasant morning— when out of nowhere, John showed up to fight the **Battle of Mirabeau**! Thanks to the element of surprise, John quickly captured both Arthur and John.

What happened next was the key to the misery that followed John for the rest of his life. If John had been a chivalrous knight of the High Middle Ages, then he would have treated his prisoners well. Instead, John locked Arthur and Hugh in dark dungeons for days at a time— with no food, no water and no bathrooms. And it wasn't just Arthur and Hugh. Before John was finished, more than twenty French nobles had died in his miserable dungeons!

This turned out to be a big mistake. From the time of William the Conqueror down through John's day, western France was always in a tug-of-war between the King of France and the King of England. To win that tug-of-war, John needed help from French nobles. But after the way John treated his prisoners, no French noble wanted to help him! In other words, John ruined everything. The Battle of Mirabeau could have been a great beginning for him; but instead, it was the beginning of the end.

SEAL OF KING JOHN

After the Battle of Mirabeau, noble after noble abandoned John. The more abandoned him, the more lands he lost in France. Near the end of 1204, John lost the most important French land of all: Normandy, home of William the Conqueror. The fall of Normandy was the end of the once-great **Angevin Empire**.

The **Angevin Empire** was the set of lands ruled by King Henry II, whose father was the Duke of Anjou (Chapter 10). As we read above, the empire included a lot of lands in France.

A King John Penny

Normandy was so important to John that he spent the next ten years fighting to take it back. But instead of taking back Normandy, John almost lost the best land he had left: England.

Like his brother Richard before him, John thought of England as a place to raise tax money for wars in France. The noble barons of England thought otherwise. After ten years of fighting for Normandy, English barons were furious about John's taxes. Not even William the Conqueror had demanded as much as John did!

It wasn't just taxes, though. The barons also complained that John wasn't a good Christian king. They even complained that he liked to flirt with their wives— despite the fact that he was already married to one of the most beautiful women in Europe, Isabella of Angouleme!

By 1215, John's English barons had had enough. That May, a group of them marched into London and seized John. At a place called Runnymede, just west of London, the barons forced their king to sign one of the best-known documents in all history: the first **Magna Carta**.

> *Magna Carta* is Latin for "Great Charter."
>
> **Charter** can mean the declaration of a new law.

What was the Magna Carta all about? Basically, it set limits on the king's power. Before now, the King of England could do whatever he pleased— except when the Church stood in his way. Now it wasn't just the Church that stood up for itself. The Magna Carta insisted that the English people had rights too!

Most of the rights in the Magna Carta were for barons. For example, the king was not to demand high taxes from his barons, nor seize a baron's land without good reason.

On the other hand, some of the rights in the Magna Carta were for all free Englishmen. For example, the king was not to seize any freeman's property without paying for it, nor jail any freeman without trial. In other words, the Magna Carta declared that all free Englishmen had rights— whether they were nobles or not!

King John signing the first Magna Carta at Runnymede on June 15, 1215.

Naturally, John hated having limits on his power. The slippery king had hardly finished reading the Magna Carta when he started looking for ways to get around it!

It wasn't long before the king and his barons were fighting again. Their next war, the **First Barons' War**, was a low point in English history. For the first time ever, England almost fell to a King of France! About half the barons in England swore loyalty to Philip II's son: Prince Louis Capet, the future King Louis VIII. To some barons, even a future King of France seemed better than their wicked King John!

The First Barons' War (1215 - 1217)

What saved England from the King of France was an unexpected death that almost no one mourned. While fighting rebel barons in the east, John caught a bad case of dysentery— in other words, diarrhea. The sickness tore through his body, making him weaker and weaker. He died in October 1216, leaving his son to take his place. The next king from the House of Plantagenet was a nine-year-old called **Henry III**.

According to legend, the last journey of King John cost England a set of priceless crown jewels. Since John's men weren't used to eastern England, they didn't know the dangers of crossing a piece of coastland called the Wash. The Wash was a strange place that was dry at low tide, but flooded with rushing currents at high tide.

The Wash was dry when John's men set out to cross it. Before they finished, though, the tide poured in— drowning John's men, and burying the crown jewels in a thick layer of mud. Even today, some treasure hunters still search the Wash for the lost crown jewels of King John.

Christian Heroes of the High Middle Ages

The High Middle Ages were a high point for the Church of Rome. As we read in Chapter 12, the popes called kings from all over Europe to fight in their crusades. With that much power, almost no one dared disagree with a pope. One who did dare was a priest from southeastern France called **Peter de Bruis**.

Peter was one of the first Christians to draw a sharp line between Scripture and **Church tradition**. Scripture, of course, means the Word of God. Church tradition, on the other hand, means something that Christians learn from the generations of Christians who came before them.

Peter de Bruis
(? – 1131?)

A **Church tradition** is a belief or practice that Christians learn from the generations that came before them, instead of learning directly from the Bible.

Peter believed that when Church tradition disagrees with Scripture, Christians should always follow Scripture. Why? Because Scripture comes from holy God; while Church tradition might come from sinful man.

The more Peter thought about it, the more he believed that certain Church traditions were just the opposite of what Scripture said. For example:

➢ Peter didn't agree with infant baptism. The Church baptized children as infants; but Peter only baptized believers who were old enough to understand why they were being baptized.

➢ Peter didn't agree with an idea called transubstantiation. The Church taught that when a priest led Holy Communion, the bread and wine changed into the body and blood of Jesus Christ. But to Peter, transubstantiation seemed to honor priests more than it honored Christ.

➢ Peter didn't agree with praying for the dead. He believed that God would judge people for their own deeds, not for the prayers of others.

Unfortunately, Peter also taught his followers to burn crosses. In Peter's eyes, the cross was a symbol of Christ's torture and death— not of His resurrection. This explains why Peter burned crosses: not because he didn't honor Christ, but because he thought crosses made poor symbols of Christ.

Of all the things Peter taught, the Church hated cross-burning most. According to legend, a mob of angry Christians killed Peter de Bruis by throwing him into one of his own bonfires.

Another medieval Christian who dared disagree with the pope was a rich Frenchman called **Peter Waldo**. Peter was quite happy being rich, until he learned this story from Mark 10:17-23:

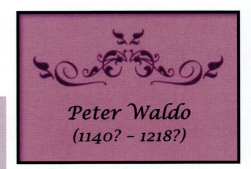

Peter Waldo
(1140? – 1218?)

> "As Jesus started on his way, a man ran up to him and fell on his knees before him. 'Good teacher,' he asked, 'what must I do to inherit eternal life?' … [Jesus said] 'Go, sell everything you have and give to the poor, and you will have treasure in heaven. Then come, follow me.' At this the man's face fell. He went away sad, because he had great wealth. Jesus looked around and said to his disciples, 'How hard it is for the rich to enter the kingdom of God!'"

Unlike the rich young man in the Gospel of Mark, Peter really did give away his whole fortune to benefit the poor. The faithful Peter Waldo went on to preach the gospel for the rest of his life.

Because the Bible had brought Peter to Christ, Peter liked to preach straight from the Bible. Unfortunately, the only Western Bible of Peter's day was the Vulgate— the Latin Bible we covered in Chapter 3. Peter wanted a Bible that his French listeners could understand. The answer, he decided, was to translate the whole New Testament into French— even though the Church of Rome said he couldn't.

Translating the Bible wasn't the only thing Peter Waldo did without Church permission. Like Peter de Bruis, Peter Waldo believed that certain Church traditions went against Scripture. He didn't believe in praying to the saints. Nor did he believe in <u>purgatory</u>— the afterworld where Christians were supposed to be <u>purged</u> of sin. What Peter Waldo did believe was that all Christians should be allowed to preach, not just priests.

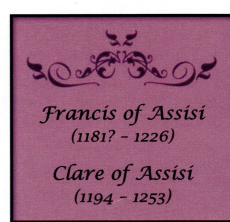

Francis of Assisi
(1181? – 1226)

Clare of Assisi
(1194 – 1253)

When Peter asked the pope about his beliefs, the pope condemned him as a heretic. Many of Peter's followers, the **Waldensians**, were burned to death for believing what Peter taught— instead of believing what the pope taught.

One medieval Christian who didn't disagree with the pope was **Francis of Assisi**. Francis was a rich young man who gave up his riches because he couldn't stand to watch the poor suffer. More than any other Christian saint, Francis is remembered as a tenderhearted servant of the poor. So are Francis' followers: an order of servant monks called the Franciscans.

Clare of Assisi was a devoted Christian girl who fell in love with Francis' beautiful preaching. Clare longed to serve the poor as Francis did; but her parents wanted her to get married like other girls. Defying her parents, Clare ran away from home and tried to join the Franciscans!

Most monks probably would have sent Clare home, but not Francis. Instead, Francis found a home for Clare in a nearby nunnery. Clare of Assisi went on to start the Order of Poor Ladies— an order of nuns that followed the Franciscans, serving wherever the monks did.

Francis of Assisi

CHAPTER 14:

The Black Death; the Hundred Years' War

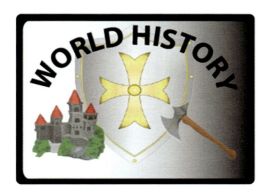

The First English Parliaments

In Chapter 13, we read how angry English barons forced King John to sign the **Magna Carta** in 1215. For the first time, an official document declared that the English people had rights— and that the king must always respect those rights.

The Magna Carta was the first pull in a long, hard tug-of-war between king and people. The kings pulled for more power; while the people pulled for more rights. Sometimes the kings won, and sometimes the people did.

We also read how King John tried to get around the Magna Carta. He had hardly finished signing it when he attacked his barons— starting a long, hard fight called the First Barons' War. When the war broke out, many English barons went looking for a new king— deciding that John would never give them their rights.

The Palace of Westminster in London, where the modern-day Parliament meets

The King of France was happy to help! The very next year, the Crown Prince of France landed in England. His name was Louis Capet; and he was the son of King John's old enemy, King Philip II of France. By mid-year, about half of all English barons had sworn loyalty to Prince Louis Capet. For a while there, it looked like all England might soon be following the King of France!

All that changed in October, when King John died of dysentery. The next King of England was John's son, a nine-year-old called Henry III. Now that John was out of the way, the barons took a fresh look at their choices. On the one hand stood a full-grown French prince; while on the other stood a half-grown English king. After a bit of thought, the barons all abandoned Prince Louis Capet— deciding that an English boy would be easier for them to control than an adult foreigner.

ꤞꤞꤞꤞꤞꤞꤞꤞꤞꤞꤞꤞꤞꤞꤞꤞꤞꤞꤞꤞꤞꤞꤞꤞꤞꤞ

The half-grown King Henry III didn't mind the Magna Carta. But when Henry grew up, he found that he didn't like the Magna Carta any more than his father had liked it.

In a king's eyes, the worst thing about the Magna Carta was that he couldn't raise taxes without permission from his barons. Like his father before him, Henry wasn't satisfied with the lands he had. He wanted to do the same thing his father had done: to use tax money raised in England to fight for more lands overseas.

More Kings from the Royal House of Plantagenet

5. King Henry III
(Reigned 1216 – 1272)

6. King Edward I
(Reigned 1272 – 1307)

7. King Edward II
(Reigned 1307 – 1327)

8. King Edward III
(Reigned 1327 – 1377)

9. King Richard II
(Reigned 1377 – 1399)

ROYAL SEAL OF KING HENRY III OF ENGLAND

*O*nce again, the king's nobles stepped in to stop him. Henry was past fifty years old in 1258, when a group of nobles met at Oxford, England to set more limits on his power. This meeting is called the Oxford Parliament; and it was one of the first English **parliaments**.

> *Parliament* comes from the Old French word *parler*, meaning "to speak."
>
> In modern times, **Parliament** is the legislature of the United Kingdom. This is the part of the government that writes law, just as Congress writes law for the United States.

The Oxford Parliament insisted that the King of England could not simply do whatever he pleased. From now on, he would have to listen to two groups of nobles: a small group called the Privy Council, and a bigger group called Parliament. This new Parliament was to meet three times each year. Nobles would come from all over England to talk about how king and council were running their country.

*L*ike the signing of the Magna Carta, the creation of Parliament was a step toward protecting the rights of all Englishmen. The goal of Parliament was the same as the goal of the Magna Carta: to stop the king from becoming a tyrant. Before making any big decisions, the king would have to listen to people from all over his country.

> Like many European kings, King Henry III hated Jews. In keeping with a decree from the pope, Henry III commanded all English Jews over the age of seven to wear yellow badges over their hearts. These Jewish badges were shaped like the two tablets of the Ten Commandments, which Moses brought down from Mount Sinai in Exodus 32:15.

At first, only nobles were invited to Parliament. Very soon, though, some commoners were invited too. In time, Parliament gave all free Englishmen a chance to take part in their government.

England under the Edwards

*T*he next king of England was one of the mightiest ever— and one of the cruelest, in the eyes of the Scots. King Edward I, son of Henry III, is mostly remembered for two things: conquering Wales, and almost conquering Scotland.

Wales, of course, is one of the three countries on Great Britain. It stands on the west side of the big island, north of Bristol Channel. Before Edward I, Wales was ruled by a Welsh prince. In 1282, though, Edward conquered the last Welsh prince— a man called Llewellyn the Last. To strengthen his hold on Wales, Edward built an **iron ring** of strong castles there.

*S*tarting then, the King of England was also the lord of Wales. Since the time of King Edward I, almost every heir to the throne of England has been titled "Prince of Wales."

*T*he story of Scotland is quite different from the story of Wales. The Scots were determined to keep their independence, no matter how hard Edward tried to take it away!

The trouble in Scotland started with a death in the Scottish royal family. In 1290, the last king from the royal **House of**

Caernarvon Castle, part of King Edward I's "iron ring" around Wales

Dunkeld died— leaving no clear heir to the throne. Naturally, Scottish nobles argued about which of them should take his place.

With its nobles all at each other's throats, Scotland was headed toward a nasty civil war. The Scots could think of only one way to stop that war. They wanted a higher noble to choose between them— someone all Scottish nobles would respect and obey.

The higher noble the Scots wanted was King Edward I of England. In 1292, the nobles invited Edward to come to Scotland and decide which of them would be its next king.

To understand what happened next, we must first go back to the rules of the feudal system. As we read in Chapter 10, feudal law started with the oath of fealty— a solemn vow in which vassals promised to obey their lords. To break the oath of fealty was one of the worst crimes a vassal could commit.

When Edward came to Scotland, the first thing he did was to demand the oath of fealty from all Scottish nobles. Why? Because in swearing the oath, they swore to obey Edward— which meant accepting Edward's decision about who would be king. After receiving the oath from every noble who would swear it, Edward chose one of them: a baron called John Balliol.

King Edward I of England

The royal **House of Dunkeld** was a dynasty that ruled Scotland from 1034 - 1290 (with a short break). Macbeth, the Scottish king made famous by the Shakespeare play, came from the House of Dunkeld.

Those oaths of fealty changed everything. Although John Balliol might call himself King of Scotland, he was only a junior king in Edward's eyes. Since John had sworn the oath of fealty to Edward, the real King of Scotland was Edward himself!

A few years later, Edward decided to test his new authority over Scotland. It so happened that Edward needed more troops for a war in France. To get them, he ordered the Scots to send him an army.

Naturally, the Scots balked. If the King of England could command Scotland's armies, then Scotland was really just a part of England— and not an independent country at all!

The Scots took a bold step to protect their independence. Instead of sending an army to fight the French, Scotland joined an **alliance** with France. In other words, the Scots promised to help protect France, and the French promised to help protect Scotland. This was the start of a long friendship between Scotland and France called the **Auld Alliance**.

THE THISTLE OF SCOTLAND

An **alliance** is a bargain in which friendly countries agree to help defend each other.

The **Auld Alliance** was a long alliance between Scotland and France against England.

Now came Edward's turn to balk. In swearing oaths to the French, the Scots broke the oaths of fealty they had sworn to Edward. To punish their oath-breaking, Edward changed his plans. Instead of attacking France that year, Edward attacked Scotland— starting the **First War of Scottish Independence**.

Edward's attack was fierce and terrible, capturing several Scottish cities in just a few months. One of those cities was the capital of Scotland: lovely **Edinburgh**.

With the fall of Edinburgh, Scotland became an **occupied** country. The English army ruled Scotland under martial law, the law of war. Edward's men showed no mercy to the Scots. They robbed them, beat them and even killed them— sometimes for no reason at all.

> To be **occupied** is to be controlled by foreign troops.

The cruelty of the English explains why a Scottish noble called **William Wallace** hated them so much. According to legend, the English murdered the girl Wallace planned to marry— a lovely lass called Marion Braidfute. Starting then, Wallace wanted nothing more than to drive the English out of Scotland forever.

> **William Wallace (1273? – 1305)**

William Wallace made a fierce enemy for the English. For one thing, he was uncommonly tall, strong and smart. For another, he was a born leader with new ideas about how to beat the English. He got off to a great start in September 1297, when he tackled a big English army at the **Battle of Stirling Bridge**.

The key to the Battle of Stirling Bridge may have been the bridge itself. According to one version of the story, the wooden bridge collapsed halfway through the battle— leaving half the English army on one side of the river, and half on the other. With half the English cut off, Wallace easily beat the other half!

All that was before Edward came. When Edward heard about the Battle of Stirling Bridge, he decided to go to Scotland and tackle Wallace himself. The next year, Edward crushed Wallace's army at the terrible **Battle of Falkirk**.

Scene from the Battle of Stirling Bridge

The Stone of Scone and King Edward's Chair

The Bible tells how Jacob laid his head on a certain stone one night, and saw angels climbing between heaven and earth (Genesis 28). When Jacob awoke, he named that spot Bethel— Hebrew for "House of God."

The Scots believed that Jacob's Pillow somehow made its way to Scotland, where it became the coronation seat for Scotland's kings. For centuries, every new King of Scotland sat on this special stone when he received his crown. They called it the **Stone of Scone**, a.k.a. the Stone of Destiny.

After conquering the Scots, Edward I wanted to show them that he was now the rightful King of Scotland. The way to do it, he decided, was to steal the Stone of Scone!

Back in England, Edward built a coronation seat of his own. It was called **King Edward's Chair**, and it had a special slot under its seat for the Stone of Scone. Starting then, anyone who sat on the coronation seat of England was also sitting on the coronation seat of Scotland!

King Edward's Chair in Westminster Abbey, London, with its slot beneath the seat for the Stone of Scone

Wallace disappeared for a while after that. He may have gone to France, trying to get more help from the French. Wherever he went, he was back in Scotland by 1304— the year he was captured and dragged off to England for trial.

When Wallace heard what the English were accusing him of, he could hardly believe his ears. They kept calling him a traitor, saying that he had broken his oath of fealty to Edward. Wallace scoffed at the very idea, saying: "I cannot be a traitor, for I owe [Edward] no allegiance. He is not my sovereign; he never received my [oath of fealty]; and whilst life is in this persecuted body, he never shall receive it."

William Wallace on trial for his life

Of course, Edward's court didn't see it that way. At trial's end, the great hero of Scottish independence was put to death in the most horrible way imaginable.

Fortunately for Scotland, Edward didn't live forever; and the next King of England, Edward II, wasn't as mighty as his father. By 1328, King Robert the Bruce had won back Scotland's independence.

The third Edward was another mighty one. King Edward III of England was the fighting king who started the Hundred Years' War— with help from his son, a famous knight called Edward the Black Prince.

The Hundred Years' War was a long struggle for the throne of France. Despite its name, it lasted well over a hundred years— all the way from 1337 – 1453. For all that time, the King England was trying hard to become King of France too!

Like the trouble in Scotland, the trouble in France started with a death in the royal family. For centuries, all kings of France had come from a royal family called the House of Capet. This was the house of King Philip II and his son, Prince Louis Capet— the same Philip and Louis who almost took England from King John (Chapter 13).

By now, though, the House of Capet was dying out. The year 1328 brought the death of its last royal: King Charles IV of France. Since Charles IV had no sons, there could be no more kings from the House of Capet.

On the other hand, Charles IV did have a sister; and that sister had a son. Charles' sister Isabella Capet had been married to an English royal: King Edward

King Edward III with his son Edward the Black Prince

II, who had just died in 1327. Isabella's son was Edward Plantagenet, who had just become King Edward III. In other words, the King of England was also the nephew of the King of France!

What an irresistible opportunity that was. When the old King of France died, leaving no sons to take his place, Edward III decided that his uncle's throne should pass to him!

Naturally, the French decided otherwise. Instead of choosing Edward as their next king, the French chose one of Charles IV's cousins: Philip Valois, who now became **King Philip VI of France**. Philip was the first king from France's next royal house, the **House of Valois**.

A few years later, Edward III demanded the throne of France— saying that he, not Philip VI, was the rightful king. The Hundred Years' War had begun.

The English did well at first. After a big win at the Battle of Crecy, fought in 1346, Edward III took back part of Normandy— the important duchy that King John lost in the early 1200s.

Then came a major interruption. The Hundred Years' War was just getting started when Europeans suffered through one of the worst natural disasters ever: the **Black Death**.

The Black Death

The Black Death was probably an **epidemic** of a very **contagious**, very deadly disease called **bubonic plague**. The name comes from **buboes**— ugly swellings that appear on victims' skin. Besides buboes, plague victims also suffered high fevers, trouble breathing and a terrible cough— among other symptoms even worse.

> An **epidemic** is a widespread disease.
>
> **Contagious** means "easy to catch."

Before the days of antibiotic medicines, doctors had no good way to treat plague. About half of all plague victims died within two to seven days!

The plague spread through grain supplies. The germs that caused plague lived inside fleas, which lived in the coats of rats and mice.

Medieval cities had big problems with rats and mice. The barns and silos where they stored their grain supplies were full of them. Each time a flea-bitten rat took a bite of grain, it left behind plague germs. After that, catching the plague was easy: all one had to do was carry home a sack of flour!

The Black Death started in the 1330s, somewhere in far-off China. From there, it inched along the Silk Road between East and West— until 1346, when it reached the Crimean Peninsula.

The Crimean Peninsula is the northern gateway to the Black Sea, which connects to the Mediterranean Sea. From wharves along the Black Sea, rats scurried up the ratlines of trade ships headed for the Mediterranean. Without knowing it, traders carried these rats to ports all around the Mediterranean. Along with the rats came their plague-infested fleas.

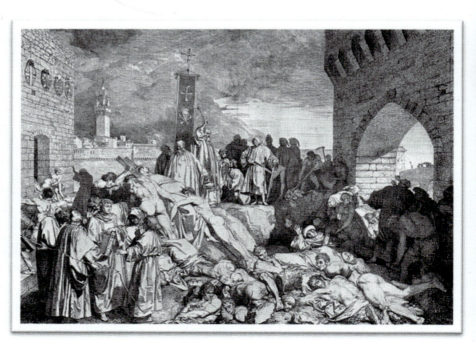

Churchmen ministering to Italian victims of the Black Death in 1348

The Black Death hit France in 1347, ten years into the Hundred Years' War. England's worst year was 1348. Both countries suffered indescribable catastrophes, losing millions of people in just a couple of years.

From France and England, the Black Death spread on to the rest of Europe. The dying didn't stop until 1351, when the plague finally ran its course. By that time, somewhere between one-third and six-tenths of all Europeans who had been alive in 1346 were dead!

Some victims of the Black Death died because their governments tried to stop the plague without knowing what caused it. For example:

➤ Some governments killed every stray dog and cat they could find, believing that stray animals spread plague. Alas, killing strays only made the plague worse. Why? Because strays killed rats, which were the real villains of the Black Death. Without dogs and cats to kill them, rats multiplied even faster.

➤ Some governments tried to stop the plague by burning houses, or even whole villages, where plague had struck. Alas, these fires killed some of the very people they were trying to protect. Uninfected families often locked themselves inside their homes, trying to avoid the plague— only to be burned out by their own governments.

The Black Death didn't strike Jews as hard as it struck Christians— perhaps because the Jews kept themselves separate from the rest of the world. When Christians noticed this, they accused Jews of causing the Black Death! Some Christians insisted that Jews must be secretly poisoning Christian wells.

Sad to say, many medieval cities beat, tortured and even killed Jews for the terrible crime of well-poisoning— even though they had no proof that Jews were poisoning wells.

The **plague doctor's costume** was a special suit that some doctors wore when they examined plague victims. Each feature of this cunning suit was designed to ward off plague:

➤ The beak-like mask was filled with sweet-smelling herbs. By filtering their breath through these masks, plague doctors hoped to block out **miasmas**— the foul airs that they believed to be the cause of plague.

➤ The heavy overcoat, scarf, gloves and boots covered every square inch of the plague doctor's body. All were coated with thick layers of wax or oil to help infection slide off.

➤ The long stick allowed plague doctors to examine plague victims without touching them.

This plague doctor's costume was made for a later epidemic than the Black Death

About fifty years after the Black Death, and about midway through the Hundred Years' War, came an important change in England's royal family.

The Royal House of Lancaster

When the mighty King Edward III started to grow old, he laid down the law about who would take his place. His oldest son, Edward the Black Prince, was first in line. After the Black Prince came the Black Prince's son: little Richard, born in 1367.

Alas, the Black Prince died in 1376— a year before his father. Even so, England stuck to the old king's plan. When Edward III died in 1377, his 10-year-old grandson took his place— becoming King Richard II.

Some Englishmen found this unfair. Why? Because the Black Prince wasn't the only son of Edward III. When Edward III died, his son John, Duke of Lancaster was still alive. When a dying king left behind a living son, his throne usually went to that son. If Edward III had followed that rule, then John of Lancaster would have been king. Instead, Edward III left his throne to a grandson.

If John of Lancaster didn't mind not being king, then his son certainly did. In 1399, John's son Henry, Duke of Lancaster invaded England, fought off the king's armies and captured the king!

After a bit of arm-twisting, Parliament agreed to make Henry king. Henry, Duke of Lancaster became King Henry IV— the first king from the new royal House of Lancaster. As for Richard II, he disappeared into some dark dungeon— where he probably died hungry and alone.

〰〰〰〰〰〰〰〰〰〰〰〰〰〰〰〰〰〰〰〰〰〰〰〰〰〰〰〰

Around the same time, France discovered a serious problem of its own— namely, that the King of France was a madman!

There is good reason why King Charles VI is also called Charles the Mad. Charles wasn't just a little bit touched in the head. Sometimes, he was completely out of his mind. One day in 1392, Charles was happily riding along— when out of nowhere, he drew his sword and started slashing at his own knights! From that day forward, no one knew when Charles might fly into a fit. There were days when he couldn't even remember his own name!

Without a sane king to hold it together, France split in two.

> Northern France went to a group called the Burgundians. Their leader was the Duke of Burgundy, a cousin to Charles the Mad.

> Southern France went to a group called the Armagnacs. Their leader was Dauphin Charles, Charles the Mad's oldest son.

> ### Kings from the Royal House of Lancaster
> **1. King Henry IV**
> (Reigned 1399 - 1413)
> **2. King Henry V**
> (Reigned 1413 - 1422)

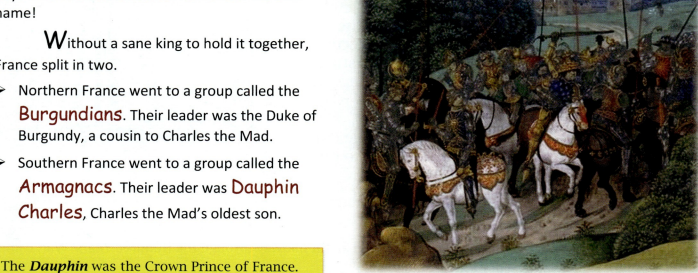

Charles the Mad attacking his own knights

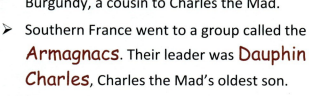
The **Dauphin** was the Crown Prince of France.

This big split meant big trouble for the French. They were already fighting the Hundred Years' War against England. Now they were fighting a civil war too!

The next King of England, **Henry V**, took advantage of France's trouble. It happened at one of the biggest battles of the whole Hundred Years' War: the famous **Battle of Agincourt**, fought in 1415.

The trouble started in August of that year, when Henry led an English army into northern France. He was hoping to take back more of Normandy, the big duchy lost by King John.

Alas, the campaign in Normandy took longer than Henry expected. After a couple of months, Henry retreated northward— back toward the part of Normandy that Edward III had taken back. But before Henry could escape, a French army slipped between him and his goal. Worse yet, that army was about six times the size of the English one— which meant that Henry would be fighting for his life!

King Henry V fighting the Battle of Agincourt

The first two keys to the Battle of Agincourt were weather and the battlefield. The fighting started on the morning after a night of heavy rain, on a field that had just been plowed. When the French knights charged onto this field, it turned to thick, sticky mud. Weighed down by their heavy plate armor, the poor French knights could hardly move— let alone fight!

The other key to the Battle of Agincourt was a powerful weapon called the **English longbow**. With the French stuck in the mud, English archers poured deadly arrows into them— killing them by the thousands. Against all odds, Henry V wound up winning the Battle of Agincourt!

With that, Henry V was well on his way toward winning the Hundred Years' War. Instead of fighting Henry V, the Burgundians joined forces with him. With Henry's help, the Burgundians drove the Armagnacs out of Paris and captured Charles the Mad! The Dauphin retreated southward, making his new capital at a place called **Chinon**.

Meanwhile, Henry forced Charles the Mad to sign an agreement called the **Treaty of Troyes**. If the French followed this treaty, then the Dauphin would never be King of France. For the treaty said that Henry V was the rightful heir of Charles the Mad— not the Dauphin!

Once the Treaty of Troyes was signed, all Henry had to do was wait for Charles the Mad to die. When he did, Henry would be King of France as well as King of England— which was the whole point of the Hundred Years' War!

The **English longbow** was the deadliest weapon of the Hundred Years' War. King Edward III had ordered all able-bodied Englishmen to practice with the longbow in their spare time. By the days of King Henry V, England had many skilled longbow archers— not only nobles, but also commoners.

It took a lot of strength to be a longbow archer. Some English longbows had a pull force of two hundred pounds! With that much force behind it, an iron arrowhead called a **bodkin** could pierce any armor of the day— even the heavy plate armor of the 1400s.

Bodkin-point arrowhead

The best wood for longbows came from a flexible tree called the yew. The English used up so many yew trees that they had to start buying them from overseas!

Alas for Henry, things didn't work out that way. A couple of years later, Henry was leading another campaign in France when he suddenly took sick. To the surprise of all, the great king died in 1422— even though he was only thirty-five years old.

Henry V left behind just one legitimate son: an 8-month-old called Henry, who now became **King Henry VI of England**. Just two months later, Charles the Mad died as well!

Now all was chaos. Following the Treaty of Troyes, the English claimed the throne of France for their boy King Henry VI. The Dauphin claimed the throne too. And so the Hundred Years' War dragged on— with Henry VI king in the north, the Dauphin king in the south, and no one king of all France! This was the sticky situation when a French peasant girl called **Joan of Arc** came on the scene.

Joan of Arc

Joan was a devoted Christian from Domremy, a little village in northeastern France. She was about ten years old in 1422, when both Henry V and Charles the Mad died.

A couple of years later, Joan started seeing visions about the Hundred Years' War and the throne of France. In Joan's mind, there was no doubt that her visions came from God. God was telling Joan that the Dauphin was the rightful King of France, and no one else! From now on, the Hundred Years' War would be a holy war for France.

Some of Joan's visions told her secrets about the war— military details that no mere peasant girl should have known. When Joan was sixteen years old, she shared some of these details with a knight's squire— who shared them with his knight. When the details turned out to be true, the knight wondered if Joan might be a prophet.

The knight took Joan to Chinon, where the Dauphin himself put her to the test. Like most peasants, Joan had never laid eyes on the Dauphin. The Dauphin's test was to remove his royal robes and blend in with everyone else— to see if Joan was prophet enough to recognize him. When Joan did, the Dauphin started to believe in her too.

Joan of Arc (1412 – 1431)

After a few more tests, the Dauphin decided to try Joan out. First he gave her a horse, a suit of armor and a banner. Then he sent her off to war, hoping she could do something about the **Siege of Orleans**.

Orleans was a fortress that guarded an important bridge over the Loire River. At the moment, Orleans was also the key to the Hundred Years' War! For the Loire River was the border between the Dauphin and his enemies, the English and the Burgundians. If his enemies took Orleans, then they took the Loire River. And if they took the Loire, then the Dauphin was in serious trouble.

Joan of Arc raising the Siege of Orleans

When Joan of Arc set out for Orleans, the Burgundians had almost surrounded it. They had also seized the *Tourelles*— a strong gatehouse that guarded the far side of the bridge. With the *Tourelles* in enemy hands, there was no way Orleans could stand for long.

Everything turned around when Joan of Arc came. For the peasant Joan breathed more life into the French people than the royal Dauphin ever had. When she paraded through the streets of Orleans, shouting that God was on France's side, every peasant in France wanted to join her. With help from Joan's peasants, the Dauphin's armies soon took back the *Tourelles* and raised the Siege of Orleans!

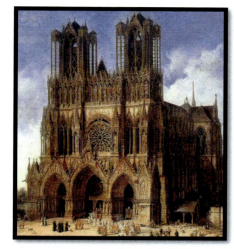

Reims Cathedral

Joan's next target was an important city called **Reims**, which stood about 80 miles northeast of Paris. The most important thing about Reims was its cathedral. For hundreds of years now, every new King of France had gone to **Reims Cathedral** to receive his crown. This was why Joan wanted Reims: so that the Dauphin could receive his crown there too. Driven by her visions, Joan insisted on taking Reims— even though it lay well inside enemy territory.

Reims soon fell to Joan, just like Orleans. Joan saw her fondest prayer answered the very next day. On July 16, 1429, the Dauphin received his crown at Reims Cathedral— becoming **King Charles VII of France**.

How unexpected it all was. In the end, it was no splendid fighting king who won the Hundred Years War for France. Instead, it was a peasant girl called Joan of Arc!

In light of everything Joan did for France, the rest of her story is sickening. One day in May 1430, the Burgundians took Joan prisoner. They would have been happy to send her home, if her king had paid them a ransom. But for some reason, Joan's beloved king wouldn't pay. So instead, the Burgundians sold Joan to their English allies. The moment the English got their hands on Joan, they put her on trial— accusing her of crimes against God and Church.

A **show trial** is a fake trial that is supposed to make a court look fair, when it really isn't.

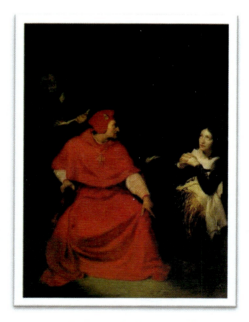

A cardinal questioning Joan of Arc in her prison cell

Like many trials in medieval times, Joan's was a **show trial**. Although the Church pretended to give Joan a fair trial, the court made its decision before it even started. Vengeful English priests called Joan a heretic for saying that her visions came from God. They also condemned her for going against God and nature; for Joan had worn battle armor, which they said was for men alone.

Even now, the King of France probably could have helped Joan if he'd wanted to. Instead, he let his great helper go. Abandoned by all, Joan of Arc suffered the awful death set aside for heretics: she was tied to a stake and burned alive.

The game of **tennis** probably started in French monasteries, where bored monks played handball against monastery walls.

The strange words used in scoring tennis probably also come from French. For example, "love"— the tennis word for zero score— may come from the French word *l'oeuf,* or "goose egg."

Seasons and Tropics

What causes the seasons of the year to change— to go from spring to summer, fall, winter and then back to spring again? The answer is the tilt of Earth's axis!

Once each year, the northern end of Earth's axis leans directly toward the sun, and the southern end directly away from the sun. This is the **summer solstice** of the Northern Hemisphere, which always falls around June 21. This solstice is the start of summer in the Northern Hemisphere, and winter in the Southern Hemisphere.

Six months later, the southern end of Earth's axis leans directly toward the sun, and the northern end directly away from the sun. This is the **winter solstice** of the Northern Hemisphere, which always falls around December 21. This solstice is the start of winter in the Northern Hemisphere, and summer in the Southern.

Earth's **axis** is the axle on which Earth rotates. It is an imaginary line that runs through the globe from North Pole to South Pole.

The tilt of Earth's axis also marks out five important lines of latitude:

1. The **equator** is the line of 0° latitude. Twice each year, the sun stands directly overhead at the equator. The first time is the **spring equinox**, which comes midway between the winter and summer solstices— always around March 20. The second time is the **fall equinox**, which comes midway between the summer and winter solstices— always around September 23.

2. The **Tropic of Cancer** is the line of 23-1/2 degrees north latitude. The sun stands directly over the Tropic of Cancer once each year, at the summer solstice of the Northern Hemisphere.

3. The **Tropic of Capricorn** is the line of 23-1/2 degrees south latitude. The sun stands directly over the Tropic of Capricorn once each year, at the summer solstice of the Southern Hemisphere.

4. The **Arctic Circle** is the line of 66-1/2 degrees north latitude. For part of each summer, the sun never sets north of the Arctic Circle— for Earth's rotation never carries that part of the globe out of the light. And for part of each winter, the sun never rises north of the Arctic Circle— for Earth's rotation never carries that part of the globe into the light.

5. The **Antarctic Circle** is the line of 66-1/2 degrees south latitude. The Antarctic Circle is the southern equivalent of the Arctic Circle in the north.

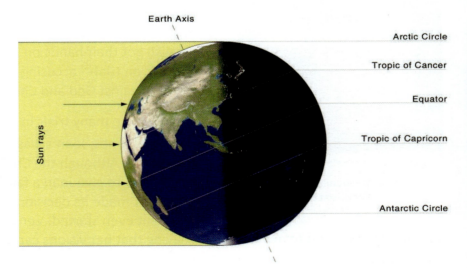

The summer solstice of the Northern Hemisphere, when the sun stands directly over the Tropic of Cancer. Notice how the whole Arctic Circle is always in the light, no matter how Earth rotates.

The End of the Hundred Years' War

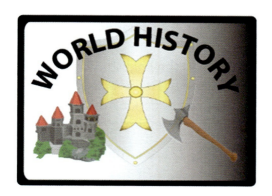

Through faith, Joan of Arc did something no mere peasant girl should have been able to do: She turned the Hundred Years' War around. Before Joan came along, it looked like **Dauphin** Charles might never be king. With Joan's help, her beloved Dauphin received his crown at Reims Cathedral in 1429— becoming King Charles VII of France.

Alas, the Hundred Years' War wasn't over; for Charles wasn't the only King of France. The King of England claimed the same title!

How could a King of England claim to be King of France? The answer goes back to the Treaty of Troyes, which we covered in Chapter 14. This important treaty said that when King **Charles the Mad** of France died, King **Henry V** of England would inherit the throne of France.

What we didn't cover is that the Treaty of Troyes was also a marriage contract. To seal the treaty, Charles the Mad had to give Henry his daughter: Princess Catherine of Valois. Henry and Catherine were married in 1420, the same year the treaty was signed. A year later, the royal couple had a little boy called Henry. As the son of Catherine of Valois, little Henry was also the grandson of Charles the Mad— a fact that would become most important later.

Little Henry was less than a year old when his father died. As his father's only heir, he now became King Henry VI of England. A few months later, Charles the Mad died too. Thanks to the Treaty of Troyes, little Henry was now King of France too!

> The **Dauphin** was the Crown Prince of France.
>
> **Charles the Mad** was King Charles VI of France— father to the Dauphin, who became King Charles VII.
>
> **Henry V** was the great English fighting king who won the Battle of Agincourt in 1415.

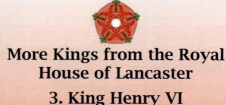

More Kings from the Royal House of Lancaster

3. King Henry VI
(Reigned 1422 - 1461, 1470 - 1471)

𝌆𝌆𝌆𝌆𝌆𝌆𝌆𝌆𝌆𝌆𝌆

Since Henry was still a baby when his father died, older men ran his kingdoms for him. The man in charge of France was his uncle John, Duke of Bedford. It was Bedford and his allies who took on Joan of Arc at Orleans and Reims, and lost (Chapter 14).

Henry was still barely a teenager in 1435, when Bedford died. The new man in charge of France was another relative: Henry's cousin Richard, Duke of York.

The boy King Henry VI with his two coats of arms: the arms of England, three lions on a field of red; and the arms of France, three *fleurs-de-lis* on a field of blue

When Henry finally grew up, he and Richard started arguing about what to do in France. Like Henry V before him, Richard wanted to go right on fighting for France— no matter what it cost. But Henry VI wasn't like his fighting father. He started trading away his French lands, as though the Hundred Years' War were already lost.

The more lands Henry VI traded away, the angrier Richard grew. He couldn't forget all the Englishmen who had given their lives for those lands— including Henry's own father, Henry V. In Richard's eyes, the fact that Henry wouldn't fight for France meant that he wasn't fit to be King of England. What England needed, Richard thought, was another brave fighting king— someone like himself!

This was the setup for some of the longest, ugliest wars in English history: the **Wars of the Roses**. The "roses" were the badges of the two rivals who fought these wars. One was the **House of York**, which was named for Richard of York. The other was the **House of Lancaster**, which was named for the family of King Henry VI.

The Wars of the Roses

The more Richard thought about it, the more certain he was that he deserved to be king— not Henry. Why? Because Richard was descended from the second son of King Edward III: Lionel, Duke of Clarence. As for Henry, he was descended from the third son of Edward III: John, Duke of Lancaster (Chapter 14). Since Richard was descended from the older son, his claim to the throne was stronger than Henry's— in a way.

On the other hand, no one from Richard's branch of the family had ever been king. Meanwhile, Henry's branch had three kings: Henry IV, Henry V and Henry VI. In this way, Henry's claim was stronger. In the end, though, it didn't matter which branch of the family had the stronger claim. It only mattered which was stronger on the battlefield!

The trouble started in 1451, when Richard of York came to Parliament with an unusual request. It so happened that Henry VI and his wife, **Queen Margaret**, had no sons yet— which meant no heirs to the throne. Richard proposed an interesting solution to this problem: He wanted Parliament to make him the official heir to Henry VI!

Naturally, Queen Margaret was furious. For Margaret was still young, and still hoped to have sons someday. To her, it looked like Richard was trying to steal the throne from her sons— which made him a traitor.

The year 1453 brought three key events. The first was that after 116 years, the Hundred Years' War finally ended! After losing a big battle that year, Henry VI had almost nothing left in France.

The second key event was that Henry VI lost his mind! Just as Charles the Mad went mad, so his grandson Henry VI went mad. It seems likely that Charles the Mad handed down his madness to Henry VI. Fortunately, Henry's madness wasn't violent like Charles the Mad's. Instead of slashing at people, Henry just lost his senses. Even so, the king was in no shape to run his country!

The name "**Wars of the Roses**" came from the badges of the two rival houses. The House of Lancaster's badge was the Red Rose of Lancaster; while the House of York's was the White Rose of York.

Richard, Duke of York (1411 – 1460)

Coat of Arms of Richard of York

The third key event was that Queen Margaret gave birth to a son: **Edward of Westminster, Prince of Wales**. Now that Henry VI had a son, Richard of York would never be heir— unless something happened to Edward of Westminster.

With the king gone mad, and his son too young to take his place, England needed a **Lord Protector of the Realm** to run its government. The question was, who should be Lord Protector?

Naturally, Richard of York wanted to be Lord Protector. But Richard was the last person Queen Margaret wanted! Margaret feared that if Richard took charge, then her son might never inherit the throne.

> A **Lord Protector of the Realm** was a lot like a **regent**. Both were trusted officers who managed the government for kings who were too young, or too sick, to manage on their own.

Just as the madness of Charles the Mad split France in two, so the madness of Henry VI split England in two. Those who stood with Richard of York were called **Yorkists**, after the House of York. Those who stood with Queen Margaret were called **Lancastrians**, after the House of Lancaster. The longer this split went on, the more Yorkists and Lancastrians hated each other.

Besides Richard of York, the most powerful Yorkist was the **Earl of Warwick**. With help from the wealthy Warwick, Richard convinced Parliament to make him Lord Protector in March 1454. This was the first link in a crazy chain of events:

➢ On Christmas Day 1454, King Henry VI suddenly came to his senses! With a sane husband back on her side, Queen Margaret soon drove Richard out of office.

➢ Now came Richard's turn to be afraid. With Henry and Margaret back in power, Richard feared that Parliament might declare him a traitor. If that happened, then any Englishman could kill Richard on sight! Rather than face that danger unprepared, Richard raised an army to defend himself.

➢ The following May, Henry VI raised an army to tackle Richard's army. Since Richard hadn't been declared a traitor yet, the king expected Richard to back down without a fight— as a loyal subject should. But Richard thought that if he backed down, then the Lancastrians might take him prisoner— or even put him to death.

Edward of Westminster, son of King Henry VI and Queen Margaret

➢ When neither side backed down, Richard and Henry fought the first battle of the Wars of the Roses: the **First Battle of St. Albans**, which happened in May 1455.

Richard's fighting experience served him well that day. In that short battle, Richard crushed Henry's army and captured Henry himself! The stress of battle made Henry lose his mind again— which made Richard Lord Protector again.

For the next few years, the government went from Yorkist to Lancastrian and back again. Whenever the king went mad, Richard was Lord Protector. Whenever the king came to his senses, Queen Margaret pushed Richard out. With every change, the hatred between Yorkists and Lancastrians grew a little bit stronger.

Henry VI King of England

Queen Margaret grew tired of all these changes. During one of the king's sane times, Margaret finally convinced Parliament to declare Richard of York a traitor!

Once again, Henry VI led an army against the Yorkists. Once again, the Yorkists beat Henry, captured him and hauled him back to London. Only this time, Richard demanded the prize he had been wanting for years: the throne of England! For the first time, Richard asked Parliament to get rid of the mad King Henry VI, and name Richard king in his place.

This was when Parliament showed how fickle it could be. Just a short time ago, Parliament had declared Richard a traitor. But now, Parliament decided to give Richard part of what he wanted. Instead of naming Richard king, Parliament did what Richard had asked back in 1451: It made him the official heir to King Henry VI.

At this, Queen Margaret exploded! This was exactly what Margaret had feared all along: that Richard would come between her son and the throne. Desperate to save her son, Queen Margaret ran away to the north— where she raised the biggest Lancastrian army yet.

This was the start of a deadly chapter in the Wars of the Roses. Before now, both sides had tried to claim the throne legally— through Parliament. Now came an all-out death struggle— with the winner taking the throne by force, and the loser going to his grave.

ꙦꙦꙦꙦꙦꙦꙦꙦꙦꙦꙦꙦꙦꙦꙦꙦꙦꙦꙦꙦꙦꙦꙦꙦꙦꙦꙦꙦꙦꙦꙦꙦ

Queen Margaret of England, a.k.a. Margaret of Anjou (1430 – 1482)

In late 1460, Richard went north to tackle Margaret's big army. Alas, Richard had no idea just how big Margaret's army was. Margaret may have hired as many as 18,000 troops— about four times Richard's numbers!

Faced with that many troops, Richard should have holed up inside his castle and waited for help to arrive. But he didn't. Instead, Richard bravely rode out to the **Battle of Wakefield**— which he soon lost.

At battle's end, the Lancastrians offered to spare Richard's life if he surrendered. But Richard refused; for he knew what would come next. Since Margaret had declared him a traitor, he felt sure that he would die a traitor's death if he surrendered. He preferred the honorable death of a soldier— which is exactly what his enemies gave him.

One way to remember the colors of the rainbow is to memorize this short description of the Battle of Wakefield: "**R**ichard **o**f **Y**ork **g**ave **b**attle **i**n **v**ain." The colors of the rainbow are **r**ed, **o**range, **y**ellow, **g**reen, **b**lue, **i**ndigo and **v**iolet.

The Battle of Wakefield (December 30, 1460)

After the Battle of Wakefield, Queen Margaret showed what a merciless enemy she could be. Instead of burying Richard's remains with honor, Margaret ordered his head cut off and set out on a spike. To top off this gruesome sight, Margaret set a paper crown on Richard's head. In her mind, a cheap paper crown was the only kind of crown Richard deserved!

If Margaret had known what was coming, then she might have shown more mercy. For the army she had just beaten wasn't the only Yorkist army. There was another one to the south, led by two great commanders. One was Richard's powerful friend, the Earl of Warwick. The other was Richard's oldest son: **Edward of York**.

With his father out of the picture, Edward was the new head of the House of York. To defend that house, Edward and Warwick marched off to fight one of the bloodiest battles in all English history: the **Battle of Towton**.

The Battle of Towton was the ultimate death struggle for the throne of England. It all started with a dramatic gesture. Just before the battle, Warwick drew his sword and killed his own horse! He wanted to show his horseless foot soldiers that he would never run away, no matter what happened. Warwick meant to either win the Battle of Towton or die trying!

The Battle of Towton (March 29, 1461)

The key to the Battle of Towton was the weather. It so happened that the battle fell on a windy, snowy day. It also happened that the wind blew away from the Yorkists, and toward the Lancastrians— which meant that Yorkist arrows flew farther than Lancastrian ones. Slowed by the wind, Lancastrian arrows never even reached Yorkist lines. Meanwhile, Yorkist arrows pierced many Lancastrians!

The Earl of Warwick killing his own horse just before the all-important Battle of Towton

When the snow-blind Lancastrians finally realized what was happening, they stopped shooting and charged. What followed was one of the ugliest scenes the world has ever witnessed. The hatred between Yorkist and Lancastrian was so bitter that no one asked for mercy, nor gave it. Thousands of fighters fell— so many that time and again, the living had to drag off the dead to make room for more fighting. Even when the beaten Lancastrians broke and ran, the Yorkists still didn't stop killing them.

Kings from the Royal House of York

1. King Edward IV
(Reigned 1461 - 1470, 1471 - 1483)

2. King Edward V
(Reigned 1483, one of the young Princes in the Tower)

2. King Richard III
(Reigned 1483 - 1485)

After losing the Battle of Towton, Queen Margaret and her son fled overseas. As for the winner, Edward of York, he became the first king from the House of York: **King Edward IV of England**.

The new king was not quite nineteen years old— almost full-grown, but still too young to run a kingdom without advice. Most of Edward's advice came from the noble who fought so hard for him at the Battle of Towton: the Earl of Warwick. Edward might never have been king without Warwick— which is why people called him **Warwick the Kingmaker**.

The first thing Warwick wanted to do was to arrange a good marriage for Edward. Unfortunately, Warwick and Edward had different ideas about what made a good marriage! Edward wanted a woman he could love; but Warwick couldn't have cared less about love. What Warwick wanted was a foreign princess— someone who could give Edward new lands and new allies overseas.

What Warwick didn't know was that he was wasting his time. Unknown to just about everyone, Edward had already fallen in love with an English beauty called **Elizabeth Woodville**. Even worse, he had already married her!

Ordinarily, a royal wedding would have been a grand affair, followed by an even grander coronation for the new queen. But Edward knew how disappointed Warwick would be with his choice of brides. Feeling guilty about it all, Edward kept his wedding secret— even from his top adviser. Imagine how uncomfortable Edward must have felt when he finally broke the bad news to Warwick!

To Warwick, the worst part of Edward's marriage wasn't the queen herself— no, it was the queen's family. Before the wedding, the Woodvilles had been minor nobles who had nothing to do with running the government. But after the wedding, Elizabeth's father became Edward's closest adviser— closer than Warwick himself. What a lousy way to treat the "Kingmaker," the man who had set him on his throne!

Elizabeth Woodville (1437? – 1492)

By 1470, Warwick had had enough of the Woodvilles. Abandoning Edward, Warwick joined forces with a most unlikely ally: his old enemy Margaret, wife of Henry VI! Nine years after the Battle of Towton, Margaret and her son were still waiting overseas— still hoping to take back what they'd lost. With Warwick's help, they got their chance. In late 1470, Warwick led Margaret's army in an attack on Edward IV.

The attack caught Edward by completely by surprise. The stunned king had to flee his own country, lest he be captured or killed. With Edward out of the picture for now, Warwick set the mad King Henry VI back on his throne!

But not for long. Less than six months after he fled, Edward IV made a comeback. His first big win came at the **Battle of Barnet**, fought in April 1471. Edward not only crushed Warwick's army, but also killed his old friend Warwick. As for old Henry VI, he went from the throne of England to a cell in the Tower of London.

Not long after the Battle of Barnet, poor old Henry VI was dead! Just how the king died, no one knows for sure; but most people suspect that the House of York had something to do with it!

Scene from the Battle of Barnet (April 14, 1471)

The month after the Battle of Barnet brought another big win for Edward: the **Battle of Tewkesbury**. Edward not only crushed Margaret's army, but also killed her son Edward of Westminster— who was just 17 years old.

After Tewkesbury, it looked like the House of York had won the Wars of the Roses! With Henry VI and Edward of Westminster both dead, both with no living sons, there could be no more kings from the House of Lancaster. King Edward IV was free and clear.

Scene from the Battle of Tewkesbury

ꕤꕤꕤꕤꕤꕤꕤꕤꕤꕤꕤꕤꕤꕤꕤꕤꕤꕤꕤꕤꕤꕤꕤꕤꕤꕤꕤꕤꕤꕤ

One of the saddest stories from the Wars of the Roses started in 1483, the year Edward IV died. The forty-year-old king left behind two sons: Edward, Prince of Wales and Richard, Duke of York. Edward was twelve years old when his father died, and Richard nine. Both were grandsons to the old Richard of York— the one who died at the Battle of Wakefield (above).

The new Richard of York lived in London with his mother, Elizabeth Woodville. As for Prince Edward, he lived in Wales with his mother's brother: Anthony Woodville.

The moment his father died, Prince Edward became **King Edward V of England**. When the big news of his father's death made it to Wales, the young king set out for London to receive his crown. At his side rode his uncle and guardian, Anthony Woodville.

Somewhere along the road to London, another uncle showed up. This uncle was called **Richard of Gloucester**; and he was a trusted brother to Edward IV— the one brother who had stood by him through thick and thin.

> One reason Edward IV trusted Richard of Gloucester so much was because he distrusted another brother: **George, Duke of Clarence**. Gloucester stayed loyal to Edward all through the Wars of the Roses. Clarence, on the other hand, switched back and forth— fighting first for Edward, then Warwick, then Edward again. In Shakespeare's *Henry VI*, the great playwright calls George, Duke of Clarence a "quicksand of deceit."

Now that Edward IV was gone, Gloucester had been named Lord Protector of the Realm. This was why he had come to meet Edward, he said. As Lord Protector, Gloucester wanted to take Edward to London himself— instead of letting Anthony Woodville take him.

The first sign that something was wrong came the following morning, when Gloucester arrested Anthony Woodville. Although Edward didn't know it yet, he would never see Woodville again!

For now, though, everything else seemed alright. Gloucester took Edward on to London, where he introduced him as King Edward V. As far as most people knew, Gloucester meant Edward no harm.

Richard of Gloucester, a.k.a.
King Richard III of England

Edward's mother knew better. When Elizabeth Woodville heard what Gloucester was doing, she rushed Richard of York to her favorite church: Westminster Abbey. Why? Because she knew that as long as Richard was alive, it would do Gloucester no good to kill Edward. For if he did, then the throne would pass to Richard— not to Gloucester. If Richard was safe, then Edward was safe. And Elizabeth trusted the Church to keep Richard safe.

Sad to say, Elizabeth misplaced her trust. For Gloucester was terribly clever, especially when he was talking to priests. Just what Gloucester said to the priests of Westminster Abbey, no one now knows. There may be many ways to explain what happened. But what seems to have happened is that Gloucester talked the priests into handing over Richard of York! Now Gloucester had both of his brother's sons, which meant that both were doomed.

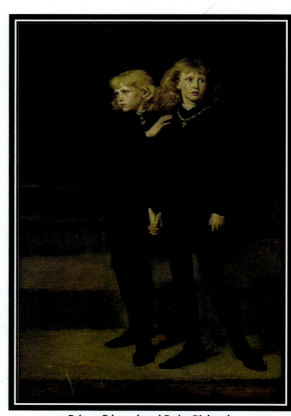

Even now, most people still didn't know what was coming. Gloucester seemed to be doing what any good Lord Protector would do: keeping the precious brothers safe. For safety's sake, Gloucester kept them in the safest fort he had. This just happened to be the **Tower of London**— the same Tower where poor old Henry VI had died!

It was only later that Gloucester's true plan came to light. And once again, it all started with a priest.

A couple of months later, a priest came out with a big announcement. He said that just before Edward IV died, the old king had confessed certain sins to him. Deathbed confessions were supposed to be secret, of course. But this one told news that the whole kingdom needed to hear!

What Edward IV confessed was that before he married Elizabeth Woodville, he had promised himself to another woman. Under Church law, this meant that Edward never should have married Elizabeth! If the Church had known, then it never would have approved Edward's marriage. In other words, Edward's marriage to Elizabeth was unlawful— which meant that his children had been born into an unlawful marriage. As unlawful children, they had no right to the throne of England!

In those days, most people thought that no priest of God would ever lie about something as sacred as the deathbed confession of a king. Three days after the priest made his announcement, a noble council took Edward off the throne, and put Gloucester in his place. All Gloucester's scheming had finally paid off. Instead of the Duke of Gloucester, he now became **King Richard III of England**!

After that, people saw less and less of the two young **Princes in the Tower**. In time, they saw nothing at all! Just what happened to the boys, no one knows for sure— just as no one knows what happened to Henry VI. But most people think the Princes in the Tower were murdered— either by Richard III himself, or on his orders.

Prince Edward and Duke Richard, the two frightened Princes in the Tower

It was partly because of the Princes in the Tower that the Wars of the Roses started up again. After the poor princes disappeared, people stopped trusting Richard III. When the Lancastrians noticed this, they looked around for someone to take Richard's place. The someone they found was called **Henry Tudor**.

When one remembers how the Wars of the Roses got started, it seems strange that Henry Tudor should try to claim the throne. One of the arguments between Yorkists and Lancastrians was about which house had the strongest claim to the throne. Yet Henry Tudor's claim wasn't strong at all!

On his father's side, Henry Tudor wasn't the son of a king, or even the grandson of a king. Instead, he was the grandson of a king's wife: Catherine of Valois, whom we met above. After Henry V died, Catherine married a Welsh soldier called Owen Tudor. Catherine and Owen had a boy called Edmund Tudor, who became the father of Henry Tudor.

Henry was only a little more royal on the side of his mother: Margaret Beaufort. Margaret was a great-granddaughter to John of Lancaster, the third son of King Edward III (above). Unfortunately, John of Lancaster hadn't married Margaret's great-grandmother until after their children were born. Because of this, an old law said that no one from Margaret's family could ever claim the throne.

But now the Lancastrians didn't care about that old law. After 30 years of bloody war, Henry Tudor was the closest thing to royalty the House of Lancaster had left. If Henry couldn't be King of England, then no Lancastrian could. They wanted him to kill Richard III and seize the throne!

Henry Tudor and his army sailed from Normandy in August 1485. They soon landed in Wales, where Henry's father and grandfather lived. Richard III led an army out to meet them. The two armies clashed at the last big battle of the Wars of the Roses: the famous **Battle of Bosworth Field**.

The key to the Battle of Bosworth was a rich noble called Thomas Stanley. Stanley was married to Henry's mother, Margaret Beaufort— which made him Henry's step-father. Knowing this, Richard thought there was a good chance that Stanley might take Henry's side. Richard couldn't let that happen, if he could help it. To keep it from happening, Richard took one of Stanley's sons hostage before the battle— threatening to kill him if Stanley took Henry's side!

For his son's sake, Stanley didn't take either side at first. He held his army out of the battle, leaving both sides guessing about what he might do.

In the middle of the battle, Richard noticed Henry riding toward Stanley with only a few bodyguards to protect him. At this, Richard charged straight at his rival— hoping to strike him down in man-to-man combat!

Alas for Richard, Stanley chose this moment to join the fight. As Richard charged past on his way toward Henry, Stanley's army swept down to attack him from behind. The last Yorkist king went down, shouting with his dying breaths: "Treason! Treason!"

Lord Stanley handing the crown of Richard III to King Henry VII after the Battle of Bosworth (August 22, 1485)

After killing Richard, Stanley picked up his crown and gave it to Henry Tudor. Right there on the battlefield, Henry Tudor became King Henry VII of England— the first king from the new royal House of Tudor.

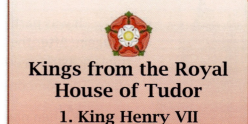
Henry's first job as king was to let everyone know that the long, horrible Wars of the Roses were finally over. One of the ways he did that was by marrying Elizabeth of York. Princess Elizabeth had been a daughter to Edward IV, and a sister to Edward V. Since Elizabeth came from the House of York, and Henry from the House of Lancaster, their marriage brought the two royal houses together. Hopefully, this meant the end of the awful wars between them!

After King Henry VII took over, he wanted special troops to guard the Tower of London. The answer was an elite army unit with two names. Its formal name was the **Yeoman Warders**; but most people called it the **Beefeaters**. This funny nickname may have meant that as the king's favorites, the Beefeaters ate juicy beef from the king's own table. In a time when few Englishmen could afford beef, this would have been a special treat!

As another sign that the Wars of the Roses were finally over, King Henry VII designed a special badge for the new House of Tudor. The **Tudor Rose** combined the badges of the two houses that had fought each other for so long: the Red Rose of Lancaster and the White Rose of York.

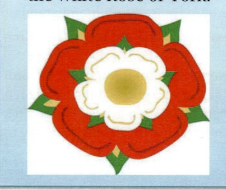

The Divine Comedy

The Divine Comedy is a long poem that describes the afterworld— in other words, the place where people go when they die. An Italian Christian called Dante Alighieri wrote *The Divine Comedy* over the years from 1308 – 1321. Since then, readers have never ceased to marvel at the images Dante created.

Dante divided *The Divine Comedy* into three parts: one for hell, one for purgatory and one for heaven. The best-known part is the Inferno, which describes hell as Dante imagined it.

Dante's hell is divided into nine circles for nine different kinds of sinners. He writes that without Christ, everyone on Earth is doomed to go to one of those nine circles. The worse the sinner, the lower the circle of hell.

Dante's first circle, Limbo, isn't for punishing sinners. Instead, Limbo is for good people who would have gone to heaven, if not for one thing: they were never baptized. Without baptism, Dante writes, even the most innocent people who ever lived can never get to heaven. The saddest sights in Limbo are the countless innocent babies who died before they could be baptized.

The ninth circle of hell is for the worst sinners of all: traitors. The devil Lucifer is there, frozen waist-deep in ice. Dante's Lucifer is a three-headed monster with three sets of jaws, each gnawing one of the worst traitors of all time. The center set gnaws Judas Iscariot, the traitor who betrayed Jesus with a kiss!

Antarctica

Antarctica is the continent where people go to find the South Pole— but only if they don't mind the cold! The South Pole is far colder than the North Pole. The North Pole lies in the Arctic Ocean, which is connected to all the other oceans— making it a bit warmer. But the South Pole lies in vast Antarctica, where there is no ocean to warm it. Thermometers on Antarctica have recorded temperatures as low as −130° Fahrenheit— more than 160° below freezing!

To reach Antarctica, ships must pass through the treacherous Southern Ocean. Glaciers and sea ice can crush any ship that isn't strong enough. The trip is so dangerous that the first explorers didn't set foot on Antarctica until 1821.

A **gargoyle** is a statue attached to the outside of a building. Early gargoyles usually looked like real animals, especially lions. Some later gargoyles, though, looked like demons from hell! Even church buildings had demonic-looking gargoyles, to remind sinners how truly terrible hell would be.

A true gargoyle is also a waterspout. Its job is to carry rainwater away from a building's foundation, usually by pouring it out of its mouth. The words "gargoyle" and "gargle" both come from the Old French word *gargouille*, meaning "throat."

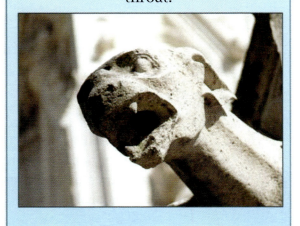

If the sea journey to Antarctica was dangerous, then the land journey to the South Pole was even worse. No one made it until ninety years later, when a Norwegian called Roald Amundsen set out across the frozen continent. Amundsen used lessons he learned years before, when he lived among the Inuit people of northern Canada. He wore fur clothes instead of wool, and rode dogsleds instead of horses or tractors. The great explorer planted the Flag of Norway at the South Pole on December 14, 1911.

Roald Amundsen and crew after planting their flag at the South Pole

The Land of the Hindus

India is the biggest country in South Asia, and one of the biggest in the world. In modern times, only six countries on Earth have more land than India: Russia, Canada, China, the United States, Brazil and Australia. And only one country has more people: China.

India used to have even more land than it does today. Until 1948, India was everything east of **Iran**, southeast of **Afghanistan** and south of **China** and **Nepal**. This whole area was called British India, and was part of the great British Empire.

This went on until 1948, when India declared independence from Britain. In that same year, India split into two parts for two big religions:

➢ The Hindu part became the **Republic of India**, or simply India.

➢ The Muslim part became **Pakistan**.

At first, Pakistan was also split into two parts: **West Pakistan** and **East Pakistan**. Then in 1971, East Pakistan won independence from West Pakistan. East Pakistan became **Bangladesh**; while West Pakistan became simply **Pakistan**.

Along the northern border of India stands a huge mountain range called the Himalayas. Nine of the ten tallest mountain peaks in the world stand in the Himalayas. The tallest of all is Mount Everest, which rises 29,029 feet above sea level!

Just south of the Himalayas lies a fertile land called the <u>Indo-Gangetic Plain</u>. This complicated name comes from the two most important rivers in India: the <u>Indus River</u> in the west, and the <u>Ganges River</u> in the east. The Ganges is so holy to so many Indians that it has a goddess to represent it: a life-giving female called Ganga.

Southern India is surrounded by huge bodies of water. The **Arabian Sea** lies to the west; the **Indian Ocean** to the south; and the **Bay of Bengal** to the east. The big island off the southern tip of India is **Sri Lanka**.

Flag of India

The capital of India is **New Delhi**.

The Indo-Gangetic Plain in purple, just south of the Himalayas

Hindus, Jains and Buddhists

The names "Indus" and "India" both come from the oldest religion in India: **Hinduism**. "India" means "Land of the Hindus." The Hindu faith is so important to India that it is hard to talk about India without talking about Hinduism.

The first thing to know about Hinduism is that Hindus are not born equal. Instead, they are born into levels called **castes**. There are four main castes, or *varnas*:

➢ The highest caste is the Brahmins— priests and teachers of the Hindu faith.

➢ Below the Brahmins stand the Ksatriyas— warriors and government officials.

➢ Below the Ksatriyas stand the Vaisyas— farmers, businessmen and skilled tradesmen.

➢ The lowest caste is the Sudras— unskilled laborers who serve the higher castes.

The people of each caste stick together, with the higher castes shunning the lower ones. Even in modern times, most Hindus never change castes, nor marry someone from a different caste.

Some Hindus are considered too lowly for any caste, even the Sudras. These are the **untouchables**, who are also called out-castes or *dalits*. Untouchables handle jobs that the higher castes won't touch— unclean jobs like sweeping streets and scrubbing toilets. Some untouchables work only at night, when no one can see them— so that upper-caste Hindus don't have to look at them!

The oldest Hindu holy book is a set of hymns called the **Rig Veda**. These hymns are written in **Sanskrit**, the language of ancient India. *Rig* is Sanskrit for "praise," and *veda* for "knowledge." In other words, the Rig Veda is a set of praise hymns filled with knowledge about the Hindu world and its gods. But it is only one of many Hindu holy books. There are many kinds of Hinduism, each with its own favorite scriptures.

Hinduism is a religion of cycles— chains of events that repeat themselves over and over. One well-known cycle is acted out by a set of gods called the **Hindu trinity**. First comes **Brahma**, the creator god who builds a new world. Second comes **Vishnu**, the preserver god who keeps that world going for a time. Third comes **Shiva**, the destroyer god who tears that world down— so that Brahma can start all over again.

Another example of a Hindu cycle is **reincarnation**, a.k.a. *samsara*. Hindus believe that every soul has always been alive, and always will be. Although bodies die, souls never do. They are simply reborn into new bodies.

Reincarnation is the only way most Hindus can ever rise above the lower castes. If a Hindu does well in one life, then he may move up to a higher caste in the next.

From left to right: Brahma the creator, Shiva the destroyer and Vishnu the preserver

The path to the higher castes lies through something called **karma**. Basically, karma is the sum of good and bad deeds one does in life. If the good outweigh the bad, then a Hindu may be reborn into a higher caste. Religious duties like meditation, prayer, and temple worship help build good karma. So do special rituals like washing in Hinduism's holiest river, the Ganges.

But the highest goal of a Hindu is not to step up to the highest caste. No, the highest goal is to rise above all castes— into something called **nirvana**.

The Hindu nirvana starts with *moksha*, which means the end of reincarnation. Hindus work toward stepping out of the endless cycle of life, death and rebirth. In rising above all that, they reach nirvana— a state of perfect peace and rest.

Nirvana is also the goal of India's second oldest religion: **Jainism**. But the Jain nirvana is different than the Hindu nirvana. Instead of breaking free from the cycle of life, Jains try to break free from the material world.

Jainism

Jains believe that the love of possessions is the root of all evil. Possessions lead to greed, which leads to theft, violence and other sins.

To avoid those sins, all Jains live by five strict vows called *mahavrata*. One vow is that they will never grow attached to material possessions. In keeping with this vow, Jains do what Christian monks like Anthony of Thebes did: they become **ascetics**. In other words, Jains own very little, eat very little and sleep very little.

Jains are also strict vegetarians. Why? Because eating meat means killing animals; and another of the five Jain vows is never to kill.

Around 500 BC, an Indian prince tried both Hinduism and Jainism— and found that neither was enough. His name was **Siddhartha Gautama**, a.k.a. **Gautama Buddha**.

Siddhartha's father was a rich king who tried to shield his precious son from the outside world. He didn't want Siddhartha to be troubled by unpleasant things like sickness, old age and death. To guard against all that, the king built three fine palaces for Siddhartha— and never let him go anywhere else! Safely tucked inside his palaces, Siddhartha had no idea that most people weren't as fortunate as he was. He thought that everyone went through life without suffering, just like him.

"Chutes and Ladders" is based on an old Indian board game called Snakes and Ladders. The Snakes and Ladders game board teaches lessons about Hinduism. The top of the board stands for **nirvana**, a state of perfect peace and rest. The ladders stand for good karma, which carries Hindus up toward nirvana. The snakes represent bad karma, which carries Hindus down away from nirvana.

An **ascetic** is someone who denies himself material things so that he can focus on spiritual things.

All that changed when Siddhartha grew up, and took his first trip outside his palaces. The suffering he saw outside horrified him! From that day forward, Siddhartha's goal in life was to find some answer to the terrible problem of suffering.

At first, Siddhartha tried the same answers that other people had already tried. Like the Hindus, Siddhartha tried meditating and doing good deeds— trying to build good karma. And like the Jains, Siddhartha became an ascetic. He cast off the riches of his princely boyhood, and made himself poor. At times, Siddhartha ate so little that he almost died!

Alas, neither Hinduism nor Jainism had the answers to Siddhartha's deepest questions. Desperate for something better, Siddhartha sat down under a tree to meditate— vowing never to rise until he learned what he needed to know.

Siddhartha Gautama deep in meditation

After forty-nine days of meditation, Siddhartha finally had an inspiration. The answer was not to be always working toward a higher caste, like the Hindus did. Nor was the answer to deny oneself everything, like the Jains did. The true answer must be a middle way between these two extremes.

With this discovery, Siddhartha Gautama became the first **Buddha**— the first **enlightened one**. Buddhists honor Siddhartha as the holy man who finally found the answer to the problem of suffering.

Buddha means "enlightened one."

Part of Siddhartha's answer lies in his **Four Noble Truths:**

➤ **Noble Truth #1:** Life is suffering.

➤ **Noble Truth #2:** Suffering starts with the desire for worldly pleasures.

➤ **Noble Truth #3:** To stop suffering, one must free oneself from desire.

➤ **Noble Truth #4:** The Noble Eightfold Path laid out by the Buddha leads to the end of desire, and therefore the end of suffering.

The eight-spoked Dharma Wheel, a symbol of the Noble Eightfold Path

The **Noble Eightfold Path** is a way of thinking, living and acting toward others. The eight steps along the path are: right view; right intention; right speech; right action; right livelihood; right effort; right mindfulness; and right concentration. Those who follow the Noble Eightfold Path are on their way to becoming enlightened buddhas, just like Siddhartha did.

Empires of Ancient and Medieval India

For most of its history, India was divided into many kingdoms. Only a few empires ever ruled more than a small part of all that is now India.

The first Indian empires all started in the north. The oldest was the Harappan civilization, which grew up in the Indus River Valley. The Harappans kept growing until around 1750 BC, when they mysteriously disappeared— as we read in Year One.

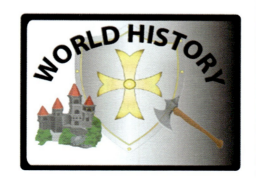

The next great Indian empire came almost 1,500 years later. Around 350 BC, a Hindu leader called **Mahapadma Nanda** built the vast **Nanda Empire**. It stretched across northern India, from the Ganges River Valley in the east almost to the Indus River Valley in the west.

The Nanda Empire lasted until 321 BC, when it was conquered by **Chandragupta Maurya**— the first emperor from the **Maurya Empire**. The Mauryas were the first to bring northern and southern India together. Chandragupta came along just after another great conqueror: a Greek-speaker called Alexander the Great (Year One).

The Maurya emperors suffered from something that didn't seem to bother most emperors: guilt. The only way to build an empire that big was to fight horrible battles that left thousands of people dead. Looking out over the battlefield, Chandragupta couldn't help feeling guilty about all the innocent lives he was destroying.

Chandragupta grew so desperate to ease his guilt that he finally changed religions— switching from Hinduism to Jainism. No one took the five vows of Jainism more seriously than Chandragupta did. After ruling one of the richest empires in the world, he now owned almost nothing. In fact, he gave up so many possessions that he wound up starving himself to death!

Chandragupta's grandson, an emperor called **Asoka**, felt just as guilty. But Asoka followed a different path. After fighting a bloody war of his own, Asoka converted to peaceful Buddhism. He spent the rest of his life spreading Buddhist ideas— not only in India, but also in Southeast Asia, China and Japan.

Buddhist missionaries setting up a lion-topped Pillar of Asoka, one of many pillars that helped spread Asoka's Buddhism

Hundreds of years passed before the next empire arose. The **Gupta Empire** started in the 300s, and ended in the 500s— which makes it the first Indian empire to last into medieval times.

The Gupta age was a Golden Age of India. The Gupta **maharajas** brought both prosperity and peace— which meant that Indians could finally stop thinking of war, and start thinking of higher things. One of those things was art. The **Ajanta Caves**, which we cover below, are the best example of great Indian art from the Golden Age of the Gupta Empire.

> **Maharaja** is Sanskrit for "great king."

The Guptas were also the first great Indian scientists and mathematicians. Unlike Greek scientists, Gupta scientists understood that Earth revolves around the sun— not the other way around! The Guptas also created the **Hindu-Arabic numeral system**: 0, 1, 2, 3, 4, 5, 6, 7, 8 and 9. If you don't think these numerals are handy, then just try multiplying Roman numerals!

If the Gupta Empire had survived, then who knows what other discoveries its scientists might have made? Unfortunately, the Guptas faced a terrible enemy: deadly raiders called the Huns (Chapter 6). Just as the Huns threatened the Romans, so too the Huns threatened the Guptas. Although the Huns never conquered the Gupta Empire, they weakened it so badly so that it finally collapsed. With that, India splintered into pieces again.

> **The Gupta Empire (About 320 - 550)**

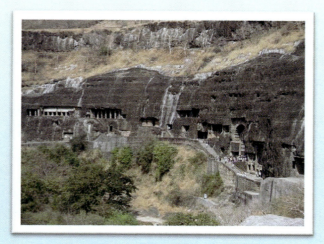

The Ajanta Caves cut into their mountainside

The **Ajanta Caves** are a set of twenty-nine manmade caves cut into a mountainside in west central India. These caves were once a great Buddhist monastery. They had everything a monk might need, from worship halls to meeting halls, offices, guest rooms, kitchens, dining rooms and bedrooms. Buddhist monks spent centuries carving them out, probably between about 200 and 600 AD.

The most stunning thing about the Ajanta Caves is all their artwork. Some walls and ceilings are carved with giant statues of the Buddha. Others are painted with giant murals that tell stories from the Buddha's life. The amount of time and care it took to craft twenty-nine such beautiful caves is almost unimaginable!

For a long time, though, there was no one to see all that art. Over the centuries, Buddhism faded out of India— forcing the monks to find new homes elsewhere. Without monks to care for the caves, the jungle grew up around them, and they were lost. They stood empty for hundreds of years, all their great art forgotten.

This went on until 1819, when an officer of the British East India was out hunting for tigers— and happened to stumble upon the Ajanta Caves! Since then, they have become the biggest tourist attraction in their part of India.

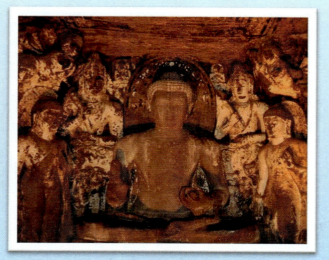

The Buddha and his bodhisattvas. A bodhisattva is an enlightened spirit who helps others reach enlightenment.

The next Indian empire was neither Hindu, Jain nor Buddhist. Instead, it was Muslim! Even though there were far more Hindu Indians than Muslim ones, Muslims ruled most of India for more than 650 years— all the way from 1206 through 1857.

Islam spread into India from the west, through Afghanistan and Persia (Iran). The first Muslim rulers of India came from Turkestan, the ancient home of the Turkish people.

In Chapter 12, we read how the Turks converted to Islam in the 900s. Just as Turkish Muslims conquered Asia Minor to their west, so they conquered India to their southeast. The Turkish sultans of India ruled from the city of Delhi, which is why their empire is called the Delhi Sultanate.

India wasn't like Turkestan, Persia or Afghanistan. In those countries, almost everyone converted to Islam— forgetting all about his old religion. But the Hindu religion was so important to so many Indians that it could never be forgotten. Even after Muslim invaders took over their country, most Indians refused to convert to Islam. They were determined to stay Hindu, no matter how much it cost them.

The Delhi Sultanate
(1206 - 1526)

The strange situation of Muslim sultans ruling a Hindu people caused a lot of trouble. As a good Muslim, the Sultan of India was supposed to stamp out all other religions. But he couldn't stamp out Hinduism; for every time he tore down a Hindu temple, Hindus rebelled. On the other hand, Muslims rebelled if the sultan didn't tear down Hindu temples— which meant that he was in trouble either way.

Rebellions weren't the Delhi sultans' only troubles. They were also troubled by two terrible invaders: Genghis Khan and Tamerlane.

Genghis Khan came from Mongolia, just north of China. In the early 1200s, Genghis set out to conquer the whole world— and almost succeeded! The mighty **Mongol Empire** threatened India many times, but never quite conquered it. See Chapter 19 for more on Genghis Khan and the Mongol Empire.

Tamerlane threatened India almost two hundred years after Genghis Khan did. This deadly menace came from **Samarkand**, a city in what is now Uzbekistan.

Tamerlane had two reasons for trying to conquer the world. First, he was a descendant of the world-conquering Genghis Khan— which meant that he wanted to rule the Mongol Empire. Second, he was a Muslim. Like many Muslim leaders of his day, Tamerlane did his best to stamp out all other religions.

This second reason was the excuse Tamerlane gave in 1398, when he led his army into India— heading for the capital, Delhi. Since the Delhi Sultanate was already Muslim, India didn't need another Muslim conqueror. But Tamerlane said that the Delhi Sultanate couldn't really be Muslim— for if it was, then why were most Indians still Hindu?

Tamerlane, a.k.a. Timur

What Tamerlane did at Delhi shows what a deadly menace he was. On his way to Delhi, Tamerlane crushed several small armies that tried to stop him. By the time he reached the city, he had taken about 100,000 Hindu prisoners.

Ordinarily, Tamerlane would have kept all these prisoners— so that he could sell them into slavery later. But with a big battle ahead of him, Tamerlane didn't want to keep his prisoners— for fear they might break free and join the other side. To save himself the trouble, Tamerlane ordered all 100,000 prisoners put to death!

The key to the battle that followed was elephants. To start the **Battle of Delhi**, the Sultan of Delhi sent 120 armored war elephants against Tamerlane. What a fearsome sight that must have made, to see that many elephants charging across the battlefield!

The Battle of Delhi (December 17, 1398)

War elephants at the Battle of Delhi

Alas for the sultan, Tamerlane knew the elephants' biggest weakness: fear of fire. He sent a crowd of camels charging toward the elephants, their backs piled high with burning wood and straw. The fires sent the terrified elephants thundering away, leaving Tamerlane to win the Battle of Delhi.

What happened next proved why Tamerlane really invaded India: not because he loved Islam, but because he loved money. After the Battle of Delhi, Tamerlane and his troops carried off a fortune in gems, gold, silver and slaves!

The Battle of Delhi might have been the end of the Delhi Sultanate, if not for what came next. When Tamerlane left India, he assigned a Muslim governor to run the country for him. Six years later, Tamerlane was on his way to conquer China when he suddenly died. Maybe the governor of India shed a few tears for Tamerlane, but probably not. Either way, the governor took over the country— becoming the next sultan of the Delhi Sultanate.

֍֍֍֍֍֍֍֍֍֍֍֍֍֍֍֍֍֍֍֍֍֍֍֍֍֍֍֍֍֍֍

The next Muslim conqueror came along more than 100 years later. His name was **Babur**; and he was a great-great-great-grandson of Tamerlane. Just as Tamerlane wanted to rule the empire of Genghis Khan, so Babur wanted to rule the empire of Tamerlane.

Babur started out fighting for the capital of Tamerlane's empire: Samarkand. When he couldn't take that, Babur switched to another country that Tamerlane had once ruled: India. The fight for India came in April 1526, when Babur tackled the Sultan of Delhi at the **First Battle of Panipat**.

The Sultan of Delhi thought he was ready for Babur. He brought tens of thousands of troops to Panipat, backed by at least 100 war elephants. Babur brought far fewer troops, and few if any war elephants.

> **Panipat** was a village about 60 miles north of Delhi.

However, Babur brought one advantage that the sultan couldn't match: **gunpowder**. Babur was the first general in India to use muskets and cannon in battle. Against terrifying new weapons like that, the sultan and his war elephants never had a chance.

That was the end for the Delhi Sultanate. In winning the First Battle of Panipat, Babur became the first emperor of a new Muslim empire in India: the **Moghul Empire**.

> **Moghul** is another version of the word "Mongol."

Matchlock Muskets

The matchlock musket was an early type of musket that first appeared around 1440. To use a matchlock, the musketeer first loaded his barrel with gunpowder and ball. He then poured a bit of gunpowder into the flash pan— a small pan attached to the outside of the barrel. A little hole called a touchhole connected the flash pan to the inside of the barrel.

The matchlock's spark came from a slow-burning fuse called slow match. A length of slow match was attached to the lock, or firing mechanism. To fire, the musketeer simply turned the burning slow match so that it lit the powder in the flash pan. If all went well, then the fire in the flash pan spread through the touchhole to the powder in the barrel— and then boom!

Matchlocks suffered from two big problems. One was that the fire in the slow match was always going out, especially in wind and rain. Later mechanisms like the snaphance and the flintlock helped solve this problem.

Another problem with matchlocks was that the fire in the flash pan didn't always spread to the barrel. This kind of misfire was called a "flash in the pan."

A matchlock mechanism with slow match

War elephants and horses terrified by Babur's cannon at the First Battle of Panipat

Babur's grandson was called **Akbar**, which means "the Great." It was the great Emperor Akbar who finally found the answer to the sticky question India still faced: how could a Muslim emperor rule a Hindu people without getting into trouble?

Like Babur before him, Akbar started as a strict Muslim who hated all other religions. But as Akbar grew older, a personal problem forced him to open his mind.

The problem was that Akbar had no sons. As of 1570, fifteen years into his reign, Akbar still had no heir to carry on his dynasty. If Akbar couldn't come up with an heir before he died, then the great Moghul Empire would probably fall. Needing a miracle, Akbar turned to someone who was supposed to be a miracle worker: a Muslim holy man called **Salim Chisti**.

When Akbar shared his problem with Salim Chisti, the holy man blessed him— promising that the emperor would soon have a son. Not long after, Akbar's wives gave him not one son, but three! In Akbar's eyes, this was proof enough that Salim Chisti really was a miracle worker. From then on, Emperor Akbar was a devoted follower of Salim Chisti.

What makes all this so important is that Salim Chisti was no average Muslim. Instead, Salim was a **Sufi**— part of a strange Muslim sect that studied visions and dreams. The Sufis were less strict than other Muslims, and much friendlier to people from other faiths. In following a Sufi leader, Akbar learned to be friendly to Hindus. Instead of tearing down Hindu temples, as Babur had done, Akbar left Hindus alone.

Naturally, Hindus were much happier with an emperor who didn't tear down their temples! Without all the trouble between Hindus and Muslims, India thrived. The Moghul Empire of Akbar and his heirs grew into one of the biggest, richest empires the world has ever seen.

Emperor Akbar

The mark of Akbar's open-minded faith was a special house of worship called the **Ibadat Khana**. Most houses of worship are for one faith only; but not this one. The Ibadat Khana was a place where holy men from all faiths came together to share their beliefs.

Of course, Akbar invited all kinds of Muslims to the Ibadat Khana. But he also invited Hindus, Jains and Buddhists. He even invited the Catholic priests who were starting to sail in from Portugal, as we'll read in Chapter 24. Akbar listened carefully to what each holy man had to say, honoring them all.

Akbar at the Ibadat Khana, surrounded by holy men of all faiths

CHAPTER 17

The Land of Qin and Han

China is one of the biggest countries in the world. In modern times, only two countries on Earth have more land than China: Russia and Canada. And no country has more people than China!

China's outline on a map looks something like a rooster. The big bird's head, beak and crest lie to the northeast, in a part of China called Manchuria. The tail lies to the west, and the belly to the southeast. The feet are two big islands: one called **Hainan**, and the other **Taiwan**. Actually, Taiwan has had a separate government since 1949— the year when most of China got a communist government.

One way to remember the geography of China is to think of a huge ramp. The high ground all lies in the west. The low ground all lies in the east, along the coast. And in between, rivers carry torrents of rainwater from high ground to low.

The high ground of western China is the highest in the world. Part of this high ground is the world's tallest mountain range: the **Himalayas**, which stand along the border with India and Nepal (Chapter 16). Another part is the huge **Tibetan Plateau**, which stands north of the Himalayas. The Tibetan Plateau averages about 15,000 feet above sea level— nearly three miles high! This fantastic height explains why Tibet is called the "Roof of the World."

A scene from the beautiful Three Gorges region of the Yangtze River Valley

The low ground of eastern China lies along four big seas. The northernmost is the Bohai Sea, which lies between China and North Korea. The next sea southward is the Yellow Sea, which lies between China and South Korea. Next comes the East China Sea, followed by the South China Sea. Beyond these four seas lies the Pacific Ocean.

Central China is a land of rushing rivers. Most of China's smaller rivers flow into one of three main river systems: the **Yellow River** in the north, the **Yangtze River** in the middle and the **Pearl River** in the south.

The capital of China is **Beijing.**

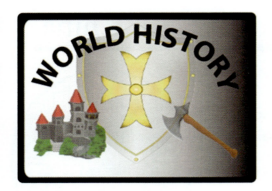

Dynasties of Ancient China

The history of China reads like a list of dynasties. The Chinese have watched dozens of dynasties rise and fall over the centuries. Most of these dynasties ruled only part of all that is now China.

The first known dynasty grew up in the Yellow River Valley. It started around 2200 BC, when King Yu the Great became the first emperor of the **Xia dynasty**.

The Xia Dynasty (about 2200 - 1750 BC)

King Yu was a river-tamer. Before his day, farming along the Yellow River was terribly risky. Farmers never knew when a flood might wash away their crops, or when a drought might stunt them. Yu used a combination of engineering genius and hard work to solve both problems. He built great dams to control flooding in wet years, and dug great canals to spread water around in dry years.

The third known dynasty was both strong and weak. On the one hand, the **Zhou dynasty** reigned for a long time— about 800 years in all! On the other hand, the Zhou Empire was falling apart for most of those 800 years. In those days, China was divided into nine provinces. Without strong emperors to keep them loyal, the leaders of the nine provinces started fighting among themselves— each hoping to become emperor himself.

The Zhou Dynasty (about 1100 - 250 BC)

A **philosophy** is a certain way of thinking about life and the world.

A **moral problem** is a question about right and wrong.

The chaos of this terrible time called for new ways of thinking. This explains why two of China's best-known **philosophies** come from Zhou dynasty times: **Confucianism** and **Taoism**.

Confucius was a traveling teacher who lived around 500 BC. In Confucius' eyes, the wars of Zhou dynasty times started with a **moral problem**. The leaders of the nine provinces were simply too greedy and proud! They cared only for themselves, and not at all for the innocent lives that were destroyed by their constant fighting. All Chinese would be better off if their leaders learned better morals.

Confucianism

Teaching good morals was a big part of Confucianism. Confucius wanted all Chinese to learn the virtues of what he called a **junzi**— Chinese for "perfect gentleman."

➢ The first Confucian virtue was *Li*— Chinese for "etiquette" or "good manners." Good Confucians were always humble and respectful toward others, never pushing themselves forward when they shouldn't.

Confucius

- A second Confucian virtue was *Xiao*— Chinese for "filial piety." "Piety" means "religion," and "filial" means "of a son." In other words, good Confucians were religious about showing respect for their parents and ancestors. They also cared deeply about their family's honor. To bring shame to one's family was the worst thing any Confucian could do.

- Above all other virtues, Confucius valued *Ren*— Chinese for "human kindness." The great philosopher wanted everyone to feel true concern for his fellow man. Good Confucians demanded justice for everyone, not just for themselves.

Confucius also taught a version of the **Golden Rule**— about five hundred years before Jesus Christ taught His! However, the Confucian Golden Rule is different from the Christian one. Christ said in Matthew 7:12, *"…do to others what you would have them do to you…"* But the Confucian Golden Rule said, *"Don't do to others what you wouldn't want them to do to you."* The difference is that Christ taught Christians to do good deeds; while Confucius taught his followers not to do bad deeds.

Sculpture of Lao-tzu

Taoism started with another great philosopher from Zhou dynasty times: **Lao-Tzu**. If you know "Star Wars," then you already know something about Taoism. Jedi philosophy comes straight from Lao-Tzu, with just a few changes for dramatic effect!

Taoism

According to Lao-Tzu, the **Tao** is a force that flows from all things that are alive, or have ever been alive. This force is not a god, exactly; but it does have a will like a god's. To get along in life, one must learn to go along with the will of the Tao. Good Taoists take life as it comes, trying not to struggle against the will of the Tao.

A *taijitu*, the common symbol for yin and yang

The Tao has two sides: a dark side called **yin**, and light side called **yang**. But the dark yin is not bad, nor is the light yang good. Instead, they are two opposite sides of the same whole. There can never be yang without yin to balance it. For example, there can never be light without darkness— for without darkness, there would be no need for light.

Good Taoists try to maintain balance between yang and yin. Among other things, this means living in harmony with others; living in harmony with nature; and eating healthy foods.

The Qin Dynasty (221 - 206 BC)

The last 250 years of the Zhou dynasty were especially hard times in China. The fighting was so intense that this part of Chinese history got a special name. It is called the **Warring States Period**; and it lasted from about 476 – 221 BC.

Near the end of the Warring States Period, one of the nine provinces rose to the top. The ruler of **Qin province** conquered more and more of the other provinces— until finally, he conquered them all. Starting in 221 BC, all China belonged to **Shi Huangdi**— the first emperor of the **Qin dynasty**.

The first thing Shi Huangdi did was to pull all China together into one country. Before now, most Chinese had seen themselves as citizens of the province where they lived. But Shi Huangdi wanted to erase the nine provinces, so that all would be loyal to him alone. One way he did that was by banning the old provinces' names— making it a crime to speak them. Starting then, all Chinese belonged to one empire!

Emperor Qin Shi Huangdi

What Shi Huangdi did probably explains how China got its name. The name "China" may come from "Qin," the name of Shi Huangdi's dynasty.

Shi Huangdi is also remembered for giant building projects— including his biggest, the **Great Wall of China**. It all started with a border problem. The northern border of China was simply too long to defend. While the army was busy guarding one part of the border, raiders would swarm across another part and steal everything in sight. That was why Shi Huangdi started the Great Wall: to defend China against raiders from the north.

Over the centuries, other emperors finished what Shi Huangdi started. By the 1300s, the Great Wall of China was an unbroken barrier more than 5,000 miles long!

An older section of the Great Wall of China

The years of China's next dynasty, the **Han dynasty**, were a Golden Age of China— a time of tremendous growth and change. For example:

> The **Silk Road** was an ancient trade route used to carry goods back and forth between the Far East and the West.

➢ The Han years saw the opening of the famous **Silk Road**, the ancient trade route between East and West. Han traders gave the West its first taste of fine materials like silk and porcelain— luxuries that only the Chinese knew how to make. The Silk Road explains why fine tableware is called "china": because the ancients couldn't buy such fine things anywhere else!

The Han Dynasty (206 BC - 220 AD)

➢ The Han years saw the first Buddhist missionaries come to China, sent by Emperor Asoka of India (Chapter 16). Although Buddhism later faded in India, it became one of the top religions in China.

➢ Han scientists invented two of China's **Four Great Inventions**: the **magnetic compass** and **paper**.

If the Qin dynasty gave China its name, then the Han dynasty gave China's biggest race its name. Even today, most Chinese see themselves as members of an ancient race called **Han Chinese**.

The **Four Great Inventions** are four marvelous technologies that the Chinese developed before any other people on Earth. The first two, the **magnetic compass** and **paper**, came in Han dynasty times. The second two, **gunpowder** and **woodblock printing**, came in Tang dynasty times (below).

Dynasties of Medieval China

After everything the Qin and Han dynasties did to pull China together, it fell apart again. The last Han emperor fell in 220 AD. For the next 360 years, different emperors ruled different parts of China; but no one ruled all China. It wasn't until 581 that someone finally pulled China back together again.

The story starts with a minor noble called **Yang Jian**. Yang started small, serving in the army of a lord in northern China. But Yang served better than most. By the time he was sixteen years old, his lord was already so pleased with him that he gave him his daughter as a bride: a thirteen-year-old noblewoman called Dugu.

Replica of a compass from Han dynasty times

The Sui Dynasty (581 - 618)

Yang was so pleased with this gift that he made Dugu a special promise. He swore that as long as Dugu lived, she would be his only wife— and that he would always stay faithful to her. Yang Jian's great marriage would turn out to be one of the keys to his great success.

In 561, Dugu gave Yang a beautiful daughter. When that daughter grew up, a northern emperor chose her as a bride for his son. When that emperor died, his son took his place— making Yang's daughter empress. How high Yang Jian had risen now— all the way from minor noble to the father of an empress!

A few years later, the new emperor died too— making Yang's daughter a widow. Since the emperor's son was too young to rule on his own, he needed a **regent** to run his government for him. The other nobles chose Yang Jian as regent, even though the new emperor wasn't his grandson.

> A **regent** is an officer who runs a government for a royal who is too young or sick to rule on his own.

A few years after that, Yang Jian tossed out that emperor and took his place. Instead of Regent Yang Jian, he became **Emperor Wen of Sui**— first emperor of the **Sui dynasty**. This was the first great Chinese dynasty of medieval times.

Even now, Yan Jian kept his promise to his wife. He could have had many mistresses; but instead, he stayed faithful to Dugu. He taught his second son, **Yang Guang**, to do the same: to honor women always. Sad to say, Yang Guang didn't learn.

After Empress Dugu died, old Yang Jian finally took a younger woman as mistress. What he didn't know was that Yang Guang wanted the same woman. Even after his father claimed her, Yang Guang kept right on chasing this same woman!

When the mistress told Yang Jian about it, the furious father sent officers to arrest his son. But Yang Guang was ready and waiting for them. When the officers arrived, Yang Guang's men turned the tables on them— arresting them instead.

After that, it is said, Yang Guang committed the worst crime a Chinese son could ever commit. He sent one of his servants to smother his old father to death!

Yang Guang didn't stop there. He also murdered his older brother, along with all eight of his brother's sons— so that none of

Yang Guang, a.k.a. Emperor Yang of Sui

them could ever stand between him and his father's throne. The strange thing about all this is that the Chinese cared more about family honor than anyone. Yet somehow, a man who murdered his own father became the second emperor of the Sui dynasty!

Besides caring nothing for his family, Yang Guang also cared nothing for the Chinese people. The cruel emperor spent countless lives on his biggest building project: the **Grand Canal of China**.

The Grand Canal started with a geography problem. The two biggest rivers in China are the Yellow and the Yangtze; and they both flow mainly from west to east. The valleys around them were naturally separate, with no good waterways between them.

> The **Grand Canal of China** is the longest manmade waterway in the world. It stretches almost 1,200 miles, starting at Beijing in the north and ending at Hangzhou in the south.

This wasn't a problem, as long as the two valleys belonged to two separate kingdoms. But when the Sui dynasty came along, it pulled the two valleys into one empire— which meant that it needed to connect them. As always, waterways were the best ways to carry heavy loads from place to place.

Since nature hadn't given them a north-south waterway, the Sui emperors built their own! The result was the longest manmade waterway in the world: the Grand Canal.

A scene from the Grand Canal of China in the 1800s

The amount of work that went into the Grand Canal is almost beyond belief. By law, every able-bodied man had to spend several months working on the huge project. Millions of Chinese came to do their part. Some dug the mountains of earth and rock that had to be moved. Others cut timber or sawed lumber for the many **locks** that had to be built. Still others built bridges over the canal, or roads alongside it. All this without bulldozers, dump trucks or other power tools. The closest thing the medieval world had to a dump truck was an ox-drawn cart!

> A **lock** is a set of water gates, pumps and valves that canal operators use to raise and lower ships.

The pressure of finishing all this work claimed many, many lives. Of the 5 or 6 million Chinese who worked to build the Grand Canal, as many as 2 or 3 million died! They died of overwork; or they died of diseases that spread in overcrowded work camps; or they died in cave-ins and drowning accidents. The Grand Canal was a big success for Yang Guang, but a tragedy for the people who built it.

The other tragedy of Sui dynasty times started with a kingdom just east of China. It was called Goguryeo; and it stood in what is now North Korea. Both Sui emperors wanted desperately to conquer Goguryeo. Both sent huge armies to fight the **Goguryeo Wars**— sometimes more than a million troops at once! Sad to say, alot of those troops never came back— like the ones who tried to cross the **Salsu River** in 612.

One day that year, the general in charge of Yang Guang's army decided to wade his troops across the Salsu— all 300,000 of them. The water was quite shallow when the Chinese set out. But when they were

> The **Salsu River** is now called the Chongchon. It flows near what is now Pyongyang, North Korea.

halfway across, the water mysteriously started rising. Unknown to the general, his enemies had opened a dam upriver— sending down a flood to wash away the Chinese. Of the 300,000 who set out, only 3,000 made it across— about 1 man in 100!

Between the Grand Canal and the Goguryeo Wars, the Chinese had had enough of Yang Guang. His empire fell into chaos, with rebellions breaking out all over.

The end came one day in 618, when Yang Guang's generals decided that it was time for their emperor to die. Not wanting to shed his royal blood themselves, they asked him to commit suicide. Yang Guang would have liked to take a painless poison, but couldn't find any on such short notice. When his generals insisted, he finally took off his scarf and handed it to a soldier— who used it to strangle him.

〰〰

The next great dynasty took over that same year, 618. The years of the Tang dynasty were another Golden Age of China— another time of peace, wealth and discovery. While the Europeans were still muddling through their Dark Ages, the Chinese were making big breakthroughs. Two of these breakthroughs were the last two of the Four Great Inventions: gunpowder and woodblock printing.

Gunpowder is a mixture of three chemicals: charcoal, sulfur and potassium nitrate. The potassium nitrate is an **oxidizer**— in other words, a source of oxygen. All fires need plenty of oxygen if they are to burn quickly. The chemical formula for potassium nitrate is KNO_3— which means that every molecule of potassium nitrate has three oxygen atoms to burn.

The Chinese thinkers who discovered gunpowder in the 800s were a special kind of scientists called **alchemists**. Alchemists were always looking for a way to turn cheap metals into precious gold. They also looked for the **Elixir of Life**— a potion that gave eternal life and youth to anyone who drank it.

Woodblock printing means carving a design into a block of wood, and then using that block to print many copies of that design. Printers who knew this art could copy books far faster than any scribe could copy them by hand.

Another benefit of woodblock printing was that every copy was the same, with none of the mistakes a scribe might make— unless the carver of the woodblock made a mistake.

Besides these great inventions, the most fascinating fact about the Tang dynasty is that one of its emperors was a woman! Although Empress Wu Zetian wasn't the only powerful woman in Chinese history, she was the only Empress Regnant. In other words, she was the only woman ever to rule China on her own, without a husband or son over her.

The ***Ballad of Mulan*** is an old poem that tells a beloved story from medieval China. Fa Mulan is the daughter of a man who was once an honored soldier, but is now too old and sick to serve. The problem is, the emperor wants a soldier from every family. The only way Mulan can save her poor father is to disguise herself as a man and go fight in his place!

The story of Fa Mulan is mostly legend. If she ever really lived, then it may have been in the days of the Sui or Tang dynasties.

Fu Mulan

All that came later, though. At first, Wu Zetian was only a low-level wife of an emperor— the kind they called a concubine. The Tang emperors had many wives, but only one empress. The rest were all concubines like Wu Zetian.

Wu's first husband was Li Shimin, a.k.a. Emperor Taizong of Tang—the second emperor of the Tang dynasty. They married when she was in her teens, and he closer to forty. Li Shimin died at age fifty-one, leaving Wu a widow at twenty-five.

At this point in her life, it looked like Wu Zetian didn't have much to look forward to. As the former wife of an emperor, she could never marry again— lest she dishonor her husband. She found herself locked in a Buddhist monastery, where monks watched over her day and night. The monks even shaved her head to keep other men from noticing her.

Shaved head or no, one man couldn't help noticing Wu Zetian. That man was Li Shimin's son: Li Zhi, a.k.a. Emperor Gaozong of Tang. Li Zhi had actually noticed Wu Zetian years before, when she was still his father's concubine. And why not? For she was much closer to Li Zhi's age than she was to his father's. Now whenever Li Zhi visited the monastery, he admired Wu Zetian from afar.

Li Shimin, a.k.a.
Emperor Taizong of Tang

Even so, Wu Zetian might never have left the monastery without the schemes of Li Zhi's wives. He had two favorites at the time: an empress called Wang, and a concubine called Xiao. Alas, Empress Wang lived in constant fear. For Xiao had given Li Zhi children; while Empress Wang had not. Without children of her own, Empress Wang feared that Li Zhi might get rid of her and make Xiao empress instead.

What Empress Wang needed, she thought, was some new woman to make Li Zhi forget about Xiao. And what better woman than the one Li Zhi had been admiring all this time: Wu Zetian? Thanks to Empress Wang's schemes, Wu Zetian didn't have to spend the rest of her life in a monastery. Instead, she came to the palace as a new concubine for Li Zhi.

Empress Wang didn't know it yet, but she had just made the biggest mistake of her life. Wu Zetian would turn out to be a far worse problem than Xiao had ever been!

Wu Zetian soon did what Empress Wang could not: She gave Li Zhi children. Every year brought a new child— first a son, then a second son, then a daughter. Every child made Empress Wang a little more jealous of Wu Zetian.

Empress Wu Zetian (624 – 705)

Then tragedy struck. After getting along fine for some time, Wu Zetian's daughter suddenly died. No one had any idea why— until a servant stepped forward to say that he had seen Empress Wang coming out of the baby's room.

What a thorny problem for the royal household! On the one hand, no one had actually seen Empress Wang hurt the baby. On the other hand, everyone knew that Empress Wang was terribly jealous of Wu Zetian. Putting two and two together, most people decided that Empress Wang must have smothered the poor girl in a fit of jealousy!

That was the beginning of the end for Empress Wang.

Wu Zetian became Empress Wu the very next year. The year after that, her oldest son became the official heir to the throne. Later, Empress Wu had both Wang and Xiao put to death!

For most of the next 30 years, Empress Wu took part in every decision her husband made. Whenever Li Zhi sat on his throne, the empress sat right behind him— so that she could whisper advice in his ear. But she always sat behind a veil, so that no one would know the Emperor of China was taking advice from a woman!

*O*f course, a few people knew who sat behind that veil. But they didn't dare criticize; for Empress Wu was a fierce enemy. Anyone who crossed her either disappeared or died.

When Li Zhi died, Empress Wu should have gone into retirement. Instead, she went right on ruling China— but still from behind the veil. Since the next emperor was her son, he usually obeyed his mother. When he stopped obeying, she simply set him aside, and made another son emperor instead.

*A*fter a few more years of pretending, Empress Wu finally stepped out from behind the veil. She ruled China in her own name for fifteen years— the only woman ever to do so!

The Chinese used dragons as symbols of power and authority. The Emperor of China sat on a special seat called the **Dragon Throne**. On flags and other emblems, a five-clawed dragon represented the emperor himself; while Dragons with fewer claws represented noblemen.

A five-clawed dragon of the flag of the Qing dynasty, which reigned from 1644 - 1912

The next great dynasty of medieval times was the Song dynasty. Like the Tang dynasty, the Song dynasty is remembered for important inventions:

➤ The Song government combined woodblock printing with economics to print the first paper money. Of course, the first counterfeiters tried to copy the first paper money the moment it was printed! The answer was to add complicated designs to its bills, making them almost impossible to copy.

The Song Dynasty (960 - 1279)

➤ The printers of Song dynasty times were the first to use movable type. Instead of carving a separate woodblock for each new page, they molded ceramic type for each character, and then fastened the characters to an iron plate. Unlike woodblocks, ceramic type could be rearranged to print new pages, and reused again and again.

➤ The engineers of Song dynasty times built the world's first iron-cased gunpowder weapons— including grenades, bombs and hand cannon. Earlier gun tubes were made of something far softer: bamboo.

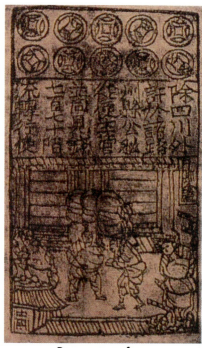

Paper money from the Song Dynasty

Like many emperors from the Far East, the first emperor of the Han dynasty saw himself as the rightful ruler of the whole world. He wanted his capital to stand at the very center of that world, so that he could reach the farthest corners without traveling too far. Not knowing where the center of the world was, he asked his scientists to measure it out for him. The spot they chose was where the Han built their capital: **Chang'an**, which is now called **Xi'an**.

Centuries later, emperors of the Sui and Tang dynasties rebuilt the ancient Han capital. The new Chang'an was a planned city laid out in a perfect rectangle, 5 miles wide and 6 miles long. In the Golden Age of the Tang years, Chang'an was probably the grandest city on Earth.

The Land of the Rising Sun

Japan is an island country in the farthest part of the Far East. Unless one is going around the world, Japan is about as far east as one can go— which is why Japan is called the **Land of the Rising Sun**.

Like the British Isles, Japan is an **archipelago**. The Japanese archipelago covers more than 4,000 islands in all; but most of Japan lies on just four main islands. From north to south, these four main islands are **Hokkaido**, **Honshu**, **Shikoku** and **Kyushu**. The biggest of the four, Honshu, is the seventh-biggest island in the world. Honshu is just a bit bigger than the island of Great Britain.

> An **archipelago** is a group of islands.

Four seas separate Japan from its closest neighbors. To the north, between Japan and **Russia**, lies the Sea of Okhotsk. To the south, between Japan and the **Philippines**, lies the Philippine Sea. To the west lie two seas. One is the Sea of Japan, which lies between Japan and **Korea**. The other is the East China Sea, which lies between Japan and **China**.

Japan is a land of mountains, volcanos, earthquakes and hot springs. The tallest mountain in Japan, **Mount Fuji**, is an active volcano. Fuji stands on Honshu, about 60 miles southwest of **Tokyo**.

> **Tokyo** is the capital of Japan.

Most Japanese don't call their homeland "Japan." Instead, they call it "Nippon" or "Nihon." "Japan" is another way of saying "Cipangu," which is the name Marco Polo learned on his famous trip to the Far East— as we'll read in Chapter 19. "Cipangu" probably meant "Kingdom of the Rising Sun."

The Heavenly Emperors of Japan

Flag of the Emperor of Japan

The history of Japan reads very differently than the history of China. Where China has had many dynasties over the centuries, Japan has had only one: the **Imperial Dynasty**, which is sometimes called the Yamato dynasty. If the legends are true, then all Japanese emperors spring from the same ancestor: **Jimmu Tenno**, the first Emperor of Japan.

Who were Jimmu Tenno's ancestors? According to legend, only some of them were human. The rest were gods. If the legends are true, then the first Emperor of Japan was descended from a goddess called **Amaterasu**.

Where did Amaterasu come from? According to legend, she sprang from a creator god called **Izanagi**. Amaterasu and Izanagi are just two of many gods whose stories are told in the oldest Japanese religion: **Shinto**.

The Shinto creation legend says that in the beginning, everything was chaos. The lighter parts of that chaos rose up to form heaven, where the gods lived. But no one lived under heaven; for everything below was still chaos.

Earth got started when the older gods sent down two younger gods, asking them to bring order to the chaos. The male god was called Izanagi, and the female Izanami.

To help the young couple with their task, the elder gods gave them a special blade called a **naginata**. Izanagi dipped this blessed blade into the chaos under heaven. When he pulled it back up, drops of matter clung to it. These drops fell back into the chaos, forming the first solid ground on Earth.

> A **naginata** was a Japanese weapon that was similar to a European halberd. Both were long poles with sharp blades at one end. The naginata used by Izanagi was called *Amenonuhoko*.

A long time later, Izanami died in childbirth. The loss of his wife left Izanagi lonely and miserable. He never stopped searching for her— not even when her trail led to Yomi, the terrifying Shinto underworld.

The underworld was so pitch-dark that Izanagi couldn't see his wife; but he could still recognize her voice. When he finally heard that familiar sound, he begged Izanami to come home. Alas, Izanami said, her husband was too late. She had already eaten the food of the underworld— which meant that she could never go back to the land of the living.

Izanami and Izanagi bringing order from the chaos under heaven

Izanagi still wanted to save Izanami. He decided to wait until she fell asleep, and then strike a light— hoping to see how he might help her. But when the light shone on her, he saw that her once-beautiful face was now riddled with decay! The sight was horrifying. Izanagi knew now that his wife was trapped in the underworld forever— and that he might be trapped there as well.

With a cry of dismay, Izanagi fled the underworld as fast as he could. His cry awakened Izanami, who was furious that her husband had seen her. Izanagi made it to the gate of the underworld in the nick of time, just before Izanami caught up to him. Breathing a sigh of relief, Izanagi rolled a huge stone over the gate and fell against it.

What happened next explains how death came into the Shinto world. Still furious with her husband, Izanami screamed through the gate how she meant to destroy his world: by dragging 1,000 people down into the underworld every day! Izanagi screamed back how he would save his world: by creating 1,500 new people every day!

After his awful ordeal in the underworld, Izanagi felt so filthy that he just had to wash. But even washing wasn't simple for someone as mighty as Izanagi. As he washed his face, three new gods were born! Amaterasu, goddess of the sun, sprang from Izanagi's left eye. Tsukuyomi, god of the moon, sprang from Izanagi's right eye. Their brother Susanoo, god of seas and storms, sprang from Izanagi's nose.

Naturally, Amaterasu and Susanoo started arguing right away. Just as storm clouds frustrate the sun, so the storm god frustrated the sun goddess.

After one bad argument with Susanoo, Amaterasu felt so angry and depressed that she hid herself in a cave. With the sun goddess sulking in her cave, refusing to come out, the sun disappeared from the sky. The other gods got so anxious that they asked Uzume, goddess of laughter, to see if she could bring Amaterasu out of her cave.

Uzume started by hanging two tempting gifts outside the cave. One was a curved piece of jade, a green jewel that is treasured in the Far East. The other was a brilliant mirror made of polished bronze.

The Mirror and the Jewel

With the jade and the mirror as bait, Uzume gathered the other gods outside the cave and started telling jokes. When they all howled with laughter, Amaterasu peered out of her cave to see what was so funny. Between the laughter of the gods and the beautiful gifts they had given her, Amaterasu cheered up enough to come out of her cave for good.

The brilliant Amaterasu coming out of her cave

This sticky problem with Amaterasu wasn't the only one Susanoo caused. Izanagi got so frustrated with his stormy son that he finally banished him to the underworld. Of course, Susanoo took his time about getting to the underworld— for after all, he had never been very obedient.

Somewhere along the way, Susanoo ran into the most terrifying monster imaginable: an eight-headed dragon that was big enough to swallow whole islands! Fortunately, Susanoo knew this dragon's weakness: it liked rice wine. Before the big fight, Susanoo prepared eight huge casks of rice wine— one for each head. After the dragon got happily drunk, Susanoo leapt out and cut off all its heads!

Susanoo didn't stop there; for he knew that some dragons can regrow their heads. Determined to kill this one for good, he kept slicing at the dragon— trying to cut it into bits so small that it could never regrow.

The problem was, one of the dragon's tails wouldn't cut. Wondering why, Susanoo slit the tail open— revealing a magnificent **sword** inside! This sword was no ordinary find. It was a real treasure— a gift worthy of a god.

Susanoo put that sword to good use. After the mirror and the jewel, he knew all about Amaterasu's weakness for beautiful objects. So instead of going to the underworld, Susanoo went home and gave the sword to Amaterasu. Amaterasu was so pleased with Susanoo's gift that she forgave him— at which Izanagi forgave him too.

The Sword in the Dragon

Susanoo slaying the dragon

ꊢꊢꊢꊢꊢꊢꊢꊢꊢꊢꊢꊢꊢꊢꊢꊢꊢꊢꊢꊢꊢꊢꊢꊢꊢꊢꊢꊢ

The three gifts from these last two legends play an important part in Japanese history. Together, these three precious possessions of Amaterasu— the sword, the mirror and the jewel— are called the **Three Sacred Treasures**.

According to legend, Amaterasu handed down the Three Sacred Treasures to her grandson Ninigi. In turn, Ninigi handed them down to his own descendant: Jimmu Tenno, the first Emperor of Japan.

Since then, every emperor has handed down these family heirlooms to the next emperor. If the legends are true, then this line has never been broken. Even today, the Japanese still keep the Three Sacred Treasures at three separate Shinto shrines. Although Shinto priests may see one treasure at a time, only the Emperor of Japan may see all Three Sacred Treasures at the same time.

An artist's vision of the Three Sacred Treasures

ꊢꊢꊢꊢꊢꊢꊢꊢꊢꊢꊢꊢꊢꊢꊢꊢꊢꊢꊢꊢꊢꊢꊢꊢꊢꊢꊢꊢꊢꊢ

From Immortal to Mortal

If the emperors of Japan come from gods, then why do they die like ordinary mortals? The legend of Ninigi, grandson to Amaterasu, explains how the emperors lost the gift of immortality.

Soon after Ninigi came down to Earth, he met a lovely young flower goddess called Sakuya. Her stunning beauty reminded Ninigi of the **chrysanthemum**, a flower that is especially treasured in Japan. Ninigi wanted to marry Sakuya at once.

Alas for Ninigi, Sakuya's father had other ideas. It so happened that Sakuya had a sister called Iwanaga, who also needed a husband. When Ninigi asked to marry Sakuya, her father offered him Iwanaga as well. The trouble was that Iwanaga was no beautiful flower goddess. Instead, she was a plain goddess of stone. Wanting nothing to do with such a plain goddess, Ninigi refused Iwanaga— but still asked for Sakuya.

Imperial Seal of Japan

Only then did Sakuya's wise old father reveal what was really going on. Flowers, the father said, are beautiful only for a short time. Stone, on the other hand, is beautiful forever. In choosing the short-lived beauty of the flower over the permanent beauty of stone, Ninigi had chosen a short life over a permanent one! Thanks to Ninigi's poor choice, all emperors of Japan lost their immortality— becoming mere mortals like everyone else.

The chrysanthemum from Ninigi's story is another important symbol of the Imperial Dynasty. The Imperial Seal of Japan is a yellow chrysanthemum; and the seat of Japan's emperors is called the Chrysanthemum Throne.

Legends like these are only part of Shinto beliefs. Another part is *kami*, or spirits. Shinto believers see *kami* in everything— not only living things like people and animals, but also non-living things like mountains, rivers and wind. To approach these kami, Shinto believers worship at special gates called **torii**. Each torii marks a border between heaven and earth, holy and unholy.

One example of a torii, a Shinto symbol of the gateway between heaven and earth

Emperors, Clans and Samurai

The first civilization in Japan started long after the first one in China. In fact, the first civilization in Japan may have come from China— led there by a Chinese magician called **Xu Fu**.

Xu Fu was a court magician who worked for the first emperor of the Qin dynasty: Shi Huangdi, whom we met in Chapter 17. Shi Huangdi was terribly worried about dying. To save himself from death, he sent Xu Fu on an important mission. He wanted him to find the **Elixir of Life**, a potion that gave eternal life and health. Alas, Xu Fu came back empty-handed— just like everyone else who searched for the Elixir of Life.

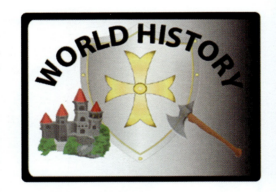

Still determined to have his elixir, an angry Shi Huangdi sent Xu Fu back out— ordering him to search again. Knowing how angry Shi Huangdi was, Xu Fu was afraid of what might happen to him if he went home empty-handed again. So instead of going home, he sailed over to Japan— where he built the first Japanese civilization. Some people think that Xu Fu and Jimmu Tenno may have been the same man!

The legend of Xu Fu may be true, or it may not be. Either way, the people of ancient Japan certainly learned a lot from the Chinese. For example, the characters used to write Japanese came from the ones used to write Chinese. Japanese characters are called

Xu Fu searching for the Elixir of Life

kanji, and Chinese characters hanzi. Early Japanese writing styles were also similar to China's. So were early Japanese law, early Japanese building styles and much more.

〰〰〰〰〰〰〰〰〰〰〰〰〰〰〰〰〰〰〰〰〰〰〰〰〰〰〰〰

Despite what all the legends say, there was no one emperor who ruled all Japan in ancient times. Instead, Japan was divided into little kingdoms— each ruled by a powerful **clan**.

It was only later, in early medieval times, that one clan started building an empire. This first empire arose in southern Honshu, around

> A **clan** is a big, powerful family.

what is now one of Japan's biggest cities: Osaka. The clan that built it was called the Yamato, which is why the Imperial Dynasty is also called the Yamato dynasty (above).

In all the long years since, the Yamato dynasty has never fallen. All Japanese emperors are descended from the first Yamato emperors. If there have been no mistakes over the centuries, then every single Emperor of Japan has had Yamato blood running in his veins!

The Yamato wasn't the only great clan, though. Over the centuries, other clans grew even more powerful than the Yamato. The first was the Soga clan, which took over around 500 AD. Then came the Fujiwara clan, which took over around 800. Later came the Taira clan, followed by the Minamoto clan. If the history of China reads like a list of dynasties, then the history of Japan reads like a list of clans!

The difference is that none of these clans got rid of the Yamato emperors. Instead, they found other things for the emperor to do. The Yamato emperors became the leaders of Shinto, the state religion of Japan. Their jobs were to meet with priests, attend ceremonies, dedicate shrines and so on.

Meanwhile, the clan leaders ran the country. Their jobs were to collect taxes, run courts, raise armies and so on. In other words, the Yamato emperors were only **figureheads**. The real power in Japan belonged to the clan leaders.

> On a ship, a **figurehead** is a carving that decorates the prow. In government, a figurehead is a leader who seems to be in charge, but really isn't. Like the figureheads on ships, the figurehead emperors of Japan were there mostly to inspire people— not to lead them.

〰〰〰〰〰〰〰〰〰〰〰〰〰〰〰〰〰〰〰〰〰〰〰〰〰〰〰〰

Another big difference between China and Japan was a Japanese fighting man called a samurai. The name *samurai* comes from the Japanese word for "servant" or "attendant." That was how the samurai got started— as skilled soldiers serving in the armies of clan leaders. Every clan needed soldiers to protect it from the other clans. The samurai were the best kind of soldiers; for fighting was their whole life.

A good samurai was almost always either fighting or training to fight. If he wasn't fighting, then he was usually thinking about fighting, writing about fighting or painting pictures of fighting. He was a master of all weapons, from bow to sword to spear; and he could fight from horseback as well as on foot.

The Japanese laid their ancient emperors to rest in huge, keyhole-shaped burial mounds called *kofun*. They honor their ancestors so much that many *kofun* have never been disturbed, even after all these centuries.

Daisen Kofun, the biggest *kofun* in Japan. This giant burial mound is the size of thirty football fields, and about 1,500 years old.

A mounted samurai wearing a horned-helmet *yoroi*, and carrying a *yumi*

Like the best knights of the West, the samurai lived by a warrior code. The knight's code was called chivalry, and the samurai code **bushido**.

Bushido had a lot to say about honor. A good samurai loved honor more than he loved life. He didn't mind dying in battle; for he knew he had to die someday. He only wanted to die well. He dreamed of a dying in glorious battle, surrounded by a crowd of enemies too big for anyone to defeat. Then he could die happy, knowing that he wouldn't be ashamed in front of his ancestors.

In fact, the samurai loved honor so much that the thought of losing a fight could be too much to bear. If a samurai had a chance to die a good death in battle, but didn't, then he might be called a coward. And no samurai could stand being called a coward. A beaten samurai had to find some way to prove his courage.

Sometimes, there was only one way to prove it: through a deadly ritual called **seppuku**, a.k.a. **hara-kiri**. The beaten samurai killed himself in the most horrible, painful way imaginable— to prove that he wasn't afraid of anything.

Honor was just as important in everyday life. If a samurai felt insulted by anyone, then he had a legal right to draw his sword and cut that person down!

In other words, Bushido was much more than a warrior code. In time, it became a way of life— not just for the samurai, but for everyone in Japan. It wasn't only the samurai who learned that honor was better than life, and shame worse than death. Everyone learned it, even mothers and children.

Samurai Equipment

Most samurai fought with two kinds of swords: a long sword called a **katana**, and a short sword called a **wakishazi**. Both were slightly curved. A third kind of samurai sword, the **tachi**, was for fighting from horseback.

The samurai bow was called a **yumi**, and the samurai spear a **yari**.

The samurai suit of armor was called a **yoroi.** The best yoroi were made from bands of steel, bound together with straps of leather to make them flexible.

Katana at top, *wakishazi* at bottom

The Japanese invented the first folding fans around 600 – 800. These first fans were simple, with paper blades pasted over thin strips of wood or bamboo.

Naturally, the samurai found ways to turn harmless folding fans into weapons! Some carried fans made of sheet metal honed to a sharp edge. Others carried a special war fan called a *tessen*. Hung on a samurai's belt, a *tessen* looked like an ordinary folded fan. But in a samurai's hand, it turned out to be a heavy iron club or blade! One advantage of these disguised weapons was that samurai could carry them where weapons weren't allowed.

Example of a *tessen*, an iron club made to look like a folded fan

The Rise of the Shoguns

All that came later, though. For a long time, the samurai remained what they were in the beginning: soldiers serving in the armies of clan leaders. It was only around 1200 that the samurai way became the only way for Japan.

It all started with a new set of rules for emperors. Some emperors didn't like spending their whole lives on the throne. The older ones dreamed of retiring to some peaceful monastery, where they could lead lives of ease and luxury. But they didn't want to give up their power, for fear they might be ignored or forgotten.

The answer was a kind of half-retirement called the **Insei system**. When an emperor was ready to retire, he let his son become the next emperor. But he didn't give his son all the powers of an emperor. Instead, he kept the highest powers for himself. Since Japanese sons always respected their fathers, the old emperor could usually force the new one to do what he wanted him to do.

The trouble started in the days of the 74th Emperor of Japan, who was called **Toba**. In 1123, Toba went into retirement— leaving his son **Sutoku** to take his place. But Toba didn't hand over his power. Thanks to the Insei system, Toba could go right on telling Sutoku what to do.

Emperor Toba (reigned 1107 – 1123)

Emperor Sutoku (reigned 1123 – 1142)

Sixteen years later, Toba's favorite young wife gave him a son called **Konoe**. Naturally, the new mother wanted nothing but the best for her son. What she wanted most was for Toba to make Konoe emperor— even though his older son, Sutoku, was still on the throne!

To please his young wife, Toba agreed. In 1142, Toba ordered Sutoku to hand the throne to his three-year-old half-brother Konoe. As an honorable son, Sutoku had to obey his father— even though he was terribly embarrassed!

The next embarrassment came thirteen years later, when Konoe died at age sixteen. With Konoe out of the way, Sutoku expected Toba to set him back on the throne. At the very least, he expected Toba to set one of Sutoku's sons on the throne. Instead, Toba chose another son of his own! The next emperor was another half-brother of Sutoku called **Go-Shirakawa**.

This was too much for Sutoku. When Toba died later that year, Sutoku attacked Go-Shirakawa— fighting to take back the throne his father had taken away. Their fight is called the **Hogen Rebellion**, and it started in 1156.

The first problem with the **Hogen Rebellion** was that neither Sutoku nor Go-Shirakawa had an army. If they were going to fight a war, then they needed the samurai armies of the clans. Sutoku hired the **Minamoto** clan to fight for him; while Go-Shirakawa hired the **Taira** clan. Without samurai armies, both emperors would have been helpless.

The Hogen Rebellion turned out to be short. Thanks to the Taira samurai, Emperor Go-Shirakawa soon won— shaming poor Sutoku yet again. With that, the Taira became the most powerful clan in Japan— the one that had won the war and saved the emperor!

Alas for the Taira, the Minamoto clan wasn't finished. The Minamoto's turn came in the next big fight: the Genpei War.

Like the Hogen Rebellion, the Genpei War started with insults to an emperor. Only this time, the insults didn't come from an older emperor. Instead, they came from the leader of the Taira clan: a samurai called Taira Kiyomori.

The man Kiyomori insulted was the 80th Emperor of Japan, who was called Takakura. The first insult came in the 1170s, when Kiyomori forced Takakura to marry one of his daughters. A few years later, that daughter had a son called Antoku— who was Kiyomori's grandson.

The second insult came when Antoku was not quite two years old. Even though Takakura was nowhere near old enough to retire, Kiyomori forced him out anyway— so that Kiyomori's grandson, little Antoku, could become emperor!

This was something new and dangerous. Although older emperors had pushed out younger ones before, no clan leader had ever done it. If this went on, then the Imperial Dynasty might be finished. To save himself, the emperor called on the only clan strong enough to tackle the Taira: the Minamoto.

The Minamoto pressed hard against the Taira, threatening to capture the emperor himself. At this, the Taira gathered up Antoku and the Three Sacred Treasures and fled. The flight of the Taira set up the biggest battle of the Genpei War: the Battle of Dan-no-ura.

The Battle of Dan-no-ura was a sea battle fought between Honshu and Kyushu. The turning point came midway through the battle, when a Taira officer suddenly switched sides. Shouting to the Minamoto, this turncoat Taira pointed out the ship that carried Antoku and his family. The Minamoto immediately turned all their bows on this ship— killing its oarsmen, and setting it adrift.

When the Taira saw their emperor's ship drifting, they

Samurai of the Taira clan drowning themselves after the Battle of Dan-no-ura

knew they were beaten. To save their honor, they did what beaten samurai were trained to do. They all leapt over the sides of their ships, where the weight of their armor dragged them straight to the bottom! One of the dead was Antoku, who was not quite seven years old.

With that, the Minamoto took over Japan. The emperor was still there, of course; but he was only a religious leader. The real leader was the head of the Minamoto clan, who soon got a new title: shogun.

A shogun was a samurai general who ruled Japan in the emperor's name. The first one took over in 1192, seven years after the Battle of Dan-no-ura. The shogun could hand down power to his heir, just like an emperor. For most of the next seven hundred years, the real power in Japan belonged to the shoguns!

The **Heike crab** is a special kind of crab found only near Japan. The odd thing about Heike crabs is that their shells look like human faces— and not just any faces, but the scowling faces of angry samurai.

Ever since the Battle of Dan-no-ura, fishermen who catch Heike crabs have automatically thrown them back. Why? Because according to legend, these crabs carry the souls of the Taira samurai who drowned themselves at the Battle of Dan-no-ura!

Another legend from the Battle of Dan-no-ura tells the fate of the Three Sacred Treasures. Near the end, it is said, the Taira samurai tried to throw all three treasures overboard— to keep the Minamoto from getting them. Without the Three Sacred Treasures, the Imperial Dynasty would be finished; for it would lose its link to the sun goddess Amaterasu.

It is also said that the Minamoto samurai leapt aboard just in time to save the jewel. Alas, they were too late to save the mirror and the sword— both of which went to the bottom. Fortunately, the mirror was shiny enough to be found by divers. But the sword may have been lost forever. Some say that the sword the Imperial Dynasty has now is only a copy of the one Susanoo found in the dragon's tail!

The Land Down Under

Australia is the smallest of the seven continents, and the second southernmost continent. The name "Australia" comes from the Latin word *australis*, or "southern." Long before European explorers discovered Australia, their maps showed a continent called *Terra Australis Incognita*— Latin for "Unknown Southern Land." The first Europeans to discover that Unknown Southern Land were the Dutch, who sighted Australia in the early 1600s.

Australia is the lowest, flattest continent— and one of the driest. About two-thirds of Australia it is too dry for most people. Most people prefer the wetter parts near the eastern and southeastern coasts— in and around cities like Sydney, Canberra and Melbourne.

One of Australia's most fascinating features is the Great Barrier Reef, which lies just off the northeastern coast. This beautiful coral reef measures about 1,600 miles long! Other well-known features include Tasmania, a big island about 150 miles south of the mainland; and the Great Australian Bight, a huge bay off the south coast.

CHAPTER 19:   The Mongol Empire

Mongolia

Mongolia is a large, **landlocked** country in East Asia. The Mongols have just two neighbors. Everything north of Mongolia belongs to Russia; while everything west, south and east of Mongolia belongs to China.

Unless you happen to be talking to a Mongol warrior, it is probably safe to say that Mongolia is not the most comfortable place to live! Most of Mongolia is too high, cold and dry for raising crops. In fact, only about one percent of Mongolia is good for crop farming. Most of the rest has only enough grass to feed wandering herds of sheep or goats. In modern times, more Mongols make their livings as miners than as farmers.

In medieval times, most Mongols made their livings as wandering herdsmen, wandering hunters or both. Either way, the Mongols were always wandering— which meant that they didn't need permanent homes. Instead, most Mongols lived in a special kind of tent called a **yurt**.

> A **landlocked** country is one with no coasts.

> The capital of Mongolia is **Ulan Bator**.

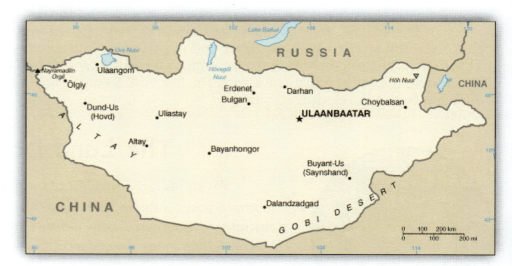

A **yurt** is a round tent made for a single family. The usual Mongol yurt had a light frame of wooden poles covered with layers of warm felt. Finding felt was no problem for the Mongols; for felt is made by crushing wool, and they had plenty of sheep. Finding wood, on the other hand, could be a big problem; for trees were few and far between on the plains of Mongolia.

The Mongols set up their yurts with their doors facing south, the direction that received the most sun throughout the day. Honored guests sat farthest from the door, where the air was warmest. Children and less honored guests sat closer to the door.

A modern-day yurt standing on a Mongolian plain near the base of the Gurvansaikhan Mountains, just north of the Gobi Desert

The Rise of Genghis Khan

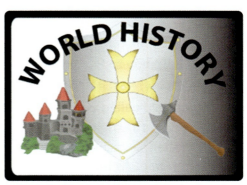

One of the very first historians, a Greek called Herodotus, wrote that hard lands produce hard peoples. If a land gives plenty of food, then its people may grow soft. But if a land gives little food, then its people will grow hard— for they will have to fight hard for every mouthful.

Since Mongolia is one of the hardest lands on Earth, the Mongols naturally became one of the hardest peoples! The harsh climate of Mongolia turned the Mongols into great warriors. From hunting **marmots** on the open plains, they learned to shoot from horseback with rarely a miss. And from spending days with no food, they learned to cross great distances quickly— carrying almost no supplies. They showed up out of nowhere, stole whatever they wanted, and then disappeared before anyone could stop them.

Marmots are big rodents that live in holes burrowed in the ground. The common groundhog is a kind of marmot.

Since their own land gave so little food, the Mongols often stole food from other lands. The people of northern China lived in constant fear of Mongol raids. These raids were the main reason why Shi Huangdi, first emperor of the Qin dynasty, started building the Great Wall of China— as we read in Chapter 17.

All through ancient times, and well into medieval times, the Mongols were divided into different tribes. The **Khamags**, the **Tatars** and the **Merkits** were just a few of the many tribes that roamed the plains of Mongolia. Without a leader to pull the tribes together, the Mongols raided each other as often as they raided the Chinese!

Mongol warriors chasing down their enemies

ⴽ ⴽ ⴽ ⴽ ⴽ ⴽ ⴽ ⴽ ⴽ ⴽ ⴽ ⴽ

The childhood years of a boy called **Temujin** taught him all about Mongol raids. In fact, Temujin might never have been born without one special raid.

Temujin's father, who was called **Yesugei**, was a leader of the Khamag Mongols. He was also a falconer— a hunter who used falcons to catch small game. Yesugei was out hunting one day when he happened to see a beautiful girl riding by in a horse-drawn cart. The horseman pulling the cart was a Merkit Mongol, and he had just married the girl.

Alas for the Merkit, he didn't stay married. Wanting the girl for himself, Yesugei chased the Merkit down and stole his wife. This tearful young woman, whose name was **Oyelun**, would go on to give Yesugei five children. Temujin was the oldest.

According to Mongol legend, Temujin was born "with fire in his eyes and light in his face." In other words, Temujin was the leader who was born to pull all Mongol tribes together! In years to come, this fearsome Mongol leader would be better known by his title: **Genghis Khan**.

Genghis Khan is a title, not a name. It is Mongolian for "great ruler."

When Temujin was nine years old, Yesugei took him to meet Oyelun's family— hoping to find a bride for him there. But they never made it they far. For along the way, a mysterious stranger invited Yesugei to meet his daughter— a 10-year-old called **Borte**.

When Yesugei looked in Borte's eyes, he saw the same fire and light Temujin had. Sensing that he had found the right bride for his son, Yesugei headed home. As for Temujin, he moved in with Borte's family; for that was the Mongol custom.

Finding a bride for his son would turn out to be the last thing Yesugei ever did. Along the road home, a group of pleasant-seeming strangers invited Yesugei to share a meal with them. What Yesugei didn't realize was that these were no strangers. Instead, they were angry Tatars who held a terrible grudge against him! Years before, Yesugei had led a raid against these very Tatars. Yesugei didn't recognize the Tatars; but they recognized him all too well. To get back at him, they mixed a bit of poison with the food they gave him— causing him to sicken and die when he got home.

This was the start of a dark time in Temujin's life. As soon as he heard about his father, Temujin rushed home to take his place. But when he got there, the leaders of his tribe had already abandoned his family— leaving poor Oyelun to feed and raise five children on her own. "Apart from our own shadows," Oyelun mourned, "we have no friends."

A Tatar elder

The family's problems only got worse as Temujin grew older. The leaders of his tribe knew that they had been wrong to abandon his family, and feared he might take revenge someday. To save themselves, they ordered the family to hand Temujin over.

Of course, the family didn't. Instead, the family put him on a horse and sent him racing into the wild. When he could ride no farther, he found a hiding place in a heavy thicket. There he sat, hoping his enemies would give up the search and go home.

Alas, they didn't. Alone in his thicket, Temujin waited nine whole days for his enemies to give up. In all that time, Temujin had not one morsel of food to sustain him. When he could stand the hunger no longer, he finally cut his way out of the thicket— allowing his enemies to capture him at last.

As a wandering people, the Mongols didn't have jails to hold prisoners. Instead, they locked them in miserable contraptions called **cangues**. A rope tied to the cangue helped Temujin's jailer keep hold of him.

But Temujin was too strong for his jailer. One summer day, Temujin jerked the rope out of his jailer's hands, hit him on the head and ran!

Not even Temujin could run far with a heavy cangue on his neck. Finding nowhere else to hide, he lay down in a rushing river— leaving only his face above the surface. After his enemies ran by, he waded down to the home of some friends— who finally helped him escape.

> A **cangue** was a set of boards locked around a prisoner's neck. No prisoner could run far carrying a heavy cangue. Nor could a prisoner feed himself; for the wide boards kept his hands from reaching his mouth.

A prisoner locked in a cangue

Temujin's escape meant that he and Borte were finally free to be married. Alas, their happiness was short-lived. For just months into their marriage, a band of Merkits kidnapped Borte! Why? Because the Merkits had never forgotten how Yesugei kidnapped Oyelun from them years before. Since Yesugei was now dead, the Merkits took their revenge by kidnapping Borte from Yesugei's son.

The key to what came next was something called *anda*— Mongolian for "blood brothers." Mongolian *anda* were special friends who vowed always to be loyal to one another, no matter what. The vows *anda* swore were the most sacred, unbreakable vows in the Mongol world.

> *Anda* is Mongolian for "blood brother."

Before setting out to take Borte back, Temujin called on his father's old *anda*— a Khamag prince called **Toghrul Khan**. Remembering the vow he had sworn to Yeseugei, Toghrul Khan promised 20,000 troops to Yeseugei's son.

Temujin also called on an *anda* of his own— another Khamag prince called **Jamukha**. With another 20,000 troops from Jamukha, Temujin had more than enough to crush the Merkits and take Borte back.

This was the turning point for Temujin. With a great victory like this under his belt, Temujin could finally take his father's place as a leader of his tribe. Thousands of Mongols joined Temujin's army— so many that he was soon as powerful as Jamukha and Toghrul Khan.

One of the secrets to Temujin's success was the way he promoted army officers. Other Mongols promoted troops from the richest, most powerful families; but not Temujin. His way was to promote the troops with the most skill and courage, so that he wound up with better officers.

A second secret to Temujin's success was the way he swallowed up other tribes. Each time Temujin conquered a new tribe, his mother adopted young princes from that tribe— making them half-brothers to Temujin. As the head of the family, Temujin automatically became the head of his half-brothers' tribes.

Temujin and Jamukha became *anda* at age eleven. To seal their vow as blood brothers, each gave the other a **knucklebone**— in other words, the anklebone of a deer or other animal.

The gift of a knucklebone was more special than it sounds. The odd shape of knucklebones meant that they could be rolled like dice. Mongol **shamans**, or spirit-talkers, rolled knucklebones to try to predict the future.

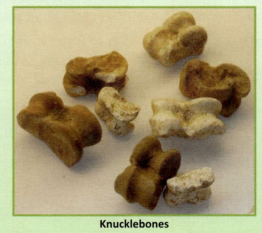

Knucklebones

The more tribes Temujin swallowed, the more he wanted to swallow. He dreamed of becoming the **Great Khan**— the one ruler who would lead all Mongol tribes.

Unfortunately, Temujin's *anda* Jamukha dreamed the same dream. The quest to be Great Khan set up a deadly contest between the two. Temujin and Jamukha might have been blood brothers before; but now they were bitter rivals for the throne.

Portrait of Genghis Khan by a Chinese artist

Twenty years later, the off-and-on war between Temujin and Jamukha ended in betrayal. One day in 1206, some of Jamukha's own men handed him over to Temujin— probably expecting rich rewards.

Temujin didn't give Jamukha's men what they expected. Instead of rewarding them, Temujin put them to death for betraying their master! Then, for the sake of old oaths, Temujin offered Jamukha his life. All he had to do was swear loyalty to Temujin, and he could live out his days in peace and comfort!

Alas, Jamukha didn't want that kind of life. If he couldn't be Great Khan, then he wanted nothing more from Temujin than a quick death. Resigned to his fate, Jamukha told his old friend:

> "As there is room for only one sun in the sky, so too there is room for only one Mongol lord."

With that, Temujin stood on top. From 1206 on, he was known by the title he had fought so long to win:

Genghis Khan, Great Ruler of the Mongols.

After conquering his fellow Mongols, Genghis Khan turned his attention to a new task: conquering his neighbors. The rise of Genghis Khan started one of the

Temujin enthroned as Genghis Khan,
Great Ruler of all Mongol tribes

most terrifying times in all history: the **Mongol invasions** of the 1200s.

This was when the harshness of Mongolia came in handy. The Mongols were so used to going without food that they didn't need to carry a lot of supplies with them. Without clunky supply wagons to slow them down, they could ride farther and faster than anyone expected them to. **Hordes** of Mongols thundered in out of nowhere, taking their enemies completely by surprise.

The invasion started with the Mongols looting and burning a village or two, killing everyone in sight. After everyone in the area was thoroughly terrified, they gave their enemies two choices: either pay **tribute** to the Great Khan, or prepare to die. If anyone defied them, then they murdered everyone— even those who wanted to pay tribute. Then they thundered off again, leaving nothing but burned cities and mounds of skulls.

> A **horde** is a swarm of enemies or pests.
>
> A **tribute** is a payment that a conqueror demands from those he conquers.

The Mongols divided their empire into sections called darugha, each run by a governor called a darughachi. The darughachi's most important job was collecting tribute payments. Any village that paid less tribute than its darughachi demanded could expect a visit from a Mongol horde!

A darughachi inspecting a tribute payment from a Russian village

Their first victims were the Chinese. Genghis attacked northern China in 1206, the same year he became Great Khan.

The timing was important. The attack fell in the middle years of one of China's great medieval dynasties: the Song dynasty. But the Song dynasty didn't rule all China. By the time Genghis came, rebellions had torn China to pieces— which meant that he could conquer it piece by piece. By 1215, all northern China belonged to the Great Khan. But he failed to conquer southern China, where the Song dynasty still ruled.

After conquering all he could in the east, Genghis turned to the west. The lands between China and the Caspian Sea were the next to fall. By 1227, the Mongol Empire stretched all the way from the Pacific Ocean in the east to the Caspian Sea in the west!

The year 1227 was a turning point for the Mongol Empire; for that was when Genghis died. Just before he died, Genghis spoke these last words to his four sons:

> "With heaven's aid I have conquered for you a huge empire. But my life was too short to achieve the conquest of the world. That task is left for you."

The Great Khan's sons tried hard to do just that: conquer the whole world. The amazing thing is, they almost succeeded. Before the end of the 1200s, the Mongol Empire was the biggest empire in all history— on land, at least. Almost all of Asia, and even a big chunk of Eastern Europe, belonged to the Mongols!

Since the Mongols were always on the move, their government needed to move with them. But the government of the Great Khan could hardly meet inside a common yurt! So instead, the Mongols built huge, movable yurts called **ordos**. Some ordos were so big and heavy that they needed teams of twenty-two oxen to pull them.

Genghis Khan taking Beijing, capital of northern China

In modern times, most foreigners look back on Genghis Khan as a monster— remembering all the millions of people he murdered. But Mongol historians like to point out that Genghis wasn't all bad. For example:

➤ Genghis brought law and order to Mongolia. His code of laws, the *Yassa*, was the first written law in Mongolian history.

➤ Genghis built a clever communications system called the *Yam*. Like the Pony Express of the old American West, the *Yam* was a set of postal stations all over the empire. Each station kept plenty of fresh horses, food and water. By riding hard from station to station, horsemen could carry messages across thousands of miles in just a few days.

➤ Genghis protected the Silk Road, the ancient trade route between West and Far East. At the height of their power, the Mongols controlled almost the whole length of the Silk Road.

The Mongols had two good reasons for protecting the Silk Road. First, they collected high tolls from traders who used it. Second, the Silk Road gave them a place to spend all their money. As a nation of raiders, the Mongols knew more about stealing fine goods than they did about making them for themselves. If they wanted fine goods, then they bought them along the Silk Road.

Genghis Khan coin

The Yuan Dynasty

As we read above, Genghis Khan didn't conquer all China. The most he could manage was northern China. Long after Genghis died, the Song dynasty was still holding on in southern China.

How did the Song dynasty stand up to Genghis Khan, when no one else could? The answer goes back to Chapter 17, where we read about a great weapon the Chinese invented in Song dynasty times: iron bombs. Song engineers were the first to pack gunpowder into iron cases. Tough as the Mongols were, even they couldn't stand up to iron-cased bombs!

Alas for China, the Great Khan's sons picked up where he left off. Even so, it was no son of Genghis who conquered southern China. Instead, it was one of his grandsons: **Kublai Khan**. The Song dynasty collapsed in 1279, when the mighty Kublai Khan finally conquered the last bits of southern China.

Kublai Khan (1215 - 1294)

Like his father and grandfather before him, Kublai Khan dreamed of conquering the whole world. After finishing off China, he set out for the countries beyond— starting with Japan.

The problem with invading Japan was crossing the Sea of Japan. Mongol warriors knew a great deal about horses, but almost nothing about ships. Kublai Khan sent two huge fleets against Japan, one in 1274 and another in 1281. Both times, huge storms called **typhoons** drove them off— drowning Mongols by the thousands. The Japanese had another name for the blessed storms that saved them from the Mongol hordes. They called them *kamikazes*— Japanese for "heavenly winds."

The losses didn't stop there. Kublai Khan also invaded both Vietnam and Burma, yet conquered neither. By the late 1200s, the Mongol Empire was as big as it would ever be.

A Chinese junk from Yuan dynasty times.

A typhoon in the East is like a hurricane in the West. Both are tropical storms that blow up in the warm waters near the equator.

When he wasn't at war, Kublai Khan enjoyed all the good things China had to offer. The Chinese had great science, beautiful art and interesting literature to share. The Mongols had none of these things, which is why Kublai enjoyed them so much. He wrote poetry in Chinese, and even converted to Chinese Buddhism.

Kublai Khan also gave himself a Chinese title. Outside China, he was still the Great Khan of the Mongols. But inside China, he was the Emperor of China. The family of Kublai Khan became the **Yuan dynasty**— the next great dynasty after the Song dynasty.

Kublai Khan's battle command center, built across the backs of four war elephants

Kublai Khan spent most of his time at his capital in northern China: Beijing. As the capital of the biggest empire on Earth, Beijing drew visitors from all over— including a pair of brothers called **Niccolo** and **Maffeo Polo**.

The Polo brothers were traders from Venice, Italy. They moved to Constantinople in the mid-1200s, not long after the Fourth Crusade. Alas, times were so hard in Constantinople that they soon moved on. Around 1260, the Polo brothers set out along the Silk Road— hoping for better fortunes.

They were still on the Silk Road in 1264, when a Mongol ambassador invited them to meet Kublai Khan. The Great Khan had never met an Italian, and wanted to know more about them. Niccolo and Maffeo finally made it to Beijing two years later, in 1266.

The Polos' trade caravan traveling the Silk Road

After talking to the Polo brothers, Kublai Khan wanted to know more about Christianity. To find out, he sent the brothers home with a letter for the pope— asking him to send two items to Beijing. One was a bit of holy oil from the Church of the Holy Sepulcher in Jerusalem. The other was a hundred Christian teachers to bring Western ideas to China.

To aid the Polo brothers in their travels, Kublai Khan gave them a special emblem called a *paiza*. The holder of a *paiza* could demand free food and fresh horses from any *Yam* station in the Mongol Empire, courtesy of the Great Khan himself. Even with their valuable *paiza*, the Polo brothers still needed three years to travel from Beijing to Italy!

The Polo brothers receiving their paiza in the court of Kublai Khan

Back in Venice, Niccolo Polo ran into someone he barely knew: his own son, whose name was **Marco Polo**! The last time they met, Marco had been hardly more than a baby. Now he was almost grown up. He was seventeen years old in 1271, when his father and uncle set out for Beijing again— taking Marco along.

Marco Polo (1254? - 1324)

Kublai Khan was so pleased to see the Polos again that they became great favorites. The Great Khan took them everywhere he went, even in wartime. Marco Polo spent almost twenty-four years in the Far East, seeing sights that no one from the West had ever seen before.

When he finally got home to Venice, Marco Polo wrote a book about all he'd seen. First published around 1300, this famous book had two titles. The author called it *The Travels of Marco Polo*; but his publishers often called it *Marvels of the World*. For the things Marco Polo had seen were truly marvelous, especially to Western eyes.

For example, Marco described the great Kublai Khan commanding half a million Mongol horsemen at once— from a tower built across the backs of four war elephants! He also described wonders of science that the West hadn't discovered yet. The Chinese had fireproof cloth made of asbestos fibers; a kind of "burning rock" called coal; and paper money that worked just as well as gold and silver coins!

Some Westerners refused to believe that the East had discovered all these wonders before the West did. In fact, some Italians were so doubtful that they gave Polo's book a third title: *Il Milione*, "The Million Lies."

But Marco Polo wasn't lying— at least, not about everything. In medieval times, Chinese technology really was better than Western technology.

〰〰〰〰〰〰〰〰〰〰〰〰〰〰〰〰〰〰〰〰〰〰〰〰〰〰〰〰〰

How did the Mongol Empire finally end? One way to mark the end is by the end of Kublai Khan; for Kublai was the last Great Khan of the whole empire.

Kublai Khan

When Kublai died in 1294, the Mongol Empire split into four parts. The **Yuan dynasty** continued to rule China. The **Chagatai Khanate** ruled the lands west of China. The **Ilkhanate** ruled the Middle East; while the **Golden Horde** ruled Western Asia and Eastern Europe. The more time passed, the less these four parts had to do with one another.

Another way to mark the end of the Mongol Empire is by the end of the Yuan dynasty. In 1368, a Han Chinese called Zhu Yuanzhang overthrew the last Yuan emperor. Zhu became the first emperor of the next great Chinese dynasty: the **Ming dynasty**.

One by one, the other pieces of the Mongol Empire all collapsed. As we read in Chapter 11, the Russians stopped paying tribute to the Golden Horde in 1480. By that time, the empire was all but gone.

When he wasn't in Beijing, Kublai Khan liked to spend time at his summer palace: a fantastic retreat called **Xanadu**. Marco Polo wrote of two palaces at Xanadu. One was made of marble, and the other of lacquered bamboo tiles. As was fitting for a Mongol lord, the bamboo palace could be taken down, hauled away and then set up again wherever the Great Khan wished!

The Ming emperors reigned from a special section of Beijing called the **Forbidden City**. The name "forbidden" came from the fact that no one could enter or leave without the emperor's permission. Part of what made the Forbidden City "forbidden" was a set of two strong barriers: a wall about 25 feet high, and a moat more than 50 yards wide.

The number 9 is special to the Chinese. Remembering this, the architects of the Forbidden City drew in 999 buildings containing a total of 9,999 rooms.

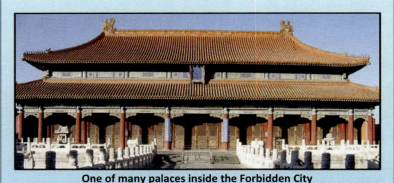

One of many palaces inside the Forbidden City

Many medieval Chinese favored an unusual kind of pet: the cricket. Some carried crickets as good luck charms. Others favored crickets for their music. Still others enjoyed crickets for a more violent reason: because they liked to watch them battle to the death.

A gourd and stopper used as a cricket cage

The Church of the East

One big difference between the Mongol Empire and other medieval empires was that the Mongols didn't have a state church. As long as they didn't miss their tribute payments, the Mongols' subjects could believe whatever they liked— whether they were Shamanist like the Mongols, Buddhist like the Chinese, or Islamic like the Turks and Persians.

Some of the Mongols' subjects followed a religion that was hardly known in the Far East: Christianity. Without meaning to, Genghis Khan brought new life to an old church that had been struggling along for centuries: the **Church of the East**, a.k.a. the **Nestorian Church**.

The name "Nestorian" came from a Syrian priest called **Nestorius**, who lived from about 386 – 450. Nestorius was chosen Archbishop of Constantinople in 428, just before the Church of Egypt split off from all other churches— as we read in Chapter 4. Nestorius got caught in the same sticky web that caught the Egyptians, but in an opposite way.

Nestorius' troubles started with one Greek word: *Theotokos*, meaning "Mother of God." This was one of the titles used for Mary, the mother of Jesus. Priests started calling Mary *Theotokos* long before Nestorius' day. But when Nestorius came along, he insisted that *Theotokos* was the wrong title for Mary. Why? Because God created all things, including Mary. If God created Mary, Nestorius asked, then how could Mary possibly be the "Mother of God"?

The strange way Nestorius answered this question was to cost him his job as Archbishop. Most Christians believed that Christ was a blend of two natures: the divine nature of God, and the human nature of man. Nestorius believed that those two natures were separate. One could say that Mary was the mother of Christ's human nature— *Christotokos*. But one could not say that Mary was the mother of Christ's divine nature— *Theotokos*. For the divine nature was part of God; and God was never born.

In other words, Nestorius taught the opposite of what Egyptian Christians taught. The Egyptians believed that Christ's divine nature absorbed his human one. But Nestorius believed that Christ's divine nature remained separate from his human one.

An icon of Mary as *Theotokos*

The problem was, most Christians believed that both were wrong!

As we read in Chapter 2, Athanasius said that Christ must be both divine and human— fully God and fully man, both at the same time. If Nestorius was right, and Christ's divine nature was never born, then it also never died on the cross— which meant that Christ never could have conquered sin and death.

Despite what old Athanasius said, Nestorius stuck to his beliefs. When the rest of the Church condemned Nestorius, he and his followers moved east— into Persia, where they joined a struggling church called the **Church of the East**.

Although the Church of the East never really thrived, it never died either. Nestorian missionaries won hearts not only in Persia, but also in India, China and even Mongolia. Since Genghis Khan didn't mind, whole Mongol tribes became Nestorian Christians. The wife of Mongke Khan, the fourth Great Khan of the Mongols, was a Nestorian Christian.

CHAPTER 20:   The Ottoman Empire

Osman's Vision

Back in Chapter 12, we read how Turkish Muslims built their first great empire: the **Great Seljuk Empire**. This chapter tells how that empire fell apart, and how the Turks went on to build an even greater one: the **Ottoman Empire**.

The Ottoman Empire would be the biggest Muslim empire of all time. It would also be the longest-lasting, standing for more than six hundred years! The name "Ottoman" comes from the man who started the empire in 1299: **Sultan Osman I**.

All that comes later, though. In early medieval times, the Turks mostly stuck to their old homeland: Turkestan, which stood between China and the Caspian Sea (below). Most Turks also stuck to their old religion— a spirit-talking one called shamanism. It wasn't until the mid-900s that the Turks switched to their new religion: Islam.

Like a lot of other Muslims, the Turks wanted to rule the whole Islamic Empire. They started moving west, conquering other Muslims as they went. The Great Seljuk Empire swallowed Persia first, then Iraq, then Syria. By 1070, it was breaking off pieces of the last Christian empire in the East: the Byzantine Empire.

Naturally, the Byzantines rode out to stop the Turks. The big showdown came in 1071, when the two enemies fought the famous **Battle of Manzikert**.

As we read in Chapter 12, Manzikert was one of the biggest disasters in the whole history of the Byzantine Empire. The emperor's army collapsed around him, allowing the Turks to capture the emperor himself! According to legend, **Sultan Alp Arslan** set his boot on the neck of the beaten emperor— making it perfectly clear which of them was master.

Scene from the Battle of Manzikert

After the Battle of Manzikert, Alp Arslan assigned one of his generals to tackle the Byzantine Empire— hoping he could take the rest of it. Meanwhile, Arslan himself rode off to fight more battles in the east.

After one of those battles, Arslan's men brought him a beaten enemy to judge. As usual, Arslan sentenced his enemy to death. But this enemy was different. When Arslan announced his sentence, the man pulled out a hidden dagger and rushed at him!

Alp Arslan (1029 – 1072)

As dangers went, this wasn't a big one. Arslan was surrounded by guards, all armed and ready to defend him. There was also Arslan himself, who had great skill with bow and arrow. To show everyone just how great, Arslan waved his guards aside— planning to shoot the man down himself.

This turned out to be a mistake. For just when Arslan released his bowstring, his foot slipped— sending his arrow wide of the mark. Before the guards could react, the rushing man plunged his dagger into Arslan's chest. So it was that the mighty sultan died, hardly a year after his great victory at Manzikert.

A **caravanserai** was a roadside inn built along a trade route of the East, like the ancient Silk Road. After a long, hot day of desert travel, traders could stop at a caravanserai to water their camels, buy supplies, bathe and sleep with a roof over their heads.

A still-standing caravanserai in Iran

Back in the west, Arslan's general was taking more and more land from the Byzantine Empire— all with no help from the Great Seljuk Empire. The longer this went on, the more the general realized that he didn't need any help. In 1077, he struck out on his own— setting up a new country called the **Sultanate of Rum**.

The Sultanate of Rum was a Muslim land in **Anatolia**, just east of the Byzantine Empire. The name "Rum" was the Turkish version of the Latin name "Rome." Like everyone else in those days, the Sultan of Rum dreamed of rebuilding the Roman Empire— with himself as emperor.

Anatolia, a.k.a. Asia Minor, is the big peninsula between the Black Sea and the Mediterranean Sea.

When other generals saw what the Sultan of Rum had done, they started breaking away too. By the mid-1090s, the Great Seljuk Empire was finished.

ꙮꙮꙮ

Meanwhile, the sultans of Rum drew closer and closer to the capital of the Byzantine Empire: lovely **Constantinople**. By about 1090, the only thing between Constantinople and the Turks was a thin strip of land and water. The Byzantine emperor grew so desperate that he sent a letter to the pope— saying that if help didn't come soon, then Constantinople might fall.

As we read in Chapter 12, the pope answered the emperor in a big way. In late 1095, Pope Urban II called on all Christians to fight a holy war against the Muslims— the war we now call the **First Crusade**.

The soldiers of the First Crusade came in two waves. The sultans of Rum had no trouble with the first wave, which was the poor peasants of the People's Crusade. But when the trained knights of the Prince's Crusade came along, they drove the sultans back— well away from Constantinople.

About 150 years later, Rum faced another mighty enemy: the **Mongol Empire**. As we read in Chapter 19, the Mongols set out to conquer the whole world— and almost succeeded! By the mid-1200s, Rum was doing what almost every other kingdom in the East was doing: paying tribute to the Mongols.

But the Mongols only conquered the eastern side of Rum. The western side stayed strong. When the eastern side collapsed, the generals of the western side declared independence from Rum— just as Rum had declared independence from the Great Seljuk Empire.

One of those western generals was Ertugrul Ghazi, who had a son called Osman. In years to come, Osman would be **Sultan Osman I**— first sultan of the **Ottoman Empire**.

When Osman was young, he paid a lot of visits to a Muslim holy man called **Sheikh Edebali**. Although Osman loved his Muslim faith, that was only one reason why he spent so much time with Edebali. The other reason was Edebali's daughter: the beautiful Mal Hatun, whom Osman longed to marry.

Osman was lying down to rest one night, thinking about his future, when a vision appeared to him. The first scene was himself and Sheikh Edebali, lying asleep side-by-side. As Osman looked on, a full moon rose from Edebali's chest, and then set in Osman's chest. Next, a huge tree pushed up from Osman's chest— its branches covered with curved leaves. The tree spread out over all three of the known continents: Asia, Europe and Africa.

Everywhere the tree spread, prosperity spread too. Fountains gushed from the tree's roots, watering great harvests. Mosques sprang up, filled with Muslims praying thanks to Allah. In the middle of it all, glittering like a diamond ring, stood the city of Constantinople. Osman was about to set this precious ring on his finger when the vision ended, and he awoke.

When Osman told Sheikh Edebali about his vision, the wise old man revealed the hidden meanings of everything he had seen:

➢ The moon represented Islam, which Edebali loved with all his heart. That love had now spread to Osman's heart— which meant that Osman was the perfect leader to build a new Muslim empire. Now that Edebali knew Osman's heart, he was happy to let him marry Mal Hatun.

➢ The great tree represented the great empire that Osman was about to build. The Ottoman Empire would one day spread out over three continents.

➢ The curved leaves represented the curved **scimitars** that Osman and his **ghazi** warriors would use to build the Ottoman Empire.

Sheikh Edebali was a special kind of Muslim called a dervish. Dervishes are mystical holy men who find Allah in visions and trances. A **whirling dervish** is one who dances a whirling dance, trying to bring on a trance that will bring him closer to Allah.

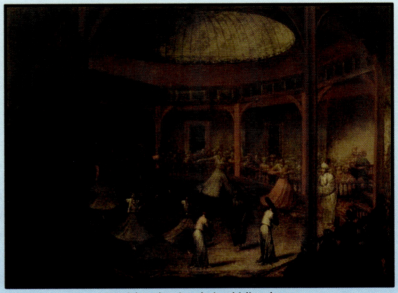

Dervishes dancing their whirling dance

A **scimitar** was a kind of curved sword used mostly by Muslim warriors.

A **ghazi** was a Muslim holy warrior who tried to spread Islam all over the world. The Turkish Muslims who fought for the Great Seljuk Empire, the Sultanate of Rum and the Ottoman Empire all thought of themselves as ghazis.

Despite all the good omens in Osman's vision, the Ottoman Empire took a long time to build. Since the mighty Mongols still ruled eastern Anatolia, Osman started in western Anatolia. In one way, the Mongols actually helped Osman. The longer the Mongols ruled the east, the more Turkish Muslims moved west to join Osman's armies.

Even so, Osman never conquered any lands in Europe or Africa. The glittering ring of Osman's vision, Constantinople, was never his to wear. Like Genghis Khan before him, Osman left the rest of the world for his sons and grandsons to conquer.

Sultan Osman I inspiring his ghazis with words from the Quran

Osman's son **Orhan** was the first to conquer lands in Europe. Sultan Orhan seized the peninsula of **Gallipoli**, southwest of Constantinople, in 1355.

Osman's grandson conquered a lot more. Sultan **Murad I** seized most of the Balkan Peninsula, the part of Europe where Constantinople stands. By the end of his reign, Constantinople was like a little Christian island in a huge Muslim sea.

> **Gallipoli** is the narrow part of Europe just across from Asia Minor. The strait in between is called the Dardanelles.

One of the secrets of Murad's success was the kind of soldiers he used. Before the 1300s, most countries didn't have **standing armies** filled with professional soldiers. Instead, they had part-time armies filled with farmers and tradesmen— ordinary men whose everyday jobs had nothing to do with fighting.

Murad had a better idea. Around 1365, he created a new kind of soldier called a **janissary**. Janissaries had the best of everything: the best weapons, the best training, the best horses and uniforms.

When a janissary tangled with an enemy farmer, the janissary usually won.

> A **standing army** is one that is always ready to fight, whether there is a war on or not.
>
> **Janissary** is Turkish for "new soldier."

Most janissaries weren't born Muslims. Instead, they were Christian boys who were taken from their parents and raised as Muslims. When an Ottoman sultan conquered a Christian land, he ordered Christian parents to hand over their boys.

The sultans called this system **devshirme**— Turkish for "child tax." Christians called it by a less flattering name: the **blood tax**.

The sultans especially wanted boys about 6 – 10 years old; for they found younger boys easier to re-train. *Devshirme* boys went from Christian homes to Muslim military schools, where their teachers raised them to be great fighters.

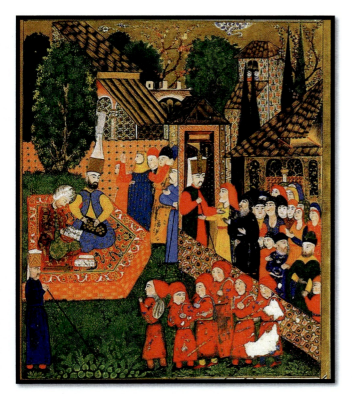

Collecting the blood tax from Christian parents

Because *devshirme* boys were young, most of them forgot all about their pasts. Hearing nothing but Turkish, they forgot their old languages. Hearing nothing but Islam, they forgot their old Christian faith. And hearing nothing but praise for the sultan, they grew up loyal to the sultan. The janissaries were the sultan's special new soldiers, raised from boyhood to fight for the sultan alone.

〰〰〰〰〰〰〰〰〰〰〰〰〰〰〰〰〰〰〰〰〰〰〰〰〰〰〰〰〰〰〰〰〰

Sultan Murad I had two strong sons. The older son, Bayezid, commanded the left wing of the sultan's armies; while the younger, Yakub, commanded the right wing. The trouble started in 1389, when Murad died in battle— without saying which of his sons would be the next sultan.

Bayezid had been waiting for something like this. When Bayezid heard that his father was dead, he sent a carefully-worded message to Yakub— saying that Yakub was to come to the sultan's tent immediately. Like the dutiful soldier he was, Yakub came— not knowing that "sultan" in the note was really his brother. The moment Yakub stepped into the tent, Bayezid's men strangled him to death!

Bayezid wasn't the first sultan who murdered his brothers on his way to the top; and he wouldn't be the last. Ottoman sultans weren't like the kings of the West, who usually handed down their thrones to their oldest sons. The sultans' way was to let their sons fight for their thrones. They felt that the last brother alive would be the strongest, which made him the right brother for the job.

〰〰〰〰〰〰〰〰〰〰〰〰〰〰〰〰〰〰〰〰〰〰〰〰〰〰〰〰〰〰〰〰

Sultan Bayezid I

For a while, it looked like Bayezid I might be the sultan who finally captured Constantinople. Bayezid laid siege to Constantinople in 1394, and kept it up for nearly eight years. Alas, Bayezid was so busy fighting in the west that he forgot to look east— where **Tamerlane** was gunning for him.

The last time we covered Tamerlane was in Chapter 16, when he sacked the capital of India: Delhi. The Ottoman Empire was next on his list. A few years after the Battle of Delhi, Tamerlane crushed Bayezid in a big fight called the Battle of Ankara. At battle's end, the beaten Bayezid was hauled off in chains! He went from the sultan's throne to a prison in Tamerlane's capital: Samarkand, where he soon died.

A few years after that, Tamerlane died too. By then, though, the Ottoman Empire was in chaos, and needed a long time to get back on its feet.

The Fall of Constantinople

Thanks to all the trouble with Tamerlane, it wasn't Bayezid I who captured Constantinople. Nor was it Bayezid's son, Sultan Mehmed I; nor even his grandson, Sultan Murad II. The one who finally captured Constantinople was Bayezid's great-grandson: **Sultan Mehmed II**, who is also called **Mehmed the Conqueror**.

How did Constantinople stand for so long against so many strong sultans? The answer is that Constantinople was probably the strongest city on Earth. The whole city was surrounded by high, strong walls that had been hundreds of years in the making. Some sections had two walls, or even three— all surrounded by a broad, deep moat. Even if an enemy managed to cross the moat and break through the first wall, he still had more walls to go.

All that was on the land side, which faced mostly to the west. On all other sides of Constantinople, attackers had to cross big bodies of water. To the south lay the **Sea of Marmara**. To the east lay the **Bosporus**, the strait that connects to the Black Sea. And to the north lay Constantinople's natural harbor: the calm, lovely **Golden Horn**.

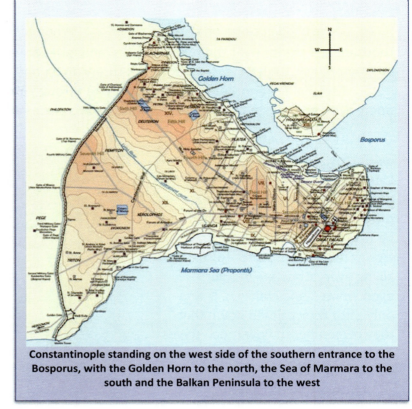

Constantinople standing on the west side of the southern entrance to the Bosporus, with the Golden Horn to the north, the Sea of Marmara to the south and the Balkan Peninsula to the west

Mehmed would have loved to sail his warships into the Golden Horn; but alas, the Byzantines wouldn't let him. Whenever he tried, they stretched a long, strong chain across the entrance. Floating logs kept the chain near the surface of the water, making it impossible to cross. And with the strong Byzantine navy defending the chain, Mehmed couldn't cut it.

Mehmed also tried **sapping**— in other words, tunneling under the city walls. With a finished tunnel, Mehmed's troops might have

Sappers were specially-trained soldiers who tunneled under city walls.

sneaked into the city and attacked the Byzantines from behind. Or they might have piled enough gunpowder under the walls to blow them sky-high! But the Byzantines had faced sappers before, and knew how to beat them. Wherever the Byzantines heard digging sounds, they dug holes of their own— collapsing the tunnels on the sappers' heads.

A super-cannon like the one Orban built for the Siege of Constantinople

When both sailors and sappers failed, Mehmed turned to a weapon that was still new in the 1400s: the cannon. Just before the **Siege of Constantinople**, a Hungarian cannon-maker called **Orban** had offered to forge a huge cannon for the city. When the Byzantines couldn't afford his price, Orban offered his cannon to Mehmed II— who was rich enough to afford any price!

The size of Orban's cannon was breathtaking. Even broken into pieces, the huge gun still needed sixty oxen and four hundred men to haul it into place. Its stone cannonballs were equally breathtaking, measuring two feet across and weighing 600 – 1,200 pounds each. With enough gunpowder behind it, a cannonball that size could smash any wall— even Constantinople's.

Smashing walls was just part of breaking into Constantinople. There was also the problem of crossing the moat, which meant either bridges or boats. Mehmed's solution was a kind of land bridge called a **causeway.** His poor troops had to dump tons of earth and rock into the moat, with the Byzantines firing down on them all the while.

A **causeway** is a land bridge made by piling earth and rock into the water.

The big day came on **May 29, 1453**. When his causeways were finally ready, Mehmed sent thousands of troops over them at once. His janissaries started surging over a wall that had been crushed by cannonballs. Each time the Byzantines threw down one janissary, two more leapt up to take his place!

Meanwhile, another set of troops broke through a small gate that someone had foolishly left half-open. With enemies pouring over the walls in two places at once, the city was doomed.

The Fall of Constantinople was an ugly scene, even for the Late Middle Ages. After waiting hundreds of years for this great prize, the Muslims were thrilled to be taking it at last! Triumphant troops raced from street to street, killing every Christian in sight— even women and children. It was only after they calmed down that they remembered how much slaves were worth. Then the Muslims started capturing instead of killing, so that they could sell their Christian captives into slavery.

The last Emperor of the Byzantines made a brave end for

Scene from the battle inside Constantinople

himself. Casting off the purple cloak that marked him as a royal, **Emperor Constantine XI** threw himself into the thickest part of the battle— and died fighting for his people.

Mehmed the Conqueror riding into Constantinople

The Fall of Constantinople was a historic milestone, the kind of event historians use to mark endings and beginnings. A lot of things ended when Constantinople fell.

One thing that ended was the Middle Ages. The Fall of Constantinople is one way to mark the end of the medieval era, and the start of the next era: the Renaissance, which we'll get to in Chapter 26.

Another thing that ended was the Byzantine Empire. It had stood for almost a thousand years, ever since the Fall of Rome back in 476. Now it stood no longer. In a way, the Roman Empire ended too; for the Byzantine Empire had started as the Eastern Roman Empire.

A third ending happened at the finest church in Constantinople: the Hagia Sophia. The grand old Hagia Sophia had been the capital of Eastern Christianity since the 500s, when old Justinian built it (Chapter 4). Now it was a church no longer! The same day Mehmed rode into Constantinople, the Hagia Sophia became a mosque. An imam started chanting the *Shahada* from its altar— saying over and over, "There is no god but Allah, and Muhammad is his prophet." After 900 years of standing for Christ, the Hagia Sophia now stood for Allah.

The Hagia Sophia with minarets added

The years to come brought more changes to the Hagia Sophia. The Christian mosaics inside were all covered with plaster and paint, after the Muslims pried out all the golden tiles. They also added four minarets, the high towers used to call Muslims to prayer five times each day.

〜〜〜〜〜〜〜〜〜〜〜〜〜〜〜〜〜〜〜〜〜〜〜〜〜〜〜〜〜

With Constantinople as its capital, the Ottoman Empire grew faster than ever. Sultan **Selim I** tripled its size, conquering Arabia, Egypt and more. After starting in Asia and spreading to Europe, the empire now spread to the third continent from Osman's vision: Africa!

Selim's son, **Sultan Suleiman I**, was probably the greatest of all Ottoman sultans. As a great historic figure, Suleiman has two historic nicknames. The East calls him **Suleiman the Lawgiver**; while the West calls him **Suleiman the Magnificent**.

Suleiman the Magnificent (1494 – 1566)

The Eastern nickname honors Suleiman as a writer of law. Like the Byzantine Emperor Justinian, and like King Henry II of England, Suleiman set up one common law over his whole empire. Even today, some Middle Eastern law is still based on the laws of Suleiman.

The Western nickname honors Suleiman for his magnificence. The Ottoman Empire was truly magnificent in Suleiman's day— not only huge, but also incredibly rich and prosperous. Muslim writers, artists and builders all did some of their best work in Suleiman's day.

One of Suleiman's many projects was the Dome of the Rock, which still stands in Jerusalem. As we read in Chapter 5, the Dome of the Rock is a shrine to the Night Journey taken by the prophet Muhammad. The original Dome of the Rock was built in the 600s, when Islam was just getting started. By Suleiman's day, that old shrine was crumbling. Suleiman restored it, making it much better than the original.

〜〜〜〜〜〜〜〜〜〜〜〜〜〜〜〜〜〜〜〜〜〜〜〜〜〜〜〜〜〜〜〜

Like all Ottoman sultans, Suleiman kept many women in his **harem**. When a harem woman had a son, the sultan usually sent both mother and son away. That way, harem women couldn't fight over the all-important question: which of their sons would be the next sultan?

> A **harem** was a special section of the palace where a sultan kept his many wives.

But one of Suleiman's women was different. Suleiman's wife **Roxelana** was so smart, pretty and fun that he couldn't bear to send her away. He kept Roxelana at his side, raising six children with her.

Since Roxelana was the sultan's favorite wife, she felt that her son should be the next sultan. The trouble was, her sons were only boys;

"Suleiman and Roxelana" by artist Anton Hickel

while some of Suleiman's sons were grown men. Roxelana was especially worried about one of Suleiman's sons— a powerful one called Mustafa. Knowing how many Ottoman sultans had murdered their own brothers, Roxelana had good reason to fear that Mustafa might murder her sons.

But not if Roxelana murdered Mustafa first!

The story of how Mustafa died is more legend than history. But if the legend is true, then Roxelana planted a false rumor about Mustafa. All of a sudden, Suleiman's spies started hearing that Mustafa was planning to rebel against his father.

Suleiman's answer was to call his son to his tent. Mustafa came quickly, having no idea that anything was wrong. The moment he stepped in, Suleiman's guards strangled him to death— with Suleiman himself calmly looking on! See Year Three for more on Suleiman the Magnificent.

Muslim Food Laws

Islamic law forbids Muslims to eat certain foods. Foods that Muslims may eat are called **halal**, Arabic for "permissible." Forbidden foods are **haram**, Arabic for "sinful."

Two kinds of foods are especially *haram*: pork and alcohol. Good Muslims never eat any food that comes from a pig. They also avoid alcohol, although not all Muslims live by this rule.

Good Muslims observe these table manners:

➤ They carefully wash their hands before and after each meal.

➤ They don't start eating until their host starts, nor stop until their host stops.

➤ They eat only with their right hands, never their left; and they always use at least 3 fingers.

➤ They do not blow their food to cool it.

➤ They stand to drink water by day, but sit or lie down to drink water by night.

Saint George

The patron saint of England didn't come from anywhere near England. Instead, Saint George came from somewhere in the Eastern Roman Empire. The Eastern Roman Empire became the Byzantine Empire, which ended with the Fall of Constantinople— as we read above.

The story of St. George is part real and part legend. The best-known legend of St. George tells how he came to slay a dragon!

As the story goes, George was wandering through North Africa when he met a hermit with a sad tale. An evil dragon had taken over the little kingdom where George now stood. The menacing worm had already eaten all the kingdom's livestock, and was now eating its way through the children. It wanted a new child to eat every day, or else it would attack the capital.

The dragon's demands gave the king a terrible choice to make every day. If he obeyed the dragon, then one child would surely die. But if he disobeyed the dragon, then his whole kingdom might die!

So far, the king had made his choice in the fairest way he could: by drawing names from a pot. But today, the hermit said, was the worst day yet— for the name that came out of the pot that day belonged to the king's own daughter. The princess was on her way to the dragon's lair that very moment, never to return.

Like the hero he was, George immediately galloped off to slay the dragon and save the princess. But this was no easy dragon to slay! When George thrust his spear at the dragon, the weapon broke against its scales. His sword was also powerless to pierce the scales. Meanwhile, poisonous smoke spewed from the dragon's mouth— almost suffocating the brave knight.

Fortunately, the smoke wasn't thick enough to hide the dragon's one weakness: a soft spot with no scales, right between breast and wing. When George stabbed this vulnerable spot, the dragon fell dead.

After ward, the king asked George how he could thank him for saving his daughter. The only thanks George wanted was this: that everyone in the whole kingdom should become a Christian!

The real story of St. George is less romantic. The future St. George was a Christian soldier who served under one of the most Christian-hating Roman emperors ever: Diocletian. When Diocletian found out about George's faith, he ordered George to give it up. When George refused, Diocletian killed him.

Greek icon of St. George the Dragon-slayer

The Caspian Sea

The Caspian Sea is an inland sea east of the Black Sea. Unlike most seas, the Caspian Sea isn't connected to the oceans of the world. Fresh water flows into the Caspian Sea from the Volga River, the Ural River and many others. But no water flows out of the Caspian Sea. The only way water leaves is by evaporation.

When water evaporates, it leaves behind mineral salts that were dissolved in it. Just as the oceans have built up salt over time, so the Caspian Sea has built up salt. The waters of the Caspian Sea average about one-third as salty as ocean water.

The Caspian Sea is a great place to catch a kind of fish called sturgeon. Russian fishermen make sturgeon eggs into a fancy food that many people never taste, because they can't afford it: caviar. Some kinds of caviar cost well over $100 per ounce!

The Dark Continent

Most of the stories we've read so far come from Europe or Asia. When we've read about Africa, it has almost always been North Africa— the part near the Mediterranean Sea. Why? Because in medieval times, few outsiders had ever seen any other part of Africa. They called it the Dark Continent, thinking of it as a mysterious place full of unknown wonders.

Africa is the hottest of the seven continents. This is because most of it lies in the tropics, the warm part of the globe between the Tropic of Cancer and the Tropic of Capricorn. Many of the hottest temperatures ever recorded come from Africa.

Africa is also the second-biggest continent, behind only Asia. The easiest way to study such a big place is to break it into regions.

The first region, North Africa, has one of the biggest, driest deserts in the world: the Sahara. Next to Antarctica, the Sahara is probably the last place on Earth where most people would want to live. Water is extremely rare in the Sahara. On the other hand, sand is extremely plentiful! High winds whip the Sahara sands into deadly sandstorms, piling them into dunes up to 500 feet high.

Only two parts of North Africa aren't part of the Sahara. One is the Nile River Valley, where one of the oldest known civilizations began. The other is the Maghreb, a mountainous region along the Mediterranean Sea. The coasts of Morocco, Algeria, Tunisia and Libya are all part of the Maghreb.

> With a total length of more than 4,100 miles, the **Nile** is the longest river in the world.

Below the Sahara, between the dry desert and the wetter lands to the south, lies a half-dry region called the Sahel. A good year in the Sahel brings just enough rain to water crops. A bad year can stunt crops, leaving people to starve.

Along the southern coast of West Africa lies a region called Guinea, which is well-known for its gold mines. Near the end of medieval times, Guinean gold helped start the Age of Discovery— as we'll read in Chapter 24.

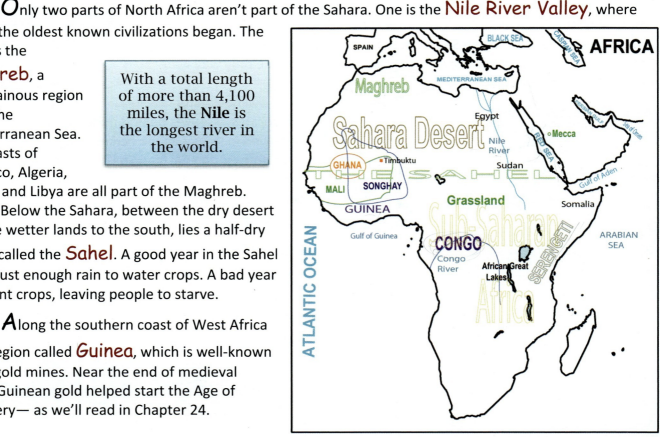

Southeast of Guinea lies a region called the **Congo**. The Congo is home to Africa's deepest jungles and wildest animals. Gorillas, leopards and pythons all live in the Congo, as do many other wild species.

East of the Congo lies the **African Great Lakes region**. The biggest lake in Africa, Lake Victoria, is also the second biggest lake in the world. Only Lake Superior in North America is bigger.

East of the African Great Lakes region lies a grassy plain called the **Serengeti**. The Serengeti is where the wild herds go to graze— including gazelles, wildebeests, zebras and more. The Serengeti is also where lions and hyenas go to prey on the herds.

A lioness taking some sun on a rock in the Serengeti

Sub-Saharan Africa is the part of Africa south of the Sahara Desert.

All these lower regions, and more besides, belong to **Sub-Saharan Africa**— the part below the Sahara Desert. The Sahara was so hot, so dry and so wide that almost no one from the north dared cross it. Until they did, Sub-Saharan Africa would always be the Dark Continent.

Medieval Empires of West Africa

Traders were especially curious about the Dark Continent. Sub-Saharan Africa offered valuable goods that everyone wanted— rare items like gold, ivory and black pepper. The question was, how could they get their hands on those goods? Badly as they wanted them, few traders dared go after them; for they all knew how deadly the Sahara could be.

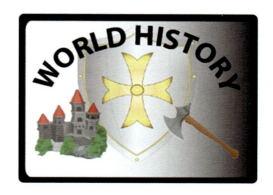

Fortunately, one kind of trader knew how to cross the Sahara without dying: the **Tuaregs**. The Tuaregs were a tough people who lived all around the Sahara, and sometimes in it. As natives of the desert, the Tuaregs had learned how to survive there— what to wear, how to travel, and where to find water.

An **oasis** is a place to find water in the middle of a desert, like a green island in a sea of sand.

A Saharan oasis in Libya

As dry as the Sahara is, it does have a few watery **oases**. However, crossing the Sahara is not as simple as hopping on a camel and setting out for the next oasis! For one thing, the sand dunes are always shifting— which makes it easy to get lost. For another, the oases lie many days apart— which makes it easy to run out of water. And in the Sahara, even a few hours without water can be enough to kill.

To solve this water problem, the Tuaregs built a small village at each oasis along their trade routes. When a **trade caravan** started to run out of water, it sent a fast rider to the next oasis ahead. The villagers there put together a water caravan, which the rider guided back to the trade caravan.

A modern-day salt caravan crossing the Sahara. A trade caravan is a group of traders who travel together for help and safety.

So far, so good. But if anything went wrong— for example, if the water caravan couldn't find the trade caravan, or found it too late— then the traders might still run out of water. Then they would all die hot, dry, sandy Saharan deaths.

~~~~~~

What did the Tuaregs buy with all that gold and ivory from sub-Saharan Africa? The answer is mostly salt. In the middle of the western Sahara, halfway between Morocco and Guinea, stood a salt mining town called Taghaza. The slaves of Taghaza worked at one of the most miserable jobs ever: mining slabs of rock salt.

What made salt mining so miserable was that salt was everywhere. Everything in Taghaza was salty, from the drinking water and the food to the miners' clothes, skin and eyes. Even the walls of the miners' huts were made from stacked slabs of rock salt. The miners' jobs were so hard that even today, when people think of jobs they'd rather not do, they speak of going "back to the salt mines."

Why did miners keep doing those miserable jobs? Because salt was so valuable— especially to the Africans of hot, humid Guinea. People who sweat a lot lose a lot of salt, and need a way to replace it. Livestock need salt to thrive. Salt is also used to preserve meat and fish, or to flavor meals.

~~~~~~

Wherever trade grew, empires also grew. Taxing trade was a great way for emperors to grow rich. Just as the Mongol Empire taxed trade along the Silk Road, so the empires of West Africa taxed trade across the Sahara.

Stacked slabs of rock salt

The medieval era saw the rises and falls of three West African empires. The first was **Ghana**; the next was **Mali**; and the last was **Songhai**. All three stood in the Sahel, just south of the Sahara. They stood between Guinea and the Sahara, collecting taxes on gold from Guinea and salt from the Sahara.

The Ghana Empire (700s - 1200s)

Just how the **Ghana Empire** got started, no one knows for sure. Some say that the first kings of Ghana were traders who came down from the north and conquered the natives. Others say that it was the natives who built Ghana. Since it all happened long ago, before anyone in West Africa learned to write, no one can say for sure.

What is sure is that Ghana had a lot of gold! A writer who visited in the 800s saw gold everywhere. Gold jewelry was only the beginning. He also saw gold swords, shields, clothes, hats— even dog collars and horse harnesses!

Between Ghana and the next empire, the **Mali Empire**, came a big change. The people of Ghana followed ancient African religions, which were different from tribe to tribe. But Mali followed an Arabian religion: **Islam**. The Muslim faith had been filtering in since the late 600s, when it finished conquering North Africa. Now it was ready to conquer Sub-Saharan Africa too.

The Mali Empire (1200s - 1500s)

The story of Mali starts with a mighty Muslim prince called **Sundiata Keita**. Sundiata belonged to the **Mandinka**, one of the first tribes in West Africa to turn Muslim. But that might have been forgotten, were it not for special storytellers called **griots**.

A griot is a kind of singing historian found only in West Africa. Griots memorize long songs full of stories and names. Before writing came to West Africa, the only way to learn what griots knew was to listen to their songs. Many important stories would have been lost without the excellent memories of griots.

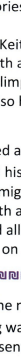

Griots from Mali. Learning history from a griot isn't like opening a book. To share what they know, griots must sing their songs from beginning to end— which can take more than a day!

According to griot legend, Sundiata Keita wasn't born mighty. In fact, he was born with a spine so crooked that he couldn't walk! He limped along until one fateful day, when one of his half-brothers insulted his poor mother— who also had a crooked spine. Sundiata longed to punish his half-brother, but needed strength to do it.

To get that strength, Sundiata asked a blacksmith for a heavy iron rod. He pulled and pulled on that iron, straining with all his might— until his spine went straight, and the iron went crooked! Now instead of a bent weakling, Sundiata was a mighty warrior with a backbone stronger than iron.

With a mighty king like that at their head, the Mandinka soon conquered all the other tribes around them. As Emperor of Mali, Sundiata Keita took on a new title: *mansa*, Mandinka for "king of kings."

The most famous mansa of Mali, **Mansa Musa**, also rose in an interesting way. The mansa before Mansa Musa wanted to explore the world. He sent two hundred ships out into the Atlantic Ocean, ordering their captains to learn as much as they could. Only one of those captains ever came back— and with a frightening story to tell. At the far edge of the Atlantic, the captain said, churned a huge whirlpool that had sucked down all the other ships. It would have sucked him down too, had he not been last in line!

The mansa thought this captain must be lying. To prove it, the mansa led an exploration of his own— this time with two thousand ships. None of them ever returned, not even the mansa's ship. With the old mansa out of the picture, his second-in-command took charge of Mali. That was Mansa Musa.

A terracotta horseman figure from Malian times

If the Ghana Empire had a lot of gold, then the Mali Empire had even more. For Mali was bigger than Ghana— big enough to swallow some of the gold mines down in Guinea. Instead of just taxing gold, Mansa Musa mined gold of his own.

The laws of Mali said that any gold nuggets found in the mines automatically belonged to the *mansa*. Others could own gold dust, but the big chunks all went straight to the emperor. On a famous world map from the 1300s, Mansa Musa eyes a gold nugget bigger than his fist!

Mansa Musa on a Spanish map published in 1375

Like all good Muslims, Mansa Musa once went on the **Hajj**— the great pilgrimage to Mecca (Chapter 5). But with that much gold, Mansa Musa's *Hajj* was like no one else's. As pocket money for his journey, his caravan carried tons of gold dust— enough to pay for a new mosque at every city where he happened to stop on a Friday night!

> The **Hajj** is a yearly pilgrimage to the place where Islam was born: Mecca, Arabia. All able-bodied Muslims must take the *Hajj* at least once in their lives.

Mansa Musa also spent gold to make Mali more Muslim. On his return from Mecca, he brought home a Muslim architect to build new mosques in Mali. He also brought home imams and books, hoping to teach his people a purer form of Islam.

ꉭꉭꉭꉭꉭꉭꉭꉭꉭꉭꉭꉭꉭꉭꉭꉭꉭꉭꉭꉭꉭꉭꉭꉭꉭꉭꉭꉭꉭꉭꉭꉭꉭꉭꉭꉭ

The Songhai Empire (1400s - 1590s)

The last medieval empire of West Africa started with a rebellion against the Mali Empire. In the mid-1400s, a breakaway people called the Songhai set up an empire of their own: the Songhai Empire.

The more time passed, the more cities Songhai seized from Mali. Two of them were the greatest cities in all West Africa, Timbuktu and Djenne. Both stood on or near the Niger River, the most important river in West Africa.

The rest of the world knew little of Timbuktu, until a Muslim called Leo Africanus pointed it out. Just as Marco Polo stunned the West with news from China, so Leo Africanus stunned the West with news from Timbuktu.

A sketch of medieval Timbuktu

According to Leo, the emperor of Songhai had a bar of solid gold that weighed almost 1,000 pounds! Leo also wrote that Timbuktu was filled with wise men; and that its people strolled casually through its streets each night, serenading one another with fine music. Ever since Leo's book, travelers have seen Timbuktu as a far-off place of mystery and wonder— hard to reach, but worth the trouble.

The Great Mosque of Djenne in modern times

Djenne is known for the biggest building in the world made of mud bricks: the **Great Mosque of Djenne**. The craftsmen of Mali and Songhai built mostly with sun-dried mud bricks, all covered with plaster. The result was a curious style of building

The logs that jut from the sides of mud-brick buildings like the Great Mosque of Djenne are called **toron**. Toron serve two purposes:
➢ One is to tie the building together.
➢ The other is provide a permanent scaffold for workers who keep the outside walls sealed with plaster. Without a tight coat of plaster, rainwater would seep in and dissolve the mud bricks.

found nowhere else in the world. Djenne is also known for the **Djenne terracotta figures,** strange statuettes that were first sculpted by artists of the Mali Empire.

A Djenne terracotta figure

Of the three great empires of medieval West Africa, Songhai was the greatest. Its territory was even bigger than Mali's, and its riches were beyond count.

Alas, the Songhai emperors didn't keep up with the times. The end came in the late 1500s, when the Sultan of Morocco needed gold to help fight off the Portuguese. The way to get it, he decided, was to steal it from the Songhai. The sultan's armies brought weapons the Songhai had never seen before: muskets and cannon. Without gunpowder weapons of their own, the poor Songhai warriors never had a chance.

So it was that the Songhai Empire collapsed, as all empires do someday. From the 1590s forward, there were no great empires in West Africa— only scattered kingdoms.

The Mamluk Sultanate of Egypt

Way back in Chapter 7, we read how the Islamic Empire carried on after the prophet Muhammad died. The first government after Muhammad was the Rashidun Caliphate, which ruled from 632 – 661. Then came the Umayyad Caliphate, which ruled from 661 – 750. Both these caliphates kept a firm grip on the whole Islamic Empire.

After that, the story gets a bit more complicated. The next caliphate was the **Abbasid Caliphate**, which took over in 750. Like the other caliphs before them, the Abbasid caliphs claimed to rule the whole Islamic Empire. But they really didn't; for the empire was falling apart. Instead of one Muslim empire, there were now many Muslim kingdoms— each ruled by a **sultan** or **emir**.

For most of the Holy Land Crusades, **Egypt** was ruled by a family of sultans called the **Ayyubid dynasty**. The Ayyubids were the heirs of Saladin, the mighty Muslim who battled Richard the Lionheart in the Third Crusade (Chapter 12). Saladin ruled not only Egypt, but also the Holy Land, Syria and part of Arabia.

Like most dynasties, the Ayyubids grew weaker over time. Some of Saladin's heirs couldn't be bothered with running Egypt. They did less and less for themselves, depending more and more on special soldiers called **Mamluks**.

The Mamluks were a lot like the janissaries of the Ottoman Empire (Chapter 20). The first Mamluks came from non-Muslim lands that were conquered by Muslims. They were taken from their parents as boys, and then raised as slave-soldiers for sultans. Just as the Ottoman sultans depended on janissaries, so the Ayyubid sultans depended on Mamluks. The Mamluks did everything for their sultans, from defending their country to running their government.

All that was fine, so long as the Mamluks stayed loyal to their sultans. The trouble started during the **Seventh Crusade**, when an Ayyubid sultan lost the Mamluks' loyalty.

The Seventh Crusade started in 1249, when **King Louis IX of France** set out across the Mediterranean Sea. Like all crusaders, Louis wanted to take back the Holy Land from the Muslims. But Louis went about it differently. He wanted to take Egypt first, and then use it as a base to take back the Holy Land.

> A **sultan** was a governor who ruled part of the Islamic Empire in the caliph's name.
>
> An **emir** was a Muslim military leader.
>
> **Mamluk** is an Arabic word that can be translated "the owned" or "slave-soldier."

Mamluk lancers. A lancer is a cavalryman armed with a lance, or long spear.

Like most of the Holy Land Crusades, the Seventh Crusade went badly for the crusaders. The trouble this time was that the Nile River was flooding when Louis landed. Instead of taking Egypt by surprise, Louis sat around for months— waiting for the water to go down so that he could attack.

By the time the water went down, the Ayyubids were more than ready for Louis. Instead of Louis capturing Egypt, the Egyptians captured Louis— and then held him for ransom! The French had to pay a fortune to save their saintly king from the Muslims.

In other words, the Seventh Crusade looked like a big win for the Ayyubids. What the Ayyubids didn't know yet was that it was also the beginning of their end!

King Louis VII of France setting out to fight the Seventh Crusade

A Mamluk warrior

While fighting the Seventh Crusade, the old Ayyubid sultan suffered a bad wound to the leg. The wound grew infected, sending poison into the sultan's blood. His doctors tried to save his life by cutting off the infected leg; but alas, it was too late.

Fortunately, the old sultan had a son to take his place. Unfortunately, the sultan's son made a foolish mistake. After everything his father's Mamluks had done for him, the new sultan should have treated them with respect; but he didn't. Instead, he ordered them to step aside— so that he could replace them with new favorites of his own.

The mighty Mamluks didn't want to let go of their might. Instead of stepping aside for the disrespectful young sultan, they simply killed him— and then set one of their own in his place! Just like that, the Ayyubid dynasty was finished. Starting in 1250, Egypt had a new government: the **Mamluk Sultanate**. The Mamluks had managed an incredible rise— all the way from slave-soldiers to sultans!

Ten years later, the Mamluk Sultanate faced one of the worst tests any government could face: a Mongol invasion. As we read in Chapter 19, the Mongol Empire started in 1206— the year Temujin became Genghis Khan. The murderous Mongols would soon conquer almost all Asia, and more besides.

Genghis was long dead by 1250, when the Mamluks took over Egypt. The latest Mongol ruler was his grandson **Mongke Khan**. Mongke sent one of his brothers, a fierce fighter called **Hulagu Khan**, to conquer the Middle East— including Egypt.

Hulagu Khan leading a Mongol horde

As always, the Mongols moved quickly. The Mamluk Sultanate was eight years old in 1258, when Hulagu Khan conquered Baghdad, Iraq— capital of the Abbasid Caliphate. Two years later, Hulagu conquered Syria as well.

The next stop was Egypt. On his way to conquer Egypt, Hulagu Khan sent this message to the Mamluks: "…You should think of what happened to other countries and submit… We have conquered vast areas, [killing] all the people. You cannot escape from the terror of our armies. Where can you flee? …Our horses are swift, our arrows sharp, our swords like thunderbolts, our hearts as hard as the mountains, our soldiers as numerous as the sand. Fortresses will not detain us, nor arms stop us. Your prayers to God will not avail against us… We will shatter your mosques and reveal the weakness of your God and then will kill your children and your old men together." Naturally, the Mamluks were terrified!

Just when they least expected it, the Mamluks had a stroke of luck. Around the same time Hulagu sent that terrifying message, he heard that Mongke Khan had died. Instead of going on to Egypt, he had to go back to Mongolia and help choose the next Great Khan. To the delight of the Mamluks, Hulagu took most of his army with him— leaving only a small army to invade Egypt.

Instead of waiting for that army, the Mamluks rode out to meet it. The Mongols and the Mamluks locked swords in the Holy Land, at a place called **Ain Jalut**. The key to the **Battle of Ain Jalut** was understanding the Mongols' favorite battle plan: the **feigned** retreat.

When facing a Mongol horde, most armies formed a Roman-style shield wall. This was a tight wall of shields bristling with long, strong spears. A well-handled spear could skewer any horse that tried to leap the shield wall.

But the Mongols were too clever to leap the shield wall. Instead, they made a feigned retreat. They started with a half-hearted try at breaking through the shield wall. When that failed, they pretended to run away in fear. Their enemies gave chase, thinking they had the Mongols on the run. Alas, this was exactly what the Mongols wanted them to do. Once their enemies left the safety of their shield wall, the Mongols turned and attacked!

Alas for the Mongols, the Mamluks found a way to turn the tables on them. Just before the Battle of Ain Jalut, the Mamluks split their army in half. The first half found a clever hiding place. The second half attacked the Mongols, and then ran away— straight toward the place where the first half was hiding. When the Mongols gave chase, the first half leapt out of hiding and crushed the Mongols!

In winning the Battle of Ain Jalut, the Mamluks did something that no one had done since before the days of Genghis Khan: they defeated a Mongol horde. Thanks to this great victory, the Mongols never conquered Egypt. The Mamluk Sultanate ruled Egypt for more than 250 years— until 1517, when it was finally conquered by Sultan Selim I of the Ottoman Empire (Chapter 20).

> ***Ain Jalut*** is Arabic for "Well of Goliath." The Battle of Ain Jalut happened at the same place where young David of Israel slew the Philistine giant Goliath of Gath (I Samuel 17).
>
> To **feign** is to pretend.

The Avignon Papacy

The Holy Land Crusades raised an important question about authority in the Christian world. The question was, who had more authority: a pope or a king?

While the Crusades lasted, the pope's authority was usually greater. The Third Crusade shows just how great. When the pope announced the Third Crusade, the three greatest kings in Europe— Frederick of Germany, Philip of France and Richard of England— all set out for the Holy Land. In other words, the pope commanded all three great kings.

The next eighty years changed all that. For as we read in Chapter 12, the Holy Land Crusades ended in failure. The four Crusader States all fell, leaving the Holy Land in Muslim hands.

After that many failures, it was hard to believe that the popes were as close to God as they said they were. Disappointed Christians started paying less attention to their popes, and more to their kings.

ꝫꝫꝫꝫꝫꝫꝫꝫꝫꝫꝫꝫꝫꝫꝫꝫꝫꝫꝫꝫꝫꝫꝫ

Thirty years after the last Holy Land Crusade, an Italian pope called **Boniface VIII** had a big argument with **King Philip IV of**

King Philip IV of France   **Pope Boniface VIII**

France over authority. The trouble started with money, as it often does. King Philip needed money to refill his empty treasury. To raise that money, Philip raised taxes on the richest organization in France: the Church.

The trouble was, the Church also needed more money. Pope Boniface wrote an angry **papal bull** against Philip— warning that if any king tried to tax the Church without permission, then the pope would have that king arrested and thrown out of the Church!

Philip answered with another blow to the pope's pocketbook. Under a new law Philip wrote, no French church could send any money at all to the Church of Rome!

Boniface answered back with his harshest words yet. In a papal bull called *Unam Sanctam*, Boniface wrote that the pope was the highest authority on Earth. If a king did wrong, then the pope had the power to judge that king. But only God had the power to judge a pope! *Unam Sanctam* ended with this strong warning about heaven and hell: "… it is absolutely necessary for salvation that every human creature be subject to the Roman [Pope]."

A **papal bull** is an open letter containing a special announcement from a pope. The name "bull" comes from *bulla*, the Latin name for the pope's official seal.

A papal bull from the 1600s with a stamped lead *bulla*

In other words, no one could be saved without the pope. If *Unam Sanctam* was right, then Philip had two choices: he could either obey the pope, or he could literally go to hell!

At this, Philip decided that enough was enough. In 1303, he sent a small army to arrest Boniface. Philip's men caught up with the pope at his home in Anagni, Italy, just outside Rome. Seizing Boniface, Philip's men threw the old man in jail for three days— giving him neither food nor water.

A French knight slapping the pope in 1303

At the end of those three days, an Italian army chased Philip's men off. Before they left, though, one of Philip's men slapped the old pope hard across the face. Between the slap, the jail time and the wound to his pride, it was all too much for Boniface. The old pope died less than a month later. The French called this episode the Anagni Slap; while the Italians called it the Outrage at Anagni.

The next pope was an Italian who served for less than a year. The pope after that was a Frenchman who did whatever King Philip asked. One thing he asked was to move the Church from Italy to France!

A **papal conclave** is a special meeting to decide who will be the next pope. When an old pope dies, the College of Cardinals locks itself inside the Sistine Chapel at Vatican City, Rome. While the cardinals vote, discuss and then vote some more, black smoke rises from the chapel's chimney. But when the cardinals finish voting, white smoke rises. The whole affair ends with the head cardinal joyfully announcing *Habemus papam*— Latin for "We have a pope!"

In 1309, Pope Clement V moved the offices of the Church from Rome, Italy to Avignon, France. This was the start of the Avignon Papacy, which was the only time when the popes didn't live in Rome. The next seven popes were all Frenchmen, and all lived at Avignon. The Avignon Papacy lasted almost seventy years, until the pope moved back to Rome in 1377.

CHAPTER 22

America before Columbus

The Americas

North America is the third-biggest of the seven continents, and South America the fourth-biggest. Together, the two Americas are much bigger than the second-biggest continent: Africa. Even together, though, the two Americas are not quite as big as the biggest continent: Asia.

Two huge bodies of water separate the Americas from Europe, Africa and Asia. The huge **Atlantic Ocean** lies east of the Americas; and the even huger **Pacific Ocean** lies west of the Americas.

Two smaller bodies of water lie between North America and South America. The northern body is the **Gulf of Mexico**, and the southern is the **Caribbean Sea**. The line between the two is mostly covered by two pieces of land. One is **Cuba**, the biggest island of the West Indies. The other is the **Yucatan Peninsula**, which juts off southern North America. In modern times, most of the Yucatan is covered by **Mexico**. But **Belize** also covers part, and **Guatemala** another part.

The narrowest part of North America is called Central America. It starts just south of the Yucatan, and ends at South America. The narrowest part of Central America is called the **Isthmus of Panama**; and it was here that American engineers built one of the toughest projects ever: the Panama Canal.

> An **isthmus** is a narrow piece of land that connects two bigger pieces.

From ancient times through early modern times, the only way ships could cross from the Atlantic to the Pacific was to sail all the way around South America. They might have sailed around North America too, if not for a big problem: The water up north was always clogged with sea ice. Either way, the journey was long, hard and risky.

The Panama Canal changed all that. The Americans took over the project in 1904, when Theodore Roosevelt was president. After ten hard years of digging and **lock**-building, the canal finally opened in 1914— the same year World War I broke out. A trip through the Panama Canal takes about half a day, and covers only about fifty miles— which is a lot better than sailing 8,000 miles around South America!

> A **lock** is a set of gates, pumps and valves built to raise and lower ships.

Empires of Middle America and South America

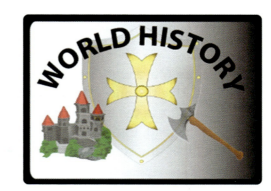

Long before Leif Ericsson, and even longer before Christopher Columbus, Native Americans built empires in the Americas. Some empires arose in **Middle America**, just above South America. Others arose in the **Andes Mountains** of western South America.

This doesn't mean that there were no empires north of Middle America, in what are now the United States and Canada. Archaeologists have found signs of fair-sized cities north of Mexico. What they haven't found are the two main signs that empires leave behind: writing and stone buildings. Without those signs, it is hard to learn much about any empires that might have grown up in the north.

> **Middle America** means Central America plus what is now Mexico.
>
> The **Andes Mountains** run about 4,350 miles from north to south, which makes them the longest mountain range in the world.

One Middle American empire left a lot of stone buildings, but very little writing. The capital of this mysterious empire was called **Teotihuacan**, and it probably got its start around 100 BC. The ruins of Teotihuacan still stand about thirty miles northeast of Mexico City, Mexico.

The people of Teotihuacan built some of the biggest buildings ever in Middle America. The biggest was an incredibly massive one called **Pyramid of the Sun**. With a base that measures about 750 feet on a side, and a height of almost 250 feet, the Pyramid of the Sun is the third biggest pyramid in the world! Only those two Egyptian giants, the Pyramids of **Khufu** and Khafre, are bigger.

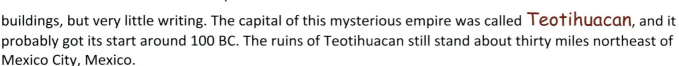

A view down Teotihuacan's Avenue of the Dead with the Pyramid of the Sun on the left

The Pyramid of the Sun and its partner, the Pyramid of the Moon, stand on a long street called the **Avenue of the Dead**. So do many other big buildings, all lined with curious paintings of Teotihuacan's gods. These paintings give clues about what the people of Teotihuacan believed; but without more writing, it is hard to know for sure.

> The **Pyramid of Khufu** is also called the Great Pyramid of Giza.

> The people of Teotihuacan may have been the first to build temples in a Middle American style called **talud-tablero**. *Talud* is Spanish for "slope," and *tablero* for "board" or "table." The walls of talud-tablero temples go back and forth between steep slopes and level tables.

Much more is known about a civilization that arose on the Yucatan Peninsula: the **Maya civilization**. For the Maya not only built temples, but also wrote down what they believed— in a set of books called the **Maya Codices**.

The Maya writing system was the best in Middle America. Like the ancient Egyptians before them, the Maya didn't use the letters of an alphabet to represent sounds. Instead, they used symbols that represented words, ideas and sometimes syllables.

Maya writing and art have taught historians a lot of strange facts about the Maya. For example, the Maya believed in strange-looking gods with peaked skulls, crossed eyes and fangs like snakes'. Maya kings were supposed to be descended from these gods.

Naturally, Maya queens wanted to make their sons look like their god ancestors. One way they did that was by tying sandwich boards to their babies' foreheads. They clamped them down hard for hours at a time, forcing their soft young skulls to grow in the peaked shape of a god's.

Another trick Maya queens tried was tying small toys close to their babies' eyes— so that in looking at the toys, their babies would grow cross-eyed. They even filed their babies' teeth into fangs!

Maya writing carved into stone

Like their neighbors in Teotihuacan, the Maya built tall temples to worship their gods. The tops of some Maya temples had round-backed pulpits for the king. The reason for the roundness was to focus the king's voice so that all could hear. When the **acoustics** worked right, a Maya king could talk down to his people with a voice that echoed from on high— as if he were a god.

The Maya built most of their temples from a special kind of rock called limestone. One of the many good qualities of limestone is that it is soft when it comes out of the quarry, but hardens in the air. In other words, fresh limestone is soft enough to cut, but then grows hard enough to make long-lasting buildings. Maya stoneworkers could cut fresh limestone into blocks so smooth that they didn't need mortar to hold them together. All they needed was their own weight!

A **codex** is a kind of hand-copied book from before the days of the printing press. The plural of codex is **codices**.

Only a few Maya Codices are still around today. Most of them were destroyed in the 1500s, when the Spaniards who conquered Middle America tried to stamp out the Maya religion.

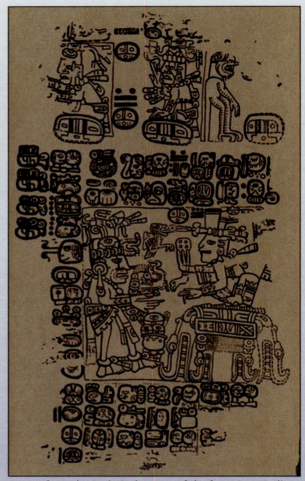

A page from the Paris Codex, one of the few Maya Codices that wasn't destroyed

Acoustics is the science of sound.

One reason the Maya built with limestone was because they were missing an important piece of technology: iron tools. Unlike other ancient peoples, most Native Americans never learned to mine iron and forge it into tools. Instead, they used cutting tools made from hard stones like **obsidian**. Since stone tools can be brittle, Maya stoneworkers worked with the softest building stone they could find: limestone.

> **Obsidian** is a hard kind of stone that comes from volcanoes.

Most Native Americans also missed two other important pieces of technology: wheels and pulleys. The Maya knew enough about wheels to use them in small ways, such as toy-making. But they never seemed to use them as tools— to roll heavy loads on a cart, or to lift them with pulley and rope.

One science the Maya did know well was astronomy— the study of the heavens. Maya astronomers followed the motions of the sun, moon and planets carefully. For example, they knew that the **solar year** lasted 365 days. Their solar calendar had 18 months of 20 days, plus 1 month of 5, for a total of 365.

Temple I at the Maya city of Tikal, with its pulpit at the top

> A **solar year** is the length of time it takes the Earth to revolve around the sun.

Another Maya calendar focused on Venus. Maya astronomers watched Venus appear as the morning star for 263 days; then disappear for 50 days; then reappear as the evening star for 263 days; and then finally disappear for 8 days. The total number of days on their Venusian calendar was 263 + 50 + 263 + 8 = 584.

In fact, one might say that the Maya were obsessed with calendars! For any given day, Maya astronomers could name a date from the solar calendar, the Venusian calendar and more. Dates were so important that they even built children's birthdays into their names.

ᴠᴠᴠ ᴠᴠᴠ ᴠᴠᴠ ᴠᴠᴠ ᴠᴠᴠ ᴠᴠᴠ ᴠᴠᴠ ᴠᴠᴠ ᴠᴠᴠ

The next great empire in Middle America was the **Aztec Empire**, which arose in what is now Mexico. But the Aztecs didn't get their start in Mexico. They sprang from an older people called the **Nahua**, who came from parts unknown.

The Maya and the Aztecs worshiped strange creator gods with the bodies of serpents and the feathers of birds. The Maya called their feathered serpent **Kukulcan**; while the Aztecs called theirs **Quetzalcoatl**.

Quetzalcoatl bridged the gap between heaven and earth. His feathers tied him to the sky, and his snakelike body to the ground. The swishing of his tail caused the wind, and the writhing of his body caused earthquakes.

Quetzalcoatl gleefully swallowing a victim

According to Aztec legend, the Nahua started as seven tribes living in seven separate caves— all hidden in a mysterious place called Chicomoztoc. Sometime later, the seven tribes moved to a second mysterious place called Aztlan. Just where either place was, no one now knows for sure; but the name "Aztec" comes from Aztlan, the lost second home of the Nahua people.

Later still, the seven tribes went looking for a third home. One by one, they all settled in the **Valley of Mexico**— the high valley where Mexico City now stands. The last tribe to arrive, the Mexica, was the one that would give Mexico its name.

By the time the Mexica reached the Valley of Mexico, the other tribes had already taken all the best land. The only land the Mexica could find was a rocky hill that no one else wanted— at a place called Chapultepec. Not satisfied with their rocky hill, the Mexica kept looking for a better land. Their priests told them to watch for a sign, promising that the god of war would show them a better place.

> The **Valley of Mexico** is a high valley in south central Mexico. The average elevation in the Valley of Mexico is over 7,300 feet, which is almost one and a half miles above sea level.

The coat of arms of Mexico, which comes from the vision of the Mexica priests

The sign came where no one expected it. Just east of Chapultepec lay a marshy lake called **Lake Texcoco**. Looking out over the lake one day, Mexica priests noticed a peculiar sight. On a little island not far from shore, a golden eagle stood perched on a prickly pear cactus— eating a snake it had just caught.

This was the sign the priests had been waiting for, they said. Since the Mexica could find no good land anywhere else, they would take the land the eagle marked for them— by filling in Lake Texcoco!

> **Lake Texcoco** was one of five marshy lakes in the Valley of Mexico. In modern times, all five have been filled in to make room for one of the biggest cities in the world: Mexico City.

The first step was to build a **causeway** over to their island. The Mexica carried in tons of earth and rock, piling it on the lake floor until they could walk across on dry land. The next step was to fill in around the island, adding more and more dry land— plus two more causeways. In time, the Mexica built their little island into a big city called Tenochtitlan.

Where did the Mexica raise crops, if all they had was an island? The lake took care of that, too. The Mexica set aside part of their lake for watery gardens called *chinampas*. These were raised planting beds just a few feet wide, with narrow canals in between. With the water that close, their crops always stayed moist— with or without rain. And with weather as warm as Mexico's, the Mexica could raise three or four crops per year!

Raising that many crops took careful planning. Mexica farmers didn't plant seeds on their *chinampas*, because raising crops from seed takes too long. Instead, they planted seeds in separate, smaller

> A **causeway** is a low land bridge made by piling earth and rock into a shallow body of water.
>
> The Aztecs deliberately left gaps in the causeways that led to Tenochtitlan. Most of the time, wooden bridges spanned these gaps. But when danger threatened, the Aztecs could raise the bridges and cut off their enemies!

seedbeds. Only after the seeds grew into seedlings did they transplant them to *chinampas*, where they grew to full size. Mexica farmers were always raising two crops at once: seeds in seedbeds, and seedlings in *chinampas*.

Of course, seedbeds also needed space. To get it, Mexica farmers wove mats out of reeds and floated them in the lake. With thin layers of soil on top, these well-watered mats made perfect seedbeds.

The Mexica tribe grew quickly, now that it had plenty of food and a good place to live. As Tenochtitlan grew, it became a capital for more than just the Mexica. Now it was the capital for a big new people called the **Aztecs**. They came from all the Nahua tribes who had once lived at Aztlan, plus more besides.

ᐱᐱᐱ ᐱᐱᐱ ᐱᐱᐱ ᐱᐱᐱ ᐱᐱᐱ ᐱᐱᐱ ᐱᐱᐱ ᐱᐱᐱ ᐱᐱᐱ

In the middle of Tenochtitlan, on the very spot where the priests saw their golden eagle, stood the place where the Aztecs worshiped: the **Sacred Precinct**. The biggest temple in the Sacred Precinct was one the Spanish called the **Templo Mayor**. This was a double temple that honored two favorite Aztec gods: **Huitzilopochtli**, god of war; and Tlaloc, god of water and storms.

A model of the Sacred Precinct inside Tenochtitlan

If even a few of the stories told about the Aztecs are true, then their worship was horribly cruel. The Aztecs would do anything to please their gods. Sadly, what pleased their gods was blood— lots and lots of human blood.

Most of that blood came from enemy soldiers. When Aztec warriors fought, they tried hard to capture their enemies, rather than kill them. But they didn't do it because they were kind. They did it because they wanted to haul their enemies back to Tenochtitlan, where they could drag them to the top of a temple and shed their blood as a sacrifice to their gods.

The cruelty of Aztec worship started with the cruelty of the gods they followed. One sign of their cruelty comes from a myth about suns. Aztec priests divided the whole history of the world into a set of eras called the **Five Suns**. Why five? Because cruel gods had destroyed the first four suns, along with everyone under them.

➤ The first sun, the Sun of Water, ended in a great flood sent by the gods. The people of that sun hid in the water, becoming the first fish.

Huitzilopochtli, the cruel war god
of the Mexica tribe

- The second sun, the Sun of Jaguars, ended when the gods sent jaguars to eat everyone and everything.

- The third sun, the Sun of Fire, ended when the gods sent a fiery rain to burn the whole world down. The people of that sun hid in the air, becoming the first birds.

- The fourth sun, the Sun of Wind, ended when the gods sent a ferocious windstorm. The people of that sun hid in trees, becoming the first monkeys.

As for the Aztecs themselves, they lived under the fifth sun: the Sun of Earthquakes. The next time the gods grew angry, they would send enough earthquakes to grind the whole world into rubble.

That was why the Aztecs shed so much blood: to keep the gods from sending earthquakes. According to one Aztec myth, two good gods had given their own blood so that the Sun of Earthquakes could begin. Now it was up to the Aztecs to keep that sun going. To do that, they had to give as much blood as those two gods gave— or so the Aztecs believed.

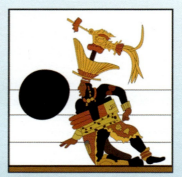

Tlatchli goal mounted on the wall of a ball court

The Middle American Ball Game

In once-forgotten cities all over Middle America, archaeologists have found playing courts for a once-forgotten team sport: *Tlatchtli*, a.k.a. the **Middle American Ball Game**. Although different peoples played different versions of *Tlatchtli* over the centuries, there were some things about it that didn't change much. One was the ball, which was always a heavy one made of solid rubber. Another was the court, which was always a narrow alley with sloped walls made of stone.

One kind of *Tlatchtli* was like a mix of basketball and soccer. As in basketball, the object of the game was to shoot a rubber ball through a high hoop. As in soccer, players couldn't use their arms to strike the ball— only their legs, hips and chests. Obviously, this made it rather difficult to score! In fact, scoring was so difficult that the first team to do it usually won.

The losers sometimes faced terrible consequences. Like everything else in Middle American life, a game of *Tlatchtli* could be tied to the gods. Each team might represent a certain god or gods. When the game was over, the winners might receive all the honor due to a god; while the losers might be sacrificed to the gods.

The last great American empire grew up in the Andes Mountains of South America. Near the middle of the Andes, in what is now **Peru**, lived a people called the Quechua. The empire started in 1438, when a king called Pachacuti pulled four Quechua kingdoms into one. He called it Tawantinsuyu, which is Quechua for "the four corners together."

> **Peru** stands in west central South America, at the heart of the Andes Mountains.
>
> **Inca** is Quechua for "ruler."

In modern times, most people call Tawantinsuyu the Inca Empire. This simpler name comes from Pachacuti's title: **Inca**, which is Quechua for "ruler" or "emperor."

The first problem with building an empire in the Andes was road-building. As the Romans learned long ago, big empires needed good roads. Without them, an emperor couldn't send troops and supplies to the far corners of his empire when he needed to.

Unfortunately, roads were hard to build in the Andes! For the Andes were high, rocky and thousands of miles long. They were also cut with countless **chasms**— gaps so deep and dangerous that only mountain climbers could cross them.

The Inca Empire
(1438 - 1533)

A **chasm** is a deep, narrow cut between two pieces of higher ground.

The answer, of course, was to build bridges. Mountain life turned the Incas into expert bridge builders. They went up and down the whole length of the Andes, building long rope bridges to fill the gaps in their roads.

The emperor kept close watch over his rope bridges. Whenever one started to sag, he ordered the ropes replaced— so that he could always count on his bridges when he needed them.

A rope bridge over a chasm in the Andes. Like other American peoples, the Incas didn't use wheeled carts. However, they did use llamas to carry heavy loads— which meant that their bridges had to be strong enough to carry loaded llamas.

The next problem with building an empire in the Andes was raising food. When Inca farmers tried planting crops on the steep slopes of the Andes, heavy rains washed everything downhill.

The answer was a trick called **terraced farms**. The Incas dug straight into the slope, carving out a level space called a terrace. A few feet downhill, they carved out a second terrace— and so on all the way down. Terracing didn't stop the rain from washing downhill; but it did slow it down enough to keep it from washing away crops.

The Incas were also expert stonemasons. Even without iron tools, they still managed to carve complicated shapes in some very hard Andean rock. Their stones

fit together so tightly that they didn't need mortar to hold them together. The weight of the stones was enough!

Besides rope bridges, terraced farms and great stonework, the Incas are known best for their gold— tons and tons of gold.

An Inca terraced farm

The fact that the Incas never learned to work with iron didn't stop them from working with gold. Inca goldsmiths made all sorts of beautiful objects— enough to fill whole rooms with gold. But they didn't make gold coins; for the Incas never traded in coin. Instead, they traded in useful items like food and cloth.

If the Incas had known how much trouble their gold would cause, then they might have left it in the ground. The trouble started in 1492, when Christopher Columbus went looking for a new way to the Far East— and instead found a whole New World. Spanish soldiers came rushing in, carrying weapons no Native American had ever seen before.

These gold-greedy soldiers are called the *conquistadors*— Spanish for "conquerors." The two most famous were **Hernan Cortes**, who conquered the Aztecs in 1521; and **Francisco Pizarro**, who conquered the Incas in 1532. See Chapter 25 for more on the conquistadors versus the Aztecs and Incas.

> The *conquistador*s were soldiers who conquered a big chunk of the New World for Spain and Portugal.

The conquistadors left no stone unturned in their frantic search for Inca gold. But they did miss one stony place: a mountain haven called **Macchu Picchu**.

Macchu Picchu is a set of about two hundred Inca buildings, all made of dry-stacked stone. It stands about fifty miles from Cusco, the Incas' capital. But Macchu Picchu stands a lot higher than Cusco, which is probably why the conquistadors missed it. Just what Macchu Picchu was for, no one now knows for sure; but it may have been a country home for Pachacuti.

The conquistadors weren't the only ones who missed Macchu Picchu. After the Inca Empire fell, everyone but the locals forgot all about the place. It lay mostly abandoned until 1911, when a Yale University professor called Hiram Bingham rediscovered it.

John Wycliffe and the Lollards

In Chapter 21, we read about an argument between a king and a pope. The King of France challenged the pope's authority over France, saying that his own authority was greater. This chapter tells how an English Bible professor challenged the pope's authority— not just over England, but over all Christians.

John Wycliffe taught Bible at Oxford, one of the two best universities in England. The more Wycliffe learned about the Bible, the more he loved it; and the more he loved it, the more he wanted to share it with others. Alas, sharing the Bible wasn't as easy as it sounded— because most people didn't know the language of the Bible.

Before Wycliffe's day, all Western Bibles were written in Latin. The only time most Christians ever heard the Bible was when their priests read to them from the **Vulgate**— the Latin Bible translated by St. Jerome (Chapter 3). Since most Christians couldn't understand Latin, it did them little good to hear the Bible read in Latin.

John Wycliffe's solution was to do something no one had ever done before: translate the Vulgate into English! Then Englishmen could read for themselves what the Bible said, instead of waiting for priests to tell them. The **Wycliffe Bible**, which he finished in the early 1380s, was the first complete Bible in the English language.

> **John Wycliffe**
> **(1330? – 1384)**

After he finished translating, Wycliffe faced two new problems. First, the pope didn't want anyone but priests reading the Bible! Why? Because he feared that without trained priests to guide them, some Christians might interpret the Bible differently than the Church interpreted it. If enough Christians did that, then the Church might split— causing the pope to lose even more authority.

Second, the printing press hadn't been invented yet— which meant that every copy of the Wycliffe Bible had to be written out by hand. Hand-copied books cost so much that few Englishmen could afford them, no matter how badly they wanted Bibles of their own.

Wycliffe's answer was to train a new kind of preacher. Since the **ordained** priests of the Catholic Church wouldn't read the Wycliffe Bible, Wycliffe gave it to un-ordained preachers who would: the **Lollards**.

> To **ordain** someone was to officially install him as a priest of the Church of Rome.

The Lollards were unofficial ministers who traveled all over England, reading the Wycliffe Bible in English to all who would listen. A Lollard might not know Latin, nor how to lead rituals like a priest; but he did know the Bible! In a time when Christians were starting to doubt the Church, the Lollards took them back to the original Word of God— spoken in a language they could understand.

John Wycliffe sending the Lollards out with the Wycliffe Bible

CHAPTER 23: The Spanish Reconquista

The Iberian Peninsula

The southern edge of Europe has three big peninsulas jutting off it. The eastern one is the Balkan Peninsula, which is home to Greece and other countries. The middle one is the Italian Peninsula, which is home to Italy. This chapter covers the western one: the **Iberian Peninsula**, which is home to Spain and Portugal.

> The name "**Iberia**" probably comes from the Ebro River, which runs across the northeast corner of the peninsula.
> *Sierra Nevada* is Spanish for "snowy mountain range."

Iberia is divided from the rest of Europe by a strong barrier: a high mountain range called the **Pyrenees**. Only a few mountain passes cut through the Pyrenees, and even those are quite high. But the Pyrenees are just one of several mountain ranges in Iberia. A second is the **Sierra Nevada of Spain**, which stands in the southeast. A third is the **Cantabrian Mountains**, which hug the northern coast.

A trip around Iberia takes one through several bodies of water. North of Iberia lies the Bay of Biscay, which opens on the Atlantic Ocean to the west. Southwest of Iberia lies the Gulf of Cadiz. To the south lies the narrow Strait of Gibraltar, which opens on the Mediterranean Sea to the east.

Well out in the Mediterranean, but still close to Iberia, lie some islands that are known around the world for their fine weather. These are the **Balearic Islands**, where temperatures are almost never too hot or too cold. Europeans love to take their vacations on the three biggest Balearic Islands: **Majorca**, **Minorca** and **Ibiza**.

The best-known mountain in Iberia is the Rock of Gibraltar, just north of the Strait of Gibraltar. Unlike the rest of Iberia, Gibraltar is neither Spanish nor Portuguese. Instead, it is British! Britain seized Gibraltar from Spain in 1705, and has never given it back.

Balearic Islands

The Re-conquest of Iberia

The last time we covered Iberia was in Chapter 7. Way back then, we read how Muslim general called Tariq bin Ziyad leapt across the Strait of Gibraltar in 711. The Christians of Iberia were completely unprepared for him. They lost battle after battle, giving up more and more ground. Within ten years, almost all Iberia was ruled by a Muslim people called the **Moors**.

Fortunately for the Christians, all was not lost. After all the Moors' victories, there was still one part of Iberia they didn't rule. Up in the northwestern corner, a Christian kingdom called **Asturias** stood strong against the Moors.

What saved Asturias was the Cantabrian Mountains (above). One day in 722, King Pelayo of Asturias lured the Moors into a certain valley in the Cantabrians. The Moors had no idea that Pelayo's army was hidden in the rocks above that valley. At just the right moment, the Christians leapt out of hiding and crushed the unsuspecting Moors— winning a famous fight called the **Battle of Covadonga**.

The Battle of Covadonga marks the start of a long, hard war called the **Spanish Reconquista**. The Christians fought to "re-conquer" Iberia from the Moors; while the Moors fought to hold onto Iberia.

Christians called the Muslims of Iberia **Moors**, and their kingdoms **Moorish**. Most of the Moors started as Berber Muslims from North Africa.

A drawing of Moorish troops from the Alhambra, a grand castle in Granada, southern Iberia

Reconquista is Spanish for "re-conquering."

Like most wars between Christians and Muslims in those days, the Reconquista was a **crusade**. In other words, it was a holy war to take back Christian lands that had been seized by Muslims. The Reconquista was to be the longest of all crusades. All told, it would last 770 years— all the way from 722 – 1492.

֍֎

Al-Andalus was another name for Muslim Iberia.

As important as the Battle of Covadonga was, it was only one win for the Christians. Everywhere else, the Moors had already won. Shrugging off their loss, the Moors settled down for a long stay in the rest of Iberia— which they called **Al-Andalus**.

At first, Al-Andalus was ruled by the Moorish generals who conquered it. But a great land like Al-Andalus was too rich to be ruled by generals for long. A Muslim royal soon showed up to claim it.

Where did that Muslim royal come from? To answer, we must go back to how the Islamic Empire carried on after the prophet Muhammad died. The first government after Muhammad was the Rashidun Caliphate, which ruled from 632 – 661. The name "Rashidun" had to do with how caliphs were chosen. It meant "rightly guided"— which meant that in the eyes of most Muslims, the Rashidun caliphs were the ones Allah wanted them to have.

The second government after Muhammad was different. It was called the <u>Umayyad</u> Caliphate, after the family that started it: the powerful <u>Umayya</u> clan. The first Umayyad caliph made a promise when he took over— saying that when he died, the throne would go to a member of Muhammad's family. But when the time came, the caliph broke his promise and set his son on the throne instead. The Umayyads became the first **dynasty** of caliphs— the first to hand down the throne from father to son.

If one dynasty could do it, then why not another? The Umayyad Caliphate ended in 750, when a rebel Arab called Abul <u>Abbas</u> As-Saffah killed the last Umayyad caliph. As-Saffah became first caliph of the next caliphate: the **Abbasid Caliphate**.

Abdul al Rahman I (731 – 788)

After killing the caliph, As-Saffah sent hunting parties to track down and kill the rest of the Umayyads. He especially wanted to kill the young prince— a 19-year-old called **Abd al-Rahman I**.

When he heard about the hunters, Abd al-Rahman gathered up what little family he had left and ran for his life. He and his brother were beside the Euphrates River, probably looking for a boat, when the hunters caught up with them. Desperate to save themselves, both brothers dove into the river.

Instead of jumping in after them, the hunters tried a trick. They called out to the brothers from the shore, promising to spare their lives if they would turn back. Abd al-Rahman knew better than to believe the hunters; but alas, his brother did not. The brother may have been too tired to go on, or he may have hoped for mercy. Whatever the reason, he swam back to the shore— where the hunters immediately murdered him. Abd al-Rahman wept for his brother all the way across the Euphrates.

Six years later, Abd al-Rahman turned up in Al-Andalus— where his royal name took him to straight to the top of the government. In 756, he declared himself **emir** of a big new country in Al-Andalus. He called it the **Emirate of Cordoba**, after its capital: Cordoba, a city in south central Iberia.

ꙥꙥꙥꙥꙥꙥꙥꙥꙥꙥꙥꙥꙥꙥꙥ

More than 150 years later, a different Abd al-Rahman gave himself a promotion. In 929, Emir **Abd al-Rahman III** decided that Cordoba should be more than just an emirate. He declared himself caliph of a new caliphate: the **Caliphate of Cordoba**. For the first time, there were two Sunni caliphates at the same time: the Abbasid in the east, and Cordoba in the west.

As caliph, Abd al-Rahman III needed a capital fit for a grand ruler. The answer was a fine new city called **Medina al-Zahara**. Abd Al-Rahman spared no expense, using only the best materials and craftsmen money could buy. In its day, Medina al-Zahara was probably one of the most beautiful cities on Earth.

> **Medina al-Zahara**, capital of the Cordoba, was a city with three tiers:
>
> ➢ On the top tier stood the Alcazar, a grand palace for the caliph. The mansions of the caliph's highest nobles also stood up top, as did the headquarters of his army.
>
> ➢ The middle tier held a mosque; a souk, or open-air market; and lovely gardens filled with fountains, flowers and exotic animals.
>
> ➢ The bottom tier held army barracks, along with stables for the caliph's beloved horses.

Part of the ruins of Medina al-Zahara

Meanwhile, up in northwestern Iberia, the little Christian Kingdom of Asturias was growing. One thing that kept Asturias growing was a special place called **Santiago de Compostela**.

Santiago is Spanish for "Saint James." The Apostle **James, son of Zebedee** is a special hero to Iberian Christians. Tradition says that after Jesus rose from the dead, James preached the gospel in faraway Iberia. If he hadn't, then the Iberians might never have heard the good news of Jesus Christ.

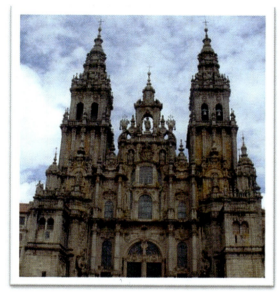

The Basilica de Santiago, a grand cathedral that stands over the tomb of St. James at Santiago de Compostela

Whether or not James really went to Iberia, he was certainly back in Jerusalem when he died. The Bible says in Acts 12:1-2 that he was killed by Herod Agrippa, King of Judea.

The next tradition picks up where the Bible leaves off. It is said that after James died, two of his followers loaded his body on a boat and sailed it back to his beloved Iberia. When they got there, they buried him in a hidden tomb made of marble. Years later, when these two loyal followers died, they were buried in that same hidden tomb.

The tomb stayed hidden for about 800 years, until 840. It is said that in that year, a Christian hermit from Asturias had a vision from God that told him exactly where to find the tomb. The hermit showed the tomb to his bishop, who in turn showed it to his king. The bishop noticed the tomb's great age, and the fact that it held three bodies. After studying the story of James and his two followers, the bishop decided that this must really be the tomb of the Apostle James!

What an incredible find this was— a real relic of a real apostle of Jesus Christ, right here in Western Europe! Before now, Christians had had to go all the way to the Holy Land to see such sights. Now they had only to go to Asturias. Thousands of them came, wandering in from all over to see the tomb of the Apostle James. And the more Christians came, the more they wanted to help their Christian brothers in Asturias fight off the Moors.

Camino de Santiago is Spanish for "Path of Saint James." The **Camino de Santiago** is a set of paths that lead to the tomb of the Apostle James at Santiago de Compostela. Even today, Christian pilgrims from around the world still follow these paths every year.

The symbol of the Camino de Santiago is the scallop shell. The many lines on the scallop represent the different paths Christians follow to reach the tomb. Just as the lines on the shell all come together, so Christians from around the world all come together in the same place.

By this time, Asturias wasn't the only Christian kingdom in Iberia. There were also Christian kingdoms in the borderland between Iberia and West Francia— a place called the **Spanish March**.

The word **march** can mean "borderland."

The story of the Spanish March goes back to another story we covered in Chapter 7. After conquering most of Iberia, the Moors tried to conquer Francia too. Fortunately for the Christians, a Frankish general called **Charles Martel** was there to stop them— at a famous fight called the **Battle of Tours**. If Martel hadn't won the Battle of Tours, then the Muslims might have conquered all Europe!

The family of Charles Martel went on to build one of the biggest empires ever: the **Carolingian Empire**. Its greatest emperor was **Charlemagne**, who took over in 768. By the early 800s, Charlemagne ruled almost all Europe. The only parts he didn't rule were some of the farthest edges— including Al-Andalus, where the Moors were still strong.

That was how the Spanish March got started. With strong enemies like the Moors on his southern border, Charlemagne needed strong armies to protect that border. To get them, he set up several **counties** in the borderland between Francia and Iberia. In time, those counties became kingdoms. The three strongest kingdoms of the Spanish March were **Navarre** in the west, **Aragon** in the center and **Catalonia** in the east.

> A **county** was a land run by a nobleman called a **count** or earl.

Meanwhile, the Kingdom of Asturias was changing. Around 910, Asturias took the name of its new capital— a city called **Leon**. The kings of Leon spun off more Christian kingdoms. East of Leon stood **Castile**, which was named for the <u>castles</u> that protected Leon from the Moors. South of Leon stood **Portugal**, which was named for the city of <u>Porto</u>.

EMBLEM OF ASTURIAS

The Spanish Reconquista wasn't 770 years of non-stop war. There were times when Christians and Muslims lived together in peace. Even in wartime, things weren't as simple as they seemed; for it wasn't always Christians fighting Muslims. Soldiers often switched sides— fighting first for Christianity, then Islam, then Christianity again. Some soldiers didn't care who they fought for, as long as they got paid.

One of the many Christians who switched sides was the greatest warrior of the Reconquista: **Rodrigo Diaz de Vivar**, better known as **El Cid**.

Rodrigo was a minor noble born in Castile around 1040. Rodrigo grew up in the Castilian army. By his mid-20s, he was already one of the most experienced generals in all Castile.

When Rodrigo was young, a king called Ferdinand I ruled both Castile and Leon. But when old Ferdinand died, his kingdoms were split. Castile, where Rodrigo lived, went to Ferdinand's oldest son **Sancho**. Leon went to Ferdinand's second son, **Alfonso**. From the moment Ferdinand died, the battle was on to see which son would come out on top: Sancho or Alfonso.

Rodrigo Diaz de Vivar, better known as El Cid (1040? – 1099)

For a while, it looked like Sancho would come out on top. With help from great soldiers like Rodrigo, Sancho won victory after victory. His greatest victory came in 1072, when he defeated Alfonso and drove him out of Leon! In fear for his life, Alfonso fled southward— seeking safety with a Muslim friend. Meanwhile, Sancho became what his father Ferdinand had been: King of both Castile and Leon.

Alas, Sancho didn't hold onto his crowns for long. Just a few months after his big win over Alfonso, Sancho was dead— murdered by an assassin!

Rodrigo was furious. Legend tells how he leapt on his horse and chased the assassin, trying to find out who had hired him. Alas, the assassin slipped out of the city through a hidden gate— leaving Rodrigo's burning question unanswered.

Even so, Rodrigo had a pretty good idea who had hired the assassin. He figured it was probably the man who had the most to gain from Sancho's death: his brother Alfonso. With Sancho dead, and with no sons to take his place, Alfonso became **King Alfonso VI of Castile and Leon**!

Rodrigo wasn't the only one who suspected Alfonso. So many people distrusted the new king that he finally had to take a sacred oath. It happened at a church called Santa Gadea in 1072. Alfonso stood at the altar with his hand on a Bible, swearing before God and man that he had nothing to do with his brother's murder.

The **Oath of Santa Gadea** was enough for most Christians; but it wasn't enough for Rodrigo. Since Rodrigo didn't trust Alfonso, Alfonso sent him away— leaving the best general in Iberia without a king to serve.

King Alfonso VI of Castile and Leon taking the Oath of Santa Gadea, swearing that he had nothing to do with the murder of his brother Sancho

By this time, the old Caliphate of Cordoba had fallen apart. But there were still plenty of smaller Muslim kingdoms in Iberia. After two Christian kings turned him away, Rodrigo offered to serve a Muslim emir— who gladly accepted!

That was how the best Christian general in Iberia came to join forces with the Muslims. When Rodrigo's Muslim troops learned what a clever general he was, they gave him a Muslim nickname: *El Sayyid*, Arabic for "the Master." Over time, *El Sayyid* shortened to **El Cid**.

> **El Cid** was a shortened version of *El Sayyid*, which is Arabic for "The Master."

Meanwhile, Alfonso VI was earning the nickname he would carry into history: **Alfonso the Valiant**. As King of Leon, Castile and more, Alfonso led the fight against Islam— swallowing up more and more Muslim kingdoms.

To save themselves from Alfonso, the Muslims called for help from outside. Help came in 1085, when a general from Muslim Morocco led a huge army into Iberia. Some say that El Cid commanded one wing of this army, and some say he didn't. Either way, the Muslims defeated Alfonso the Valiant at the

Battle of Sagrajas, fought in 1086.

Now came Alfonso's turn to be desperate. The year after his big loss, Alfonso swallowed his pride and begged El Cid to come back to the Christian side!

Since El Cid still didn't trust Alfonso, he didn't exactly fight for Castile. But he did turn against his Muslim allies. He spent the rest of his life trying to carve out a Christian kingdom around **Valencia**, a city in eastern Iberia. A soldier to the end, El Cid went down fighting the Muslims in 1099.

The next great leader of the Reconquista was born more than 100 years after Alfonso the Valiant. Around 1180, **King Alfonso VIII of Castile** started pressing hard against the Muslims— seizing more and more of their kingdoms.

Once again, the Muslims called for help from outside. In 1195, another general from Muslim Morocco defeated another Alfonso. Alfonso VIII lost so many troops in the **Disaster at Alarcos** that he needed years to grow strong again.

Now came the Christians' turn to call for help from outside. Help came in the 1210s, when **Pope Innocent III** ordered a big crusade against the Muslims of Iberia. The pope's call brought together Christian knights from all over— not only Castile, but also Leon, Portugal, Navarre and Aragon. Even French knights came down to join the crusade, complaining about the horrible heat south of the Pyrenees.

> **Pope Innocent III** was the same pope who ordered the Fourth Crusade (Chapter 12). He was also the pope who told King John of England that he didn't have to obey the Magna Carta (Chapter 13).

The first problem was finding the enemy. The Muslims had set up camp in the mountains of southern Iberia, where there were very few roads. The crusaders had no idea how to reach them— until they met a local shepherd, who of course knew all about the mountains. This shepherd showed them a little-known mountain pass that led straight to the Muslim camp.

Terrible dangers awaited the crusaders at the far side of that pass. For one thing, the Muslim army turned out to be far bigger than theirs— perhaps five times bigger! For another, the Muslim general had built a strong defense for himself. A ring of 3,000 camels and 10,000 slaves surrounded the general, all chained together to keep them from running away.

The nervous general clutched a scimitar in one hand and a Quran (Muslim holy book) in the other. As the crusaders closed in on his circle, the general screamed out promises from the Quran. If his soldiers died fighting for Islam, he said, then they would surely go to heaven. But if they ran away, then they would surely go to hell!

Scene from the Battle of Las Navas de Tolosa (July 16, 1212)

Despite the general's threats, the crusaders broke through the circle. When the general finally gave up and ran off, Alfonso VIII won one of the greatest victories of the whole Reconquista: the famous **Battle of Las Navas de Tolosa**.

The next hero of the Reconquista was Alfonso VIII's grandson, **King Ferdinand III of Castile**. Ferdinand conquered almost everything the Muslims had left. By 1238, they were down to just one kingdom in Iberia: the **Emirate of Granada**.

Granada stood along the southern coast of Iberia, east of the Rock of Gibraltar. Two advantages helped keep Granada strong. One was the Sierra Nevada mountains (above), which made a strong barrier between Granada and Castile. The other was the Strait of Gibraltar, which was the only seaway between the Mediterranean and the Atlantic. The traders who passed through the Strait of Gibraltar paid a fortune in taxes to Granada. The Emir of Granada sent part of that fortune to the King of Castile. By paying tribute every year, Granada survived for another 250 years— long after every other Muslim kingdom in Iberia was gone.

King Ferdinand III of Castile

The job of conquering this last Muslim kingdom, Granada, fell to two famous royals called Ferdinand and Isabella. **Princess Isabella of Castile** was born in 1451, and **Prince Ferdinand of Aragon** in 1452. By this time, the kingdoms of Castile, Aragon and Portugal were the three strongest in Iberia. Portugal held western Iberia, and Castile the center. Aragon held eastern Iberia, plus lands over in Italy.

Isabella was a daughter to King John II of Castile. The princess hardly knew her father; for he died when she was only three. The next king was Isabella's much-older half-brother, who now became **King Enrique IV of Castile.**

Iberia before 1492, with Portugal in tan, Castile in red, Aragon in bright green and Granada in dark green

As the new head of the family, Enrique was supposed to arrange a good marriage for his sister. But Enrique didn't see Isabella as a sister. Instead, he saw her as a chess piece— a pawn to be sacrificed by her king. Almost every noble in Europe dreamed of marrying a princess as rich as Isabella. Enrique promised her first to one, then to another— trading her for whatever he needed most at the time.

Isabella's first fiancé was the one she would wind up marrying: Ferdinand of Aragon. Enrique promised Isabella to Ferdinand when they were both very young, hoping to bring Castile and Aragon together.

But when Isabella was ten years old, Enrique changed his mind. Now instead of marrying Ferdinand, Isabella was supposed to marry Charles of Navarre— a man thirty years older than she! Four years later, Enrique changed his mind again. Now the 14-year-old Isabella was supposed to marry a 42-year-old called Pedro Giron— a wealthy warrior who could help Enrique fight his battles. Isabella probably would have married Pedro, if he hadn't died on his way to claim her.

Three years after that, Enrique changed his mind yet again— promising Isabella to King Alfonso V of Portugal. This was probably the worst match yet, for a couple of reasons. First, Alfonso was almost twenty years older than Isabella. Second, Alfonso's first wife died young— maybe because Alfonso poisoned her! Enrique still wasn't finished. When Isabella refused to marry Alfonso, Enrique promised her to a brother of the King of France!

With that, Isabella decided to take matters into her own hands. One day when she was 18 years old, Isabella lied her way out of Enrique's castle. She told him that she was going to visit the grave of her younger brother; but she really wasn't. Instead, she was going to a secret meeting with Ferdinand of Aragon!

Although Isabella had never met Ferdinand face-to-face, she had secretly traded letters with him. After reading those letters, Isabella felt sure that Ferdinand would make a better husband than anyone Enrique might choose. This is what Isabella's secret meeting was for: to arrange her marriage with Ferdinand.

Queen Isabella I of Castile

The meeting was just as secret on Ferdinand's side. To enter Castile in secret, the rich young Ferdinand disguised himself as a servant to poor trader!

Ferdinand and Isabella were married in October 1469, just a few days after their secret meeting. After that, all the young royals had to do was wait. Enrique died in 1474, leaving Isabella as Queen of Castile. Ferdinand's father died in 1479, leaving Ferdinand as King of Aragon. In years to come, the two great kingdoms of Castile and Aragon would combine to form an even greater kingdom: Spain.

The marriage of Ferdinand and Isabella was the beginning of the end for the Emirate of Granada. Both royals were crusaders, strong Christians who were driven to defeat the Muslims. The war on Granada started in 1482, just three years after Ferdinand became king.

Ten years later, it was all over. The last Emir of Granada surrendered in 1492, handing over the last Muslim kingdom in Iberia. After 770 years, the Spanish Reconquista was finally finished!

The following year, the emir left Iberia forever— headed for Muslim Morocco. On his way out, the beaten emir stopped to look back at all the Muslims had lost. The sad sight brought tears to his eyes. His moment of tears infuriated his old mother, who exploded at him:

> "You are weeping like a woman for something that you could not defend like a man!"

With one last sigh, the last emir turned his back on Granada for the last time. The mountain pass where he looked back is still called The Last Sigh of the Moor.

The last Emir of Granada looking back on his lost kingdom with longing

One of the treasures the Emir of Granada couldn't stand losing was a stunning castle called the **Alhambra**. Granada had spent a fortune on the Alhambra, using only the finest materials and craftsmen money could buy. Nothing about the Alhambra was plain! Everywhere one turned, surprising beauties met the eye.

Many of those beauties were a kind of Muslim pattern art called **arabesques**. Since Islamic law forbade idol worship, and since carvings of people and animals tended to look like idols, Muslim artists didn't carve people and animals. Instead, they carved mostly vines, leaves and flowers, all woven in never-ending patterns. Some artists deliberately carved small mistakes into otherwise-perfect arabesques— to remind their fellow Muslims that only Allah was perfect.

Great castles like the Alhambra and the Alcazar of Medina al-Zahara marked Granada as one of the most advanced kingdoms on Earth. In some ways, Granada was more advanced than the Christian kingdoms that took over in 1492.

A view from a lovely court inside the Alhambra

The Spanish Inquisition

Ferdinand and Isabella were devoted to the Catholic Church. Their devotion showed in the special nickname they bore: *Los Reyes Catolicos*, Spanish for "The Catholic Monarchs."

As devoted Christians, the Catholic Monarchs wanted their people to be devoted too. But in trying to make their people more Christian, the Catholic Monarchs did things that hardly seem Christlike— especially to modern eyes.

When Isabella was young, she made all her confessions to a priest called Tomas de Torquemada. The two became close friends. Even after Isabella became queen, Tomas was often at her side, sharing his thoughts with her.

Tomas thought a lot about two kinds of people: Moriscos and Marranos. Moriscos were Muslims who switched to Christianity; while Marranos were Jews who switched to Christianity. Hopefully, some switched because they truly believed in Christ. But there were also some who switched for a more self-serving reason: because Christian kings had conquered them, and they wanted to please their new kings.

What Tomas didn't like about Moriscos and Marranos was that some of them only pretended to be Christians. In public, they did everything Christians did— attending church, taking communion and so

Tomas de Torquemada,
Grand Inquisitor of Castile

Emblem of the Inquisition

on. But in private, some of them still followed their old religions. Some even told Christians that Islam or Judaism was better than Christianity. Tomas warned Isabella that if she didn't get rid of these pretend Christians, then Castile would never be as Christian as she wanted it to be.

The solution to this problem, Tomas said, was a new court. With permission from the pope, Tomas and Isabella set up a Church court to hunt down false Christians. Tomas was the first **Grand Inquisitor** of this new court, which was called the **Spanish Inquisition**. It started in 1483, nine years before the fall of Granada.

> The **Spanish Inquisition** was a special Church court that started in Castile, and later spread to other parts of the Spanish Empire. The main mission of the Inquisition was to hunt down people who pretended to be Christians, but secretly weren't.

When the Inquisition came to a new town, the first thing that happened was a **Mass**— a special church service that always included communion. During this service, the inquisitors asked all good Catholics to examine themselves and confess their sins. They also asked them to examine their neighbors, to see if any of them might be false Christians.

Next came the accusations. Any Christian could accuse anyone of anything, without ever having to face the one he accused. If a Christian believed that his neighbor might secretly be a Muslim or Jew, then he had only to tell the inquisitors.

Then came the trials. The inquisitors asked tough questions, trying to trick the accused into saying something wrong. One might ask a Morisco, "Why don't you buy wine? Is it because you still follow Islamic law, like the Muslim you really are?" Or one might ask a Marrano: "Why do you buy extra food on Friday afternoons? Is it because you still keep the Sabbath on Saturdays, like the Jew you really are?" If an inquisitor didn't get the answer he wanted, then he might torture the accused until he did.

Last of all came a dreaded Mass called the **Auto-da-Fe**, or "Act of Faith." If the inquisitors decided that the accused was lying, then they ordered him punished. Some victims of the Spanish Inquisition were strangled to death; while others were burned alive.

> The **Alhambra Decree** was a 1492 law that expelled all Jews from Aragon and Castile.

Because the Inquisition was a Christian court, it had no authority over anyone who still called himself a Jew or Muslim. Even so, the Inquisition caused no end of trouble for Jews and Muslims.

The worst trouble for Jews was a law called the **Alhambra Decree**. In 1492, just after they captured Granada, Ferdinand and Isabella suddenly banished all Jews from their kingdoms! The Alhambra Decree gave every Jew in Castile and Aragon just four months to get out. The worst of it was, they couldn't take any money with them. They had to find new homes in new countries, starting with little more than the clothes on their backs. As awful as this was, it was just one of many times when the Jews of the **Diaspora** were forced to pack up and leave.

The worst trouble for Muslims was a new Grand Inquisitor called **Jimenez de Cisneros**. In 1502, Cisneros gave the last Muslims in Castile a hard choice: Either become Christians or get out. Cisneros also burned every Muslim book he could find, doing his best to stamp out Islam.

> The **Diaspora** was the scattering of the Jews.
> The descendants of the Jews expelled by Ferdinand and Isabella are called **Sephardi Jews**. Some Sephardi Jews still speak a form of Spanish.

CHAPTER 24:

Explorers from Portugal and Spain

The Age of Discovery

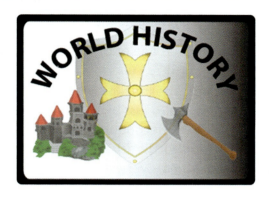

In medieval times, Europeans knew just three of the seven continents: Europe, Asia and Africa. Europe, of course, they knew well. They also knew West Asia and North Africa; for both of those touched the Mediterranean Sea. But few Europeans had

ever ventured beyond West Asia, to far-off countries like India and China. And almost no Europeans had ever seen any part of Africa south of the Sahara Desert.

Far-off places can be tempting. Europeans got curious about East Asia around 1300, when Marco Polo wrote his famous *Marvels of the World* (Chapter 19). They got curious about West Africa a few years later, when they heard about all the gold Mansa Musa spent on his *hajj* to Mecca (Chapter 21). The more Europeans heard about these wonders, the more they wanted to go to these far-off places.

One reason to go was for trade. China had luxuries that no one in Europe knew how to make— exotic goods like silk cloth and porcelain tableware. India had tea and spices that Europeans loved. West Africa had bountiful gold and beautiful ivory. If European traders could only get their hands on these goods, then they could sell them for fortunes back home.

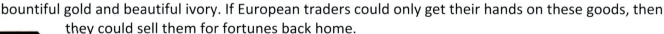

Another reason to go was for faith. As disciples of Jesus Christ, Europeans had a duty to "make disciples of all nations"— as the Bible says in Matthew 28:19. To medieval Christians, "making disciples" often meant bringing people under the authority of the pope.

The question was, how could Europeans get to these far-off places? It made little sense to go by land; for the roads over land were terrible. Marco Polo's father had taken four whole years to get from Constantinople to Beijing. And only a few Tuaregs knew how to cross the Sahara without dying of thirst!

Besides, heavy loads were hard to carry by land. As always, water was the best way to carry heavy loads. If traders wanted to bring back heavy loads from far-off places, then they would have to go by ship.

Replicas of Christopher Columbus' three ships, *Santa Maria*, *Nina* and *Pinta*, in a photo from 1912

This is how the **Age of Discovery** began. In the early 1400s, Europeans started sailing farther and farther from home— looking for new ways to reach the far-off parts of the world. They had no idea just how much they would find.

ꟲꟲꟲꟲꟲꟲꟲꟲꟲꟲꟲꟲꟲꟲꟲꟲꟲꟲꟲꟲꟲꟲꟲꟲꟲꟲꟲꟲ

The Age of Discovery started during the Spanish Reconquista. As we read in Chapter 23, the Reconquista was a long crusade to take Iberia back from the Muslims. The longer it went on, the more lands the Christians took back. By the mid-1200s, the Muslims were down to just one kingdom in Iberia: the Emirate of Granada.

The Reconquista pushed a lot of Muslims across the Mediterranean Sea, into North Africa. The problem was, some Muslims didn't stay in North Africa. Every so often, Muslim pirates sailed over and raided the coasts of Iberia— especially the Portuguese coast. These were the first **Barbary Pirates**, Muslim pirates from the **Barbary Coast**.

"A Barbary Pirate" by artist Pier Mola

The **Barbary Coast** was the whole coast of North Africa west of Egypt. The name "Barbary" comes from the natives of that part of the world, who were called "Berbers."

One of the Barbary Pirates' favorite things to steal was people. They were famous for kidnapping Christians and selling them in Muslim slave markets. Their victims disappeared by the thousands, never to be seen again.

The Portuguese soon figured out where the Barbary Pirates were coming from. It turned out that most of them started from a Muslim port called **Ceuta**. Ceuta stood near the east end of the Strait of Gibraltar, just across from the Rock of Gibraltar.

King John I of Portugal had a plan for fixing all this: He wanted to seize Ceuta from the Muslims. If he could manage it, then two good things would happen. First, the Barbary Pirates would lose their main base— which might put a stop to their raids. Second, Portugal would gain a rich port with tons of gold. For not all gold from West Africa went to emperors like Mansa Musa. A lot of it wound up with Muslim traders in Ceuta.

The first part of John's plan went well. In 1415, his forces sailed over and seized Ceuta— forcing the Barbary Pirates out.

Alas, the second part of John's plan didn't work out. For when Ceuta went Christian, Muslim traders found other places to take their gold. Despite winning Ceuta, the Portuguese were no closer to all that West African gold— until the king's son had an idea.

Infante Henry was the fourth son of King John I. In Portugal and Spain, only the oldest son carried the title "prince." The others were all *infantes*— younger sons who never expected to be king.

Since Henry would never be king, he turned his attention to other things— like that West African gold. The way to get it, he thought, was to do something no one had dared do before now: sail around the west coast of Africa. If he could manage that, then the Portuguese wouldn't have to buy

Infante Henry of Portugal, a.k.a. Henry the Navigator (1394 – 1460)

gold from traders in North Africa. Instead, they could get it from the source— straight from the gold mines south of the Sahara. The *infante*'s idea earned him an unusual nickname: **Henry the Navigator**.

Henry's nickname doesn't mean that he personally sailed around the west coast of Africa. Instead, Henry made it easier for others to sail. One way he did that was by building a kind of sailors' college— a place where Portuguese sailors could learn the new science of navigation. Henry also hired mapmakers to draw the best, most accurate maps the world had yet seen. The better the maps, the more sailors knew about hidden dangers that might wreck their ships.

**Henry the Navigator
(1394 – 1460)**

B esides making better sailors and better maps, Henry also made better ships. He wanted none of the slow, heavy ships that traders used on the

A caravel rigged with triangular lateen sails

Mediterranean Sea. Instead, he built lighter, faster ships called **caravels**.

Caravels had two or three masts, all rigged with triangular sails called **lateens**. By moving their lateens from side to side, caravels could make the most of whatever wind they had. They were also more maneuverable than older ships, which made them better for exploring the shallow shores and rivers along the west coast of Africa.

ꍏꍏꍏꍏꍏꍏꍏꍏꍏꍏꍏꍏꍏꍏꍏꍏꍏꍏꍏꍏꍏꍏꍏꍏꍏꍏꍏꍏꍏ

T he first great find of the Age of Discovery came in 1419, four years after Portugal seized Ceuta. That was when a sailing captain called **John Goncalves Zarco** discovered an island group where not a single person lived. It was called **Madeira**, and it stood about 500 miles off the west coast of Morocco. After Portugal planted a colony there, Madeira grew famous for its fine wine.

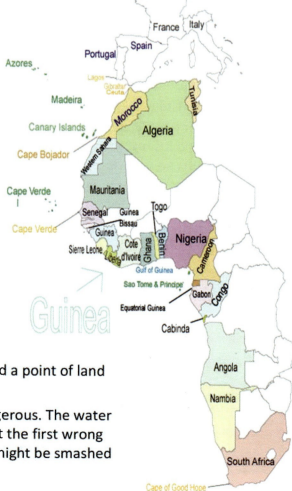

The next big island group to the south didn't need discovering. Since the **Canary Islands** lie near the coast of Morocco, plenty of people already lived there. It was Castile, not Portugal, that built the first European colonies on the Canaries.

T he next big obstacle for Henry the Navigator stood between the Canaries and the coast. Although it didn't look like much on the map, Henry's men needed a long time to get around a point of land called **Cape Bojador**.

The first problem with Cape Bojador was that it was dangerous. The water was shallow there, full of hidden rocks that could smash a ship at the first wrong turn. And if a storm blew up at the wrong moment, then a ship might be smashed anyway— wrong turn or no.

The second problem with Cape Bojador was in sailors' minds. They had all heard legends like the one Mansa Musa told— how a great whirlpool at the edge of the Atlantic sucked down thousands of Malian ships (Chapter 21). There were also legends of boiling seas in the hot south, and of falling off the edge of the sea. In the minds of superstitious sailors, passing Cape Bojador seemed like suicide!

Despite all these dangers, both real and imagined, a Portuguese called **Gil Eanes** finally sailed past Cape Bojador in 1434.

Even after all that, the discoveries came slowly. Twenty-six more years passed before **Antonio de Noli** found the next big island group to the south: the **Cape Verde Islands**. Like Madeira, the Cape Verdes were empty of people— until 1460, when Portugal built its first colony there.

The year 1460 was also when Henry the Navigator died. It was only after Henry's passing that the Portuguese found what they had been searching for since 1415: West African gold. Soon after Henry died, the Portuguese finally rounded the corner that led to **Guinea**. At last, they had reached the famous gold mines of Mansa Musa!

As quick as they could, the Portuguese built a trading post in Guinea. They called it *El Mina*, Portuguese for "The Mine," after the gold mines nearby. It stood just off the Gulf of Guinea, along the coast of what is now the **Republic of Ghana**.

A little later, King John II of Portugal built a strong castle to defend El Mina. **Elmina Castle** became the capital of an important colony called the **Portuguese Gold Coast**. Many a trader made his fortune at the Gold Coast— not only from gold, but also from ivory and slaves.

With growing colonies spread out on islands and coasts thousands of miles apart, Portugal was more than just a kingdom. It was becoming the first overseas empire of the Age of Discovery: the **Portuguese Empire**.

No sailing ship can sail directly into the wind; for the wind will simply blow the ship backward, out of control. Even so, a maneuverable ship like a caravel can still travel upwind. Instead of sailing straight into the wind, sailors **"tack"** back and forth across the wind. The long, slow process of tacking into the wind is called **beating to windward**.

Guinea was a gold-rich region along the southern coast of West Africa.

The **Republic of Ghana** stands on different ground than the old Ghana Empire, which we covered in Chapter 21.

Elmina Castle, capital of the Portuguese Gold Coast

The Portuguese Empire didn't stop at the Gold Coast. Now that the Portuguese had a big colony down in Guinea, they also had more ships and supplies farther south. These were just what explorers needed to sail on around Africa, toward their next goal: India.

At first, no one knew if sailing to India was even possible. For all anyone knew, the Indian Ocean might be an inland sea surrounded by land.

The man who proved otherwise was a clever Portuguese called **Bartolomeu Dias**. In 1488, Dias finally sailed around the southern tip of Africa— proving that ships really could sail from the Atlantic Ocean to the Indian Ocean.

> Bartolomeu Dias was the first European to round a famous spot called **Cape of Good Hope**, which stands near the southern tip of Africa. But it was not Dias who chose the cape's cheery name. The first time Dias passed it, he marked "Cape of Storms" on his map— after some strong storms that blew him off course. It was King John II of Portugal who changed the name, fearing that Dias' gloomy name might frighten others off.

> **Ferdinand** was King of Aragon, and **Isabella** Queen of Castile. These were the two kingdoms that would soon unite to form the Kingdom of Spain.

When **Ferdinand** and **Isabella** heard what Dias had done, they started to worry. The Gold Coast was already making King John II of Portugal filthy rich. Now he was well on his way to India, where he might grow richer still. With that much money, John might be able to drive Ferdinand and Isabella off their thrones!

It wouldn't be the first time a King of Portugal had tried. In Chapter 23, we read how Isabella inherited the throne of Castile from her half-brother: King Enrique IV, who died in 1474. What we didn't read is that Isabella didn't inherit her throne without a fight. There were some Castilians who preferred Enrique's daughter: a 13-year-old called Juana.

One of Isabella's old fiancés tried to take advantage of the situation. In that same year of 1475, **King Alfonso V of Portugal** burst into Castile and married Juana— even though he was Juana's uncle, not to mention thirty years older than she! Of course, Alfonso didn't marry Juana for love. He only married her so that he could claim the throne of Castile through her. Alfonso's bold move touched off a five-year fight called the

Flag of Portugal

War of the Castilian Succession.

The outcome of this war was most important to the Age of Discovery. Although Isabella won the war on land, Alfonso won the war at sea— which meant that Portugal kept its colonies overseas. The only colonies Castile kept were the ones on the Canary Islands.

Without colonies farther south, the Castilians could never reach India the way the Portuguese could— by sailing around Africa. If Isabella and Ferdinand wanted to trade in India, then they would have to find some other way to get there.

King Alfonso V of Portugal

Which is where a famous explorer called

Christopher Columbus comes into the story.

Columbus was probably born in **Genoa**, a republic along the northwest coast of Italy. The richest families of Genoa all earned their livings at sea. Columbus went to sea as a boy, and stayed there for the rest of his life. By the time he reached his mid-20s, Columbus was already an experienced ship's captain.

What made Columbus different from other captains was his love of reading. When most captains were relaxing, Columbus was reading every book he could find— especially books

Christopher Columbus

Christopher Columbus
(1451 – 1506)

about geography. The Age of Discovery was an exciting time for geography, with new maps showing new places every year. Some of those maps showed the farthest places on Earth: China and Japan.

The problem was, the distances on the maps were only guesses. In those days, no one knew for sure how big the world was, or how far away China and Japan might really be. And of course, no map showed the Americas— for Columbus hadn't discovered the Americas yet!

Columbus tried to fill in the guesses on those maps with real figures. Based on his reading, and on letters from other mapmakers, Columbus figured the following: that if a ship sailed due west from the Canary Islands, then it might strike Japan in about 3,000 miles.

What an idea! If Columbus was right, then Japan was only about half as far from Europe as the

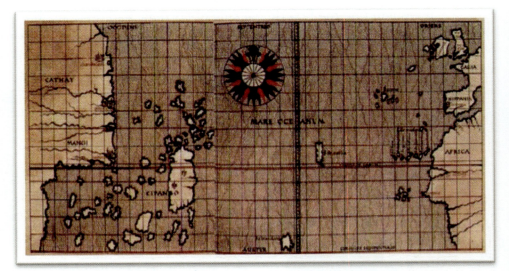

A map drawn by Italian geographer Paolo Toscanelli in 1463. The map shows Europe and Africa on the right, China and Japan on the left, and the "Ocean Sea" in between.

southern tip of Africa was. That would mean that ships shouldn't bother sailing around Africa to reach the Far East. If Columbus was right, then they should sail around the world to the west!

Of course, Columbus wasn't right. The real distance from the Canary Islands to Japan is more like 12,000 miles than 3,000. If the Americas hadn't stood in Columbus' way, then he would have starved to death long before he reached Japan!

At the time, though, Columbus had no idea how wrong he was. The only way to know for sure was to go see. To do that, Columbus needed some rich ruler to give him two things: permission and money.

The first ruler Columbus asked was King John II of Portugal. Since the Portuguese were so determined to reach India, John seemed like a good choice. But John turned Columbus away, for a couple of reasons. First, explorers like Bartolomeu Dias were already well on their way toward sailing around Africa. Second, John's scientists warned him that Columbus' calculations were wrong— which turned out to be quite true!

After trying a few other rulers, Columbus turned to King John's biggest rivals: Ferdinand and Isabella. With Portugal blocking the way around Africa, Ferdinand and Isabella desperately needed another way to reach India— which was exactly what Columbus offered.

Alas, Columbus' timing was wrong. When Columbus first spoke to Ferdinand and Isabella, they were still fighting the Spanish Reconquista (Chapter 23). With an expensive war on, they couldn't afford to waste money on an expedition that might not work.

"Columbus before the Queen" by artist Emanuel Leutze

Even so, Ferdinand and Isabella didn't want Columbus taking his ideas anywhere else. Instead of turning him away, they offered him a small salary and told him to wait.

After the caravel, the next great new ship design was the **carrack**. Carracks were bigger, taller and heavier than caravels, which meant that they could carry more supplies. Any crew that planned to sail thousands of miles without stopping needed plenty of supplies!

It all came together in one most important year: 1492. Ferdinand and Isabella finally finished the Spanish Reconquista that January. Now that the war wasn't draining their treasury, they could afford to give Columbus the answer he wanted— the "yes" he'd been seeking for seven years, ever since 1485.

Columbus used the money Ferdinand and Isabella gave him to hire three ships: Nina, Pinta and Santa Maria. *Nina* and *Pinta* were probably caravels; while *Santa Maria* was probably a newer, bigger kind of ship called a **carrack**.

Columbus led his three ships out of Palos, Castile on August 3, 1492. After a short stop at the Canary Islands, they sailed west on September 6.

Five weeks later, in the dark of the morning of October 12, one of Columbus' lookouts spotted a flickering light that could only be one thing: a fire burning on dry land.

The West Indies

The first land Columbus found wasn't North America, Central America or South America. Instead, Columbus found the arc of islands that divides the Atlantic Ocean from the Caribbean Sea. Needing a name for these new islands, Europeans called them the **West Indies**.

Why "West Indies"? Because Columbus believed that he was somewhere near the place he was really looking for: India. The same hope showed in what Europeans called the natives of the islands: "Indians." As long as he lived, Columbus never admitted that the West Indies were really nowhere near India— although he did admit some doubts near the end.

The West Indies are divided into three main island groups: the Greater Antilles, the Lesser Antilles and the Lucayan Archipelago.

➤ The **Greater Antilles** are mainly four big islands: **Cuba**, **Jamaica**, **Hispaniola** and **Puerto Rico**. The far smaller **Cayman Islands**, which lie west of Jamaica, also belong to the Greater Antilles.

➤ The **Lesser Antilles** are a string of smaller islands that start east of Puerto Rico, arc to the south for about 500 miles, and then turn west along the northern coast of South America. This string starts with the **Virgin Islands**, and ends with the "ABC islands": **Aruba**, **Bonaire** and **Curacao**, just off the northern coast of Venezuela.

➤ The **Lucayan Archipelago** lies just north of the Greater Antilles. The **Bahamas**, where Columbus first struck land, are part of the Lucayan Archipelago.

Just which of the Bahamas Columbus struck first, no one is quite sure. It may have been a Bahamian island called **San Salvador**. Whichever it was, the natives he met there were peaceful and primitive. Many of them walked around completely naked. Like the Maya, Aztecs and Incas, they used no iron, wheels or pulleys (Chapter 22).

After exploring the Bahamas for a while, Columbus moved on to the big island of Cuba. The last stops of this first voyage were on the island of **Hispaniola**.

> Modern-day **Hispaniola** is divided between two countries: **Haiti** and the **Dominican Republic**.

The New World

The trouble started on Christmas Day 1492, when *Santa Maria* ran aground off the northern coast of Hispaniola. Try as he might, Columbus couldn't float his flagship off the bottom. In a few hours, *Santa Maria* broke up— leaving Columbus and crew thousands of miles from home, with too few ships to carry them all back!

Fortunately, thirty-nine crewmen volunteered to stay behind. These brave men used lumber from the wreck of *Santa Maria* to build the very first European colony in the New World. They called it **La Navidad**, Spanish for "Christmas," after the Christmas day wreck of *Santa Maria*.

Back home in Castile, Columbus dazzled Ferdinand and Isabella with all the wonders he collected on his first voyage. He'd brought home strange new plants, a few natives— and even a bit of gold.

To say that the Spaniards were excited would be a huge understatement. At the mere mention of the word "gold," every soldier in Spain was ready to board ship for the New World! With the Spanish Reconquista over, soldiers had been wondering what they would do next. Now they knew: they would go to the New World and find fortunes in gold.

Thanks to all the excitement, Columbus' second expedition was far bigger than his first. Seventeen ships, carrying about 1,200 colonists in all, sailed with Columbus on his second voyage to the West Indies.

Columbus returned to *La Navidad* in November 1493, eleven months after he'd left. With so many ships to pay for,

Columbus needed a lot of money on this second voyage; so he was hoping to find happy colonists telling glad tales of all the gold they'd found. Instead, he found the colonists all dead! The long, ugly war between Spaniards and Native Americans had begun.

〰〰〰〰〰〰〰〰〰〰〰〰〰〰〰〰〰〰〰〰〰〰〰〰〰〰〰

Just when Europe was starting to recover from the shocking news of Spain's discoveries, Portugal started making headlines again.

➢ In 1498, a Portuguese explorer called **Vasco da Gama** finally sailed around Africa— all the way to India! After building a trading post at Calicut, India, the Portuguese started sending trade **armadas** to India every year.

➢ In 1500, the leader of the second Portuguese India Armada made a huge discovery. Oddly enough, this discovery wasn't anywhere near India. What **Pedro Alvares Cabral** discovered was **Brazil**, South America! This explains why it was Portugal, not Spain, that built colonies in Brazil.

The next big discovery was another Spanish one. In 1513, a Spaniard called **Ponce de Leon** became the first European ever to set foot in **Florida**. The usual story about Ponce de Leon is that he went looking for the Fountain of Youth— a mythical fountain that brought eternal youth and health to all

Christopher Columbus made four voyages to the West Indies in all. He touched land in South America on his third voyage, and spent part of his fourth exploring Central America.

Columbus spent another part of his fourth voyage stranded on Jamaica, depending on the natives to bring him food. Naturally, the natives started grumbling about how much Columbus and crew were eating. If the Spaniards were going to survive, then they needed a way to keep the food coming.

Columbus soon found one. In looking at his almanac, Columbus noticed that a lunar eclipse was coming soon— which gave him an idea. He warned the natives that if they stopped bringing him food, then he would take the moon away from them! When the moon went dark just like Columbus said, the natives were so scared that they gladly brought him whatever he needed.

Columbus frightening the natives with his tall tale about the eclipse

Armada means "fleet of armed ships" in both Spanish and Portuguese.

who drank from it. But the usual story is probably make-believe. What Ponce de Leon was really looking for was a way out of Christopher Columbus' shadow.

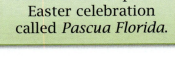

Juan Ponce de Leon was a young army officer who moved to the West in 1493, on Columbus' second voyage. Like everyone else on that voyage, Juan dreamed of getting rich. He thought his dream had come true in 1509, when the Governor of Hispaniola named him Governor of Puerto Rico.

Two years later, all Juan's hopes came crashing down. Although Christopher Columbus died in 1506, his son Diego could still name governors for all the islands his father had discovered. When Diego Columbus came to Puerto Rico, he named a new Governor of Puerto Rico— leaving Juan out of a job.

Juan realized that if he was ever going to be a governor again, then it would have to be in some place that Columbus hadn't discovered. In early 1513, Juan set out to find such an island. As he hopped from island to island in the Bahamas, the natives told him about a much bigger land to the west. Thanks to the natives, he discovered Florida that Easter!

The name **"Florida"** comes from a Spanish Easter celebration called *Pascua Florida*.

The Western Schism

In Chapter 21, we read how the pope moved from Rome to Avignon, France. The **Avignon Papacy** went on for nearly seventy years, from 1309 – 1377. This chapter tells how the pope finally moved back to Rome.

The story starts with an Italian nun called **Catherine of Siena**. Around 1370, Catherine started pleading with the French pope over in Avignon— telling him that he was making a big mistake. She said that the Lord was angry about the Avignon Papacy, and wanted the pope back in Rome right away!

Catherine of Siena

After seven years of pleading, Catherine finally got her way. To the delight of every Italian, Pope Gregory XI moved from Avignon to Rome in 1377. The Avignon Papacy was over, or so it seemed.

Unfortunately, the beloved Pope Gregory XI died the following year; and the next pope, Urban VI, wasn't beloved at all. The fiery Urban made his cardinals so angry that they elected a new pope to replace him. Alas for the cardinals, Urban wouldn't leave! After trying in vain to take his seat in Rome, the new pope gave up and moved to Avignon. Now there were two popes at the same time: one in Rome, and another in Avignon!

For the next forty years, the Church did little else but argue over which was the true pope. Since Avignon was in France, most Frenchmen followed the Avignon popes. Most other countries followed the Roman popes. This time of two popes is called the **Western Schism**. With each pope calling the other a heretic, the Church was a mess!

A **schism** is a church split.

The Western Schism was about forty years old in 1417, when three things changed. First, two Roman popes stepped down at once— for by this time, there were three popes! Second, a committee called the Council of Constance excommunicated the Avignon pope. Third, the same committee elected a new Roman pope that everyone could accept. The Avignon pope didn't step down; but he did lose most of his followers. When he died in 1423, few Christians even noticed.

CHAPTER 25:

Slavery in the New World; the Conquistadors

A Bright Beginning Gone Bad

In Chapter 24, we read how Christopher Columbus lost his **flagship**. It happened on Christmas Day 1492, when *Santa Maria* accidentally **ran aground** off the northern coast of Hispaniola.

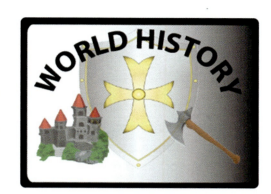

> An admiral's **flagship** is the lead ship of his fleet.
>
> To **run aground** is to strike bottom.

The accident never should have happened. Columbus' journal says that the wind was still that Christmas Eve, and the sea as smooth as glass. No one expected trouble on a night so calm. Thinking all was well, Columbus left an officer in charge of the rudder and went off to bed at 11 p.m. He certainly deserved a good night's sleep; for he hadn't slept at all the night before.

Unfortunately, Columbus wasn't the only one sleeping. After Columbus went off to bed, the officer in charge decided that he deserved sleep as well. He handed off the rudder to a younger sailor— probably thinking to himself, "What could possibly go wrong?"

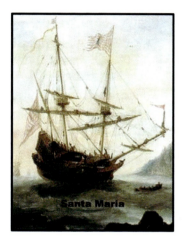

Santa Maria

Something soon went very wrong indeed. If the older, more experienced sailor had stayed at the rudder, then he might have noticed the telltale signs of shallow water ahead. The younger sailor noticed nothing— until around midnight, when he felt the sickening crunch of *Santa Maria* hitting bottom!

Columbus had to save *Santa Maria* if he could. His best chance was to make her as light as possible, in hopes that she might float off the bottom. He tried throwing her cannon overboard, and even chopping down her masts. Alas, she was still too heavy to float; for the accident had split her seams, filling her hold with water. Despite everything Columbus tried, *Santa Maria* finally broke up.

Fortunately, Columbus had a friend nearby. The natives of Hispaniola were a people called the

Taino. When Columbus came, the big island was divided into five sections— each ruled by a Taino chief called a *cacique*. The chief for northwestern Hispaniola was Columbus' friend: a kindly man called **Guacanagari**.

When Guacanagari heard that Columbus was in trouble, he leapt into action. Taino canoes swarmed around the dying *Santa Maria*, saving everything they could. Without all the tools and supplies the Taino carried ashore for him, Columbus might never have made it home from his first voyage.

"Landing of Columbus" by John Vanderlyn

What Columbus liked best about Guacanagari and his people was that they weren't greedy. The Taino could have stolen anything they wanted from *Santa Maria* that night. They must have been tempted by the fascinating trinkets the Spaniards had brought to trade— all the beads, bells and so on. Yet they stole nothing. And when the shipwrecked Spaniards needed a place to stay, the chief offered them the two best houses in his village. Columbus wrote to Ferdinand and Isabella:

"I assure your Highnesses that there is no better land nor people. They love their neighbors as themselves, and their speech is the sweetest and gentlest in the world…"

After a bright beginning like that, the Spaniards and the Taino might have become great friends— if not for what happened next. Columbus soon sailed home, leaving behind a little colony called *La Navidad*. When he came back eleven months later, he hoped to find *La Navidad* thriving. Instead, he found the little fort in ruins— and the colonists all dead! What on Earth had gone wrong, Columbus wondered?

Guacanagari knew. According to Columbus' friend, the colonists of *La Navidad* had kidnapped some Taino women from one of the other chiefs. The furious chief had answered by destroying the little fort, killing every Spaniard inside! These were the first blows in a long, ugly war that would leave thousands of innocent people dead— most of them Taino.

The biggest battle of that war came in 1495, while Columbus was still on his second voyage. With an expensive expedition to pay for, Columbus needed a lot of gold on this second voyage. To get it, he pressed inland— trying to seize the mines where the Taino found their gold. Only one chief fought for Columbus: Guacanagari. The other four chiefs joined forces against Columbus, hoping to drive him off Hispaniola. The two armies clashed at the **Battle of Santo Cerro**, which is named for a hill overlooking the gold mines.

The Battle of Santo Cerro started badly for the Spaniards. Back in 1492, Columbus had believed that he could conquer all Hispaniola with just a few well-armed Spaniards. Now he worried that his whole army might not be enough! Even sharp steel and cannon were no match for thousands of Taino attacking at once. Instead of gaining ground, Columbus lost ground— retreating farther uphill every day.

After several days of losses, Columbus feared that the next day might be his last on Earth. Instead of going to sleep that night, Columbus planted a big wooden cross on Santo Cerro, and spent the night praying.

The Battle of Santo Cerro (1495)

While Columbus was praying, one of his priests was having a vision. The priest saw the Taino try to burn Columbus' cross down; but the fire wouldn't catch. He also saw them try to chop the cross down, and then pull it down; but the cross wouldn't fall. Finally, the priest saw the Virgin Mary and the Baby Jesus standing beside Columbus' cross— both of them bathed in white light.

At sunrise the next day, Columbus got the shock of his life: The Taino army was gone! Instead of pressing their attack, the Taino had melted away. Just why they left, no one now knows for sure. But Columbus thought he knew why. To him, the priest's vision meant that Christ and His Church would never be driven off Hispaniola!

"The Virgin of Navigators"
by Alejo Fernandez

Whether Columbus was right or not, the Taino never again raised such a big army against him. The Spaniards seized more and more land, conquering more and more Taino.

As a conquered people, the Taino had to do as they were told. Columbus ordered all Taino over fourteen years old to bring him a certain amount of gold dust every month. If they didn't, then the Spaniards punished them in horrible ways. Columbus also sent Taino back to Castile to be sold at slave auctions. Within 25 years after Columbus first landed on Hispaniola, only a few Taino remained alive on the whole island.

Meanwhile, the Portuguese were making slaves of a different kind of people: Africans. In Chapter 24, we read about a gold-trading colony called the Portuguese Gold Coast. Sad to say, gold wasn't all the Portuguese traded there. They also traded African slaves. Thousands of Africans were carried off by Portuguese slave ships, never to see their homes and families again.

Of course, slavery was nothing new. Ever since ancient times, there had been many ways to become a slave. One way was to lose a battle; for the winners often sold the losers into slavery. Another way was to be kidnapped by the Barbary Pirates, or by other criminals looking for quick cash. Yet another way was to owe a lot of money. When poor people couldn't pay their debts, they sometimes had no choice but to sell themselves into slavery.

"The Slave Trade" by artist Francois-Auguste Biard

Alas, the Age of Discovery made slavery much worse. With growing colonies at Madeira, the Cape Verdes, Brazil and more, Portuguese farmers were hungry for more slaves. They used them for clearing land, tending crops, loading ships and countless other jobs.

Slavery got even worse when the Spaniards started building their empire. Just a few years after Columbus, slave ships were already sailing to the West Indies— following a sea route called the **Middle Passage**. The unlucky slaves aboard those ships were on their way to do one of the hardest jobs ever: raising **sugarcane** in the West Indies.

> The **Middle Passage** was a sea route that slave ships used to carry slaves from West Africa to the West Indies.

We've read why so many Spaniards moved to the New World: because they were obsessed with finding gold. The West Indies disappointed them; for they didn't find a lot of gold there. The gold mines Columbus won at the Battle of Santo Cerro all ran empty in a few years. After that, the Spaniards needed a new way to earn their livings.

> **Sugarcane** is a tropical plant with a thick stalk. When the stalk is pressed between heavy rollers, sweet juice comes out. Cane juice can be processed to make molasses and sugar.

For many, that new way was farming sugarcane. The West Indies turned out to be the perfect place to raise sugarcane. The climate was hot, and the soil just right.

African slaves cutting sugarcane while an overseer looks on

The problem was that raising sugarcane took a lot of hard work. Besides planting, tending and cutting plants, there were also endless jobs like pressing stalks, refining juice, barreling molasses and loading ships. The less a farmer paid for these jobs, the more money was left over for the farmer— which is why the Spaniards bought so many African slaves.

What did the world do with so much molasses? Mostly, the world turned it into rum. Any kind of sugar can be fermented and distilled to make alcohol. Distilleries in Europe could turn molasses from the West Indies into a sweet rum that customers loved.

Sugarcane, rum and slaves— these were the three corners of an ugly new business called the **Triangle Trade**. A song from the musical play "1776" tells the whole story of the Triangle Trade in just five words: "Molasses to Rum to Slaves."

➤ Farmers in the West Indies raised sugarcane, turned it into molasses and shipped it off to Europe.

➤ Factories in Europe turned molasses into rum and shipped it off to Africa.

➤ Traders in Africa traded rum for slaves, and then shipped slaves off to the West Indies to grow more sugarcane.

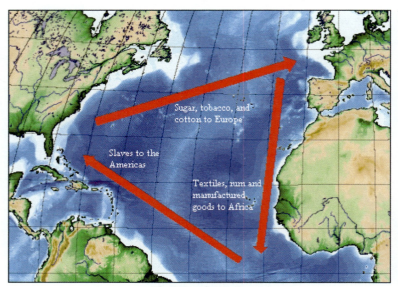
The Triangle Trade

The Door of No Return

After buying or capturing African slaves, traders herded them into strong buildings to wait for the next slave auction. One such building was Elmina Castle, which guarded the Portuguese Gold Coast (Chapter 24). Another was the Fort of St. John the Baptist of Whydah, which stood in what is now Benin.

After the auction, the poor slaves were locked inside again until it was time to board ship for the West Indies. When the big day finally came, they passed through one last door on their way out of the building. Doors like these became symbols of the sad fact that these slaves were leaving home forever, never to see their families again. Some call these symbols "Doors of No Return"; while others call them "Portals of Sorrow."

A Door of No Return

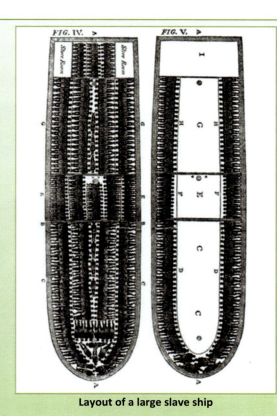

Layout of a large slave ship

Slave Ships

The ugly job of carrying so many slaves to the West Indies required a special kind of ship. Instead of the usual cargo hold, slave ships had special decks built just for slaves. The ceilings of these decks were often less than five feet high. Some carried slaves lying down, crowded in head-to-foot. Other carried slaves sitting up, crowded in back-to-chest. Slavers almost never let slaves up on the main deck, for fear they might take over the ship.

The journey from West Africa to the West Indies usually took about two months. Imagine spending two whole months chained in the same place— unable to move, even to go to the bathroom. Imagine being seasick, hot, filthy and crowded for that whole time. Imagine the person next to you dying of a fever, as slaves often did. Imagine knowing all the while that you will never see your home and family again. Imagine being sold off the moment you step ashore— as if you were a piece of property, instead of a human being. These were just some of the many horrors of slave ships and slavery.

The Conquistadors

Between searching for gold and raising sugarcane, brave young Spaniards had two ways to strike it rich in the West Indies. So naturally, they came by the thousands. After taking over Hispaniola, they moved on to Cuba, Puerto Rico and other islands. These were the Spanish **conquistadors**— the soldiers who conquered the New World for Spain.

After the West Indies, the conquistadors moved on to **Middle America**— in other words, Central America and Mexico. The first to build a colony in Middle America was a conquistador called **Vasco Nunez de Balboa**.

> *Conquistador* is Spanish for "conqueror."
>
> **Middle America** means Central America plus what is now Mexico.

Balboa was a third son born to a family of minor nobles in Spain. In that place and time, the oldest son inherited almost all the family fortune. With no hope of an inheritance, Balboa decided to move to the West Indies— hoping to find fortune a different way.

The first way Balboa found fortune was through a law called the *Quinto Real*— Spanish for "King's Fifth." The king gave certain nobles permits to search certain parts of the New World for gold. In exchange, those nobles gave the king one-fifth of any gold they found. Since Balboa wasn't rich enough to have a permit of his own, he worked for a noble who did have one.

> *Quinto Real* is Spanish for "King's Fifth." Under a Spanish law called the Quinto Real, the King of Spain automatically received one-fifth of any gold, silver or other precious metals found anywhere in his empire.

After five years' work, Balboa had enough gold to buy a big farm on Hispaniola. Alas, Balboa was no good at farming. He borrowed a lot of money trying to save his farm, and wound up losing both money and farm!

Balboa was in so much trouble that he finally did something desperate. Sneaking aboard a conquistador's ship, he hid himself in an empty barrel— hoping to start a new life somewhere else. It almost didn't work; for when the captain found out, he almost cast Balboa away on the nearest island! In the end, though, the captain let Balboa join his crew.

Balboa made a much better conquistador than he did a farmer. Just a few years after he hid in that barrel, Balboa was already the governor of a little colony. His capital, Dariena, stood near the northern end of what is now the border between Panama and Colombia.

One day in 1513, a Native American prince told Governor Balboa about an "other sea" on the far side of Panama. Since the distance was only about 70 miles, Balboa decided to march over and see it for himself. When he got there, he became the first Spaniard ever to cast eyes on this other sea— which turned out to be the Pacific Ocean!

What happened next was the kind of scene all conquistadors loved. Striding out into the water, Balboa dramatically raised his sword and claimed the entire Pacific coast for the Spanish Empire! If Balboa was right, then the west coasts of Central America, South America and North America all belonged to Spain.

Of course, Balboa wasn't right. The people who really owned those coasts were the Native Americans who lived there. Even so, Balboa's expedition made Spain the first country in Europe to claim part of the Pacific coast.

Balboa claiming every shore of the Pacific for the Spanish Empire

꧁꧁꧁꧁꧁꧁꧁꧁꧁꧁꧁꧁꧁꧁꧁꧁꧁꧁꧁꧁꧁꧁꧁꧁꧁꧁꧁꧁꧁꧁꧁꧁꧁꧁꧁

Our next great conquistador, Hernan Cortes, started out as another minor noble who moved to the West Indies as a young man— hoping to strike it rich. Cortes spent five years helping his governor conquer the biggest island of the West Indies: Cuba.

The job of conquering Cuba was just about finished in 1519, when Cortes' governor trusted him with a new mission. His orders were to sail over to Mexico, conquer the natives and claim the whole land in the governor's name.

Alas for the governor, Cortes had other ideas. When he reached Mexico, Cortes wrote a letter to the King of Spain— asking him to make Mexico a separate colony, with Cortes himself as governor!

Without waiting for the king's answer, Cortes set out for the capital of the Aztec Empire. As we read in Chapter 22, the Aztecs ruled from a beautiful island city called Tenochtitlan.

On his way to Tenochtitlan, Cortes learned a fact that would prove most useful to him. It turned out that the Aztecs' neighbors all hated them, and would be happy to see them conquered. Why? Because the Aztecs had a cruel habit of kidnapping their neighbors and sacrificing them to their gods! The Aztecs were about to pay a high price for all the horrible things they'd done to their neighbors.

Hernan Cortes (1485? – 1547)

The ruler of the Aztecs, Emperor **Montezuma II**, acted strangely around Cortes. After all he'd heard about the Spaniards, Montezuma must have

known that Cortes was up to no good. But instead of standing up to Cortes, Montezuma welcomed him as a friend. He invited Cortes to stay at one of the best palaces in Tenochtitlan; and he also gave him many gifts, including a fortune in gold.

One of the gifts Montezuma gave was especially interesting. For some reason, he gave Cortes the headdress of Quetzalcoatl— the feathered serpent god of the Aztecs. In Spanish eyes, this gift could mean only one thing: that Montezuma saw Cortes as a god!

Cortes meeting Montezuma and the Aztecs

Some historians call this wishful thinking— saying that Montezuma was only pretending to honor Cortes. What he was really doing, they say, was watching and waiting— trying to learn more about Cortes, so that he could destroy him later.

The emperor's many gifts to Cortes didn't buy him much. Instead of honoring Montezuma, Cortes seized him and held him hostage. With their emperor in enemy hands, the Aztecs didn't dare attack the Spaniards— for fear Cortes might kill him. The most they could do was to riot outside the palace, shouting for Cortes to set their emperor free.

MONTEZUMA.

A **causeway** is a land bridge made by piling earth and rock into the water.

If the Spanish version of the story is true, then the Aztecs' riots led to big trouble. According to the Spaniards, Cortes sent Montezuma out on a balcony, ordering him to calm his people down. But the Aztecs were in no mood to calm down. They wanted Montezuma to stand up to Cortes, not act like Cortes' puppet. When Montezuma showed up on that balcony, saying just what Cortes wanted him to say, the Aztecs stoned their own emperor to death!

Once again, some historians say this story is wrong. They believe that the Spaniards murdered Montezuma themselves, and then lied about it to cover up their cruelty!

Either way, the death of the emperor put the Spaniards in serious trouble. Without Montezuma to hold them off, the Aztecs would surely kill every Spaniard in Tenochtitlan. Desperate to save themselves, the Spaniards planned to sneak out of the city under cover of darkness.

Alas for the Spaniards, the Aztecs were ready and waiting for them. Although they left as quietly as possible, the Aztecs soon spotted them. As the Spaniards sped over the **causeway** toward shore, Aztec warriors bore down on them in canoes.

The luckiest Spaniards that night were the ones on horseback, like Cortes himself. Many horsemen were saved by the speed of their mounts. As for the poor men on foot, almost all of them died on **La Noche Triste**— "The Sad Night" when Cortes and his troops tried to escape.

The saddest thing about *La Noche Triste* was the way Cortes' foot soldiers died. Before they left, Cortes let them stuff their packs with as much gold as they could carry. But when the Aztecs stormed the causeway, they drove the foot soldiers into the lake— where the weight of all that gold carried them straight to the bottom. They had taken the gold because they thought it would buy them richer lives. Instead, gold wound up ending their lives.

Cortes spent the next several months raising an army against the Aztecs. Only a fraction of his soldiers were Spaniards. The rest were all the Aztecs' angry neighbors. Less than a year after *La Noche Triste*, Cortes laid siege to Tenochtitlan— cutting off all supplies from outside the city.

The Aztecs might have held on a lot longer, if not for a second enemy: disease. Ever since the Spaniards came, the Aztecs had been sicker than usual. Without meaning to, the Spaniards had brought deadly diseases to the New World— especially **smallpox**. Soon after *La Noche Triste*, a smallpox epidemic swept through Tenochtitlan. Thousands of Aztecs died, and many others were too sick to work.

Faced with two such deadly enemies, Cortes and smallpox, the empire collapsed. The last Emperor of the Aztecs surrendered to Hernan Cortes in August 1521.

〽〽〽〽〽〽〽〽〽〽〽〽〽〽〽〽〽〽〽〽〽〽〽〽〽〽〽〽〽〽〽〽

In conquering the Aztecs, Cortes became the richest conquistador so far. But there was one conquistador who became even richer: **Francisco Pizarro**. Pizarro started as an officer in the army of Vasco Nunez de Balboa, whom we met above. When a Native American prince told Balboa about the "other sea," Pizarro was right there listening.

That same prince said something that was even more interesting to Pizarro. He spoke of a far-off kingdom that had more gold than any kingdom in Middle America. It stood way down south, in the Andes Mountains of South America. Obviously, he was talking about the Inca Empire. Right then and there, Pizarro decided to either conquer the Incas or die trying!

Pizarro's first problem was finding the Incas. He needed three expeditions to South America before he finally found a usable road into the Andes.

Pizarro's second problem was finding out how to beat the Incas. The size of his expedition was pitiful— less than two hundred Spaniards, versus tens of thousands of Incas! On the other hand, the Spaniards had two advantages over the Incas:

Smallpox was a virus that brought on a terrible skin rash, severe breathing problems and worse. The worst form of smallpox killed about 4 out of every 10 people who caught it.

The reason why smallpox killed so many Aztecs, but so few Spaniards, was because Spaniards were used to it. The Spaniards had grown up in Europe, where smallpox was common— which meant that their immune systems knew how to fight it. But the Aztecs had grown up in America, where no one had ever faced smallpox before.

The Aztecs weren't the only ones who died of smallpox. The disease struck cities and villages all over the Americas, killing countless thousands. Just how many Native Americans died of smallpox, no one knows; but it may be that smallpox killed more than the conquistadors did.

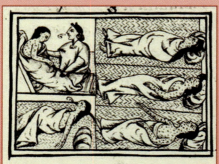

Native Americans dying of smallpox

Francisco Pizarro (1475 – 1541)

Francisco Pizarro
(1475? - 1541)

- The first advantage was that Pizarro's men carried weapons the Incas had never seen before: thundering cannon and muskets that were sure to terrify Inca warriors.
- The second advantage was that when Pizarro showed up, the Incas were just finishing a civil war between two rival emperors. The war had killed many Incas, leaving the empire weaker than before.

Inca Atahualpa (1502? – 1533)

The winner of this civil war was **Inca Atahualpa**, whom Pizarro met in November 1532. Pizarro made sure to get to the meeting place early. That way, he could hide most of his men behind buildings— ready to leap out and attack. The moment Atahualpa arrived, Pizarro sent a priest to read him the **Spanish Requirement of 1513**.

Like all Spaniards, the conquistadors were supposed to be good Christians. So how could they treat Native Americans as cruelly as they did? The answer lies in an important paper called the **Spanish Requirement of 1513**, a.k.a. *El Requerimiento*.

The Requirement explained that in the beginning, God created Adam and Eve. All people on Earth were children of Adam and Eve, no matter where they lived. As God's creatures, all people had a duty to obey God.

According to the Requirement, the only way to obey God was to obey the Catholic Church. The man God had chosen to rule His people was the Apostle Peter— the first pope, the head of the Church. When Peter died, he handed down his authority to the next pope. That pope handed down his authority to the next, and so on— all the way down to the present-day pope. Now the pope had given the Americas to the King of Spain. This meant that if Native Americans didn't obey the King of Spain, then they were going against God!

*O*f course, Pizarro didn't forget about the gold. Besides reading the Requirement, Pizarro's priest also told Atahualpa that he must pay the King of Spain a lot of gold— starting right now.

At this, Atahualpa laughed in the priest's face! With thousands of troops at his back, Atahualpa saw no reason to fear so few Spaniards. Instead of obeying, he tossed away the small book of Scripture the priest gave him— swearing that he would never pay tribute.

Tossing away Scripture was just the sign Pizarro had been waiting for. Now that Atahualpa had disobeyed God, Pizarro's men leapt out of hiding and blasted the Incas. Most of them ran off, leaving Pizarro to capture Atahualpa! After that, Pizarro did to Atahualpa just what Cortes had done to Montezuma. He held Atahualpa hostage, threatening to kill him if the Incas attacked.

The building where Pizarro held Atahualpa hostage was about the size of a one-car garage. Its name, the **Ransom Room**, comes from a bargain Atahualpa struck with the gold-hungry Pizarro. Atahualpa promised that if Pizarro would spare his life, then the Incas would fill the Ransom Room with gold. They would also fill two rooms just like it with silver, and give the whole lot to Pizarro. With that much treasure, Pizarro would be the richest conquistador ever!

The Ransom Room where Pizarro held Atahualpa

The Incas held up their end of the bargain, giving Pizarro the huge fortune Atahualpa promised. Sad to say, Pizarro didn't hold up his end. Instead of letting Atahualpa live, Pizarro placed him on trial— accusing him of going against God and Church. His punishment was to be strangled to death.

Without an emperor to hold it together, the Inca Empire collapsed. It happened in 1532, eleven years after the Aztec Empire collapsed.

Around the World in Three Years

Ferdinand Magellan (1480? – 1521)

In Chapter 24, we read how the Portuguese finally made it to India. It happened in 1498, when Vasco da Gama built a trading post there.

After da Gama, the Portuguese sailed on beyond India. There was so much more to discover! The Portuguese were especially excited about the **Spice Islands** east of India. These were the only places in the world where traders could buy cinnamon, nutmeg and cloves— valuable spices that sold for fortunes back in Europe.

The **Spice Islands** were part of what is now Indonesia.

That was how a great explorer called Ferdinand Magellan got his start: as a Portuguese naval officer defending trading posts in India and the Spice Islands. Later, Magellan got in trouble with the Portuguese; so he went to work for the Spanish. Magellan promised Spain the same thing Columbus had promised: that he could reach the Far East by sailing around the world to the west. He planned to sail around the southern tip of South America, just as Bartolomeu Dias had sailed around the southern tip of Africa.

Magellan set out in 1519, the same year Cortes invaded Mexico. After a long, dangerous sail, Magellan and crew finally found their way around South America. Once they reached the Pacific, the Far East couldn't be far off— or so Magellan hoped.

Alas, Magellan was as wrong as Columbus had been. He was expecting to strike land in a few thousand miles, which he hoped to cover in less than two months. The real distance was closer to 10,000 miles— which took four months! Since Magellan carried only two months' worth of food, his starving men had to eat anything they could find— including rat meat and boiled leather. Even the survivors were half-dead when they finally pulled up to their first island: Guam.

Continuing west from Guam, Magellan ran into the Philippines— where he made his last mistake. On one of the Philippines, a friendly chief asked Magellan to help him fight a war. Magellan agreed, probably thinking that the natives' primitive weapons were no match for Spanish steel. Alas, he was wrong. Instead of winning the war for his friend, the great navigator Ferdinand Magellan went down fighting.

After that, one of Magellan's ship's captains took over. It was actually Juan Sebastian Elcano, not Ferdinand Magellan, who finished the first full voyage around the world. Magellan had sailed out of Spain with five ships and 270 men. Three years later, Elcano sailed back to Spain with just one ship— and only 18 men!

Victoria, the only ship from Magellan's expedition that made it back to Spain

John Hus

Back in Chapter 22, we read about a Christian professor from Oxford, England called John Wycliffe. This chapter tells of a priest who loved John Wycliffe's teaching, and what happened to him because of it.

John Hus was a priest and professor at the University of **Prague**, Bohemia. As a Catholic priest, Hus was supposed to obey the Catholic Church. But Hus didn't always agree

> **Prague** is the capital of what is now the Czech Republic.

with the Catholic Church, especially after he read John Wycliffe. Like Wycliffe, Hus believed that the Bible was more important than Church tradition. He also believed in holding church services in a language his people could understand. In Hus' case, that language was Czech.

The archbishop in charge of Bohemia did everything he could think of to change Hus' mind. He tried ordering all Wycliffe's books burned. When that failed, the archbishop excommunicated Hus. By order of the archbishop, no Christian was to have anything to do with John Hus.

But the people of Bohemia didn't obey; for they loved John Hus, and hated their stuffy archbishop. Instead of leaving the Church as ordered, Hus kept right on teaching what John Wycliffe had taught— and in Czech, not Latin.

The Church finally did to John Hus what it had almost done to John Wycliffe. In 1414, the **Council of Constance** charged Hus with heresy and put him on trial.

> The trial of John Hus happened at the **Council of Constance**, Germany in 1414 - 1415. This was the same church council that would soon end the Western Schism (Chapter 24).

The trial of John Hus was no real trial; for no one defended Hus. The priests simply read out their accusations, announced that Hus was wrong, and then ordered him to change his beliefs. Hus answered that he would be happy to change his beliefs if anyone could prove him wrong. But they would have to prove it from the Bible; for Hus believed in the Bible, not in Church tradition.

When the Church couldn't change Hus' mind, it sent him to his death. Executioners stripped off his priestly robes and buried him up to his neck in a pile of wood and straw. On his head they set a mocking paper crown labelled "Leader of Heretics." When they set fire to the pile, the faithful John Hus suffered the awful death reserved for traitors and heretics: being burned alive.

John Hus (1369? – 1415)

John Hus using a Bible to defend himself at the Council of Constance

CHAPTER 26:

The Printing Revolution; the Renaissance in Florence

The End of Medieval Times

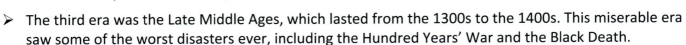

Way back at the beginning of this book, we learned that the medieval era can be divided into three shorter eras:

➢ The first era was the Dark Ages, which lasted from the 400s to the 1000s. This era saw the birth of Islam, the Viking invasions and the rise of Charlemagne.

➢ The second era was the High Middle Ages, which lasted from the 1000s to the 1300s. This was the era of knights, castles, the Norman Conquest and the Holy Land Crusades.

➢ The third era was the Late Middle Ages, which lasted from the 1300s to the 1400s. This miserable era saw some of the worst disasters ever, including the Hundred Years' War and the Black Death.

We also learned why the Dark Ages are called "dark": because for a while, the bright light of Greek and Roman learning went dark in Western Europe. Doctors forgot how to heal; engineers forgot how to build great buildings; and sculptors forgot how to carve fine art.

Learning was the biggest difference between the medieval era and the next era of history: the **Renaissance**. Renaissance is French for "rebirth." In this case, the name means a rebirth of learning. The idea is that sometime during the Late Middle Ages, Europeans started re-learning all the Greek and Roman knowledge their ancestors had forgotten.

> The **Renaissance** was the next era after the medieval era. Renaissance times started in the 1400s, and lasted into the early 1600s.

Where is the line between the medieval era and the Renaissance? The answer is that there is no one line. Instead, different historians point to different lines.

Some historians point to the **Age of Discovery**. It started around 1415, when Henry the Navigator went looking for a way around West Africa (Chapter 24). By sailing out into the unknown, Europeans left behind the old superstitions of medieval times— crazy stories about boiling seas to the south and giant whirlpools at the edge of the Atlantic.

Other historians point to the **Fall of Constantinople**. It happened in 1453, when the Ottoman Empire finally conquered the Byzantine Empire (Chapter 20). As the capital of a Greek-speaking empire, Constantinople was also the capital of Greek learning. When the Ottomans took Constantinople, some Greek scholars moved to Western Europe— bringing along some ancient learning that had been forgotten in the West.

Still other historians point to an invention that would turn out to be terribly important: the **movable-type printing press**.

Leonardo da Vinci (1452 – 1519), a leading thinker of the Renaissance

The Printing Revolution

In medieval times, books were so expensive that only the richest people owned them. The average household owned no books, not even a family Bible. Of course, the average household also had no use for books. Why? Because most people couldn't read!

Part of the problem was that books were so expensive. In those days, the usual way of making books was to copy them by hand— which could take a very long time. The average **scribe** needed a whole year just to copy out one Bible. Since scribes had to be paid, every Bible cost at least a year's wages for one man. Add in paper, bookbinding and profit, and a Bible might cost two years' wages— or even three. Imagine spending your whole salary for three years just to buy one Bible!

A scribe at work with quill and ink in a monastery scriptorium

There was also woodblock printing. A printer could carve a page into a flat block of wood, coat it with ink and then press it onto paper to print a page.

Alas, woodblocks came with problems of their own. One problem was that each block could take days to carve. Another was that each block printed only one page, not the hundreds of pages that went into Bibles. Worst of all, woodblocks wore out— forcing the tired printer to carve new ones! Woodblock printing was fine for a few pages, but not for long books like the Bible.

Johannes Gutenberg (1398? – 1468)

All these problems went away around 1450, when a German printer called **Johannes Gutenberg** dreamed up a better way. Just where Gutenberg got his ideas, no one knows for sure. His father seems to have worked with the **mint** at Mainz, Germany— which means that Gutenberg might have spent time at the mint. As a boy with talented hands, Gutenberg might have picked up useful skills from the coin-makers at the mint. He might have learned how to engrave words and pictures; how to make molds and pour molten metal into them; and how to strike many copies of the same coin.

A **mint** is where a government makes its coins.

Years later, Gutenberg discovered that printing pages could be a lot like minting coins. One by one, Gutenberg's great ideas answered all the problems that had made woodblock printing so slow and expensive.

Johannes Gutenberg
(1398? - 1468)

Gutenberg's best idea was **movable metal type**. Instead of carving pages into wood, he molded individual letters out of metal. Then he clamped his letters to a plate, coated them with ink, and pressed them onto paper to print a page.

What a difference movable type made! Setting a page in movable type took only a few hours, far less than carving a page in wood. Since Gutenberg's type was movable, he could re-arrange it to print as many pages as he liked. And since his type was made of metal, it lasted far longer than wood.

Movable metal type

The movable-type printing press spread like wildfire. Less than fifty years after Gutenberg invented it, print shops all over Europe were churning out books in different languages. And the more books they printed, the more people learned to read.

That was how the Renaissance started: with reading. Reading changed everything. In fact, reading changed so many things that it was like a revolution— which is why this part of history is called the **Printing Revolution**.

The first things reading changed were news and politics. Before the printing press, most people heard only the news their kings wanted them to hear. After the printing press, people could read books and newspapers— which sometimes contained news their kings didn't want them to hear. More news meant more power for average citizens.

Reading also changed science. Before the printing press, most scientists had no idea what other scientists were working on. One might spend years working on a problem, only to find that someone else had already solved it. After the printing press, scientists could publish their work in books and journals. Without new books on geography, Columbus might never have discovered the New World!

Reading even changed Christianity. Before the printing press, all Western Bibles were copied in Latin. Since most people didn't know Latin, the only people who could read the Bible were the few who did know it— mainly priests and scholars.

The pope wanted to keep it that way. As we read in Chapter 22, the Church tried hard to stop John Wycliffe from translating the Bible into English. The pope didn't want people reading the Bible on their own— for fear that if they did, then they might interpret the Bible differently than the Church did.

The Gutenberg Bibles

The Printing Revolution started sometime before 1455, when Johannes Gutenberg printed a set of books called the Gutenberg Bibles. These were the first full books ever done on a movable-type printing press, at least in Europe. Gutenberg printed and bound about 175 in all. The 48 Gutenberg Bibles that are still around are some of the rarest, most valuable books in the world.

One of Gutenberg's worries was that buyers might find his machine-printed Bibles too plain. Some of them were used to illuminated manuscripts, which had flowery illustrations done by hand (Chapter 3). To make his Bibles more attractive, Gutenberg hired artists to go through and hand-decorate certain letters. He also coated the edges of their pages with a thin layer of gold.

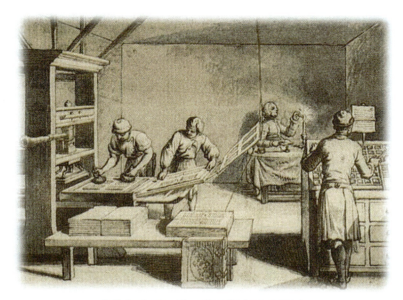

A Gutenberg-style printer's shop at work

The pope's fear turned out to be quite right. In 1517, a Bible-loving German called **Martin Luther** started complaining that the Church was wrong about certain things. Before the printing press, most people wouldn't have read one word of all that Luther wrote. After the printing press, many people read Luther— and agreed with what they read. Luther went on to lead the biggest split in the whole history of the Church: the **Protestant Reformation**, which we'll cover in Chapter 27.

The Renaissance in Florence

But we are getting ahead of ourselves. The Renaissance didn't start with Protestants in Germany, but with Catholics in Italy. The **Cradle of the Renaissance** was **Florence**, a beautiful city in northern Italy.

Renaissance Italy was a broken place. Since the end of Roman times, no one had ever ruled all Italy— although some had claimed to. It was all split into pieces, each with a different ruler.

Northern Italy, where Florence stood, was especially broken. When the Renaissance began, northern Italy was divided into a dozen or more countries. Some belonged to the Holy Roman Empire, while others were more or less independent **republics**.

At the beginning of Renaissance times, three republics of northern Italy were bigger

> A **republic** is a country governed by representatives who are elected by the people.

than all the others. The first was Venice; the second Genoa; and the third Florence.

Italy is a land of mountains. The spine of Italy is a long mountain chain called the Apennines. It runs almost all the way down the Italian Peninsula, which means that no one in Italy is ever far from a mountain. The marble quarried from the Apennines is some of the most beautiful stone in all the world.

On the northern edge of Italy stands the biggest mountain range in Europe: the Alps. This part of Italy has some beautiful mountain lakes, including the three biggest: Lake Garda, Lake Maggiore and Lake Como. The tallest mountain in Europe, Mount Blanc, stands near the corner where Italy, France and Switzerland meet.

Even the islands around Italy are mountainous. The big island of Sicily, which sits at the toe of the Italian boot, is home to the tallest active volcano in Europe: Mount Etna.

"A View of Mount Blanc" by artist Karl Friedrich Schinkel

As a republic, Florence didn't follow the old feudal system we covered in Chapter 10— with all its lords, vassals and oaths of fealty. Instead, Florence elected its leaders. When election time came, the names of the leading men of Florence were all written on little slips of paper. The slips were rolled up, tied off and placed in a leather bag. An election officer reached into the bag and pulled out several names. These were the men who sat on the governing council, which was called the Signoria of Florence.

The question was, who were the "leading men of Florence"— the ones whose names went into the bag? The answer is that they were all masters in one of Florence's many trade guilds.

A trade guild was a group of men that controlled a specific business in a specific town. For example, everyone who made or sold wool in Florence belonged to a wool makers' guild. Trade guilds were especially important in Florence. No one could work a respectable job without first joining a trade guild.

All guild men stood at one of three levels: apprentice, journeyman or master. An apprentice was an unskilled tradesman who was just starting out. A journeyman was a skilled tradesman who journeyed from shop to shop, practicing and learning more about his trade. A master was a highly skilled tradesman with enough experience to open his own shop— provided he could find the money.

Money was the key to becoming a master. Without it, a journeyman might stay a journeyman all his life. The only journeymen who could afford to open their own shops were the ones with rich families or friends. In other words, only the rich could become guild masters.

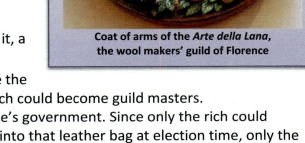

Coat of arms of the *Arte della Lana*, the wool makers' guild of Florence

The guild system played an important part in Florence's government. Since only the rich could become guild masters, and since only masters' names went into that leather bag at election time, only the rich could sit on the Signoria of Florence. In other words, Florence was ruled by the rich.

That doesn't mean that Florence wasn't a republic. However, it does mean that Florence wasn't a **democratic** republic like the United States. In a democratic republic, all citizens may take part in the government— rich or poor. Since the poor couldn't take part in the government of Florence, it was more of a **plutocracy**— a government run by the rich.

> **Democracy** means "the people rule."
> **Plutocracy** means "the wealthy rule."

When the Renaissance began, the richest man in Florence was Cosimo de Medici. Cosimo was the head of the Medici family, and a master of the bankers' guild.

The Medicis had a great talent for managing money. Cosimo's father had built his family bank, the Medici Bank, into the richest business in all Europe. Cosimo carried on his father's work when he inherited the Medici Bank.

Cosimo de Medici (1389 – 1464)

Cosimo de Medici
(1389 - 1464)

With that much money, Cosimo could do almost anything he liked. Fortunately for Florence, Cosimo de Medici was an energetic man who liked a great many things— starting with learning.

Cosimo's money came to him at an important time. The Fall of Constantinople happened in 1453, when he was at his richest. With the Byzantine Empire collapsing, the Greek scholars of Constantinople needed somewhere to go. Cosimo gave them just what they needed: a new college called the **Platonic Academy of Florence**.

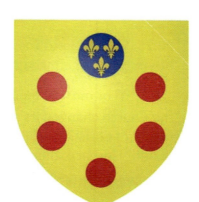

The Medici family coat of arms

The Platonic Academy started around 1462, when Cosimo started bringing in Greek scholars from Constantinople. The name "Platonic" came from Plato, a great philosopher of ancient Greece. The Platonic Academy taught ideas from ancient Greece and Rome, which a lot of Westerners had forgotten.

Cosimo also liked beautiful buildings and art. In fact, some of the best Renaissance art might never have been created without him. He was the first great **art patron** of the Renaissance— the first to spend a fortune on fine art.

> An **art patron** is a rich person who spends part of his fortune to help talented artists create fine art.

Why did artists need patrons? Because fine art costs a fortune to create! Even the most talented artists on Earth are not born knowing how to create great art. The patron must find talented young artists, and then pay older artists to train them. This means paying for food, clothes, travel and so on— not only for the artist himself, but also for his fussy teacher. Then there are the artist's studio, his assistants, his choice materials, his expensive tools— the list is endless. No one could afford all that better than Cosimo de Medici.

Why did Cosimo spend so much on art? First, because he truly loved fine art. Second, because he loved the amazing skills of the artists who created fine art. Third, because he loved Florence— which meant that he loved spending money on it. Cosimo spent two huge fortunes on Florence: one on fine art, and another on fine buildings. Between the two, Cosimo left Florence far more beautiful than he found it.

Cosimo also bought art for selfish reasons. One reason was that he wanted to be remembered forever, as he said in this famous quote:

> "All those things have given me the greatest satisfaction and contentment because they are not only for the honor of God but are likewise for my own remembrance. For fifty years, I have done nothing else but earn money and spend money; and it became clear that spending money gives me greater pleasure than earning it."

Another selfish reason started with Cosimo's banking job. Before Cosimo's day, most Christians didn't think much of bankers. Why? Because bankers made some of their money by **usury**— in other words, by charging interest on money loaned to the poor. The Bible frowns on usury, as it says in Exodus

> **Usury** means charging too much interest on money loaned to the poor.

This stunning statue of John the Baptist was carved by Donatello, a great Renaissance artist and friend of Cosimo de Medici

22:25: "If you lend money to one of my people among you who is needy, do not treat it like a business deal; charge no interest."

For most of medieval times, the Church frowned on usury too. But when the Renaissance came, the Church changed its mind— partly because of big donations from rich bankers like the Medicis. Even so, plenty of Christians still didn't trust bankers. Cosimo knew that if he didn't spend part of his fortune to benefit Florence, then the people of Florence might turn against him.

೫೫೫೫೫೫೫೫೫೫೫೫೫೫೫೫೫೫೫೫೫೫೫೫೫೫೫೫೫೫೫೫೫೫೫೫

When old Cosimo de Medici died, Florence moved on to its next great art patron: his grandson **Lorenzo de Medici**. Two of the greatest artists of the Renaissance, Leonardo da Vinci and Michelangelo, were personal friends of Lorenzo's. Michelangelo may have even lived with Lorenzo for a time.

Alas, the wealth of Lorenzo de Medici bought him more than just great art. It also bought him deadly enemies called the **Pazzis**.

The Medici Bank wasn't the only bank in Florence. There were also the Pazzi Bank, which was owned by the Pazzi family; and the Salviati Bank, by the Salviati family. Both families were terribly jealous of the Medicis.

The Pazzis also had a second reason for hating the Medicis: because they saw Lorenzo as a tyrant. Florence was supposed to be a republic, not a dictatorship. Yet whatever Lorenzo wanted done, the government did— just as if he were a king! Elections couldn't stop Lorenzo from meddling with the government; for no guild master dared criticize someone as rich and powerful as he. Even if Lorenzo couldn't control the elections, he could still control the guild masters who won those elections— or so the Pazzis said.

Right or wrong, the Pazzis dreamed up a bold plan for getting rid of Lorenzo. In the spring of 1478, they decided to murder two Medicis: not only Lorenzo, but also his younger brother Giuliano. With both Medici men out of the way, the Pazzis would be the new leaders of Florence— or so they hoped.

Lorenzo de Medici (1449 - 1492)

Portrait of Lorenzo de Medici with Florence in the background

Their first plan was a quiet one. The Pazzis knew that the Medicis were going to Rome for the pope's special service on Easter Sunday, 1478. So they thought: Why not murder the brothers in Rome? The farther they were from home when they died, the sooner the people of Florence would forget about them.

Unfortunately for the Pazzis, this first plan didn't work out. For some reason, the Medicis decided not to go to Rome that year— which meant that the Pazzis needed a new plan.

Their second plan was more daring. The Pazzis wanted to kill both brothers at once, but couldn't think of a time when both brothers were sure to be together. Until they asked themselves: Why not kill them in church? Both brothers went to Sunday Mass at the **Duomo**, a huge church in the middle of Florence. The Pazzis decided to kill them at the Duomo, in front of 10,000 people!

Portrait of Giuliano de Medici by Sandro Botticelli

The Pazzi Conspiracy (1478)

When the big Sunday came, the brothers were separated. Lorenzo stood near the front of the Duomo, and Giuliano near the back. Seeing this, the attackers also split up. They planned to wait until the priest reached a certain moment in the Mass, and then all strike at once.

When that moment in the Mass came, Francesco de Pazzi turned, raised his dagger and stabbed Giuliano de Medici. He kept on stabbing until the young man was dead.

Francesco de Pazzi striking down Giuliano de Medici

The attack in the front of the church didn't go as well; for Lorenzo sensed what was coming. Just when the Pazzis were about to stab him, Lorenzo raised his arm enough to block their daggers. Although his arm was badly cut, Lorenzo managed to stay ahead of his enemies long enough to lock himself inside a room of the Duomo. There the wounded man stood, waiting to see what the Pazzis would do next.

Since the Pazzis couldn't get to Lorenzo, they went ahead with the rest of their plan. They started parading through Florence, shouting that the Medici tyrants were dead at last. They expected the people of Florence to rejoice with them; but instead, people were furious with them.

A little later, the wounded Lorenzo walked out of the Duomo— very much alive. At this, Florence exploded on the Pazzis. Every attacker was hanged to death, along with everyone who might have known about the attack. Even worse, every Pazzi was banished from Florence forever!

Obviously, the Pazzis were wrong about how the people of Florence felt. Instead of hating the Medicis for their riches, they honored the Medicis for making Florence such a beautiful place to live.

The Bonfire of the Vanities

How quickly the times can change. While Lorenzo de Medici lived, Florence thrived. But when Lorenzo lay down to die, all Italy was about to come on very hard times. At Lorenzo's bedside sat the man who would lead Florence through some of those hard times: a strange priest called **Girolamo Savonarola**.

**Girolamo Savonarola
(1452 - 1498)**

The two men could hardly have been more different. Savonarola was a strict monk who believed in self-denial and simple living. He ate next to nothing, slept in a plain monk's cell, and wore a hair shirt to remind him of Christ's suffering. Lorenzo, on the other hand, was probably the richest man in Italy. He enjoyed every luxury that money could buy, including the best art collection in the world.

How could two men who were so different become friends? The answer starts with trouble between Florence and the pope. The first trouble was that the pope's country, the **Papal States**, was a rival to Florence. The pope was always trying to gain ground for the Papal States by taking it from Florence.

The second trouble was that the Church went a little bit crazy when the Renaissance started. Every

> The **Papal States** were a country in central Italy that was run by the pope (Chapter 7).

Michelangelo's "Moses"

All Christians agree on certain things. For example, all Christians agree that Jesus Christ is the Son of God, and that He "came into the world to save sinners" (I Timothy 1:15).

    The question is, what happens when Christians disagree? The answer is that the church often splits. We've already covered several **schisms** over the centuries:

> A **schism** is a church split.

> ➤ In Chapter 4, we read how the Church of Egypt split off from the rest of the Church around 451. The Church of Egypt was also called the Coptic Orthodox Church.

> ➤ In Chapter 19, we read how the Church of the East split off from the rest of the Church around that same time. The Church of the East was also called the Nestorian Church.

> ➤ In Chapter 8, we read how the Eastern Orthodox Church split off from the Roman Catholic Church around 1054. This huge split is called the East-West Schism or the Great Schism.

> ➤ Roman Catholics even split with themselves for a time. In Chapter 24, we read how the Church went through the Western Schism of 1378 – 1417— a time when there were two or three popes at once.

This chapter covers the biggest church split of all: the **Protestant Reformation**, which started with a German monk called **Martin Luther** in 1517.

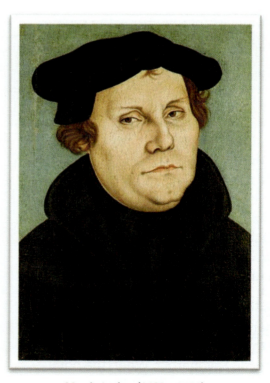

Martin Luther (1483 – 1546)

The Renaissance Popes

Martin Luther didn't set out to split the Church. At first, he only wanted to reform the Church— in other words, fix what was wrong with it. The first things Luther wanted to fix were the **Renaissance popes**.

    The Renaissance popes were the popes who led the Church through the Renaissance, which happened in the 1400s and 1500s. What was so bad about the Renaissance popes? In Luther's eyes, their biggest problem was greed. That was why Luther wanted to reform the church: because instead of following God, the Renaissance popes spent all their time raising money for fancy church buildings.

    By the time the Renaissance got started, the glory of ancient Rome was a thousand years in the past. What had once been a grand city was now a crumbling ruin. The Church didn't think a ruined city made a fitting capital for the whole Christian world. It wanted to rebuild Rome, so that Christians wouldn't have to be ashamed of it.

    The problem was, the Renaissance popes weren't satisfied with just rebuilding Rome. They wanted nothing but the best new buildings, all decorated with the greatest works of the most talented artists. The best example was a grand new church called **Saint Peter's Basilica.**

St. Peter's is a huge, beautiful church that still stands in Vatican City, Rome. Like the public square on which it stands, St. Peter's is named for the most famous of the twelve apostles: the Apostle Peter.

Peter was terribly important to Roman Catholics. His importance started with Matthew 16:19, where Christ said to Peter: "I will give you the keys of the kingdom of heaven." Some Christians took this to mean that Peter could decide who went to heaven and who didn't.

According to Roman Catholic tradition, Peter was first pope— the first head of all Christian churches. When Peter died, he handed down his power to the next pope in line. Every new pope inherited the awesome power that Christ had given Peter.

That was why the Renaissance popes built St. Peter's Basilica: as a symbol of the power they inherited from Peter. Naturally, they wanted that symbol to be as big and impressive as possible. The floors of St. Peter's covered more than five acres, and its dome soared over four hundred feet high!

St. Peter's Basilica took 120 years to build, from 1506 – 1626. Some of the marble used to build it came from the ruins of the old Roman Coliseum.

Even better than the building itself was the art inside. Every single space was filled with the most beautiful art imaginable. Some of the best artists who ever lived did their best work at St. Peter's Basilica— famous names like Michelangelo, Raphael and Bernini.

What Martin Luther didn't like about all this was that it cost too much. In Luther's eyes, St. Peter's Basilica was a symbol of the popes' greed, not of their authority! Why on Earth was the Church spending so much money on itself, Luther wondered— when that money should be going to help the poor?

Greed also showed in the way the Renaissance popes handed out jobs in the Church. Luther felt that the best jobs should go to the people who were best for those jobs. But the Renaissance popes didn't care who was best for a job. They cared only about money, power, and helping their families rise to the top. Since popes weren't supposed to have children, the best jobs usually went to their nephews— even if their nephews had never worked in the Church before. If no nephew wanted a job, then the Renaissance popes sold it to the highest bidder— again, even if he had never worked in the Church.

A view inside St. Peter's Basilica

Pope Julius II, the "Warrior Pope" who reigned from 1503 – 1513

The worst thing about the Renaissance popes was their wars. As unbelievable as it sounds, some popes strapped on swords and led armies into bloody battle. The worst was **Pope Julius II**, who fought so many wars that he was nicknamed the "Warrior Pope."

An unknown author wrote a funny story about Pope Julius. It is called **Julius Excluded from Heaven**; and it appeared in 1514, the year after the Warrior Pope died.

The story starts with Pope Julius standing outside the gates of heaven. Behind him stand thousands of soldiers who have died fighting his wars, all hoping to go to heaven with him. Like the popes of the Crusades, Julius has promised that all who die fighting for the Church will get there— no matter what sins they might have committed before.

The problem is, the gates won't open. Julius is fussing with the key to his private treasure chest, thinking that this same key ought to unlock the gates of heaven. But for some reason he can't understand, the key won't work. Julius is about to try breaking down the gates when Peter peers out a window and asks:

Peter: But oh…. what a sewer-stench is this! …Who are you, and what do you want?

Julius: Open the door, will you? …And if you were really doing your job, it should have been open long ago, and decorated with all the heraldry of heaven.

Peter: …What sort of unnatural arrangement is it, that while you wear the robes of a priest of God, under them you are dressed in the bloody armor of a warrior?

Julius: Enough words, I say. If you don't hurry up and open the gates, then I'll unleash my thunderbolt of excommunication with which I used to terrify great kings on earth and their kingdoms too…

Peter: Perhaps you used to terrify people with that bluster, but it counts for nothing here. Here we deal only in the truth. This is a fortress to be captured with good deeds, not ugly words.

Besides being funny, "Julius Excluded from Heaven" also made a serious point. Why wouldn't the key to Julius' treasure chest unlock the gates of heaven? Because heavenly treasures are nothing like earthly treasures, as Christ says in Matthew 6:19-20:

> "Do not store up for yourselves treasures on earth, where moth and rust destroy, and where thieves break in and steal. But store up for yourselves treasures in heaven, where neither moth nor rust destroys…"

The Renaissance popes seemed to forget this. The pope was supposed to be Christ's representative on Earth; but popes like Julius acted nothing like Christ.

Although no one knows for sure, "Julius Excluded from Heaven" may have been written by a Dutch author called **Desiderius Erasmus**. Why does everyone think so? Because "Julius" sounds a lot like **In Praise of Folly**, which Erasmus certainly wrote.

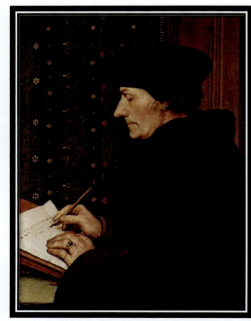

Desiderius Erasmus (1466 – 1536)

"In Praise of Folly" was another funny-but-serious work that pointed out problems in the Church. In Erasmus' eyes, it wasn't just the Renaissance popes who had gone wrong—no, it was the whole Church. He criticized everyone, from monks to friars, priests, bishops, cardinals, and even scholars like himself. In Erasmus' eyes, they all had forgotten what it really means to follow Christ.

But for all his mocking words against the Church, there was one thing Erasmus would never do. No matter what happened, Erasmus would never leave the Church. Erasmus wanted to reform the Church, not tear it down—as we'll read in Chapter 34.

Martin Luther

At first, Martin Luther wanted the same thing Erasmus wanted: to reform the Church. It was only later, after years of trying, that he gave up on the Roman Catholic Church— deciding that it was too broken to be reformed.

Martin grew up in Eisleben, a town in Saxony, Germany. Martin's father, Hans Luther, wanted his son to become a rich lawyer. He sent him to the best schools he could find, trying to prepare him for the tough challenges of law school. Alas for his father, Martin wasn't interested in law. What Martin wanted to know was how God forgave sin.

As a young man, Martin often suffered through something he called **Afflictions**. These were terrible times when the fear of dying was more than Martin could stand. He knew very well that he was a miserable sinner. He also knew how God punished sinners: by sending them to hell when they died. Knowing all this, Martin was terrified that he might die and go to hell before God forgave his sins.

Like all Christians, Martin also knew that he could confess his sins in church. Whenever he confessed, his priests assured him that his sins were forgiven. This was supposed to make him feel better; but for some reason, it didn't. Despite the comforting words of his priests, Martin never felt sure that he was truly forgiven.

Luther wearing the tonsure, a monk's hairstyle

It was fear of death and hell that made Martin Luther a monk. One day when Martin was 21 years old, a bolt of lightning struck terrifyingly close to him. Afraid for his life, Martin shouted this vow to the mother of the Virgin Mary: "Save me, St. Anna, and I shall become a monk!" When the storm didn't kill him, Martin kept his vow— much to his father's disappointment.

A few years later, Luther took his first classes at the University of Wittenberg, Germany. A few years after that, Wittenberg hired Luther to teach Bible. Luther would remain a professor of Bible at the University of Wittenberg for the rest of his life.

While preparing lessons for his Bible students, Luther found himself drawn to a certain scripture over and over. That scripture was Romans 1:17, which reads:

"For in the gospel the righteousness of God is revealed — a righteousness that is by faith from first to last, just as it is written: 'The righteous will live by faith.'"

Right there in the Bible, Luther finally found the answer to the Afflictions that had troubled him for so long. What does "righteousness" mean? Before now, Luther had always believed that being righteous meant doing good deeds. The way to heaven was to work hard at doing good deeds; for that was the only way to buy God's forgiveness. Or at least, that was what Luther had always thought.

But that wasn't what Romans 1:17 said. Instead, it said that "righteousness is by faith from first to last." In other words, righteousness doesn't come from doing good deeds. Rather, righteousness comes from faith. The people God forgives are the ones who have faith in his Son, the Savior Jesus Christ.

What a relief! For the first time in his life, Martin understood that he didn't need to work his way into heaven. If he had faith in Jesus Christ, then he was already on his way to heaven!

ꕙꕙꕙꕙꕙꕙꕙꕙꕙꕙꕙꕙꕙꕙꕙꕙꕙꕙꕙꕙꕙꕙꕙꕙꕙꕙꕙꕙꕙꕙꕙꕙꕙꕙꕙꕙꕙꕙ

Luther's new understanding came at an important time. It so happened that when Luther was just becoming a monk, the Renaissance popes were just laying the foundations of St. Peter's Basilica (above). **Pope Leo X**, the pope after Julius II, needed a fortune to pay for this huge new church. To get it, Leo struck a deal with the new Archbishop of Mainz— the head of all German churches.

The pope's deal started with something called **indulgences**. An indulgence was a special paper that was supposed to have special powers over sin. The Church said that since the pope held the keys to heaven, he had the power to set sinners free from the penalties of their sin. If a sinner received an indulgence from the pope, then he would never have to pay for his sin— or so the Church said.

Pope Leo put that power to work for the Archbishop of Mainz. The pope's part of the deal was to send the archbishop indulgences. The archbishop's part was to send priests all over Germany, handing out indulgences to Christians who donated money to the Church. Half the money would go to the archbishop, and the other half to the pope.

One of the priests the archbishop sent was a clever one called **Johann Tetzel**. Tetzel acted more like a salesman than a priest. To hear him talk, indulgences were like tickets to heaven. If a sinner would only buy an indulgence, then he would never again have to worry about going to hell!

Tetzel saved his best sales pitch for a place called **purgatory**. The Church taught that most Christians didn't go straight to heaven when they died. Instead they went to purgatory, where they were purged of their sin. Only after they paid for their sins in purgatory could they move on to heaven.

All Christians who had lost loved ones worried about purgatory. Believers mourned to think of their dear mothers, fathers and grandparents suffering in purgatory when they could be in heaven.

A mocking picture of Johann Tetzel (1465 – 1519) with one hand on a money chest. Behind Tetzel are indulgences for sale at different prices.

A **coffer** was a collection box.

But now Tetzel said that believers no longer need mourn no longer! Besides buying an indulgence for oneself, one could also buy an indulgence for a lost loved one in purgatory. The moment the Church received the money, that lost loved one would leap out of purgatory and go straight to heaven! To make his point as clear as possible, Tetzel wrote this little rhyme about indulgences:

> "As soon as the coin in the **coffer** rings,
> the soul from purgatory springs!"

Tetzel's little rhyme horrified Martin Luther. To his ears, it sounded like the pope was selling God's forgiveness— as if sinners could buy their way into heaven! But this was the exact opposite of what the Bible said. It promised that forgiveness was a gift from God, freely given to all who had faith in Jesus Christ.

The Diet of Worms

It was mostly because of indulgences that Martin Luther wrote his best-known work: the Ninety-five Theses on the Power and Efficacy of Indulgences. Tradition says that Luther published his Ninety-five Theses by nailing them to the door of All Saints' Church in Wittenberg. He did it on October 31, 1517, which was the eve of All Saints' Day. Although no one knew it yet, that was the first day of the Protestant Reformation.

What did the Ninety-five Theses say? Basically, they said that the Church had no right to sell God's forgiveness. Luther wrote that forgiveness was for all true Christians, not just the ones who could afford special indulgences from the pope.

> A **thesis** is a statement to be defended in a debate or argument. **Theses** is the plural of thesis.
> **Efficacy** means effectiveness. A thing is efficacious if it actually does what it is supposed to be able to do.

Luther also wrote that indulgences were causing the poor to suffer. Why? Because instead of donating to the poor, Christians were spending all their extra money on indulgences. Even the poorest Christians, the ones who couldn't afford food some days, were spending what little they had on indulgences— believing that they couldn't get to heaven without them.

Meanwhile, the pope was one of the richest men on Earth. Why didn't the pope spend his own money to build his precious basilica, Luther wondered— instead of stealing food from the very mouths of the poor?

Martin Luther nailing his Ninety-five Theses to the door of All Saints' Church in Wittenberg, Germany (October 31, 1517)

The Ninety-five Theses were Martin Luther's first step down a dangerous path. He knew very well what could happen to priests who spoke out against the Church. Anyone who criticized the pope could be declared a heretic and burned to death. It had already happened to John Hus in 1415 (Chapter 25), and to Girolamo Savonarola in 1498 (Chapter 26). The same thing might happen to Luther if he wasn't careful— or even if he was.

The pope was certainly no friend to Luther. If Leo X had had his way, then no one would have heard another word out of him! In 1518, the year after the Ninety-five Theses, the pope sent a message to Germany— ordering Luther's fellow monks to cast him out.

Any other time, the monks probably would have obeyed. Alas for the pope, times were different now. For Martin Luther was a beloved German scholar; while Leo X was an Italian pope with a reputation for greed. Instead of casting Luther out, his fellow monks invited him to tell them more of what he had learned from the Bible.

When Luther did, it turned out that indulgences weren't the only things he didn't like about the Church. In fact, Luther disliked a great many things!

The thing Luther disliked most was the Church's teaching about **salvation**. It seemed to him that Church believed in **salvation by works**. In other words, the Church seemed to think that the only way Christians could be saved was by obeying the Ten Commandments perfectly. If a person was perfect, then even a perfect God couldn't find fault. Then God would have to let that person into heaven; for he or she would have earned it.

Although salvation by works might sound reasonable, it wasn't what the Bible taught. Instead, the Bible taught **salvation by faith**. What Luther read in Romans was that no one was saved by good works. The Ten Commandments were so hard to follow that only one Person could do it perfectly. That Person was Christ, the Son of God. The way to be saved was not by doing good works, but by faith in Christ.

Martin Luther appearing before an angry cardinal

The more time passed, the longer Luther's list of dislikes grew. He didn't like praying to the saints— not even the Church's favorite saint, the Virgin Mary. Nor did he like adoring relics of the saints.

Luther also complained about the **Mass**, which was how the Church celebrated Holy Communion. He believed that communion was supposed to honor the awesome sacrifice Christ made when He gave His life for sinners on the cross. But now the Church had turned communion into a tool. Priests taught that there was only one way to stay in God's good graces: by taking Mass with a priest. Anyone who disagreed with the Church could be barred from Mass, which meant that he was headed for hell.

How had the Church gone so far wrong, in Luther's eyes? The answer starts with something called **Sacred Tradition**. The Church didn't just follow the Bible. It also followed **traditions** that came from outside the Bible. For example, the Bible says nothing about monks; and yet Christian monks had been around since the time of Anthony of Thebes (Chapter 3). The Church called honored traditions like these Sacred Tradition. It believed that Sacred Tradition was just as holy as the Bible— just as much a part of what all Christians should believe.

The problem, Luther said, was that some of these traditions went against the Bible. One tradition was especially upsetting to a Bible professor like Luther: Why did the Church insist on reading the Bible in Latin, when so few Christians understood Latin? Luther wanted Christians to read the Bible for themselves, in their own languages. He believed that when they did, they would see what he had already seen: that Sacred Tradition often went against the Bible.

This line of thinking led to one of Luther's biggest ideas: Sola Scriptura, or "Scripture alone." Luther believed that the Bible alone was inspired by God, and that Sacred Tradition wasn't inspired at all. For the Bible came from holy God, Who was always generous and righteous. Whereas Sacred Tradition came through unholy man, who was often greedy and corrupt.

Sola Scriptura meant that when Sacred Tradition went against the Bible, Christians should always follow the Bible— never Sacred Tradition. The Bible had never led Christians wrong. Meanwhile, Sacred Tradition had led to the greedy Renaissance popes— who were wrong about almost everything, in Luther's eyes!

> **Sola Scriptura** is Latin for "Scripture Alone."

Johann von Eck, Luther's opponent at the Leipzig Debate

〰〰〰〰〰〰〰〰〰〰〰〰〰〰〰〰〰〰〰〰〰〰〰〰〰〰〰〰〰

As we read above, Luther didn't set out to split the Church. He only wanted to change the Church's mind about certain things, so that it wouldn't go against the Bible anymore.

Sad to say, things didn't work out that way. For the more Luther criticized the Church, the angrier the Church grew. Instead of changing its ways, the Church wanted to change Luther—possibly by killing him.

One of the first signs that the Church was out for blood came in 1519, when a smart priest called **Johann von Eck** challenged Luther to debate him in public. In the middle of the Leipzig Debate, von Eck asked Luther a tricky question. What did Luther think of **John Hus**, von Eck wanted to know?

As we read in Chapter 25, John Hus was a Bohemian priest who had been condemned as a heretic in 1415. Von Eck's question about Hus put Luther in a tough spot. On the one hand, Luther believed that Hus had been right about many things— as von Eck knew very well. If Luther said that Hus was wrong, then he would be admitting that he himself was also wrong. On the other hand, the Church had burned Hus to death. If Luther said that Hus was right, then the Church might burn Luther too!

A **papal bull** was a sealed letter containing a special statement from the pope.

The cover of *Exsurge Domine*, the first papal bull against Martin Luther (1520)

As usual, Luther made the brave choice: admitting that he agreed with John Hus. From that moment on, von Eck was determined to bring Luther down.

In 1520, the year after the Leipzig Debate, Pope Leo X wrote a **papal bull** against Martin Luther. By order of the pope, Christians were not to read anything written by Martin Luther. Instead, they were to burn Luther's writings. As for Luther himself, the pope gave him sixty days to take back all the ugly things he'd written about the Church.

With papal bull in hand, von Eck rode triumphantly back to Germany— planning to burn Luther's books in big public bonfires. But he soon learned that Germans didn't want to burn Luther's books. In fact, some Germans muttered about burning von Eck instead! The German people loved their feisty Martin Luther so much that he didn't need to burn his books. Instead, he burned a copy of the papal bull!

A few months later, Pope Leo wrote a second papal bull against Luther. This time, the pope declared Luther an enemy of the Church— an "infected animal" who wanted to spread his sickness through the whole flock. No faithful Christian was to have anything to do with Martin Luther, nor with any of Luther's friends. In the eyes of the Church, all **Lutherans** were heretics!

The pope didn't say that Luther should be burned to death. What he did say was that Luther should get the same punishment other heretics had gotten. Since the Church had burned John Hus, Luther was pretty sure that the pope wanted to burn him too.

> A **Lutheran** was a follower of Martin Luther.

This second papal bull set up one of the most dramatic scenes of the whole Reformation. After the way his first papal bull failed, the pope knew that no one would obey the second either. For Luther had many friends in Germany, while the pope had few. If the pope wanted Luther arrested, then he needed someone powerful to do it for him.

The someone the pope chose was one of the most powerful men who ever lived: **Holy Roman Emperor Charles V**, who was also **King Charles I of Spain**. Charles Habsburg was a loyal Catholic who believed in a strong Catholic Church. Since Martin Luther posed a danger to that Church, Charles summoned him to appear at the **Diet of Worms**.

> The **Diet of Worms** was a special meeting of the German government held at Worms, Germany in 1521.

Despite its funny-sounding name, the Diet of Worms had nothing to do with eating worms! A diet was a meeting of the German government; while Worms was a city in Germany. In other words, the Diet of Worms was a government meeting in Worms, Germany. This special meeting had one main purpose: to try Martin Luther for crimes against the Church.

Luther's trial started like the trial of John Hus, or like a trial run by the Spanish Inquisition. Such trials were nothing like modern-day trials. The court didn't have to decide whether Luther was guilty or innocent; for the pope had already found him guilty. All the court had to decide was how Luther should be punished. The only difference at Luther's trial was the people. A crowd of Germans gathered outside the diet, threatening to riot if anything happened to Luther!

The priests who tried Martin Luther didn't want him making any long speeches against the Church. To keep him quiet, they asked him just two quick questions. Pointing at a pile of Luther's books, they asked: Did you write these books? And, will you recant all the lies in these books— in other words, take back everything you wrote?

Martin Luther defending himself at the Diet of Worms

Of course, Luther had to admit that he had written the pile of books. But when it came to the second question, Luther asked for one more day to think about his answer. The priests would have liked to say "no," but couldn't— for fear of Luther's friends outside.

The Luther Rose, a symbol of the Lutheran Church

The next day turned out just as the priests had feared. Instead of taking back what he had written, Luther told the whole world what he thought of the Catholic Church. He spoke furiously against the pope, accusing him of greedily lining his own pockets while the poor suffered. Luther's dramatic speech ended:

> "I cannot and I will not recant. Here I stand; I can do no other. God help me."

After a speech like that, many loyal Catholics felt that Luther should be put to death right away. But the Holy Roman Emperor had promised not to arrest Luther just then; and he kept his promise. Even so, Luther's friends felt that he would be safer if he went into hiding for a while. He spent most of the next year at Wartburg Castle in Eisenach, Germany, where he worked on his German translation of the New Testament.

By the time Luther went home to Wittenberg, the Protestant Reformation was in full swing. Churches all over Germany were leaving the Catholic Church and setting out on their own. Luther spent the rest of his life teaching, writing and building a new German church:

the **Lutheran Church**.

෴෴෴෴෴෴෴෴෴෴෴෴෴෴෴෴෴෴෴෴෴෴෴෴෴෴෴෴෴෴෴෴

One big difference between Catholics and Lutherans was that there were no Lutheran monks or nuns. Since the Bible said nothing about monks, Luther and his friends released all monks and nuns from their vows. After that, Luther was free to do something he never could have done as a monk: get married.

Luther's future wife started school in a nunnery when she was five or six years old. Not all girls who went to nunnery schools went on to become nuns. But **Katharina von Bora** did, taking her nun's vows when she was about sixteen.

Katharina was eighteen when the Reformation started. Although older nuns didn't want younger nuns reading Luther's books, Katharina and her friends found ways to get their hands on them. The bold ideas of Martin Luther took hold in the young nuns' hearts, just as they were taking hold in hearts all over Germany.

Katharina von Bora (1499 – 1552)

When Luther said that there would be no Lutheran monks or nuns, Katharina and her friends wanted to break their vows and go home. But the older nuns held them back, insisting that they must keep their vows before God. Desperate to escape the nunnery, Katharina wrote a letter to the man who had inspired her new faith: Martin Luther himself.

Luther came up with a simple plan to rescue the trapped girls. It so happened that Luther knew the fish-seller who sold to Katharina's nunnery. The man often went into the nunnery with wagonloads of barreled fish, and then left with empty barrels. Luther's idea was to fill those empty barrels with one girl each! On Easter Eve, 1523, Katharina and her friends rode that smelly fish wagon out of their nunnery prison.

Martin and Katharina soon fell in love. But at first, Martin wasn't sure he should marry; for he feared that the Reformation was changing things too fast. After all, he and Katharina had both sworn before God that they would never marry. Even if the Church was wrong about monks and nuns, they might still be wrong to break their word.

In the end, Luther decided that the vows taken by monks and nuns were just more Catholic traditions that went against the Bible. The couple married in 1525, and went on to have six children.

CHAPTER 28

The Renaissance in Art

Amazing Artists of the Renaissance

In Chapter 26, we read that Florence, Italy was a great place to be a **Renaissance** artist. One reason was Cosimo de Medici, who made a fortune running the great Medici Bank. The Medicis spent a big part of that fortune making Florence more beautiful. Some of their money paid for fine art, and some for fine buildings.

That doesn't mean that the Renaissance in art started with Cosimo de Medici. It actually started well before his day, sometime in the early 1300s. By the time Cosimo came along, the art world had already changed a lot. Renaissance art looked nothing like art from early medieval times.

> The **Renaissance** was the next era after the medieval era. The name is French for "re-birth."

One difference between medieval art and Renaissance art started with a difference in the Church. The medieval Church didn't approve of art that looked too much like real life. Why? Because it didn't want to break the Second Commandment, in which God warned: "You shall not make for yourself an image in the form of anything in heaven above or on the earth beneath or in the waters below. You shall not bow down to them or worship them; for I, the Lord your God, am a jealous God…"

Out of respect for God, medieval artists were careful not to make their images too realistic. Instead, they kept them flat and unrealistic— so that viewers would worship the God behind the images, and not the images themselves.

All that changed when the Renaissance came along. The Renaissance popes threw out all those old ideas, forgetting all about the Second Commandment! They spent fortunes on fine art, filling their churches and monasteries with the most realistic paintings and sculptures money could buy.

A quote from Pope Nicholas V explains why the Church changed its mind. According to this Renaissance pope, all that fine art had an important purpose. Its job was "to strengthen the weak faith of the populace by the greatness of that which it sees." In other words, Renaissance churches were built to impress. One look at a magnificent church like St. Peter's Basilica, and no one could doubt that the pope was truly the heir of St. Peter!

Two paintings of Mary and the baby Jesus in two very different styles. On the left is a flat Eastern Orthodox icon from the 900s. On the right is a realistic painting done by the great Renaissance artist Raphael in 1505.

Our first great Renaissance artist, **Giotto di Bondone**, was born more than 100 years before Cosimo de Medici. Young Giotto came from a shepherding family near Florence. He probably would have been a shepherd like his father, if he hadn't run into a professional artist one day. The artist's name was Cimabue, and he was looking for young talent to work in his studio. When Cimabue saw the lifelike pictures Giotto drew of his sheep, he decided to take the boy in and train him.

Giotto di Bondone
(1267? – 1337)

The student soon surpassed his teacher. One day when Cimabue stepped out of the studio, Giotto played a trick on him. He painted a housefly on the canvas Cimabue was working on, making it so lifelike that it seemed ready to take off. When Cimabue came back, he swatted at the fly several times before he saw that it was only a painting!

Many of the stories in this chapter come from a set of biographies called *Lives of the Most Excellent Painters, Sculptors and Architects*. This famous book was written by Giorgio Vasari (1511 – 1574), who was a Renaissance artist himself. Vasari was also a personal friend to Michelangelo.

That was Giotto's gift: creating lifelike paintings. His style was like a stepping stone between old and new, between the flat style of medieval times and the lifelike style of the Renaissance. For example, the faces in Giotto's paintings showed strong feelings—unlike medieval icons, which showed little feeling at all.

Like many Renaissance artists, Giotto was more than just a great painter. He was also a great architect! The same artist's eye that made Giotto so good at painting also made him good at designing buildings.

In 1296, the city of Florence started building a huge new church. Its full name was Cathedral of Saint

"The Kiss of Judas" by Giotto, from the Arena Chapel in Padua, Italy. A yellow-robed Judas stands at center, betraying Jesus with a kiss on the night before the crucifixion. A red-robed Peter stands at left, cutting off a servant's ear (Matthew 26:48-51).

Mary of the Flowers; but most people just called it Florence Cathedral. Later, people called it by an even shorter name: the **Duomo**, after its dome-shaped roof. This was the same Duomo where the Pazzi family would one day murder Giuliano de Medici, and try to murder Lorenzo de Medici too (Chapter 26).

Giotto's part of the Duomo was a beautiful bell tower called a campanile. Like most Renaissance cathedrals, though, the Duomo took a long time to build. **Giotto's Campanile** was hardly begun in 1337, the year Giotto died.

Our next great Renaissance artist, **Filippo Brunelleschi**, built the best-known part of the Duomo: its domed roof. Domes are hard to build, especially big ones like the Duomo's. If the builder doesn't know what he's doing, then the weight of the dome can cause the bottom to spread— bringing the top crashing down.

The ancient Greeks and Romans knew how to build domes. One of the biggest domes in the world covered an ancient Roman building called the Pantheon. Another covered the Hagia Sophia in Constantinople, which was built in the 500s. By Brunelleschi's day, though, no one had built a dome that big for a very long time.

Florence's dome story started in 1418, when the city held a contest to see who would build the one over Florence Cathedral. By this time, Brunelleschi had been studying the dome problem for years— partly in Rome, where he had gone to study Roman architecture. He knew exactly how he wanted to build the dome, and had even built a model to test his ideas. According to Brunelleschi, this model proved that he was the right architect to build the dome.

Florence Cathedral, better known as the Duomo. The domed roof built by Brunelleschi stands at right, the bell tower by Giotto at left.

Naturally, the other architects all wanted to see Brunelleschi's model. But Brunelleschi refused, saying that he didn't want the others learning his secrets. Instead, Brunelleschi announced a challenge. The man to build the dome, he said, should be the one who could figure out how to make a chicken egg stand on one end!

This seemed to be a problem that no one could solve. Until Brunelleschi solved it— by striking the egg lightly on a table, making a flat end for it to stand on. The other architects howled at Brunelleschi, saying that they could all do that! To which Brunelleschi replied, "Of course you could— now that I have shown you how. Just as you could all build the dome after I showed you my model." The city fathers gave Brunelleschi the job.

> Brunelleschi finished the Duomo in 1436, about 16 years after he started. This was 140 years after its foundations were laid, and 42 years before the Pazzi Conspiracy (Chapter 26).
>
> About four million bricks went into the dome. Brunelleschi chose bricks because they were lighter than stone.

Our next great Renaissance artist, **Donatello**, was a close friend to Brunelleschi. When Brunelleschi went to Rome to study Roman architecture, Donatello went with him.

While Brunelleschi studied architecture, Donatello studied sculpture. When he got back to Florence, Donatello became the first great sculptor of the Renaissance— a grand master whose works were as good as anything ever carved by the ancient Greeks or Romans.

Cosimo de Medici admired Donatello's sculpting skills so much that he didn't want him doing anything else. If the great artist had to waste time on other things, like selling his art to earn a living, then there would be fewer sculptures for Cosimo to enjoy.

Donatello
(1386? – 1466)

To keep Donatello at work, Cosimo gave him more money than he could ever need or use. The great sculptor grew so used to having money that he never worried about it. If Donatello's other friends needed money, then they simply borrowed it from an open basket in his studio. He trusted his friends so much that they didn't even need to ask.

〰〰〰〰〰〰〰〰〰〰〰〰〰〰〰〰〰〰〰〰〰〰〰〰〰〰〰〰〰〰〰〰〰

Our next great Renaissance artist, **Fra Filippo Lippi**, wasn't as trustworthy as Donatello. Cosimo de Medici never worried about wasting money on Donatello; for Donatello was always hard at work. But Cosimo worried a lot about wasting money on Fra Lippi. Although Fra Lippi was supposed to be a priest, he was always falling in love with some young woman. And whenever he fell in love, he forgot all about his painting.

Cosimo once grew so frustrated with Fra Lippi that he locked him inside his house, hoping to get more work out of him. Lippi answered by tying some bedsheets together to make a rope, and then using the rope to climb out a window. Even the richest man in Italy couldn't keep Fra Lippi from his women— not if he wanted the

Donatello's statue of the prophet Habakkuk. This statue is also called *Zuccone***, Italian for "Pumpkin" or "Bald Man."**

Fra Filippo Lippi
(1406? – 1469)

beautiful paintings that only Fra Lippi could create.

While working in a church one day, Fra Lippi happened to meet a beautiful young woman called Lucrezia Buti. Lucretia's parents had sent her to live with some nuns, probably thinking that she would be safe with nuns! But Lippi was thinking of his latest masterpiece, "**Madonna and Child with Two Angels**"; and he needed a model for the Virgin Mary. When he saw Lucrezia, he begged the nuns to let her model for him— promising to bring her back as soon as his masterpiece was finished.

Lucrezia never went back to the nuns, as Fra Lippi had promised. But she did give Fra Lippi a son: **Filippino Lippi**, who turned out to be as talented as his father!

"Madonna and Child with Two Angels" by Fra Lippi

Sandro Botticelli
(1445? – 1510)

Our next great Renaissance artist, Sandro Botticelli, came along a bit later. Lorenzo de Medici, grandson to Cosimo, paid for some of Botticelli's great works.

By this time, Renaissance artists were branching out.

The beautiful face of Venus from Botticelli's "Birth of Venus"

Besides Christian art, Botticelli also painted Roman gods and goddesses. Botticelli's "**Birth of Venus**" is one of the best-known paintings of all time.

Botticelli would live to regret painting non-Christian art. Like Lorenzo de Medici, Botticelli lived in the time of Girolamo Savonarola— the strict monk who ruled Florence for a while (Chapter 26). When Savonarola preached that non-Christian art was wrong, Botticelli believed him. Some say that Botticelli gave up painting for good, and may have burned some of his best paintings in the famous Bonfire of the Vanities.

〰〰〰〰〰〰〰〰〰〰〰〰

Our next great Renaissance artist was much more than an artist. Leonardo da Vinci was a true Renaissance Man, a genius in both art and science.

Leonardo started as an apprentice to an artist called Andrea del Verrocchio. Like other master artists, Verrocchio sometimes let his apprentices paint backgrounds for him. That way, the master could spend more time on his main subject.

This Botticelli painting, "The Temptation of Christ," comes from the Sistine Chapel in Vatican City, Rome. The background shows three temptations from Matthew 4:1-11. At top left, Satan tempts a starving Jesus to turn stones into bread. At top center, Satan tempts Jesus to throw Himself down from the top of the Temple— knowing that angels will save Him. And at top right, Satan offers Jesus the whole world if He will only bow to Satan.

But when Leonardo painted backgrounds, Verrocchio wished he hadn't. For Leonardo painted so beautifully that Verrocchio grew ashamed of his own paintings. He finally switched to a different kind of art: casting big statues in bronze. This was good news for Leonardo; for it meant that he could learn sculpture as well as painting.

Some of the best Leonardo stories tell of art that fell apart on him, or that he never finished in the first place. For example, the Duke of Milan, Italy once hired Leonardo to cast

Leonardo da Vinci
(1452 - 1519)

a huge **equestrian statue** of the duke's war hero father. Leonardo spent ten years at the project, working on it off and on.

Finally, Leonardo finished a clay version of the horse part of his statue— which he called the Great Mare. He had only to create the molds, and he would be ready to cast the Great Mare in bronze. The Duke of Milan set aside seventy tons of bronze for the job, thinking that the biggest equestrian statue in the world would soon be his.

All that was before the Italian Wars. In 1494, King Charles VIII of France passed through Milan on his way to invade southern Italy. With a war starting up, the duke decided that he needed weapons more than he needed statues. Instead of pouring his seventy tons of bronze into Leonardo's Great Mare, he poured it into cannon!

A few years later, the French army used the clay Great Mare as a target for cannon practice. They smashed it to bits, ending all hope that Leonardo would ever finish his Great Mare.

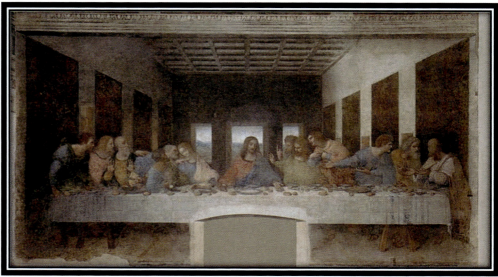

"The Last Supper" by Leonardo da Vinci. This huge, beautiful mural filled the end wall of a monastery dining room, as if the monks were sharing a meal with Christ and His apostles. Alas, the painting was hardly finished when it started flaking off the wall— thanks to a new kind of primer Leonardo used. Later, someone cut a doorway through the wall where Jesus' feet had been.

Fortunately, not all Leonardo stories end badly. One of them ends with what may be the most famous painting in the world: the **Mona Lisa**.

In 1503, a rich trader from Florence hired Leonardo to paint a portrait of his wife, whose name was Elisabetta del Giocondo. Ever since Leonardo painted the Mona Lisa, art lovers have wondered: What is the story behind that little smile on Elisabetta's face? Is she feeling pleased with herself, or perhaps irritated with someone else? She may have felt like laughing; for it is said that Leonardo hired clowns to keep Elisabetta smiling through all the long hours it took to paint her.

If Elisabetta's husband was expecting a nice portrait to hang in his home, then he was disappointed. Leonardo liked his Mona Lisa so much that he kept her with him for the rest of his life. Because Leonardo died in France, the Mona Lisa now hangs at the Louvre Museum in Paris, France.

"Mona Lisa" by Leonardo da Vinci

Our next great Renaissance artist may have been the greatest artist who ever lived. Michelangelo Buonarroti was born and raised near Florence, where Lorenzo de Medici was still training great artists. He was still quite young when Lorenzo recognized his breathtaking talent. With money and training provided by Lorenzo, young Michelangelo learned to chisel and polish sculptures of astonishing beauty.

Michelangelo was not yet twenty-five years old, and living in Rome, when he carved one of the most beautiful sculpture ever: his **Pieta**. This was Michelangelo's vision of Mary grieving over the crucified Jesus. The heart-touching Pieta now stands in St. Peter's Basilica at Vatican City, Rome.

Oddly enough, the Pieta is the only sculpture Michelangelo ever signed. This is because the Pieta taught the great artist a lesson about pride. When the Pieta was first finished, everyone in Rome crowded around to see it— including Michelangelo himself. But the artist didn't introduce himself; for he wanted to hear what people said about his work when he wasn't around.

Michelangelo expected to be pleased by what he heard; but instead, he was infuriated. When someone asked what great artist had carved this magnificent sculpture, the man who answered named the wrong artist! Naturally, Michelangelo didn't want some other artist taking credit for his best work— which is why he signed the Pieta. On a thin sash across Mary's robe, he chiseled in Latin: "Made by Michelangelo Buonarroti of Florence."

"Pieta" by Michelangelo in St. Peter's Basilica

Michelangelo Buonarroti
(1475? – 1564)

Later, Michelangelo was ashamed of himself. As a Christian artist, he was supposed to be working for the glory of God; but in signing the Pieta, he proved that he was really working for his own glory. He vowed right then never to sign another work.

Michelangelo was not yet thirty years old when he carved his next masterpiece: a six-ton, seventeen-foot-tall sculpture called the **David**. The city fathers had planned to set this sculpture on the roof of Florence Cathedral. But when they saw the finished David, they knew that it was too beautiful to set so far away. They set it down on the public square, where everyone could enjoy it.

David, of course, was the greatest King of Israel. But before he was king, David killed a giant called Goliath— as we read in 1 Samuel 17. Michelangelo's David looks at Goliath with disdain, furious with him for defying the living God. His sling rests on his shoulder, ready to strike.

The head of Michelangelo's "David"

In 1508, the Warrior Pope Julius II needed a great artist to paint the huge, arched ceiling of the **Sistine Chapel**. His first thought was to hire the greatest artist of all, Michelangelo. But Michelangelo begged off, saying that he was better at sculpting than he was at painting.

That might have been the end of it, if Michelangelo's rivals hadn't been so jealous of him. Some of them wanted very much for Michelangelo to paint the Sistine Chapel Ceiling. Why? Because they thought he would ruin it, which would also ruin his great reputation. They were secretly laughing as they pestered the pope, who pestered Michelangelo until he finally took the job.

Betting against Michelangelo was always a mistake. Instead of ruining the Sistine Chapel Ceiling, Michelangelo made it a masterpiece. He spent four uncomfortable years plastering and painting the huge ceiling. With his neck stretched back and his arms straining overhead, he thoughtfully recreated dozens of scenes from the Old Testament. His only helpers were the few workmen who built scaffolds for him, or who mixed and carried plaster.

Inside the Sistine Chapel

"God Divides Light from Darkness," one of many Michelangelo paintings on the Sistine Chapel Ceiling. Michelangelo would have looked a lot like this as he strained to plaster and paint the huge ceiling.

A *sacra conversazione*, or "holy conversation," was a special kind of painting that showed the Virgin Mary speaking with other saints. Although the baby Jesus was always with Mary, the *sacra conversazione* focused on Mary. Roman Catholics believed that if they prayed to Mary, then Mary would pray to Jesus for them.

"Altarpiece of San Marco," a *sacra conversazione* by Renaissance artist Fra Angelico

The Radical Reformation

In Chapter 27, we read how Martin Luther nailed his Ninety-five Theses to the door of All Saints' Church in Wittenberg, Germany. It happened on October 31, 1517— the first day of the Protestant Reformation.

Three and a half years later, Luther had to defend himself at a government meeting called the Diet of Worms. The Holy Roman Emperor wanted Luther to take back all the ugly things he had written about the Catholic Church. But Luther refused, saying: "Here I stand; I can do no other. God help me."

Starting then, Martin Luther was a wanted man. Loyal Catholics wanted to put him to death for criticizing pope and Church. The good news was that the emperor had promised not to arrest Luther at the Diet of Worms. The bad news was that he made no such promise after the diet. In fact, the emperor soon offered a big reward to anyone who would arrest Luther for him!

That was just what happened to Luther on his way home: He was arrested. While Luther was riding through a forest, a band of masked men rushed out from behind the trees and seized him!

Fortunately, these masked men weren't after the emperor's reward. Instead, they worked for one of Luther's friends— a rich noble called Frederick the Wise, Duke of Saxony. Frederick wanted them to make it look like Luther had been arrested, so that everyone else would stop chasing him. Luther spent most of the next year in hiding, working on his German translation of the Bible.

Wartburg Castle in Eisenach, Germany, where Luther hid in 1521 – 1522. This was the same castle where Princess Elizabeth of Hungary once lived (Chapter 11).

Meanwhile, back at Luther's home town of Wittenberg, big changes were brewing. What a strange, exciting time this was for Germany! Before now, all Christian churches had followed the Sacred Tradition of the Catholic Church. But now Luther's churches didn't believe in Sacred Tradition. Instead, Lutherans believed in **Sola Scriptura**— the idea that the Bible alone was inspired by God. In other words, Lutherans could forget about Sacred Tradition. They could throw out all their old ideas, and build a whole new church— one that was based on the Bible alone.

The problem was, some Christians wanted bigger changes than Luther did. While Luther hid at the Wartburg, a former priest called **Andreas Carlstadt** led his churches for him. Much to Luther's alarm, Carlstadt turned out to be a **radical**— the kind of person who wanted big changes fast.

> **Sola Scriptura** is Latin for "Scripture Alone."
>
> A **conservative** is someone who wants to continue old traditions.
>
> A **radical** is someone who wants to throw out old traditions.

In other words, there were two reformations going on at the same time. One was the Protestant Reformation, which was led by Luther and his friends. The other was the **Radical Reformation**, which was led by radicals who wanted to go farther than Luther did. Now that Luther had broken all the rules for them, there was no telling how far the radicals might go!

On the one hand, Luther and Carlstadt agreed about many things. Neither of them saw any monks or nuns in the Bible, which is why the Lutheran church had neither. Every monastery and nunnery in Wittenberg closed, setting all the monks and nuns free from their vows. One of those vows was the vow of chastity, which said that monks could never be involved with women. Carlstadt married in early 1522, before Luther even came out of hiding. Luther married an ex-nun called Katharina von Bora in 1525, as we read in Chapter 27.

On the other hand, Carlstadt wanted to tear all art out of every church in Germany! He wanted none of the fine art that the Renaissance popes loved so much; for he believed that it broke the Second Commandment. But Luther wanted his churches to keep some of their art; for he believed that Christians are saved by faith in Christ, not by strictly following the Ten Commandments.

The biggest question was how Christians should celebrate Holy Communion. Here again, other reformers wanted bigger changes than Luther did. See Chapter 30 for more on communion.

Currents and Columbus

The oceans are never still. Strong currents are always on the move, driven by strong forces like heat from the sun and the rotation of the Earth. During the Age of Discovery, smart sailors like Christopher Columbus used these currents to speed them on their journeys.

Between the continents, ocean currents move in giant swirls called **gyres**. The gyres north of the equator all swirl clockwise; while the gyres south of the equator all swirl counter-clockwise. For example, the South Atlantic has the **South Atlantic Gyre**, which swirls counter-clockwise. The North Atlantic has the **North Atlantic Gyre**, which swirls clockwise.

Without the North Atlantic Gyre, Christopher Columbus might never have made it to the West Indies and back. Columbus' first voyage was a clockwise journey around the North Atlantic. When Columbus set out from Spain, the gyre carried him down to the Canary Islands. When he set out from the Canaries, the gyre carried him across to the West Indies. And when he set out from the West Indies, he sailed north for a while— far enough for the gyre to pick him up and carry him back to Spain.

The farther south one sails, the less land stands in the way of ocean currents. Without continents to block them, the currents of the far south swirl swift and strong! This explains the funny nickname sailors use for the southern seas: They call them the **Washing Machine**.

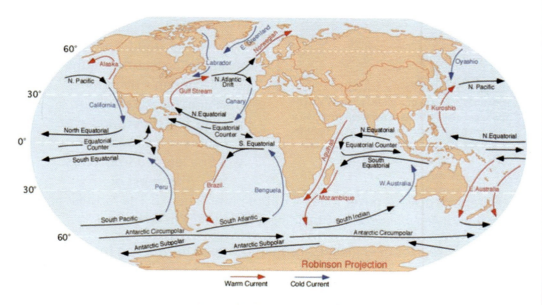

A map of major ocean currents

CHAPTER 29

The Renaissance in Science

The Renaissance Man

The Renaissance was a time of big ideas. Explorers like Christopher Columbus had big ideas about the globe. Reformers like Martin Luther had big ideas about the Church. Artists like Michelangelo had big ideas about many things, from art to the Bible, building science and more.

All these big ideas were part of what made Renaissance art so special. The best art was the kind that drew people in, making them think in new and different ways. To make that kind of art, an artist had to know all kinds of things— which meant that he had to be a **Renaissance Man**.

> A **Renaissance Man** was someone who knew a lot about many subjects.

What was a Renaissance Man? Basically, it was someone who knew everything! Renaissance men studied all subjects— not only art, but also religion, philosophy, science, engineering and more. The best example of a Renaissance Man was probably **Leonardo da Vinci**, who knew just about everything a man of his day could know.

Leonardo's learning started with his art. To make better paintings, Leonardo needed to know more about how things were put together. The way to find out was by **dissecting** animals, and then drawing pictures of what he found inside. He filled notebook after notebook with sketches of the bones, muscles and tendons hidden under animal hides.

> To **dissect** something is to cut it open and see what's inside.

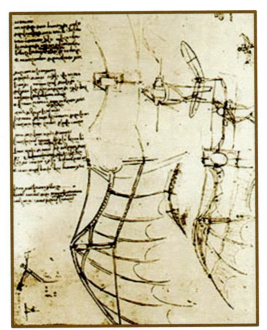

Leonardo's sketch of a glider wing, which he modeled after a bat's wing. Leonardo had a strange habit of writing notes from right to left across the page— possibly because he was left-handed.

Leonardo used what he learned from the animal world to help engineer a mechanical world. For example, he was one of the first to design a flying machine. He sketched out parachutes, gliders and even helicopters— all based on what he learned from birds.

Alas, most of Leonardo's designs never made it out of his notebooks. The farthest he got with flying was probably building and testing a parachute.

Like a lot of engineers, Leonardo wound up working for the military. He designed movable walls to defend the city of Milan, Italy. He also designed a portable bridge that could be set up quickly, with no need for nails or bolts.

A possible self-portrait of Leonardo da Vinci

The Copernican Revolution

The Renaissance was a scary time for one kind of Renaissance Man: the **astronomer**. The more astronomers learned about the heavens, the more they got in trouble. Their troubles came from men who thought they already knew all about heaven: the leaders of the Roman Catholic Church.

Before modern times, astronomy and religion always went together. Why? Because both try to answer the same questions. How did this world come to be? Are there other worlds like this one? How might this world end someday? From ancient times down through modern times, people have always looked to heaven for answers to deep questions like these.

The Church had answers to all these questions. Some of its answers came from the Bible; but a lot of them were borrowed from the science of the ancient Greeks.

Greek science started with five **elements**. The first four were the worldly elements: earth, water, air and fire. The Greeks believed that everything in the world was some mixture of these four basic elements.

An **element** is a basic building block of matter.

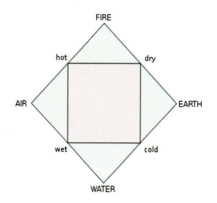

As for the fifth element, it was out of this world. According to **Aristotle**, all heaven was made of a curious element called **ether**. The first four elements were for humans; but the fifth element, ether, was for the gods.

Aristotle was an ancient Greek professor who personally taught Alexander the Great.

Ether came in many kinds. The planets were one kind of ether, and the stars another. A third kind of ether filled the space between the stars and planets. Ether was the ground the gods walked on, the lights in the gods' skies and the air the gods breathed.

Two properties of ether are especially important to remember. One is that ether was perfect; and the other is that ether never changed. The stuff of Earth might be broken, dirty and imperfect; but the stuff of heaven was smooth, clean and perfect. The stuff of Earth might be here today and gone tomorrow; but the stuff of heaven was as unchanging as the immortal gods. If Aristotle was right about ether, then nothing in the heavens could ever change.

If the heavens never changed, then why did the stars and planets move? The answer came from the most important Greek astronomer of all: **Claudius Ptolemy** of Alexandria, Egypt.

According to Ptolemy, the universe is divided into different-sized spheres. The smaller spheres are nested inside the bigger ones. The center sphere is the material world, home of the four material elements. Earth is lowest. Water floats over earth; air floats over water; and fire floats over air.

Next come the heavenly spheres— all made of ether, which floats over all. The first heavenly sphere contains the moon. Then come the spheres of Mercury, Venus and the Sun, followed by Mars and the other planets. Beyond all these, and much bigger than the rest, is the sphere that contains the stars.

Claudius Ptolemy (100? – 170?) using a quadrant to measure the positions of the stars

The heavenly spheres all turn around the material world, like an invisible set of gears. It is the turning of the spheres that causes the planets and stars to move through Earth's sky!

What causes the spheres to move? The answer lies beyond. Beyond the sphere of the stars lies an even bigger sphere called the **Prime Mover**. Beyond the Prime Mover lies the highest heaven, which Greeks called **Empyrean**. Ptolemy believed that some powerful force in the Empyrean moved the Prime Mover. In turn, the Prime Mover moved all the other spheres.

The Catholic Church had no problem with most of Ptolemy's ideas. Of course, no Christian could believe in the many gods of the Greeks. But Christians could easily believe that God the Father lived in the highest heaven, moving the Prime Mover!

The Church especially liked the idea that Earth stood at the center of the heavenly spheres. If Earth was the center, then mankind must be the center of Creation— the main reason why God created everything else. The idea that the Earth stood still, and that the sun moved around it, also seemed to agree with Bible verses like these:

One illustration of the heavenly spheres. The Latin words outside the Prime Mover read "The Heavenly Empyrean, Home of God and all the Elect."

> "[God] set the earth on its foundations; it can never be moved."
>
> —Psalm 104:5
>
> "The sun rises and the sun sets, and hurries back to where it rises."
>
> —Ecclesiastes 1:5

The idea that the Earth is the center of the universe, and that the sun, planets and stars all revolve around the Earth, is called the **geocentric** model of the heavens. From ancient times through medieval times, almost everyone in the West used the geocentric model. Almost no one thought the geocentric model might be wrong— that is, until Copernicus came along.

Nicolaus Copernicus was a Renaissance Man from the University of Krakow, Poland. His years of study made him an expert at astronomy, mathematics and more. Unlike other astronomers of his day, Copernicus saw many reasons why the geocentric model might be wrong!

> The prefix **geo-** means "Earth." **Geocentric** means "Earth-centered."

Some of Copernicus' reasons started with the orbit of Mars. For example, Copernicus noticed that Mars seemed to move forward across the night sky sometimes, and backward at other times. But Mars was supposed to be attached to a smooth-turning, never-changing heavenly sphere. If that was true, then how could it change directions?

Nicolaus Copernicus (1473 - 1543)

Another problem Copernicus noticed was that Mars changed its brightness— becoming first brighter, then dimmer. This probably meant that Mars was sometimes closer to Earth, and sometimes farther away. How could this be, if Mars was attached to a perfectly round heavenly sphere?

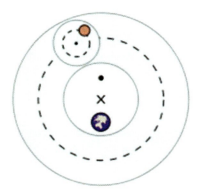

A more detailed view of Ptolemy's system

Ptolemy had answers for both these questions. In Ptolemy's model of the universe, the planets weren't attached to their planetary spheres. Instead, they were attached to smaller spheres that turned inside their planetary spheres. Like ink pens on a Spirograph, the planets moved forward, backward and then forward again— just as Mars appeared to do. They also moved closer, and then farther away— again, just like Mars.

Copernicus didn't like Ptolemy's answers, for a couple of reasons. First, the math that went with all these spheres was endlessly complicated. Second, the answers were usually wrong. Even when all the math was done, the planets were rarely where Ptolemy's model said they would be.

Instead of sticking with Ptolemy's answers, Copernicus came up with different ones. Around 1514, Copernicus wrote a short book called *Commentariolus*, or *Little Commentary*. In it, Copernicus asked: What if the geocentric model of the heavens is wrong? What if a **heliocentric model** is closer to the truth?

In other words, what if Earth isn't the center of the heavens? Instead, what if the sun is the center— and what if Earth, Mars and all the other planets really orbit the sun? Then Copernicus' problems with Mars would be easy to explain. If Mars stood farther from the sun than Earth did, then Mars might take longer to orbit the sun. Earth would catch up to Mars, and then pass it by— making it appear that Mars was moving backward. And of course, Mars would appear brighter when it was closer to Earth, and dimmer when farther away.

> The prefix **helio-** means "sun." **Heliocentric** means "sun-centered."

But then, why did the sun appear to rise and set? According to Copernicus, it wasn't because the sun revolved around the Earth. Instead, it was because the Earth rotated on its axis once each day. The rotation of the Earth also explained why the stars appeared to move. Instead of the stars turning over the Earth, the Earth turned under the stars— bringing new ones into view as it twisted its way through space.

"Astronomer Copernicus" by artist Jan Matejko

Copernicus was careful with his *Little Commentary*. He knew very well that astronomy and religion go together; and he also knew that the Church would punish him if it didn't like what he wrote. Knowing all this, he saved his book for a few astronomer friends— people he knew he could trust.

With help from these friends, Copernicus finally worked out the math to back up his new model of the heavens. His last book, *On the Revolutions of the Celestial Spheres*, was published in 1543— almost 30 years after *Little Commentary*. According to legend, Copernicus saw the first copy of his finished book on the same day he died.

Alas, Copernicus' model of the heavens turned out to be far from perfect. In placing the sun at the center, he set aside one bad old rule of Greek science: the geocentric idea. But he kept another bad old rule: the idea that the planets move in perfect circles. Since the planets don't move in perfect circles, Copernicus' math wound up as complicated as Ptolemy's— and almost as wrong.

ּׁ‎ℸℸℸℸℸℸℸℸℸℸℸℸℸℸℸℸℸℸℸℸℸℸℸℸℸℸℸℸℸℸℸℸℸ

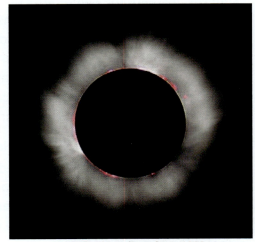

Our next great Renaissance astronomer, **Tycho Brahe**, was born three years after Copernicus died. Tycho started out as a bright young student at the University of Copenhagen, Denmark. What drew Tycho to astronomy was a heavenly happening called a **total solar eclipse**.

One day in 1559, when Tycho was thirteen years old, the moon happened to pass directly in front of the sun. At the time, the moon was as close to Earth as it ever gets— which meant that it looked as big as it ever does. At that size, the moon completely blocked the sun. It turned day as black as night, alarming both man and beast. Birds plunged from the sky in terror. People ran for cover, thinking the end of the world had come.

A total solar eclipse from 1999, photo courtesy Luc Viatour

But no Renaissance Man ran for cover. For by now, astronomers knew just when every eclipse would happen. In fact, almanacs had been publishing the correct dates and times of the next eclipse since before Christopher Columbus. That was what drew Tycho Brahe to astronomy: the fact that it worked! Tycho longed to know this marvelous science that could predict heavenly happenings so perfectly.

Tycho Brahe
(1546 - 1601)

But then Tycho's beloved science disappointed him. The problem came in 1563, when Jupiter and Saturn were about to appear very close to one another. Tycho checked two astronomical tables to see just when this would happen: one table based on Ptolemy, and another based on Copernicus. To Tycho's horror, both tables were wrong! Ptolemy missed the date by a month, while Copernicus missed it by several days. These weren't the kind of perfect predictions Tycho was looking for.

Tycho had a good idea why both tables were wrong: because they were based on wrong measurements.

Both Ptolemy and Copernicus based their math on measurements taken by astronomers over the years. To understand a planet's orbit, astronomers measured two angles: altitude and azimuth. Altitude was the angle between planet and horizon; while azimuth was the angle between planet and north. They recorded these angles night after night, year after year— whenever the skies were clear enough to see the planets.

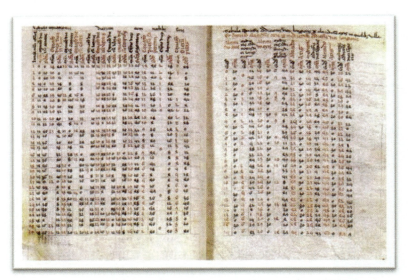

Two pages from the Alfonsine Tables, old astronomical tables based on the geocentric model of the heavens

The problem was the way astronomers measured those angles. Before Tycho, astronomers measured altitude with hand-held instruments called **quadrants**. On small devices like these, the distance from one degree to the next was only about one millimeter. This meant that a millimeter's mistake could throw a measurement off by a whole degree. But in astronomy, even fractions of a degree count! The tiniest error can be huge for an astronomer.

Tycho knew how to fix this problem. Instead of using hand-held instruments, Tycho built instruments that filled whole rooms! On a room-sized quadrant like Tycho's, the distance from one degree to the next was more like two centimeters— which made it much easier to measure angles accurately. In fact, Tycho measured his angles to within one-sixtieth of one degree.

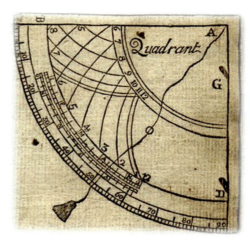

A hand-held quadrant for measuring altitude

That was Tycho Brahe's biggest gift to astronomy: accurate measurements. He spent his life recording the most complete and accurate astronomical charts the world had ever seen. But charts weren't Tycho's only contribution. He also challenged another bad old idea from Greek science: the idea that ether never changed.

In 1572, astronomers noticed a new light in the constellation Cassiopeia. Although they didn't know it at the time, they were watching a dying star called a supernova.

Since the ether wasn't supposed to change, most astronomers said that this new light couldn't be coming from a star. They thought that anything that changed must be in the same sphere as Earth. The problem was, Tycho proved that the new light never moved— which meant that it must be in the same sphere as the stars. How could there be a new star, if heavenly ether never changed?

Tycho Brahe with a room-sized quadrant

൰൰൰൰൰൰൰൰൰൰൰൰

In 1600, Tycho hired a brilliant German mathematician called

> The fun-loving Tycho Brahe kept two unusual helpers at his observatory. One was a dwarf called Jepp, who Tycho believed could see the future. The other was a tame elk who entertained Tycho's rich friends at parties. According to Tycho, his elk drank so much beer at a party one night that it got drunk, fell down a flight of stairs and died!

Johannes Kepler to help him with his calculations. A year later, Tycho died— leaving his great astronomical charts in Kepler's hands. It was Kepler who finally found what every astronomer had been wanting for years: a near-perfect way to predict the orbits of the planets.

Like Copernicus, Kepler was most interested in the orbit of Mars. Fortunately, Tycho had left him excellent measurements of Mars' orbit. Kepler filled book after book with long, complicated math— trying to find some formula that would fit Tycho's measurements.

Before he could find his formula, Kepler had to set aside one more bad old idea from Greek science: the idea that planets always move in perfect circles. For what Kepler learned is that the planets don't move in circles. Instead, they move in **ellipses**— which is what he proved

in **Kepler's Laws of Planetary Motion**.

> An **ellipse** is a special kind of oval.

- Kepler's First Law basically says that all planets revolve around the sun in ellipse-shaped orbits.
- Kepler's Second Law basically says that planets orbit faster when they are closer to the sun, and slower when they are farther away.
- Kepler's Third Law gave him a way to measure the solar system. If Kepler knew the size of one planet's orbit, then he could figure out the sizes of all the other planets' orbits.

Johannes Kepler
(1571 - 1630)

Johannes Kepler

Besides his three laws, Kepler also offered a better idea about what caused the planets to move. Kepler didn't believe in a Prime Mover out beyond the heavenly spheres. Instead, he believed that the force that moved the planets must come from the sun.

Obviously, Kepler was talking about gravity! But Kepler didn't truly understand gravity. The one who finally explained the law of gravity was an English scientist called **Sir Isaac Newton**. Newton wouldn't be born until 1642, twelve years after Kepler died.

The Galileo Affair

Like many astronomers, Johannes Kepler had trouble with the Church along the way. But Kepler's troubles were nothing compared to the troubles of **Galileo Galilei**.

Galileo was a sharp-witted, sharp-tongued Italian born in Pisa. His father was a lute player who blended math with music. As a boy, Galileo watched his father experiment with his lute— trying to understand exactly how the length and tension of his strings affected their pitch. As a grown man, Galileo believed what his father believed: that the best way to understand the world was through experiments and measurements.

Galileo was known best for his telescopes. He didn't invent the telescope; for that was done in a Dutch eyeglass shop around 1608. However, Galileo immediately improved the telescope's design. He was also the first scientist anywhere to use telescopes for serious astronomy.

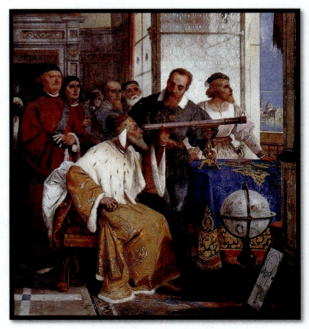

Galileo showing the leader of Venice how to use a telescope

The telescope was only about two years old in 1610, when Galileo published a little book called "Starry Messenger." The new instrument had already taught him things about the heavens that Ptolemy wouldn't have believed. For example:

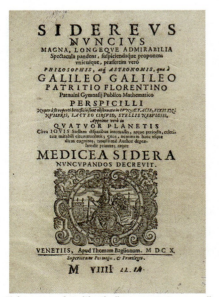

Title page of Galileo's "Starry Messenger"

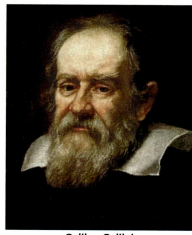

> When Galileo turned his telescope on the moon, he saw that it wasn't smooth at all. Instead, it was dotted with craters and rocks. Obviously, the heavenly ether wasn't as perfect as Ptolemy said it was!

> When Galileo turned this telescope toward Jupiter, he saw at least four moons orbiting the big planet. Obviously, Ptolemy had been wrong to say that everything revolved around the Earth!

Galileo Galilei

Not everything Galileo wrote came as a surprise. After all, some of his ideas were no different than Copernicus' or Kepler's; and some of those had already been around for almost a hundred years.

The difference was that Galileo didn't just suggest that the Earth might revolve around the sun. No, Galileo insisted that the Earth must revolve around the sun— and that anyone who didn't believe it was a stubborn old fool!

That kind of talk raised a lot of eyebrows in the Church. Priests and bishops complained that Galileo was going against the Bible. For example, Joshua 10: 13 tells of a special day when the Israelites needed more time to defeat the Amorites. To give it to them, the Lord stopped the sun and moon:

"So the sun stood still, and the moon stopped, till the nation avenged itself on its enemies."

How could the sun stand still, the Church asked, if it wasn't moving in the first place? In other words, Galileo must be wrong! No matter what Galileo said, or what his telescope showed, the sun must really revolve around the Earth. The Bible said so.

**Galileo Galilei
(1564 - 1642)**

When Galileo didn't change his mind, the Church sent the **Roman Inquisition** to deal with him. The Roman Inquisition was another powerful Church court— something like the Spanish Inquisition, but for a different purpose (Chapter 23). Galileo would face the Inquisition twice, once in 1616 and again in 1632.

Like other Church courts, the Roman Inquisition didn't waste time arguing with the accused. It simply announced that the accused was wrong, and then ordered him to change his beliefs. The first time Galileo faced the Inquisition, the court ordered him to shut his mouth and stop his pen. He was to neither speak nor write one more word about the Earth revolving around the sun. As a Catholic who lived in Italy, and hoped to live there for many more years, Galileo had no choice but to obey.

Years later, Galileo decided he was too old to waste time arguing with the stubborn Church. The time had come to write something more daring than "Starry Messenger." Galileo called his new book *Dialogue Concerning the Two Chief World Systems*; and he published it in 1632.

Galileo's *Dialogue* was a made-up talk between three made-up men. The first man was a smart scientist who proved that the Earth revolved around the sun, leaving no doubt at all. The second man believed the first. But the third man was a stubborn old fool who refused to believe, no matter how great the proof.

When churchmen read the *Dialogue*, they were furious with Galileo. They couldn't help noticing that the stubborn old fool sounded a lot like a churchman— maybe even the pope himself!

**Drawing from the frontispiece
of Galileo's "Dialogue"**

"Galileo facing the Roman Inquisition" by Cristiano Banti

The Inquisition was hard on Galileo this time. All his books were banned, all Christians forbidden to read them. Meanwhile, Galileo became a prisoner. The court place him under house arrest, ordering him to stay in his house until the court decided to let him out.

There was also a third punishment. Before ordering Galileo out of its sight for the last time, the court commanded him to speak these words aloud: "The Earth does not move."

Under threat of torture and death, Galileo had no choice but to obey. So he said it: "The Earth does not move." But he wasn't finished. It is said that the stubborn scientist added these words under his breath: "And yet it moves."

Old Galileo stayed in his house for ten years, getting deafer and blinder all the time. Even so, those were the years when he earned an honored title: **Father of the Scientific Method**.

The Scientific Method was a better way to do science than the tired old ways of the Greeks. Greek scientists started with philosophy, and worked from there. For example, Ptolemy believed in perfect heavenly spheres because he believed that the heavens must be as perfect as the gods. But Galileo was different. Instead of starting with philosophy, he started with experiments and measurements. He wanted to know the heavens as they really were, not as he believed they should be.

More about Diets

In Chapter 27, we read how Martin Luther faced the **Diet** of Worms in 1521. This chapter tells of more such diets, and how they changed the Reformation in Germany. All these diets were ordered by the same man: **Holy Roman Emperor Charles V**, who was also **King Charles I of Spain**. Charles was a loyal Catholic who wanted to stop the Reformation before it got out of hand.

The next diets after the Diet of Worms were the **Diets of Nuremberg**, held in 1522 – 1524. The emperor's orders at Nuremberg were clear: he wanted Martin Luther arrested, and all his books burned. The same was true for every Lutheran preacher in Germany: The emperor wanted them all arrested. Without powerful friends, Luther certainly would have been arrested— and probably burned to death like John Hus.

> A **diet** was a meeting of the German government.

Holy Roman Emperor Charles V, a.k.a. King Charles I of Spain

But then everything changed. Soon after the Diets of Nuremberg, the Ottoman Empire invaded Eastern Europe! The King of Hungary was killed by the most powerful sultan ever, Suleiman the Magnificent. If the emperor was going to keep Suleiman out of Germany, then he needed every German soldier he could find— including Lutheran soldiers.

The emperor knew that the Lutherans would never fight for him if he didn't ease up on them. Much as he didn't want to, he compromised with the Lutherans at the next diet: the First Diet of Speyer, held in 1526.

This first compromise between Catholics and Lutherans was called *cuius regio, eius religio*— Latin for "whoever's region, his religion." In other words, each part of the Holy Roman Empire would follow the religion of the noble who led that part. If a leader was Catholic, then his part of the empire would be Catholic. If he was Lutheran, then his part would be Lutheran.

> *Cuius regio, eius religio* is Latin for "whoever's region, his religion."

This compromise worked well enough, until the emperor took it back. Between 1526 and 1529, the emperor won a big victory in the Italian Wars. Although Suleiman still threatened, the emperor felt stronger than before— strong enough to break his compromise with the Lutherans.

The bad news came at the Second Diet of Speyer, held in 1529. The emperor announced that he was taking away *cuius regio, eius religio*— trying to force all Lutherans back into the Catholic Church!

Naturally, the Lutherans were furious. As the Second Diet of Speyer wound down, twenty-one Lutheran nobles wrote a letter of protest to the emperor. Part of this letter read:

> "We are determined by God's grace and aid to abide by God's Word alone… as it is contained in the Scriptures of the Old and New Testaments, without anything added to it. This Word alone should be preached, and nothing that is contrary to it. It is the only truth."

In other words, Lutherans insisted on following the Bible alone. They would never go back to the Catholic Church, no matter what the emperor might do to them! The name Protestant comes from those twenty-one Lutherans' letter of protest, which is called the Protestation at Speyer.

The Memorial Church of the Protestation, built in Speyer, Germany as a memorial to the Protestation at Speyer

Different Kinds of Maps

The world is a very big place, and there is much to know about it. To tell all there is to know on one map would be impossible. So instead, mapmakers create special maps that tell part of what there is to know.

One common kind of map is the physical map. Physical maps focus on a region's physical features— things like coastlines, rivers, mountains and valleys.

Some physical maps focus on more specific features. For example:

➤ A **topographic map** shows different elevations in different colors. Lower ground often appears in shades of green, with higher ground in shades of brown.

➤ A **climate map** focuses on weather patterns. One climate map might show a region's average temperature. Another might show average yearly rainfall, or the directions of prevailing winds.

CHAPTER 30:

The Reformation beyond Germany

In Chapter 27, we read where the Protestant Reformation got started: in Wittenberg, Germany, where Martin Luther lived. If the Catholic Church had had its way, then the Reformation would have ended in Germany too! The pope tried hard to stop Lutheran ideas from spreading. When the pope failed, the Holy Roman Emperor tried too— as we read in Chapter 29.

Nothing worked. Despite everything Catholics tried, the Reformation spread— first to Switzerland, then to France, the Netherlands, England and beyond.

The Swiss Reformation

Down in **Switzerland**, the story of the Reformation started with a strong-willed Swiss called **Ulrich Zwingli**. Like all early leaders of the Reformation, Zwingli started out Catholic. On his 35th birthday, Zwingli became the chief priest of the biggest church in the biggest city in Switzerland: Zurich. The date was January 1, 1519. Fourteen months had passed since Martin Luther nailed his Ninety-five Theses to a church door in Wittenberg. The Diet of Worms was still more than two years ahead.

From his first day as chief priest, Zwingli didn't preach the way other Catholics preached. Most priests preached moral lessons called homilies; but Zwingli preached straight from the Bible. In this way, Zwingli was a lot like Luther. Both Zwingli and Luther believed in *Sola Scriptura*— the idea that the Bible alone is inspired by God.

> **Switzerland** is a mountainous country in Central Europe. Its neighbors are Germany to the north, Austria to the east, Italy to the south and France to the west.

In other ways, Zwingli and Luther were quite different. Zwingli felt that Luther didn't take the Reformation far enough. He wanted to change the church faster than Luther did, and in bigger ways.

> *Sola Scriptura* is Latin for "Scripture Alone."
>
> A **radical** is someone who wants big changes fast.
>
> A **tradition** is something that has been done for a long time, handed down from generation to generation.

Why did Luther move slower than Zwingli? Partly because he was worried about the **Radical** Reformation. As we read in Chapter 28, radical Christians wanted to toss out all Catholic **traditions** right away. Luther wanted to slow the radicals down, lest they throw out things they shouldn't. The Lutheran rule was to keep any tradition that didn't go against the Bible.

Zwingli was more radical than Luther. His rule was that if a tradition didn't come straight from the Bible, then it was automatically wrong. He wanted to build a whole new church, basing everything he did on the Bible alone.

Ulrich Zwingli (1484 – 1531)

Ulrich Zwingli (1484 - 1531)

The first tradition Zwingli tossed out was a food law. The Catholic Church had special laws for the season before Easter, which it called **Lent**. As Easter drew near, all Christians were supposed to give up the luxury of eating meat— to remind them how Christ gave up everything for them on the cross.

The season of **Lent** falls in the 40 days leading up to Easter.

Zwingli's food ideas came from I Corinthians 8, which talks about Christians and food. The Apostle Paul said that Christians were free to eat whatever food they liked, even food that had been sacrificed to idols. The only reason not to eat certain foods was if eating them might weaken someone else's faith.

That was just what Zwingli told his followers. He didn't say that they should meat during Lent, nor did he say that they shouldn't. Instead, he said that Christians are free to choose— which led to a strange happening called the **Affair of the Sausages**.

A Swiss printer called Christoph Froschauer took Zwingli's words to heart. When Lent came around in 1522, Froschauer hosted a friendly meal for workers in his print shop. On the menu that day was a food that no good Catholic was supposed to eat during Lent: sausage! Nowadays, gnawing a bit of sausage might not seem like a big deal. But in those days, it was a very big deal. By eating sausage during Lent, Froschauer was deliberately breaking Church law.

As for Zwingli, he didn't eat Froschauer's sausages himself; but he did say that Froschauer had every right to eat them. Since Zwingli was still a priest at the time, he was as guilty of breaking Church law as Froschauer was.

ℼℼ

The Affair of the Sausages marked the first time Zwingli deliberately broke the laws of the Catholic Church. He would soon break many other Church laws, starting with ones about buildings and ceremonies.

In reading through his Bible, Zwingli saw a lot of differences between Biblical churches and the Catholic Church. The churches in the Bible were all poor, as Christ Himself was poor. But the Catholic Church was rich and fancy, full of fine art and grand ceremonies. If Zwingli wanted to get back to the Bible, then he would have to make his churches more like Biblical ones.

The first step was to make his church buildings as plain as possible, without tearing them down. The murals on his walls were all covered with clean white paint. The sculptures were all hauled out. **Stained glass** windows were replaced with clear glass. Even expensive pipe organs were torn out— which was especially hard for Zwingli, who loved his church music. But he was willing to make the sacrifice; for he wanted no idols in his churches. All he wanted was the simple kind of worship found in the Bible.

The next step was to make his church services more like Biblical ones— starting with Holy Communion. Zwingli saw a lot of problems with the Mass, which was the way Catholics celebrated communion. Like all Protestants, He felt that the Mass was far different from what Christ meant communion to be.

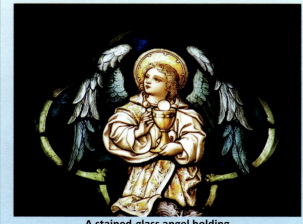

Medieval churches used **stained glass** windows to illustrate Bible stories for Christians who couldn't read. They were a "Poor Man's Bible," the only kind of Bible that the poor could understand.

A stained-glass angel holding the elements of Holy Communion

Zwingli's problem with the Mass started with an idea called **transubstantiation**. The Church said that during the Mass, the bread and wine of communion truly changed into the body and blood of

Jesus Christ. By taking the Mass, believers were taking part in Christ's sacrifice on the cross.

What Zwingli didn't like about transubstantiation was that he couldn't find it in the Bible. What he could find was Luke 22:19, where Christ said: "This is my body given for you; do this in remembrance of me." That was how Zwingli saw communion: as a way to remember how Christ sacrificed Himself for sinners on the cross. He believed that the bread and wine were symbols of Christ, not His real body and blood.

Protestants call Zwingli's ideas about communion **memorialism**, meaning remembrance.

The *Grossmunster*, Zwingli's main church in Zurich

Communion with Zwingli was nothing like a Catholic Mass. Where priests rang bells and burned incense, Zwingli spoke plain words from the Bible. And where priests used fancy plates and cups made of gold, Zwingli used plain wooden ones. He also held communion less often— only a few times a year, instead of one or more times each week. He wanted his people learning from the Bible, not watching priests put on grand ceremonies.

Oddly enough, Zwingli's ideas about communion led to an argument with someone who should have been his friend: Martin Luther.

The story starts with the Second Diet of Speyer. As we read in Chapter 29, the Holy Roman Emperor ordered all Lutherans to go back to the Catholic Church; and the Lutherans wouldn't go. From then on, the Lutherans were sure the emperor would attack them someday. Whenever he did, they would need help. And who better to help the Lutherans than their fellow Protestants down in Switzerland?

Unfortunately, the Lutherans disagreed with Swiss Protestants about certain things. If they didn't start agreeing, then the Swiss might not come when the Lutherans needed them— which might mean disaster.

That was the thinking behind a special meeting called the **Marburg Colloquy**. In late 1529, a German noble called **Philip of Hesse** arranged a special meeting between Luther and Zwingli. He wanted the two leaders to work out their differences, so that their two churches could help each other when the time came.

The biggest arguments at the Marburg Colloquy were all about communion. Like Zwingli, Luther had problems with the Mass. But Luther also had problems with Zwingli's kind of communion: memorialism.

The Marburg Colloquy (1529)

Why didn't Luther like memorialism? Because to him, the bread and wine were more than just symbols. He didn't believe that the bread and wine changed into the body and blood of Christ; but he did believe that Christ

Luther, Zwingli and others at the Marburg Colloquy

was in the bread and wine somehow. Protestants call Luther's ideas about communion **consubstantiation**. He believed that Christ was "in, with and under" the elements of communion.

Back and forth the two men argued. Luther brought up Mark 14:22, where Christ said: "Take [this bread]; this <u>is</u> my body." The word "is" made it clear to Luther what Christ meant: that the bread really is Christ's body. But Zwingli wasn't convinced. He brought up John 15:5, where Christ said "I am the vine." Did Luther think that Christ really was a vine, Zwingli asked? Or is the vine a symbol of Christ, just as the bread is a symbol of Christ's body?

Of course, Luther and Zwingli agreed on many other things. But this one thing was enough to wreck their meeting. The two men never agreed about communion, and never became friends.

Zwingli could have used more friends. In that same year of 1529, a civil war broke out between two kinds of Swiss: Swiss Protestants who followed Zwingli, and Swiss Catholics who stuck with the Catholic Church.

Without Lutheran allies, the Swiss Protestants were badly outnumbered. The great Ulrich Zwingli died in battle against the Swiss Catholics in 1531.

"The Murder of Ulrich Zwingli" by artist Karl Jauslin

The Reformed Church

Our next great figure from the Reformation also lived in Switzerland. But John Calvin was born in France, not Switzerland. Calvin started as a **Huguenot**, which was what French Protestants were called. He only moved to Switzerland after the Huguenots ran into big trouble.

> A **Huguenot** was a French Protestant.

When the Reformation started in 1517, Francis I was King of France. Like Holy Roman Emperor Charles V, King Francis I was a loyal Catholic. But unlike Charles, Francis didn't order all Huguenots back into the Catholic Church— at least, not at first.

Why not? Partly because Charles and Francis were bitter enemies. Anything that made Charles weaker made Francis stronger. Since Protestants made Charles weaker, Francis left the Huguenots alone for a while. It was only later, after the Huguenots pulled a stunt called the Affair of the Placards, that Francis changed his mind.

John Calvin (1509 – 1564)

King Francis I of France (1494 – 1547)

A Huguenot Cross, with its four French fleur-de-lis and one Holy Spirit dove

Like a lot of troubles in Reformation times, the Affair of the **Placards** started with the **Mass**. No Protestant liked the Mass. Sometimes, the Huguenots disliked the Mass so much that they just had to say something about it.

One night in 1534, the Huguenots quietly hung placards all over five French cities. When Catholics got up the next morning, they read this at the top of the Huguenot placards: "True Articles on the Horrible, Great and Intolerable Abuses of the Popish Mass." Down below, they read why the Huguenots hated the Mass so much. The placards said that the Mass was more like a pagan sacrifice than a Christian worship service. Naturally, Catholics were furious.

Even so, the Huguenots might have gotten away with hanging their placards— if not for something that happened in Paris. Somehow, some Huguenot managed to hang a placard right outside King Francis' bedroom! Whoever did it probably hoped that Francis would read the placard, and maybe believe what it said about the Mass. Instead, Francis was terrified. He shuddered to think how close the Huguenots had been to his bedroom, and how easily they might have killed him.

Thanks to that one placard, the Huguenots got the opposite of what they hoped for. Instead of becoming a Huguenot, Francis became the Huguenots' worst enemy. He started rounding them up and tossing them in jail, getting ready for a big event he was planning.

Three months after the placards went up, the Catholic Church put on a special parade in Paris. King Francis himself rode through the streets, stopping every so often to greet his people. Wherever he stopped, his executioners tortured Huguenots with fire until they died in agony.

Meanwhile, other Huguenots were rushing to get out of France. Many fled to Swiss cities just across the border, like Geneva and Basel. One Huguenot who fled to Basel was John Calvin.

〰〰〰〰〰〰〰〰〰〰〰〰〰〰〰〰〰〰〰〰〰

John Calvin was still on the run, and still living in Basel, when he published the first edition of his greatest work:

John Calvin (1509 - 1564)

"Portrait of Young John Calvin" on display at the University of Geneva

Institutes of the Christian Religion, a.k.a. the Institutes.

The Institutes spelled out Calvin's **theology**— in other words, everything he believed about God and the Bible.

What made the *Institutes* so special was Calvin's brilliant thinking. His followers thought the *Institutes* were the best explanation of Christian theology ever written. Thanks to the *Institutes*, Calvin became the father of a new kind of Protestant church: Reformed churches.

Theology is the study of God.

Reformed churches stress three main ideas. First, they stress Sola Scriptura— the idea that the Bible alone is the inspired Word of God (Chapter 27). Second, Reformed churches stress the sovereignty of God. Sovereignty means that all power and authority belong to God! As the Creator of the world, God may do with His world whatever He chooses to do.

Third, Reformed churches stress the grace of God. What is grace? In theology, "grace" means a gift from God that isn't earned or deserved.

Reformed churches teach that no one deserves to be saved. Calvin believed in original sin, which means that all people are born into the sin of Adam (Chapter 3). They are all so wrapped up in sin that they cannot possibly earn God's forgiveness.

Original sin explains why grace is so important to Reformed churches. On the one hand, no one deserves to be saved. On the other hand, God loves his people so much that He wants to save some anyway. Because God is sovereign, He can choose to save sinners who don't deserve it. In other words, salvation is all up to God— from beginning to end, with no help from man.

Bible students use the word **TULIP** to remember the ideas in Calvin's *Institutes*. Each letter stands for a different point of Calvin's theology:

T is for <u>T</u>otal Depravity
U is for <u>U</u>nconditional Election
L is for <u>L</u>imited Atonement
I is for <u>I</u>rresistible Grace
P is for <u>P</u>erseverance of the Saints

Within a year after Calvin first published the *Institutes*, a fellow Huguenot called William Farel invited him to Geneva, Switzerland. Except for a three-year break, Calvin stayed in Geneva for the rest of his life.

The longer Calvin stayed, the more powerful he became. By the 1540s, Calvin practically ran Geneva— much like the pope ran the Papal States, or like Savonarola ran Florence for a while (Chapter 26).

Calvin had a vision for Geneva. He wanted it to be the Protestant Rome— the leading city of the Protestant Church, as Rome was the leading city of the Catholic Church. But Calvin didn't want to be a Protestant pope; for he didn't believe in popes. Instead, he wanted Geneva to be a beacon to others— a shining example of what a Christian city should be.

He started by writing tough new laws for Geneva. Like Savonarola, Calvin frowned on anything that drew people's attention away from God. Also like Savonarola, Calvin was terribly strict. His laws reached into every heart in Geneva, trying to make them all live up to his vision.

For example, Genevans were not to eat too much. They were not to put on too much makeup, wear their hair in fancy styles, or buy clothing that looked too luxurious. They were to sing no non-Christian songs, only Christian ones; and they were not to dance. Nor were they to play any game that involved rolling dice.

The Reformation Wall in Geneva shows four famous figures. The first is William Farel, who first invited Calvin to Geneva. Next comes Calvin himself, followed by Theodore Beza of Geneva and John Knox of Scotland. Notice how strict they all look!

Most of all, Genevans were to go to church! The law said that every Genevan must go to church every Sunday. They must also sit quietly and respectfully, paying close attention to the sermon.

The punishments for breaking these laws could be severe. For singing non-Christian songs, one's tongue might be pierced with an awl. For laughing in church, one might go to jail.

The worst punishments were for crimes against God. Any blasphemer who cursed God, or any heretic who taught wrong ideas about God, was in danger of death. The Church of Geneva sometimes burned heretics to death, just like the Catholic Church did. The best-known burning at Geneva happened to a doctor called **Michael Servetus**.

Servetus was a Renaissance Man, the kind of thinker who dreamed up new ideas on many subjects. His greatest gifts probably lay in medicine. Of all the doctors in Europe, Servetus was the first to understand something called **pulmonary circulation**.

Michael Servetus (1511 – 1553)

Like all Renaissance men, Servetus was interested in religion too. As a boy, he loved the Catholic Church. But as a young man, he grew disgusted with the Renaissance popes— which was why he became a Protestant.

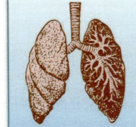

"Pulmonary" means "having to do with the lungs." **Pulmonary circulation** means that blood flows from the heart to the lungs, where it picks up oxygen. Oxygen-filled blood then flows back to the heart to be pumped out to the rest of the body.

The Reformation excited Servetus. To a man filled with new ideas, it seemed like a perfect time to throw out all the bad old ideas that had led the Catholic Church astray.

Unfortunately, Servetus chose the wrong idea to throw out. He was twenty years old in 1531, when he published a book called *On the Errors of the Trinity*. Servetus was convinced that the Holy Trinity was one of the bad old ideas that had led the Catholic Church astray. In other words, he didn't believe that God exists in three persons: God the Father, God the Son and God the Holy Spirit.

Almost no one agreed with Servetus. Catholics and Protestants disagreed about many things, but not this. On the Holy Trinity, there was no difference between Protestants and Catholics. All Christians believed in God the Father, God the Son and God the Holy Spirit. In other words, Servetus was an enemy to all Christians— Protestant or Catholic.

Sometime in the 1540s, Servetus started writing letters to Calvin— trying to convince him that the Holy Trinity was wrong. At first, Calvin wrote friendly letters back— trying to show him how the Bible points to the Trinity.

Along with one of these friendly letters, Calvin sent a copy of his own best work: the *Institutes*. Much to Calvin's dismay, Servetus sent the *Institutes* back to him— all marked up with negative comments. Not even Calvin's best work could convince Servetus that the Holy Trinity was true!

After several years of this, Calvin finally decided that nothing would ever change Servetus' mind. He started to see Servetus as a dangerous heretic who was bent on tearing down the Reformed church. In a letter to a friend, Calvin wrote this about Servetus:

"…if he comes here, if my authority is worth anything, I will never permit him to depart alive."

Much to Calvin's surprise, Servetus did wind up coming to Geneva. It happened in 1553, after Servetus was arrested on charges of heresy— not in a Protestant city, but in a Catholic one. Somehow, Servetus managed to escape from jail and get out of that city. But instead of going somewhere safe, Servetus went to Geneva— where he turned up in the pews of Calvin's own church! True to his word, Calvin had Servetus arrested and charged with heresy.

Since Servetus wasn't a citizen of Geneva, the court had no legal power to execute him. The court did have the power to banish Servetus, but chose not to. It could have sent him back where he came from, where the Catholic Church probably would have executed him. Instead, the court ordered Servetus burned to death in Geneva— along with the pile of books he'd written against the Trinity.

Why? Because to Calvin, Servetus was like a wolf in his pasture, tearing at his helpless sheep. Calvin wanted his people to hear Biblical truth, not lies meant to tear down the church.

To some people, though, the burning of Michael Servetus marked Calvin as a **hypocrite**. After all, why had Calvin come to Geneva in the first place? Wasn't it because French Catholics were burning Huguenots to death for heresy? Now Calvin was burning Servetus for heresy. So how were Reformed churches any better than the Catholic Church?

> A **hypocrite** is someone who expects other people to have good morals, but doesn't have good morals himself.

The French Wars of Religion

John Calvin was wise to leave France when he did. Times were already bad for the Huguenots in 1534, when the Affair of the Placards pushed Calvin out. Later, though, times got even worse.

The trouble this time started with a horrible happening called the **Massacre of Vassy**. One day in 1562, a Catholic duke happened to be leading an army through the town of Vassy, France. Since it was Sunday, the Huguenots of Vassy were having a church service. Since they were Huguenots, they were having it in a barn— for Huguenots weren't allowed to use Catholic church buildings.

Exactly what happened that day, no one now knows for sure. One version of the story says that the duke ordered his troops to stop the Huguenots' service. When the Huguenots fought back, the duke set fire to the barn— burning dozens of defenseless Huguenots to death.

The Massacre of Vassy was the first battle in a long set of wars called the **French Wars of Religion**. These horrible wars were to last more than thirty years, all the way from 1562 – 1598. In all that time, the Huguenots never came close to winning— mostly because they were always outnumbered. Only one King of France was ever a Huguenot, and even that one had to turn Catholic to keep his throne.

Out of all the horrible happenings of the French Wars of Religion, the most horrible was one called the **St. Bartholomew's Day Massacre**. One night in August 1572, some Catholics in Paris made a surprise attack against the Huguenots— trying to hunt down and kill every Huguenot in the city. Exactly who planned the attack, no one now knows for sure. Whoever it was, the idea soon spread to other cities. Before it was over, as many as 10,000 Huguenots lay dead.

But the Huguenots weren't beaten; for they still held a few cities. The most important Huguenot city was **La Rochelle**, a port on the west coast.

Since the Huguenots weren't wanted in France, they started sailing out of La Rochelle— hoping to find new homes where they could live in peace. Some Huguenots sailed all the way to North America, where they built two colonies. One was Charlesfort, which stood on what is now Parris Island, South Carolina. The other was Fort Caroline, which stood in what is now Jacksonville, Florida. Sad to say, neither colony lasted very long— as we'll read in Year Three.

The French Wars of Religion ended, sort of, with a law called the **Edict of Nantes**. For the sake of peace, the Catholics finally gave the Huguenots part of the freedom they wanted. From 1598 forward, the Huguenots were free to worship in any French city where they already worshiped. But they couldn't worship in Paris; for the Catholics of Paris still hated Huguenots as much as ever.

The Huguenots weren't the only Frenchmen in the New World. In the mid-1500s, King Francis I— the same Francis who gave Calvin so much trouble— sent an explorer called **Jacques Cartier** to North America. Thanks to Cartier, the French were the first Europeans to claim a huge part of North America: **Canada**.

Jacques Cartier (1491 – 1557)

Like other early explorers, Cartier started out looking for a new way to reach the Far East. But he was also interested in hidden treasures that might make him rich, like gold and diamonds. He grew a lot more interested on his second trip to Canada, when Native Americans told him of a mysterious kingdom farther north— one that had all the gold and diamonds anyone could want.

Cartier thought he'd hit the jackpot. On his third trip to Canada, he stuffed his holds with what he thought were gold and diamond ores. Alas, Cartier didn't know his minerals. When he got back to France, his "gold" turned out to be worthless iron pyrite— a.k.a. "fool's gold." And his "diamonds" turned out to be worthless quartz! See Year Three for more on Cartier.

An **inuksuk** is a Native American landmark made of stacked stones. In the vast, frozen tundra of northern Canada, one stretch of ground looked a lot like any other. The Inuit people solved this problem by building inuksuk markers to guide them.

A man-shaped inuksuk in Quebec Province, Canada

DISCOVERIES IN THE NORTH

CHAPTER 31

King Henry VIII; the English Reformation

The English Reformation

The Protestant Reformation came to different countries in different ways. In Germany and Switzerland, it started with arguments over theology. Protestant leaders like Martin Luther, Ulrich Zwingli and John Calvin believed that the Catholic Church taught wrong ideas about God and the Bible.

The English Reformation wasn't like that. Instead of starting with theology, the English Reformation started with arguments about Church law and politics. The main reason it started was because the King of England wanted to divorce his wife, and the Catholic Church wouldn't let him!

Way back in Chapter 15, we read how Henry Tudor won the Wars of the Roses. It happened at the Battle of Bosworth Field, when Henry defeated and killed King Richard III. The end of Richard was also the end of his royal house, the House of York. Right there on the battlefield, Henry Tudor became **King Henry VII**— the first king from the new royal **House of Tudor**.

If the House of Tudor was going to last, then Henry VII needed sons to take his place when he was gone. Fortunately, Henry's queen gave him what the English call "an heir and a spare." In other words, Henry had two sons. His eldest son **Arthur, Prince of Wales** was the official heir to the throne. His second son **Henry, Duke of York** was there to take Arthur's place, in case anything should happen to him.

As a future King of England, Prince Arthur attracted a powerful bride. He was fifteen years old in 1501, when he married Princess **Catherine of Aragon**. Catherine was a daughter to two of the most powerful people in the world: King **Ferdinand of Aragon** and Queen **Isabella of Castile**.

Prince Arthur Tudor, elder brother to the future King Henry VIII

Kings and Queens from the Royal House of Tudor

1. King Henry VII
(Reigned 1485 – 1509)

2. King Henry VIII
(Reigned 1509 – 1547)

3. King Edward VI
(Reigned 1547 – 1553)

4. Lady Jane Grey
(Reigned 9 days in 1553)

5. Queen Mary I
(Reigned 1553 – 1558)

6. Queen Elizabeth I
(Reigned 1558 – 1603)

The wedding was hardly over when tragedy struck. Just six months after they were married, both Arthur and Catherine came down with a mysterious fever called **sweating sickness**. Catherine got over her fever; but Arthur got worse. Despite everything his doctors tried, Arthur died— leaving Catherine a widow at age sixteen.

The House of Tudor might have been in big trouble, if not for the king's spare heir. In 1502, the 11-year-old Henry, Duke of York became the new Prince of Wales— the official heir to King Henry VII.

As for Catherine, no one was quite sure what do with her. The same things that had made Catherine a good match for Arthur would also make her a good match for Henry. The problem was, the Catholic Church said that brothers couldn't marry their brothers' wives. This Church law was partly based on Leviticus 21:20, which reads: "If a man marries his brother's wife, it is an act of impurity; he has dishonored his brother. They will be childless" [underline added].

But the Church sometimes bent its rules, especially for royals. Since Catherine had no children with Arthur, the Church gave Henry special permission to marry his brother's widow. The wedding happened in 1509— two months after Henry VII died, and his seventeen-year-old son became **King Henry VIII**.

Catherine's first job as queen was to give Henry sons. Like his father before him, Henry wanted at least two strong sons to carry on the House of Tudor after he was gone.

Sadly, Catherine couldn't seem to bear a healthy child. She was pregnant many times; but each time, the poor child died.

The couple had been married almost seven years when Catherine finally gave birth to a healthy child. Much to Henry's disappointment, that child was a daughter: **Mary Tudor**.

After one more failed pregnancy, Catherine stopped getting pregnant. It was starting to look like Catherine would never give Henry the sons he wanted so desperately.

Catherine of Aragon, 1st wife to Henry VIII. Catherine gave birth to Mary Tudor, the future Queen Mary I.

The King's Great Matter

As King of England, Henry VIII was used to getting what he wanted. Since Catherine couldn't give him sons, Henry wanted to divorce Catherine and marry someone who could. The question was, how could he get a divorce? The Catholic Church didn't usually allow divorce, especially after a couple had a child. If Henry wanted a divorce anyway, then he was going to have to give the Church a good excuse.

The excuse Henry needed came from his dead brother Arthur. One day on 1527, an English **ambassador** rode into Rome with an urgent message for the pope. The King of England was troubled by a guilty conscience, the ambassador said. Henry knew now that he should never have married his brother's widow. After all, didn't Leviticus 20:21 spell out what would happen to a man who married his brother's widow? The Bible said, "they will be childless." Surely this explained why Catherine couldn't give Henry sons?

An **ambassador** is a government officer who deals with foreign governments.

Fortunately, the ambassador said, the pope had the power to save Henry. If the pope **annulled** Henry's marriage, then it would be as if he had never married his brother's widow!

Any other time, the pope

> An **annulment** is a special kind of divorce. The Church dissolves the marriage, making it as if the couple never married in the first place.

probably would have done as Henry asked. For Henry was a loyal Catholic king, the kind who defended the Church against Martin Luther. Back in 1521, Henry had criticized Luther in a long paper called "Defense of the Seven Sacraments." For this, the grateful pope had given Henry the title *Fidei Defensor*— Latin for "Defender of the Faith."

Portrait of King Henry VIII from the studio of Hans Holbein the Younger

Just now, though, the pope couldn't do as Henry asked. It so happened that the Papal States were at war with the Holy Roman Empire. Emperor Charles V was winning, which meant that the pope had to do what Charles told him. It also happened that Charles was a nephew to Henry's wife, Catherine of Aragon. Charles' mother was Joanna of Castile, an older sister to Catherine. When Charles heard that Henry wanted to divorce his aunt, he ordered the pope to turn him down!

Even so, Henry could still think of two ways out. First, he could convince Catherine to take the vows of a nun. If she did, then she would become a bride of Christ— which would set Henry free. Second, he could convince Catherine to ask for a divorce too. Her family was so powerful that no one would stand in her way, if she only asked.

Alas for Henry, Catherine wouldn't go along with either idea— mostly because of her daughter Mary. For if Catherine stopped being queen, then Mary would stop being a princess!

Catherine of Aragon on her knees before Henry VIII in an English church court, begging him not to divorce her

When both the pope and Catherine turned him down, Henry turned to his home church. In 1529, English bishops held a special court to decide: Should the Church give Henry his divorce, or shouldn't it?

Catherine played her hand skillfully. When the queen came to court, she threw herself on her knees before the king— begging him not to divorce her. Any bishop with a heart couldn't help feeling sorry for her. Next, Catherine asked that the trial be moved to Rome. Now Henry's bishops had a tough choice to make: Should they follow their pope, or follow their king?

Much to Henry's dismay, they chose the pope! Instead of giving Henry his divorce, the bishops moved the case to Rome— where they knew he would never win.

That was the last straw for Henry. In his mind, no foreigner had any right to tell a King of England what to do! If a foreign church was going to try, then Henry would have to make some big changes in the English church.

The first step was to get rid of old churchmen who were still loyal to the pope, and replace them with new churchmen who were loyal to their king. That way, Henry would be sure to win his next case in church court.

The next step was a new law called the Statute in Restraint of Appeals. Starting in 1533, it was illegal to do what Catherine had done: to **appeal** to the pope. From now on, the pope would have no authority over English church courts. Whatever England decided would be final.

> To **appeal** a court's decision is to ask a higher court to change the first court's decision.

The last step was another new law called the Act of Supremacy. Basically, this law created a whole new English church— completely separate from the Roman Catholic Church. This was the start of the **Church of England**, a.k.a. the **Anglican Church**.

As a separate church, the Church of England needed a separate leader. The Act of Supremacy made the King of England the supreme head of the Church of England, just as he was the head of government. In other words, the king had all authority over the Church of England; while the pope had no authority at all.

Meanwhile, Henry took another try at his divorce. In May 1533, the Church of England held a new court to hear Henry's case for divorce. Just as Henry hoped, the court annulled his marriage— saying that he never should have married his brother's widow in the first place. The heartbroken Catherine of Aragon lived less than three years after her divorce. She died alone, forbidden even to see her daughter Mary.

Anne Boleyn, 2nd wife to King Henry VIII. Anne gave birth to Elizabeth Tudor, the future Queen Elizabeth I.

As for Henry, he got a new wife. For years now, he had been hoping to marry a smart, beautiful young woman called **Anne Boleyn**. Now that his first marriage was finally over, Henry was free to start his second.

More Reasons for the English Reformation

The king's divorce was only the first reason for the English Reformation. There were also many other reasons. In fact, English Christians found as many reasons to complain about the Catholic Church as German and Swiss Christians found.

One complaint was that priests had gotten greedy. Everything they did came with a price tag, from baptisms to weddings to burials. When believers said they couldn't pay, priests threatened them— saying that if they didn't come up with the money, then they wouldn't go to heaven when they died!

Another complaint was that English monasteries had gone bad. By this time, English monks lived nothing like Anthony of Thebes (Chapter 3). Instead of seeking God, they sought pleasure. Instead of eating little, they grew fat. Instead of working hard to support themselves, they lived off donations.

Over the years, those donations had made English monasteries fabulously rich. Just before the English Reformation, monasteries owned about one-third of all farmland in England— not to mention a fortune in gold, silver and precious gems.

The monasteries' fortune was tempting to Henry, who always needed more money for the royal treasury. He soon found a way to kill two birds with one stone— to fix England's monasteries and fill his treasury at the same time.

It all started with something called the **visitations of the monasteries**. As supreme head of the Church of England, the king was also head of England's monasteries. If the monasteries had gone bad, then it was Henry's job to fix them. He sent inspectors to every monastery in England, ordering them to close the monastery if they found any problems.

With so many things going wrong, Henry's inspectors had no trouble finding plenty of problems. Over the next few years, King Henry VIII closed almost every monastery in England— about 800 in all! The monk's way of life was over in England, at least for now.

Part of Reading Abbey, one of many monasteries that fell into ruins after the Dissolution of the Monasteries

The **Dissolution of the Monasteries** took about five years, from 1536 – 1541.

As for the monasteries' money and property, it all went straight to the king's treasury. If a local church wanted to use a monastery's buildings, then it could buy them from the treasury. If not, then the buildings might be left to rot.

The most money came from the biggest shrine in England: the

> A **shrine** is a memorial to an honored Catholic saint.

Shrine of St. Thomas Becket, which stood inside Canterbury Cathedral. Becket was an old Archbishop of Canterbury from the 1100s. Back in Chapter 13, we read how Becket argued with King Henry II over common law. We also read what happened to Becket in the end— how four of the king's knights burst in and killed him, right there on the altar of Canterbury Cathedral.

Thomas Becket and the knights

Since then, the Catholic Church had built a shrine to Becket— calling him a saint. Now when Christians confessed their sins, priests sent them on pilgrimages to the Shrine of St. Thomas Becket. Part of every pilgrimage was donating something to the shrine. With that many donations, Becket's shrine was now the richest in England!

King Henry VIII hated that shrine. Why? Because Becket had defied a King of England, and defended the Catholic Church. With the English Reformation going on, Henry wanted his people to do just the opposite: to defy the Catholic Church, and defend their king.

The answer, Henry decided, was to rewrite history. In 1538, he asked the Church of England to re-try the case between Thomas Becket and King Henry II— even though it was almost 400 years old! Since the Church of England answered to Henry VIII, the outcome was never in doubt. The new court decided that the old court had been wrong— and that Thomas Becket was no saint.

Once the court ruled his way, Henry tore down Becket's shrine and hauled off all its treasures. According to legend, the loot filled more than twenty wagons!

〰〰〰〰〰〰〰〰〰〰〰〰〰〰〰〰〰〰〰〰〰〰〰〰〰〰〰〰〰〰

The English were torn over all these changes. Some of them were delighted to go Protestant; while others were determined to stay Catholic. A great scholar called **William Tyndale** came down on the Protestant side.

Tyndale turned against the Catholic Church long before Henry VIII did. The English Reformation hadn't started yet in the early 1520s, when Tyndale started his life's work: translating the whole Bible into English. Before now, English churches had used the same Bible all other Western churches used: a Latin one called the **Vulgate**. Tyndale wanted to give Englishmen a Bible they could read for themselves.

William Tyndale (1492? - 1536)

We've read how the Catholic Church felt about this. It didn't want average Christians reading the Bible, for fear they might interpret it differently than the Church did. A priest told Tyndale that translating the Bible was a mistake— saying that it would be better for Christians to forget God's law than to forget the pope's. Tyndale answered:

"I defy the pope, and all his laws; and if God spares my life, in a few years, I will cause the boy that drives the plow to know more of the Scriptures than you do!"

Strange though it may seem, Tyndale got in more trouble after the English Reformation than he did before. When Henry VIII started asking for a divorce, Tyndale criticized him— saying that divorce went against the Bible. When the king's men caught up with Tyndale, they put him to death.

〰〰〰〰〰〰〰〰〰〰〰〰〰〰〰〰〰〰〰〰〰〰〰〰

Sir Thomas More also paid a high price for criticizing the king's divorce. But More was the opposite of Tyndale. Where Tyndale wanted England to go Protestant, More wanted it to stay Catholic.

More was a close adviser to Henry VIII. Before the English Reformation, the two men were great friends. When Martin Luther criticized the Catholic Church, both More and Henry criticized Luther right back.

The trouble started when Henry changed his mind, and started pulling away from the Catholic Church. More couldn't go along with Henry on this.

WILLIAM TYNDALE

The **Vulgate** was the Latin Bible translated by St. Jerome in the 300s (Chapter 3).

The Lord gave William Tyndale a great gift for languages. According to legend, Tyndale knew eight languages so well that he could speak or write any of them as well as he could English!

The **Tyndale Bible** wasn't the first English Bible; for John Wycliffe came out with one in the late 1300s. But the Wycliffe Bible was translated from the Vulgate, which made it a translation of a translation. The Tyndale Bible was the first English Bible that was translated directly from the three ancient tongues of the Bible: Greek, Hebrew and Aramaic.

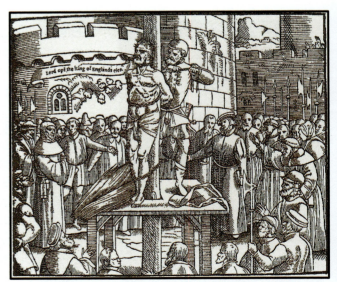

This picture from *Foxe's Book of Martyrs* shows William Tyndale about to burn at the stake, saying "Lord, open the King of England's eyes."

Although he understood that the Church had its problems, he wanted to fix those problems— not tear the Church apart.

The final blow came when the Church of England split from the Catholic Church (above). As a good Catholic, More didn't want to work for a non-Catholic government. He resigned his government job in 1532, the year before Henry divorced his first wife.

Sir Thomas More
(1478 - 1535)

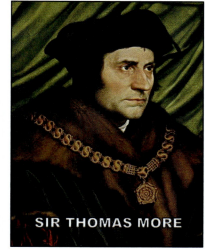

SIR THOMAS MORE

Even then, the two men might have stayed friends— if not for Henry's second wife. Anne Boleyn had waited a long time to become queen, and expected everyone to be as happy about it as she was. When Thomas More didn't show up at her coronation ceremony, she was furious with him. It was partly to please Anne that Henry charged his old friend with treason, sent him to the Tower of London and then put him to death.

William Tyndale and Thomas More weren't the only ones Henry put to death. No King of England executed more people than Henry VIII. Not even his own wives were safe from the executioner, as two of them were about to find out.

Divorced, Beheaded, Died...

After her wedding, Anne Boleyn went straight to work on her most important job: giving Henry children. Fortunately, Anne got pregnant right away; and the pregnancy went well. After all his troubles, Henry felt sure that he was about to get the son he'd been wanting for so long.

How wrong he was. Imagine Henry's disappointment when Anne's baby turned out to be another daughter: **Elizabeth Tudor**. What came next was even more disappointing. After Elizabeth, Anne's babies started dying— just as Catherine's had died!

After two lost babies, Henry feared that Anne would never give him the son he needed so desperately. He decided to get rid of her— but not in the long, drawn-out way he had gotten rid of Catherine. They were in their third year of marriage in 1536, when the king's men came to arrest Anne!

What was Anne's crime? According to the king's men, she had been caught carrying on with other men. To betray the king in that way was **treason**, a crime that carried the death penalty. Anne went from a

Sir Thomas More was a special kind of scholar called a **Renaissance humanist**. Humanists believed the opposite of what Protestant leaders like Luther, Zwingli and Calvin believed. Protestants taught original sin— the idea that all people were born into sin. But humanists taught that people were born good, and could become even better.

In other words, humanists believed in human progress. Thomas More believed that with good government, people could build a much better world— maybe even a heaven on earth.

That was the thinking behind More's best-known book, a work of fiction called *Utopia*. Utopia was a make-believe island where good government had already solved all of society's problems.

Since most of society's problems started with greed, the government of Utopia removed the reasons for greed. For example, there was no private property on Utopia. Instead, everyone shared everything.

VTOPIAE INSVLAE FIGVRA

An illustration from Sir Thomas More's *Utopia*

beautiful palace to an ugly cell in the Tower of London, where she waited to hear what Henry's court would decide.

The court wasn't sure what to do. On the one hand, the evidence against Anne was weak. On the other hand, everyone knew that the king wanted his wife dead. Since Henry VIII always got what he wanted, the court finally gave it to him— sentencing Anne Boleyn to death.

The whole ugly business took less than three weeks. The only mercy Henry showed his wife was this: Instead of his usual executioner, Henry hired an expert swordsman from France. That way, he could be sure Anne's head would come off in one stroke.

Poor Anne had been dead less than two weeks when her heartless widow married one of her **ladies-in-waiting**. Henry's third wife, Jane Seymour, was just what Henry was looking for: quiet, respectful and able to have sons. In October 1537, Jane finally gave Henry the boy he had been wanting for so long: **Edward Tudor**.

A **lady-in-waiting** was a helper who waited on a queen.

Sadly, the stress of giving birth ruined Jane Seymour's health. She died just days after she gave birth to Edward.

Jane Seymour, 3rd wife to Henry VIII. Jane gave birth to Edward Tudor, the future King Edward VI.

Around this time, Henry VIII started having health problems of his own. One problem was that he was getting on towards fifty years old. Another problem was that in 1536, when Anne Boleyn was still alive, Henry suffered a bad fall in a jousting tournament. Before his fall, Henry was strong, athletic and handsome. After his fall, Henry started to grow lazy, fat— and rather hideous.

Henry's next marriage had to do with politics. With the Reformation going on, there was always the danger of war between Protestant countries and Catholic ones. Since England was now Protestant, and so were parts of Germany, Henry's advisers wanted him to marry a German princess. That way, England would be sure to have German allies if it needed them.

Politics or no, Henry still wanted a beautiful young bride. To find one, he hired one of the best painters in Europe: a portrait artist called **Hans Holbein the Younger**. Holbein's job was to trek around Europe, painting portraits of princesses for Henry to approve.

Henry finally settled on a portrait he liked. The woman he wanted was Anne of Cleves, daughter to the Duke of Cleves. Cleves was a good-sized German duchy on the Rhine River, over near the Netherlands.

What with painting portraits and arranging the marriage, a long time passed before Anne came to England. By the time she did, the politics had changed— which meant that England didn't need German allies as much as before.

Hans Holbein the Younger's portrait of Anne of Cleves, 4th wife to King Henry VIII.

There was also a second problem. When Henry finally met Anne in person, he was disappointed in her— deciding that she wasn't as beautiful as her portrait.

Disappointed or no, Henry still married Anne; for the Germans would have been furious with him if he hadn't. After the wedding, though, he immediately looked for a way out of his unwanted marriage.

Henry soon found one. A few months into the marriage, Anne admitted that she had once been betrothed to a German prince. She also admitted she had never broken that betrothal properly, which meant that she never should have married Henry. True or not, it was all the excuse Henry needed to annul the marriage. To save Anne embarrassment, Henry gave her a comforting title: "The King's Beloved Sister." He also gave her a comfortable income.

After Anne of Cleves, Henry went back to English brides. His fifth wife, Catherine Howard, was a lively young woman who had been a lady-in-waiting to Anne of Cleves. Henry and Catherine were married less than three weeks after his divorce from Anne.

By this time, Henry was far too old and fat to make a good husband for a lively young woman. Less than two years into her marriage, Catherine Howard was accused of the same crime Anne Boleyn was accused of: carrying on with other men. She was not yet twenty years old when Henry had her beheaded.

Catherine Howard, 5th wife to King Henry VIII

Henry's sixth and last wife, Catherine Parr, was the opposite of Catherine Howard. Where Catherine Howard was young and silly, Catherine Parr was mature and thoughtful. Even so, Catherine Parr almost didn't survive the murderous Henry VIII.

The problem this time was religion. Catherine Parr happened to be a strong Protestant— unlike Henry, who still loved some of the old Catholic traditions. The year before Henry died, some of his Catholic-leaning friends almost talked him into arresting Catherine. If Catherine hadn't talked Henry out of it, then she might have wound up just like Anne Boleyn and Catherine Howard!

Catherine Parr, 6th and last wife to King Henry VIII

The Six Wives of King Henry VIII

1. **Catherine of Aragon** (married 1509 - 1533)
2. **Anne Boleyn** (married 1533 - 1536)
3. **Jane Seymour** (married 1536 - 1537)
4. **Anne of Cleves** (married 1540)
5. **Catherine Howard** (married 1540 - 1541)
6. **Catherine Parr** (married 1543 - 1547)

One way to remember the names of Henry's six wives is with this saying: "Henry married three Catherines and two Annes, but only one Jane."

One way to remember the fates of Henry's wives is with this verse: "Divorced, beheaded, died; divorced, beheaded, survived."

Both Catherine Parr and Anne of Cleves outlived Henry VIII, who was fifty-five years old when he died in 1547.

The Church of England never gave up some of its old Catholic traditions. For example, both Catholics and Anglicans still fast during Lent— the forty-day season leading up to Easter.

Lent begins with a special day called Ash Wednesday. The Tuesday before Lent is called Shrove Tuesday; for that is when Anglicans are shriven of their sins. To be shriven is to confess and receive forgiveness, which is how Anglicans prepare for Lent.

Shrove Tuesday is also called Pancake Tuesday. On the last Tuesday before Lent, Anglicans eat a big meal to get ready for all the fasting ahead. Since eggs, butter and fat are all forbidden during Lent, they eat a lot of pancakes that day. That way, they use up all the ingredients that might otherwise go to waste.

The French version of Shrove Tuesday is *Mardi Gras*, or "Fat Tuesday." Catholic countries like France often had a longer, rowdier celebration in the weeks leading up to Lent.

Like many kings of his day, Henry VIII made silver-colored coins with his face on them. To save money on these coins, Henry's mint first struck them out of cheap copper, and then coated them with a thin layer of precious silver.

After passing from purse to purse for a while, the silver started to wear off. The copper underneath started to show through, especially on Henry's nose. This explains how King Henry VIII got an unflattering nickname: "Old Coppernose."

A coin from the reign of King Henry VIII, photo courtesy Classical Numismatic Group, Inc.

Bodies of Water around the British Isles

A trip around the British Isles takes one through several bodies of water. The biggest, of course, is the **Atlantic Ocean** to the west. The next biggest is the **North Sea**, which lies to the east and north. Besides these, there are also:

➤ The **Irish Sea**, which lies between Ireland and northern England.

➤ The **Celtic Sea**, between Ireland and southern England.

➤ **St. George's Channel**, which connects the Irish Sea to the Celtic Sea.

➤ **Bristol Channel**, a big inlet between Wales and southwestern England. The British Isles' biggest river, the **Severn**, flows into Bristol Channel.

➤ The **English Channel**, which lies between England and France. The narrowest section of the English Channel is called the **Strait of Dover**. This is where most travelers go to cross over from England to France and back.

BRITISH ISLES

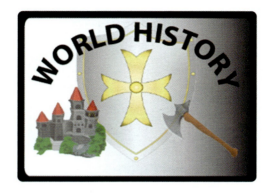

The Protestant Josiah

In Chapter 31, we read that King Henry VIII had three children from three different wives. The oldest, **Mary Tudor**, was born to Henry's first wife: Catherine of Aragon. The middle child, **Elizabeth Tudor**, was born to Henry's second wife: Anne Boleyn. And the youngest, **Edward Tudor**, was born to Henry's third wife: Jane Seymour. Between the three of them, the children of Henry VIII decided which the Church of England would be: Catholic or Protestant.

Mary wanted it to be Catholic. Why? Because her mother was a daughter to Ferdinand and Isabella, the "Catholic Monarchs" of Spain. Coming from family like that, Mary could never be anything but Catholic.

Elizabeth and Edward were different. Since they were both children when their mothers died, they were mostly raised by their father's sixth wife: Catherine Parr, who was as Protestant as Catherine of Aragon was Catholic.

The Old Palace at Hatfield House in Hertfordshire, just north of London. Elizabeth and Edward Tudor grew up at Hatfield House.

Mary was seventeen years old in 1533, when little Elizabeth was born. The grown-up princess had many reasons to resent her baby sister. First, Mary's father had divorced her mother to marry Elizabeth's mother. Second, Mary's father had split with her beloved Catholic Church— mostly for the same reason. Third, the divorce made Mary an **illegitimate child**— which meant that she wasn't a princess anymore. Instead of having a palace and servants of her own, Mary became a servant in Elizabeth's palace.

Elizabeth's turn was coming, though. She was still a toddler in 1536, the year Henry beheaded her mother! The disgraceful death of Anne Boleyn made Elizabeth an illegitimate child, just like Mary.

An **illegitimate child** is one who is born while his or her parents aren't married.

It was in 1537 that Henry's third child came along. As the only boy, Edward Tudor was sure to be the next monarch. Henry VIII would do anything for Edward, whom he called his "whole realm's most priceless jewel."

Kings and Queens from the Royal House of Tudor

1. King Henry VII
(Reigned 1485 – 1509)

2. King Henry VIII
(Reigned 1509 – 1547)

3. King Edward VI
(Reigned 1547 – 1553)

4. Lady Jane Grey
(Reigned 9 days in 1553)

5. Queen Mary I
(Reigned 1553 – 1558)

6. Queen Elizabeth I
(Reigned 1558 – 1603)

In fact, Henry even fought a war for Edward. Starting in 1543, England battled Scotland in a war with a funny name: the **War of the Rough Wooing**. The person being **wooed** was a little girl called **Mary, Queen of Scots**.

> To be **wooed** is to be courted for marriage.

Mary was the only child of King James V of Scotland. She was just six days old when her father died, leaving his baby daughter on the throne of Scotland.

Edward Tudor in 1547, around the time his father Henry VIII died

From the moment Mary was born, Henry VIII wanted her as a bride for his son. English kings had been trying to take over Scotland for more than 200 years now. If Edward Tudor married Mary, Queen of Scots, then Henry might finally succeed— without firing a shot!

Mary, Queen of Scots (1542 – 1587)

Of course, the Scots knew just what Henry was up to; and they didn't want him taking over Scotland. Instead of handing over their queen, the Scots asked the French to help them.

The price of France's help was the Queen herself. Little Mary, Queen of Scots went off to live in France, where she would grow up to marry a French prince. Meanwhile, the French helped the Scots fight the English off. Henry never took over Scotland, much as he wanted to.

ϯ ϯ

The mean, murderous old Henry VIII finally died in 1547. Edward Tudor was just nine years old when he took his father's place— becoming **King Edward VI**.

> As a young prince, Edward Tudor was probably assigned a **whipping boy** to take punishments for him. Most teachers in those days didn't hesitate to whip students who misbehaved. But no one dared whip Edward Tudor; for all were terrified of Edward's father, King Henry VIII. Instead of whipping Edward himself, Edward's teachers whipped his whipping boy.
>
> Teachers often chose a prince's best friend to be his whipping boy. That way, the prince would try harder to behave— if only to save his friend from suffering.

> A **regent** is an officer who runs the government for a king who is too young, or too sick, to run it for himself.

Since Edward was too young to run the country himself, a Council of **Regents** ran it for him. The leader of this council was called the Lord Protector of England. While his job lasted, the Lord Protector would be the most powerful man in England— far more powerful than the boy king.

These were dangerous times for the House of Tudor. With Henry VIII gone, the Tudors were down to just three people: the little boy Edward, his grown sister Mary, and his teenaged sister Elizabeth. By this time, Mary and Elizabeth were princesses again. Even so, no woman had ever ruled England in her own name. If anything should happen to Edward VI, then some nobleman from another family might easily take his place— especially if that nobleman was married to Mary or Elizabeth. A strange character called **Thomas Seymour** tried to do just that.

The king's mother, Jane Seymour, had two older brothers: Edward Seymour and Thomas Seymour. As uncles of the king, both Seymours were on the Council of Regents. As the older uncle, Edward Seymour got the top job: Lord Protector. Like many younger brothers, Thomas was terribly jealous of his older brother. He would do almost anything to take Edward Seymour's place.

It so happened that Thomas Seymour was close friends with the sixth and last wife of Henry VIII, Catherine Parr. In fact, Thomas and Catherine were so close that they had almost married back in 1543. But when Henry decided to marry Catherine, he sent Thomas overseas to get him out of the way.

Thomas returned to England in 1547, the year Henry died. Later that year, Thomas took his first steps toward taking his brother's place. Unfortunately, Thomas took some crazy missteps along the way:

➤ Just four months after Henry VIII died, Thomas married his old friend Catherine Parr. Loyal Englishmen saw this quick wedding as an insult to the king's memory.

➤ After the wedding, Thomas moved in with Catherine. Since Elizabeth was still living with Catherine at the time, Thomas also moved in with Elizabeth. Even though Thomas had just married Catherine, he flirted shamelessly with the 14-year-old Elizabeth. He may have offered to marry Elizabeth, and her sister Mary too— even though he was already married to Catherine! Catherine finally sent Elizabeth off to keep her husband away from her.

➤ Thomas also tried to get closer to Edward. As a member of the Council of Regents, Thomas knew that the young king wanted more money than he was given. He secretly gave Edward extra money, trying to get on his good side.

➤ To get that extra money, Thomas made secret deals with pirates. This Thomas could easily do; for he was not only a regent, but also Lord High Admiral of the Royal Navy.

Thomas Seymour (1508? – 1549), uncle to King Edward VI

➤ When Thomas' brother found out about the secret pirate deals, he got ready to arrest Thomas. This led to the craziest misstep yet. When Thomas heard that he was about to be arrested, he tried to sneak into the king's bedroom— carrying a loaded pistol! Just what Thomas was planning to do there, no one knows for sure. Whatever it was, it didn't work out— for as he tried to sneak in, he accidentally woke one of the king's dogs. To keep the dog off him, Thomas pulled out his pistol and shot it!

Imagine trying to explain why you have just shot the king's dog outside the king's bedroom in the middle of the night! Nothing Thomas could say made any difference. He went straight to the Tower of London, where he was beheaded for treason in March 1549.

The fact that Edward VI was only a boy didn't stop him from playing a big part in the **English Reformation**. It was Henry VIII who split the Church of England from the Catholic Church. But it was Edward VI who made the Church of England truly Protestant— with help from his friend **Thomas Cranmer, Archbishop of Canterbury.**

> The **English Reformation** was the long process of splitting the Church of England from the Catholic Church (Chapter 31).

The Archbishop of Canterbury was the head bishop of all English churches. Thomas Cranmer became archbishop in 1532, when Henry VIII was still king. One of his first jobs as archbishop was to help Henry divorce Catherine of Aragon (Chapter 31).

Cranmer also had a more important job: guiding the Church of England through the Protestant Reformation. After Henry's split with Rome, the Church of England had a chance to become a whole new kind of church. Thomas Cranmer helped decide what that new church would be.

Like Luther and Zwingli, Cranmer wanted his new church to be more like the churches in the Bible. But Cranmer had to be careful; for he knew that Henry wouldn't hesitate to behead him if he made a mistake.

Henry was happy to make certain changes. For example, Henry shut down all of England's monasteries— partly because he wanted their money for his royal treasury (Chapter 31).

Archbishop Thomas Cranmer (1489 – 1556)

Henry VIII handing the Great Bible to his bishops

Henry also brought a new Bible to the Church of England. The year 1539 saw the first printing of the **Great Bible**— the first English Bible ever authorized by a King of England. The Great Bible was mostly the work of William Tyndale, whom we met in Chapter 31. Oddly enough, Henry executed Tyndale three years before the Great Bible came out!

But the biggest changes to the Church of England came under King Edward VI. Unlike Henry, Edward was a strong Protestant who wanted nothing to do with the old Catholic traditions. He believed that those traditions were the very opposite of what God wanted.

The tradition Edward hated most was the **Mass**, which was how Catholics celebrated Holy Communion. In Protestant eyes, all the bells and incense in the Mass made it more like a pagan sacrifice than Christian worship. Protestants also didn't believe in a Catholic idea called transubstantiation. Catholics believed that during the Mass, the bread and wine of communion truly changed into the body and blood of Jesus Christ (Chapter 30).

Edward's answer was to outlaw the Mass. In 1549, Parliament passed the first of several laws called the **Act of Uniformity**. Starting then, no English church was to hold a Catholic Mass. Instead, they were to follow the Protestant communion service in a new book by Thomas Cranmer: the **Book of Common Prayer**.

The **Book of Common Prayer** was a worship book written for the Church of England by Archbishop Thomas Cranmer. Besides the communion service, the Book of Common Prayer also had services for baptisms, weddings, funerals and more— all written out word-for-word, exactly as Cranmer wanted them spoken.

Although the Book of Common Prayer has changed over the years, the Church of England still uses parts of Cranmer's work. So do two churches that sprang from the Church of England: the Episcopal Church and the Methodist Church.

Banning the Mass was just one of many things Edward did to make the Church of England more Protestant. He also ordered all services spoken in English, not Latin. And unlike Catholic priests, English priests were free to marry and have children— just like all other Christians.

ᛏᛏᛏᛏᛏᛏᛏᛏᛏᛏᛏᛏᛏᛏᛏᛏᛏᛏᛏᛏᛏᛏᛏᛏᛏᛏᛏᛏᛏᛏᛏᛏᛏᛏ

The story of King Edward VI has a sad ending. In early 1553, when he was still just fifteen years old, Edward came down with a bad cough. Instead of getting better, Edward got worse. By May, Edward's doctors had to admit the awful truth: that the young King of England would soon die.

After months of miserable health, Edward didn't mind dying. But he did mind what would happen to the Church of England after he died. Since Edward had no children, his oldest sister Mary would inherit his throne. Since Mary was Catholic, the Church of England would be Catholic again— after everything Edward had done to make it Protestant!

Edward couldn't let that happen. To save his beloved church, Edward tried to change the law just before he died. Instead of leaving the throne to his Catholic sister, Edward tried to leave it to a Protestant: a sixteen-year-old called the **Lady Jane Grey**.

Who on Earth was Jane Grey, and how could she possibly claim the throne of England? The first answer is that on her mother's side, Jane was a granddaughter to the youngest sister of King Henry VIII. In other words, Jane was Edward's first cousin, one generation removed— which gave her a small claim to the throne.

The second answer may be more important. Besides being a cousin to the king, Jane Grey was also the wife of **Guildford Dudley**— son of **John Dudley**, head of the Council of Regents.

By this time, Lord Protector Edward Seymour had been beheaded for treason— just like his brother Thomas Seymour (above). The new head of the Council of Regents was John Dudley, Duke of Northumberland. Since the king was so sick, John Dudley had a lot to say about the king's decisions.

Like Edward VI, John Dudley wanted Jane Grey to be queen because she was a Protestant. But Dudley also had another reason for wanting Jane Grey: because she was his daughter-in-law. If Jane became queen, then Dudley's son might become king through her. At the very least, Dudley's grandson would be king. Then the dying House of Tudor would give way to a new royal house: the House of Dudley!

Alas for the Dudleys, things didn't work out that way.

> Thomas Cranmer liked to call King Edward VI the **"Protestant Josiah."** The first Josiah was a young king of Judah, the southern kingdom of the Israelites. Josiah's grandfather, King Manasseh of Judah, was a wicked king who led his people away from God— teaching them to worship idols instead. When the good King Josiah came along, he led his people back to God. That was Thomas Cranmer's hope for the boy King Edward VI: that he would lead his people back to God, just as Josiah had.

A possible portrait of Lady Jane Grey, the "Nine Days Queen" (1537 – 1554)

Guildford Dudley (1535? – 1554)

Bloody Mary

John Dudley's troubles started on July 9, 1553, three days after Edward VI died. That was when Dudley finally told Jane Grey that she was the new Queen of England. Before then, Jane hadn't even known that Edward was dead!

The reason Jane didn't know was because Dudley had been keeping Edward's death secret. Most people expected Edward's sister, Mary Tudor, to be the next queen. If Jane was to be queen instead, then Dudley would have to do something about Mary— and fast.

He was already working on it. Dudley had sent for Mary days before, asking her to come see her brother one last time before he died. Once Mary reached London, she would be at Dudley's mercy. If Mary tried to claim the throne, then Dudley could lock her in the Tower of London until the trouble blew over.

John Dudley, Duke of Northumberland (1504? – 1553)

Alas for Dudley, Mary had more friends than he knew. Before Mary reached London, her friends warned her that she was walking into a trap— that Edward was already dead, that Jane Grey was already queen, and that Dudley meant to lock her up as soon as she reached London!

Mary's friends may have saved her life. Instead of going to London, she went to the east coast of England. From there, she had two choices. If she could, then she would raise an army and take the throne by force. If she couldn't, then she could still run to her relatives across the North Sea. As a granddaughter to Ferdinand and Isabella, she had many Catholic relatives who would gladly protect her.

As it turned out, Mary had no trouble raising an army. All Englishmen knew Mary's story; and most of them felt sorry for the rough way her father had treated her. On the other hand, few Englishmen had even heard of Jane Grey.

Meanwhile, John Dudley was having trouble raising an army of his own. When the Council of Regents heard about Mary's army, it immediately turned its back on him. Sensing that all was lost, Dudley gave up without a fight. He was beheaded for treason a month later.

As for poor Jane Grey, she went from a grand palace to a miserable cell in the Tower of London. She had been queen, sort of, for just about nine days— from July 10 – 19, 1553. Meanwhile, Mary Tudor became **Queen Mary I of England**— the first woman ever to rule England in her own name.

Queen Mary I, a.k.a. Bloody Mary, entering London with her sister Elizabeth Tudor

The five years of Mary's reign were terrible years for English Protestants. Before Mary, many Englishmen weren't sure whether they wanted to be Catholic or Protestant. After Mary, most Englishmen were quite sure that they didn't want to be Catholic!

What was so bad about Mary? First, she undid everything Henry VIII and Edward VI had done. After almost twenty years of independence, the Church of England went back under the Catholic Church. The Catholic Mass came back, and the Book of Common Prayer was set aside.

That was only the beginning. As a good Catholic, Mary wanted a Catholic husband to give her Catholic sons. That way, a Catholic would be sure to inherit her throne when she was gone. The husband Mary chose was one of the most powerful Catholics alive: **Philip of Spain**.

Philip was the son of King Charles I of Spain, who was also Holy Roman Emperor Charles V. By this time, Charles was getting ready to retire— leaving Philip to take over as King of Spain. If Mary and Philip were married, then Philip would become King of England too— which would make him even more powerful than he already was.

Queen Mary I, a.k.a. "Bloody Mary"

Even Catholic Englishmen thought that was a terrible idea. The Spanish Empire was already huge, and getting huger. If Philip became King of England, then poor England might be swallowed up by Spain— losing its independence forever! As for Protestants, they were all dead set against the marriage— which was why they started **Wyatt's Rebellion**.

Sir Thomas Wyatt was a well-known military man and Member of Parliament. Like most Englishmen of his day, Wyatt had been born Catholic. But Wyatt had also been to Spain, where he had seen the awful **Spanish Inquisition** with his own eyes (Chapter 23). After a sight like that, the last thing Wyatt wanted was a Spanish King of England— least of all Philip of Spain, whose family had started the Inquisition.

The plan for Wyatt's Rebellion was to replace Mary with her younger sister: Elizabeth Tudor. If the rebels could manage that, then their troubles would be over— or so

Sir Thomas Wyatt (1521 – 1554)

they hoped. For Elizabeth was a Protestant; and no good Protestant would ever marry Philip of Spain.

The Spanish Inquisition was a cruel church court set up by Ferdinand and Isabella to hunt down heretics. The Inquisition was famous for two things: torturing people until they confessed to heresy, and then burning them to death.

Alas for Wyatt, his rebellion had hardly started when Mary's spies found out about it. He was on his way to fight when he was captured, and then later beheaded.

Wyatt's Rebellion was also bad news for Jane Grey. Although Jane had nothing to do with the rebellion, her father Henry Grey did— which put them both in trouble. Jane was watching from a window one awful day in February 1554, when her husband Guildford Dudley was beheaded. Later that same day, she was beheaded herself. She was not yet eighteen years old.

Queen Mary I of England married Philip of Spain later that same year, 1554. The year after that, Sir Thomas Wyatt's worst fears came true. With Philip of Spain at her side, Mary brought her own version of the Spanish Inquisition to England. This is when Mary earned the nickname she would carry into history: Bloody Mary.

"The Execution of Lady Jane Grey" by artist Paul Delaroche. The helpful priest at Jane's side is guiding her to the executioner's block, which poor Jane can't see through her blindfold.

A **heresy** is a false teaching that threatens the Church.

In 1555, Mary ordered her church courts to put Protestants on trial for **heresy**. Any Protestant who wanted to save himself had to swear two things: that the Catholic Church was the only true Church of God, and that the Catholic Mass was the right way to celebrate communion. Just as in Roman times, Christians faced a tough choice. They could either lie to save themselves, or suffer one of the worst punishments imaginable: being burned alive.

The poor Protestants who Mary killed are called the Marian martyrs. Exactly how many Marian martyrs there were, no one now knows for sure. Some say no more than about three hundred; while others say far more.

Two Marian martyrs in a sketch from Foxe's book

Fortunately, Mary didn't catch every Protestant on her list. There were some who escaped overseas, finding safety in Protestant cities like Geneva. There they sat, waiting to see if things would ever get better back home. These too got a name: the Marian exiles.

A **martyr** is someone who dies for his or her faith.

An **exile** is someone who can't live in his home country.

The stories of the Marian martyrs were told by a Marian exile. In 1563, a writer called John Foxe published the first edition of his life's work: Foxe's Book of Martyrs. This long book is packed with details about the great faith of the Marian martyrs, and how they suffered and died for that faith. One of the best-known stories in Foxe's book is about an old friend of King Edward's: Thomas Cranmer, the Protestant Archbishop of Canterbury.

Mary Tudor had twenty years' worth of reasons to hate Thomas Cranmer. The first reason came in 1533, when he helped her father divorce her mother. The worst reason came in 1553, when he tried to help the Lady Jane Grey become Queen of England. More reasons came later that year, when he tried to stop Mary from turning the Church of England Catholic again. Mary soon grew so tired of Cranmer that she had him locked up and put on trial.

Cranmer's trial was long and miserable. The priests who handled it kept promising that all would be forgiven, if he would only take back all the ugly things he'd said about Catholics. After two torturous years, Cranmer finally did what they asked. With his right hand, he signed a confession saying just what Catholics wanted him to say.

If the Catholic Church had followed its own law, then Cranmer's confession would have saved his life. But the new Archbishop of Canterbury wanted to make an example of Cranmer. He wanted him to tell the world how wrong Protestants were, out loud and in public. The plan was to let Cranmer preach one last sermon, and then put him to death like all the other Marian martyrs.

This woodblock illustration from *Foxe's Book of Martyrs* shows Thomas Cranmer thrusting his right hand into Bloody Mary's fire

The archbishop thought he knew what was coming. Before the day of the sermon, Cranmer wrote out every word he planned to say— all about how wrong Protestants were.

But when the big day arrived, Cranmer didn't preach the sermon he'd written. Instead, he said that he'd only signed that Catholic confession to save his life. Now that he was about to die anyway, he could tell the world what he truly believed: that Catholics were wrong, and Protestants were right!

Naturally, the archbishop was furious. He ordered Cranmer burned alive that same day. As the flames rose in front of him, Cranmer bravely thrust his right hand into the hot fire. Despite the unbearable pain, he left it there as it blackened and burned— to punish it for signing a Catholic confession that he didn't believe.

Bloody Mary went right on torturing and burning Protestants as long as she lived. Fortunately for Protestants, Bloody Mary didn't live very long.

One day in November 1558, a horseman raced into a part of London called Smithfield. Smithfield was where many Protestants went to die in Mary's fires. Several of them were tied to stakes there that day, waiting for Mary's executioners to set them alight.

Imagine their relief when the horseman shouted his big news: that Bloody Mary had just died! Since Mary had signed their death warrants, the warrants expired when Mary died— which meant that the Protestants could go on living!

An **ermine** is a kind of weasel with special fur. Ermine fur is brown in summer; but in winter, it turns white to blend in with the snow. The only part that isn't white is the tip of the tail, which stays black year-round.

White fur was so rare and valuable that ermine became a symbol of royalty. In cold countries like England, royals wore beautiful coronation robes lined with warm, white ermine fur. The short black lines in these robes' linings were the ermines' black tails, stitched in right alongside their white fur.

Queen Elizabeth I in a coronation robe lined with ermine fur

CHURCH HISTORY

The Anabaptist Movement

Sad to say, Bloody Mary wasn't the only one who burned Protestants alive. Both Protestants and Catholics burned a group of Christians called **Anabaptists**.

The Anabaptist story starts with the Bible. Before the Reformation, most Christians never read the Bible— nor even heard much of it. But things were different now. Between the Reformation and the printing press, more people were reading the Bible than ever before. The problem was, not everyone who read the Bible understood it the same way.

> **Anabaptist** means "to baptize again." Instead of baptizing people as infants, Anabaptists only baptized people who were old enough to understand the gospel. Since most of the people they baptized had already been baptized as infants, their enemies called them "re-baptizers."

Anabaptists were especially interested in the **Sermon on the Mount**, which Jesus delivers in Matthew 5 – 7. They thought a lot about Matthew 5:33-34, where Jesus says:

> "… you have heard that it was said to the people long ago, 'Do not break your oath, but fulfill to the Lord the vows you have made.' But I tell you, do not swear an oath at all…"

Most Christians didn't take Jesus' words literally. They assumed that some oaths were necessary, especially the oath of fealty to one's king or queen. To Anabaptists, though, Jesus meant exactly what He said: that true Christians must never swear any oath for any reason.

Another example comes from Matthew 5:38-39, where Jesus says:

> "You have heard that it was said, 'Eye for eye, and tooth for tooth.' But I tell you, do not resist an evil person. If anyone slaps you on the right cheek, turn to them the other cheek also."

Again, most Christians didn't take Jesus' words literally; for they assumed that some kinds of fighting were necessary. If criminals attacked Christians, then surely Christian police must protect them? And if an enemy attacked a Christian kingdom, then surely Christian soldiers must defend that kingdom? To Anabaptists, though, Jesus meant exactly what he said: that true Christians must never fight for any reason.

"Sermon on the Mount"
by Carl Bloch

Another Anabaptist idea had to do with kingdoms and loyalties. In Anabaptist eyes, there was no such thing as a Christian kingdom on Earth. All true Christians belonged to just one kingdom: The Kingdom of Heaven. Since no one can serve two masters (Matthew 6:24), Anabaptists chose to serve their heavenly king— which meant ignoring their worldly kings.

As citizens of heaven, Anabaptists cut ties with all worldly kingdoms. Since they wouldn't swear oaths, they couldn't swear in court like everyone else. And since they wouldn't fight, they couldn't be policemen, nor serve in armies like everyone else.

In most Christians' eyes, this made all Anabaptists traitors! Those who refused to fight for their countries were tortured and killed wherever they lived. Many, many Anabaptists died horrible deaths for their faith.

> Just as *Foxe's Book of Martyrs* tells stories of the Marian martyrs, so a book called **Martyrs' Mirror** tells stories of the many Anabaptist martyrs who died for their faith.
>
> The modern-day **Mennonite Church** is descended from those early Anabaptist churches. Its name comes from a leader called <u>Menno</u> Simons, who lived from 1496 - 1561.

The Last of the Tudors

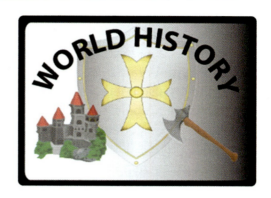

In Chapter 32, we read how John Dudley tried to trick Mary Tudor. Dudley was head of the Council of Regents for Mary's brother, King Edward VI. When Edward was about to die, Dudley sent Mary an urgent message— asking her to come to London and see her brother one last time. But that wasn't really why Dudley wanted Mary in London. The real reason was that Dudley didn't want Mary to be queen. When she got to London, he planned to lock her up and set Jane Grey on the throne instead!

What we didn't read is that Dudley also laid a trap for Mary's sister: Elizabeth Tudor. He sent the same message to Elizabeth that he sent to Mary, asking her to come and see her brother one last time.

Neither sister was fooled. When Dudley's messenger came to Elizabeth's door, she pretended that she was too sick to travel. As for Mary, she started raising an army against Dudley. When the Council of Regents took Mary's side, Dudley surrendered without a fight— leaving Mary on top. She rode into London on August 3, 1553, ready to be crowned Queen of England.

Mary didn't ride alone that day. Her sister Elizabeth rode into London right beside her, showing all the world that she wanted Mary to be queen. For now, it looked like Mary and Elizabeth were great friends— even though Mary was Catholic, and Elizabeth Protestant.

Meanwhile, Mary started undoing everything her brother had done. As a Catholic queen, she was determined to make the Church of England Catholic again. She was also determined to marry one of the most powerful Catholics in the world: Philip of Spain, son to King Charles I of Spain.

Protestants were just as determined to stop Mary. Her reign was just getting started in January 1554, when Sir Thomas Wyatt led a rebellion against her!

Princess Elizabeth Tudor in her teens

Mary's spies were way ahead of Wyatt. They started going through his mail, hoping to find out what he was up to. They soon found a letter that explained everything. Wyatt was planning to get rid of the Catholic Mary, and set the Protestant Elizabeth in her place.

Of all the details in Wyatt's letter, the most interesting one was the name on the envelope. It was addressed to Elizabeth!

Naturally, Mary's spies suspected that Elizabeth was part of Wyatt's Rebellion. She awoke to the sound of them pounding on her door. Pretending to be sick did Elizabeth no good this time. The queen's men hauled her off to a most notorious prison: the **Tower of London**.

The trip to the Tower must have been terrifying for Elizabeth. For one thing, the Tower was where her mother had been beheaded. Just like Anne Boleyn, Elizabeth entered the

Tower by the **Traitors' Gate**— a water gate that opened on the Thames River. Noble prisoners were often brought in through the Traitor's Gate, to avoid trouble with the crowds on the streets.

The route to the Traitors' Gate went under the famous **London Bridge**. In those days, London Bridge was a wide stone bridge lined with wooden shops. With Wyatt's Rebellion going on, London Bridge was also lined with something else: the heads of beheaded rebels! Mary's spies set the heads there to remind everyone how the Crown of England punished rebels. Elizabeth may have recognized some of the nobles' heads as she passed by.

Fortunately for Elizabeth, nothing in Wyatt's letter proved that she was involved in Wyatt's Rebellion. All the letter proved was that Wyatt wanted Elizabeth to be queen. Mary's spies questioned Elizabeth day after day, desperate to prove that she had ordered the rebellion. If they had found any proof, then Mary surely would have beheaded her sister. But they never did.

Even so, Elizabeth wasn't out of danger. There were plenty of Catholics who wanted to behead her anyway! Why? Because Elizabeth was the last Protestant Tudor. With her out of the way, there would be no Protestants left to claim the throne.

The Tower of London was a famous castle started by William the Conqueror after the Norman Conquest. King Henry VI died in the Tower of London, as did the Princes in the Tower (Chapter 15).

The Tower of London with the Traitors' Gate opening on the Thames River. London Bridge stands in the background.

Fortunately for Elizabeth, Philip of Spain didn't want her beheaded. Philip feared that he might be blamed for Elizabeth's death, which would make it even harder for him to be King of England. For this reason and others, Mary decided to spare Elizabeth— but only just barely.

After two months in the Tower of London, Elizabeth spent about a year under house arrest. She and Mary got along better after that. But there was always the chance that "Bloody Mary" might change her mind and kill her Protestant sister.

That chance ended in 1558, when Mary died at age forty-two. Since Mary had no children, her sister took her place. The 25-year-old Elizabeth Tudor became Queen Elizabeth I, the last monarch from the royal House of Tudor. This was the start of an important time called the Elizabethan Era.

The Elizabethan Religious Settlement

Elizabeth's first job as queen was to answer a religious question: Was England Catholic or Protestant? This question had been tearing England apart since before Elizabeth was born. It was Henry VIII who broke with the Catholic Church— mostly because he wanted a divorce, and the pope wouldn't give it to him. Henry's son Edward VI made the Church of England strictly Protestant, only to have Mary turn it strictly Catholic again.

CHURCH HISTORY

The years of Mary's reign were some of the worst ever in England. "Bloody Mary" brought her own version of the Spanish Inquisition to England, hunting down Protestants and burning them to death. After that, Protestants and Catholics hated each other more than ever. If Englishmen were ever going to trust each other again, then Elizabeth had to decide: Was England Catholic, Protestant or in between?

Fortunately, Elizabeth was less fussy about religion than either Edward or Mary. She knew that if Protestants and Catholics were going to get along, then they would have to do something neither wanted to do: they would have to **compromise**.

Elizabeth set two main goals for her compromise. First, she wanted all Englishmen to worship together in the same churches. A strong **state church** was one of the keys to a strong country, and Elizabeth knew it. Second, she wanted all Englishmen to be loyal to queen and country.

> To **compromise** is to give away part of what one wants to gain another part.
>
> A **state church** is one that is supported by the government.

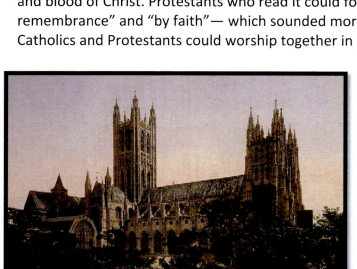

As always, the biggest problem was Holy Communion. How could Catholics and Protestants celebrate communion together? Protestants hated all the bells and incense that went into a Catholic Mass. They also hated transubstantiation— the idea that during the Mass, the bread and wine actually changed into the body and blood of Jesus Christ (Chapter 30). But to Catholics, transubstantiation was the whole point of communion.

Elizabeth's answer was a small change to the **Book of Common Prayer**. In 1559, the year after she became queen, the Church of England updated its Book of Common Prayer. The new communion service said:

> "The body of our Lord Jesus Christ, which was given for thee, preserve thy body and soul… Take and eat this in remembrance that Christ died for thee, and feed on Him in thy heart by faith with thanksgiving" [underlines added].

> The **Book of Common Prayer** was a worship book that was first written for the Church of England by Archbishop Thomas Cranmer in the days of King Edward VI.

Catholics who read this service could focus on the words "feed on Him"— which sounded like the bread and wine really were the body and blood of Christ. Protestants who read it could focus on the words "in remembrance" and "by faith"— which sounded more Protestant. If both sides behaved themselves, then Catholics and Protestants could worship together in peace. The Church of England took a middle way between the two faiths— based partly on the Bible, and partly on the old Catholic traditions.

But there was one idea on which Elizabeth refused to compromise. Like her father before her, Elizabeth wrote a law called the Act of Supremacy (Chapter 31). After five years under Bloody Mary, the Church of England went independent again— completely separate from the Catholic Church. All Englishmen were to forget about the pope and follow their queen.

This means that whatever else it was, the Church of England certainly wasn't Catholic. For a key part of being Catholic was following the pope, which loyal Englishmen no longer did.

Canterbury Cathedral, home of the Archbishop of Canterbury

England versus Spain in the New World

The English got off to a late start in the New World. Like the Spaniards, they sent their first ships to the New World in the late 1400s. But unlike the Spaniards, the English waited almost 100 years to build their first colonies there. And even then, their first colonies didn't last.

The first explorer they sent to the New World wasn't even an Englishman. In 1496, King Henry VII hired an Italian sea captain called **John Cabot** to do for England what Columbus had already done for Spain: find new lands full of riches.

In those days, no one knew that Columbus had discovered a whole New World. Like Columbus, Cabot was trying to reach the Far East by sailing westward around the globe. He had no idea that the Americas were standing in his way.

Cabot added a twist to Columbus' ideas. Columbus tried to circle the globe near the equator; but Cabot wanted to circle it in the north. He figured that the distance around the globe must be shorter in the north, which should mean a shorter trip to the Far East.

Cabot sailed due west from Bristol, England in May 1497. After passing Iceland, then Greenland on his right, Cabot struck land somewhere in northeastern North America— probably in what is now Newfoundland, Canada.

Wherever he may have landed, Cabot claimed the whole east coast of North America for England. Years later, England would base its claim to North America on the idea that John Cabot got there first— before any other European explorer.

〰〰〰〰〰〰〰〰〰〰〰〰〰〰〰〰〰〰〰〰〰〰〰〰〰〰〰〰〰

Meanwhile, the Spanish had already built their first colonies in the West Indies— and were already getting rich. Back in Chapter 25, we read how Columbus took over the gold mines on Hispaniola: by winning the strange **Battle of Santo Cerro**. That battle happened in 1495, two years before John Cabot found Newfoundland. The Spaniards were already mining gold and shipping it home before the English even made it to Newfoundland.

Hispaniola was just the start. Over the next thirty years, the **Spanish conquistadors** conquered all the main islands of the West Indies. Most of Middle America fell in 1521, when Hernan Cortes conquered the Aztec Empire— winning a huge fortune. Part of South America fell in 1532, when Francisco Pizarro conquered the Inca Empire— winning an even huger fortune.

After conquering, the Spaniards switched to mining. Around 1546, they discovered one of the richest silver mines ever: a mountain called Cerro de Potosi, which

From an Italian mural featuring Giovanni Caboto, a.k.a. John Cabot (1450? – 1499?)

> The **Spanish conquistadors** were the soldiers who conquered the West Indies, Middle America and part of South America for the Spanish Empire.

stood in what is now Bolivia. Cerro de Potosi was so full of silver that it almost seemed to be made of the stuff.

Mining was a big part of what made the Spanish Empire so rich. Under a Spanish law called the **Quinto Real**, one-fifth of all treasure went straight to the King of Spain. By the 1550s, the Spaniards were shipping tons of silver and gold from the New World to Spain every year.

> **Quinto Real** is Spanish for "King's Fifth." Spanish law said that one-fifth of all precious metals from the New World automatically went to the King of Spain.

Naturally, shiploads of silver and gold made tempting targets for pirates— which is why the Spaniards didn't send cargo ships alone. Instead, they sent fast warships to protect slow cargo ships along the way. These combinations of cargo ships and warships are called the **Spanish treasure fleets**. By Elizabeth's day, the Spaniards were running one or two treasure fleets to and from the New World every year— making themselves richer all the time.

The richer Spain grew, the more Elizabeth worried. Why? Because Catholic Spain was an enemy to all Protestants. The new King of Spain was Bloody Mary's old husband: Philip of Spain, who was now **King Philip II**. Philip II turned out to be just like his father, Charles I— just as determined to make all countries Catholic again. He was already battling Protestants in the Netherlands, just across the North Sea from England. Elizabeth feared that if she didn't do something to stop the Spanish treasure fleets, then Philip might do the same in England.

> The **Spanish treasure fleets** were groups of ships that carried silver, gold and other treasures from the New World to Spain. Anywhere from 20 - 50 ships traveled together, trying to protect each other from pirates.

The question was, what to do? How could England possibly stop the Spanish treasure fleets without going to war against Spain— which was the very thing Elizabeth didn't want?

The answer was something called a **privateer**. A <u>privateer</u> was the captain of a <u>privately</u>-owned ship with a special mission: to attack enemy trade ships.

Privateers were a bit like pirates, and a bit like navy captains. Like pirates, privateers stole cargoes from enemy ships— which sometimes meant killing enemy sailors. Like navy captains, they attacked their country's enemies on orders from their government.

Spanish ships at the port of Nombre de Dios, Panama

The difference between piracy and privateering was that privateers helped Elizabeth shift the blame. Whenever privateers attacked, the Spaniards sent ambassadors to complain to Elizabeth. But Elizabeth never admitted that her privateers worked for her. Instead, she pretended not to know them. "Whoever attacked you doesn't work for me," she would tell the ambassadors. "He must be a lawless pirate. How very unfortunate for you."

The greatest of all English privateers was **Sir Francis Drake**, who captained a powerful warship called *Golden Hind*. Drake was a patriotic Protestant who hated Catholics all his life— especially Spanish Catholics.

One reason Drake hated Spaniards was because of something that happened in 1568. That year, Drake was aboard one of several English trade ships that showed up in the Spanish port of Veracruz, Mexico. Drake and his friends had brought cargo to sell— a cargo that probably included slaves from Africa.

If the cargo did include slaves, then that would explain what the Spaniards did next. In those days, all slave traders needed special permission from the Crown of Spain. Since no Englishman had permission, the Spaniards let fly with their cannon!

If Drake hadn't known how to swim, then he would have gone down with his ship then and there. Since he did know, he swam to safety— escaping on one of two English ships the Spaniards didn't sink. From that day forward, Drake was a deadly enemy to all Spaniards.

Sir Francis Drake (1540? – 1596)

A few years later, Drake went back to the New World for revenge. One day in 1573, Drake left his ships at anchor while he led an attack inland. His target was a Spanish mule train headed for **Nombre de Dios**, a port in Panama. The mules were staggering under the weight of a huge treasure, all of it bound for a Spanish treasure fleet.

The attack was a huge success. When it was over, Drake and his men made off with twenty or thirty tons of treasure— so much that they couldn't carry it all! They had to bury most of it, and then come back later for their buried pirate treasure. Since England didn't have treasure fleets like Spain's, Queen Elizabeth was extremely pleased with her share of the treasure from Nombre de Dios.

A few years later, Drake set out on the greatest mission of his life. In 1578, Drake sailed around the southern tip of South America— hoping to take the Spaniards by surprise. The Spaniards were getting used to attacks in the Atlantic by now; but no one had ever attacked them in the Pacific before.

Since the Spaniards had never needed defenses in the Pacific, they were all but defenseless there. In a few months, *Golden Hind* was stuffed with stolen treasure. The problem now was, how could Drake get all that treasure home without being captured?

With his ships getting leaky, Drake needed to stop for repairs— while also avoiding the Spaniards. He sailed far to the north, well beyond where the Spaniards usually sailed.

At some hidden spot on the west coast of North America, Drake built a repair base called *Nova Albion*— Latin for "New Britain." Nova Albion may have stood at what is now Drakes Bay, California, just north of San Francisco Bay. Wherever it was, Nova Albion was the first English base on the west coast of North America!

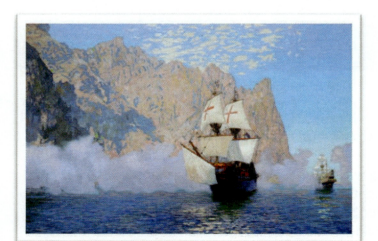

Golden Hind **off the coast of what is now California**

Once he finished his repairs, Drake needed a safe route home. After all he'd stolen from the Spaniards, he wanted to keep well away from all the Spanish ports in South America. Instead of sailing south, this incredible seaman sailed west— all the way around the world!

Drake finally made it back to England in 1580, three years after he set out. The amount of treasure he brought home was astonishing. Queen Elizabeth's share alone was a huge fortune. In fact, it was worth about as much as the taxes she collected from all England that year!

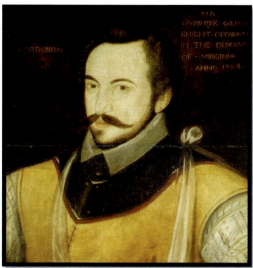

Portrait of Sir Humphrey Gilbert (1539? – 1583)

〰〰〰〰〰〰〰〰〰〰〰〰〰〰〰〰〰〰〰〰〰〰〰〰〰〰〰〰

As far as anyone knows, Francis Drake left no colonists behind at Nova Albion. If he had, then Nova Albion might have been the first English colony in North America. Instead, Nova Albion was a temporary base.

The first English colony wasn't far behind. In August 1583, **Sir Humphrey Gilbert** tried to build a colony on Newfoundland— the island John Cabot discovered back in 1497.

The first thing Cabot had noticed about Newfoundland was all fish there. In places, the codfish were so thick that catching them was ridiculously easy. All a fisherman had to do was lower a basket into the water, and it came up full of cod! From Cabot's day on, fishing ships sailed to Newfoundland every summer— not just English ships, but also French and Dutch ones. They stayed until fall, when they sailed home with holds full of salted fish. Why did no one stay year-round? Because Newfoundland winters were ridiculously cold! The harbors at Newfoundland froze solid every winter, especially on the north side of the island. Although Europeans visited Newfoundland every year, they built no colonies there— until Sir Humphrey Gilbert came along.

In 1578, Queen Elizabeth issued a **royal charter** with Gilbert's name on it. Gilbert had the queen's permission to build an English colony in any "heathen and barbarous lands not… inhabited by Christian people." This charter was to last six years.

Gilbert's six years were almost up before he finally scraped together enough money to go to Newfoundland. Upon reaching Newfoundland in August 1583, Gilbert officially took possession of the big island in the name of the queen. From now on, Gilbert said, Newfoundland belonged to England alone.

Unfortunately, Gilbert couldn't stay in Newfoundland. Like everyone else, he had to go home; for he wasn't ready for the bitter cold of a Newfoundland winter.

> A **royal charter** was a paper granting a certain person permission to do a certain thing in the queen's name.

DISCOVERIES IN THE NORTH

BAFFIN BAY

GREENLAND

Iceland

Norwegian Sea

DAVIS STRAIT

STRAIT OF DENMARK

HUDSON STRAIT

HUDSON BAY

LABRADOR SEA

Scotland

North Sea

Ireland

England

Quebec

LAKE SUPERIOR

Ontario

NEW FOUNDLAND

Gulf of St. Lawrence

St John's

English Channel

France

LAKE HURON

LAKE MICHIGAN

LAKE ONTARIO

LAKE ERIE

Nova Scotia

ATLANTIC OCEAN

Portugal

Spain

NORTH AMERICA

ROANOKE ISLAND

SPAIN

AFRICA

Gilbert was on his way home when tragedy struck. A storm wrecked his small ship, and he was lost at sea. Without Gilbert, the first English colony in the New World disappeared.

〰〰〰〰〰〰〰〰〰〰〰〰〰〰〰〰〰〰〰〰〰〰〰〰〰

With Gilbert gone and his charter expired, Queen Elizabeth issued a new charter for a new colony. This one went to a charming friend of the queen called **Sir Walter Raleigh**. Unlike Gilbert, Walter Raleigh didn't go to the New World himself— at least, not at first. Instead, he paid ship's captains and governors to build his colony for him.

Sir Walter Raleigh (1554? – 1618)

Raleigh chose a risky place for his first colony. It was called **Roanoke Island**; and it stood just off the coast of what is now North Carolina— dangerously close to the West Indies, where the Spanish Empire ruled.

Raleigh had two good reasons for choosing Roanoke Island. First, he wanted his colony to be reasonably close to Spanish shipping— so that English privateers could use it as a base. Second, the natives of Roanoke Island had already found copper there; and Raleigh hoped to find more. Although copper wasn't as pricey as gold or silver, it was still a valuable resource— something the colony might use to pay for itself.

The first group of colonists reached **Roanoke Colony** in July 1585. After poking around a bit, they built a small wooden fort near the northern end of

NATIVE COPPER

the island. Since the island was only about two miles wide and eight miles long, the natives were never far away. Fortunately, most of them were friendly enough at first.

The trouble started when a silver cup that belonged to the colony went missing. The saddest story about Roanoke Colony is how many people had to suffer and die over one silver cup!

Although they didn't know for sure, the colonists believed that a native from a certain village must have stolen the cup. Bent on punishing this crime, the colonists marched into the village and commanded the thief to step forward. When no one stepped forward, they burned the whole village to the ground— along with all the food the villagers had stored for winter!

Needless to say, the natives were a lot less friendly after that. When the ships that had brought the colonists left, the natives attacked the fort!

After fighting off the attack, the colonists were afraid to stay on Roanoke any longer. When Francis Drake happened to drop by with a small fleet, they begged him to take them home— which Drake did. Roanoke Colony was abandoned, for now.

The Roanoke colonists who returned to England with Sir Francis Drake in 1586 carried three important plants with them: tobacco, potatoes and maize (also called Indian corn). All these plants were well-known in the Americas, but completely unknown in England.

The first time Sir Walter Raleigh smoked a bit of tobacco from Roanoke, a servant doused him with water— thinking that his lord's head must have somehow caught fire.

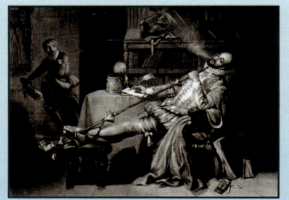
Raleigh's servant preparing to douse his lord's head

A week later, the ships that had brought the colonists returned to find an empty fort. Their captain left fifteen brave soldiers on Roanoke, mostly to keep the fort out of enemy hands. Everyone else sailed off again.

Raleigh's next expedition reached Roanoke the following year, 1587. By now, Raleigh was planning to start a new colony farther north. The only reason the new colonists stopped at Roanoke was to pick up the fifteen soldiers who'd been left at the fort.

Alas, there were no soldiers to pick up! By the time the new colonists reached Roanoke, all that remained of those fifteen soldiers was one human skeleton. The gruesome sight made the colonists glad that Raleigh had given up on Roanoke, and that they wouldn't have to stay in that dreadful place.

Then came a nasty shock. When the colonists tried to board ship again, the captain refused to let them— saying that they would have to stay after all! Just what the captain was thinking, no one knows for sure. The only sure thing is that he abandoned 150-plus colonists and their governor, John White, on Roanoke Island.

The trouble between English and Native American soon started up again. Even so, things weren't all bad. The day of August 18, 1587 brought good news of the first English child born in America: Governor White's granddaughter, baby Virginia Dare.

Baby Virginia Dare being baptized at Roanoke Colony

A little later, though, the trouble grew so bad that Governor White took a bold risk. The colony happened to have a small fishing ship, so small that most people wouldn't dare cross the Atlantic in it. But John White dared. In late 1587, White and a few others set out across the Atlantic in that tiny fishing ship. They somehow made it home to England, where White begged Raleigh to send more help to his troubled colony.

Alas, this was a terrible time to beg any Englishman for help. For by now, war had broken out between England and Spain! See Chapter 34 for more on the terrifying Anglo-Spanish War.

Thanks to the Anglo-Spanish War, White didn't make it back to Roanoke in 1588— nor in 1589. Almost three whole years passed before he finally made it back. He returned to Roanoke Island on August 18, 1590— which just happened to be the third birthday of his granddaughter, little Virginia Dare.

Governor John White of Roanoke Colony at the empty fort

If White was hoping to walk in on his granddaughter's birthday party, then he was disappointed. For when he came to the fort, not one of the 115-plus colonists he'd left behind was anywhere to be seen!

The first place White searched was the fort itself. He noticed that its walls had been strengthened, and its plank houses taken down. Other than that, the only clue White could find was a single word carved on a post: "Croatoan," the name of a nearby island.

Naturally, White wanted to search Croatoan too. But when his fleet captain tried, bad weather him off. Since White had no fleet of his own, his search was over. Neither he nor any other Englishman ever saw the Roanoke colonists again.

So began one of the great mysteries of colonial times: What on Earth happened to the **Lost Colony of Roanoke**? After all the trouble between English and Native American, it would be no surprise if the natives killed the colonists. But then, why were the houses taken down? The natives had never built anything out of planks before. Why would they bother taking down plank houses?

The answer is only another guess. It may be that the Roanoke colonists took their houses down themselves, to turn the planks into ships. If they did build ships and sail for home, then they might have been lost at sea— just like Sir Humphrey Gilbert. Without new evidence, the world will never know.

The Bard of Avon

The Elizabethan Era was a fun time to be English. Besides all the fascinating news about Francis Drake and Walter Raleigh, there were also the plays of William Shakespeare to enjoy!

Shakespeare grew up in Stratford-upon-Avon, a town about 100 miles northwest of London. He was eighteen years old when he married a Stratford woman called Anne Hathaway. Although the couple had three children together, William spent little time with them. For the family stayed in Stratford; while William moved to London to work in theater.

Like most theater men, Shakespeare did a little bit of everything— from acting to singing, dancing and costuming. What he did best, though, was writing plays. In 24 years, from about 1590 – 1613, Shakespeare wrote 37 or more long plays. Most were performed by a theater company that Shakespeare partly owned: the Lord Chamberlain's Men, which often played for the queen herself. Besides plays, Shakespeare also wrote beautiful poetry. Many English teachers consider Shakespeare one of the best English writers ever.

Some Shakespeare plays tell dramatic stories from English history. For example, "The Tragedy of King Richard III" tells how Richard, Duke of Gloucester killed the Princes in the Tower— and how Henry Tudor later killed Richard at the Battle of Bosworth Field (Chapter 15). But historians are careful not to trust Shakespeare too far. Since real life was often too dull for the stage, Shakespeare invented juicy details to liven up his history plays.

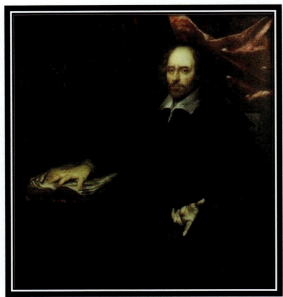

One mark of Shakespeare's greatness is that he left the English language better than he found it. If he needed words that he couldn't find in English, then he simply made them up! In 37 plays, Shakespeare added more than 1700 words to the English language. He also added many well-known English phrases— including "All's well that ends well"; "One fell swoop"; "Brevity is the soul of wit"; "Parting is such sweet sorrow"; "Dead as a doornail"; "For goodness' sake"; "Wild-goose chase"; "Love is blind"; and more.

William Shakespeare (1564 – 1616)

CHAPTER 34:

The Spanish Armada; the Counter-reformation

The Schmalkaldic War

The last time we read about the Reformation in Germany was in Chapter 29, where we covered a lot of diets. A German diet was a government meeting, not a food menu. Starting in the 1520s, every diet was like a tug-of-war between Protestants and Catholics. The Lutherans pulled for freedom of religion; while Holy Roman Emperor Charles V pulled to force all Lutherans back into the Catholic Church.

For a while, it looked like the Lutherans might win. In 1526, the First Diet of Speyer set up a compromise called *cuius regio, eius religio*— Latin for "whoever's region, his religion." In other words, each part of the Holy Roman Empire would follow the religion of the noble who led that part. If a leader was Catholic, then his part of the empire would be Catholic. But if a leader was Lutheran, then his part would be Lutheran.

> A **Lutheran** was a follower of Martin Luther, the first leader of the Protestant Reformation.
>
> **Holy Roman Emperor Charles V** was also King Charles I of Spain.

All that changed at the Second Diet of Speyer, which happened in 1529. That was when Charles V took back his compromise, ordering all Lutherans back into the Catholic Church. As for the heretic Martin Luther, Charles ordered all loyal Catholics to hunt him down, arrest him and burn every copy of his books!

What saved the Lutherans from Charles V was an attack by Muslims. In that same year of 1529, Sultan Suleiman the Magnificent invaded the Holy Roman Empire again— just as he'd done back in 1526. Only this time, Suleiman came a lot closer. As we read in Chapter 20, the Ottomans laid siege to one of Charles' most prized possessions: Vienna, Austria.

Fortunately for Charles, the Siege of Vienna turned out to be a failure. Even so, Suleiman succeeded in making Charles nervous. After the Siege of Vienna, the emperor wanted every soldier he could get— even Lutheran ones. He feared he might not get the Lutherans unless he compromised with them again. Much as he didn't want to, Charles invited them to yet another diet: the Diet of Augsburg, held in 1530.

The Lutherans had big plans for the Diet of Augsburg. They felt strongly about sticking to the Bible, as Martin Luther had taught them. They wanted the emperor to know exactly what they believed, and why they could never go back to the Catholic Church.

Holy Roman Emperor Charles V (1500 – 1558)

This portrait shows signs of the "Habsburg jaw," a jutting jaw that ran in Charles' family.

The best way to tell him was with a new statement of faith. Just before the Diet of Augsburg, a friend of Luther's called Philip Melanchthon wrote down everything good Lutherans were supposed to believe, along with all their complaints against the Catholic Church— in an important document called the **Augsburg Confession**. Five hundred years later, the Augsburg Confession is still the main statement of faith for the Lutheran Church.

A scene from the Diet of Augsburg

Most of the complaints in the Augsburg Confession were ones we covered in Chapter 27. The Lutherans didn't approve of the Renaissance popes, the Catholic Mass, or the fact that Catholic priests couldn't marry. Nor did they approve of monks, nuns, monasteries or nunneries.

Most of all, Lutherans didn't approve of any church that taught salvation by works. The Augsburg Confession said that Lutherans believed in salvation by faith, not by works of the Law.

As always, the Lutherans' ideas came straight from the Bible. For Lutherans also believed in Sola Scriptura— the idea that the Bible alone is inspired by God, and that the Sacred Tradition of the Catholic Church isn't inspired at all.

Charles V didn't care how much Lutherans loved the Bible. What Charles did care about was authority. He wanted all Germans united under one strong state church: the Catholic Church. Since the Lutherans refused to rejoin, and Charles refused to compromise, the Diet of Augsburg went nowhere.

Now the Lutherans were in more trouble than ever. After the Diet of Augsburg, they all knew that Charles V would try to force them back into the Catholic Church someday. To protect themselves, they set up an alliance called the **Schmalkaldic League**. Starting in 1531, the Lutheran parts of the empire all agreed: If Charles V attacked one of them, then they would all fight to protect that one.

> The name **Schmalkaldic League** comes from the town in central Germany where the league was formed: Schmalkalden.

Coat of Arms of Holy Roman Emperor Charles V

It took fifteen years, but it finally happened. In 1546, Charles V sent a huge army against the Schmalkaldic League. The worst battle of the **Scmalkaldic War** was the last one: the **Battle of Muhlberg**, fought in April 1547. When this awful battle was over, about half the Schmalkaldic League's army lay dead!

With losses that bad, the league was powerless to resist the emperor any longer. The war was over, and the Lutherans had lost. If arguments about faith could be settled on the battlefield, then the Schmalkaldic War would have stamped out the Lutheran faith forever!

Alas for Charles, his big win came too late. For by this time, the Lutheran faith had grown too strong to tear out of German hearts. No matter how Charles tried, the Lutheran parts of the Holy Roman Empire simply wouldn't go back to the Catholic Church. In the end, Charles was forced to do what he had refused to do back in 1530: compromise with the Lutherans.

Charles' last compromise was the **Peace of Augsburg**, signed in 1555. After thirty years of arguing and fighting, the Holy Roman Empire finally went back to what it had had in 1526: *cuius regio, eius religio*. If a leader was Catholic, then his part of the Holy Roman Empire would be Catholic. But if a leader was Lutheran, then his part would be Lutheran— with a few exceptions.

If only the Peace of Augsburg could have ended all the trouble between Protestants and Catholics! Alas, it didn't. Starting in 1618, the Holy Roman Empire would be torn by one of the worst wars ever: the Thirty Years' War.

But that was too far in the future for Charles to see. For now, the Peace of Augsburg was his cue to retire. After all, he'd been leading two empires ever since he was a teenager! His German empire went to his brother, who became Holy Roman Emperor Ferdinand I. The Spanish Empire and the Low Countries went to his son, who became **King Philip II of Spain**— the same Philip who was married to Bloody Mary for a while.

After settling his affairs, Emperor Charles V retired to a clock-filled apartment at a monastery in Yuste, Spain. Why clocks? Because Charles had been fascinated with clocks all his life. He loved to take them apart, study their mechanisms and put them back together.

Clocks have changed quite a bit since Charles' day. For example, most of Charles' clocks didn't have minute hands. Instead, they had one dial to mark the hour, and another to mark the quarter hour. His favorite clocks also had dials to mark the movements of the moon and stars.

The Anglo-Spanish War

King Philip II was a chip off the old block. Like his father before him, he was determined to force everyone back into the Catholic Church. He couldn't force the Holy Roman Empire; for he

didn't inherit that. But he could try to force a land he did inherit: the **Low Countries**, just west of the Holy Roman Empire.

By the time Philip took over, the Reformation was strong in the Low Countries— especially in the north. The Lutheran faith had spread over from the Holy Roman Empire; and the Reformed faith of John Calvin had spread over from Switzerland (Chapter 30). Even the Anabaptist faith was strong in the Low Countries; for the great Anabaptist Menno Simons came from there (Chapter 32). All these different kinds of Protestants had at least one thing in common: none of them wanted to be Catholic ever again.

"The Low Countries" is an old name for the low-lying part of Europe west of Germany. This land is now split between three countries: the Netherlands, Belgium and Luxembourg. The Netherlands and Belgium lie just across the North Sea from England.

The people of the Low Countries speak three main languages. Dutch is most common in the north, in what is now the Netherlands. Flemish is most common in the center, in what is now northern Belgium. French is most common in the south, in what is now southern Belgium.

When Philip tried to force them, the Low Countries fought back— starting a long war called the **Dutch Revolt**. This brave rebellion started in 1566, and didn't end until 1648.

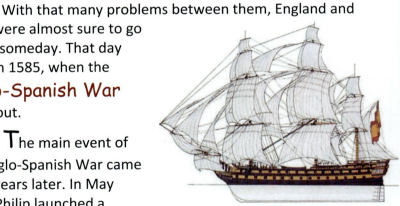

As neighbors to the Dutch, the English could hardly help being dragged into the Dutch Revolt. Why? Because whenever Dutch ships got in trouble with the Spanish, they fled to English ports. The English could have turned them away, but chose not to— partly because the English were Protestants too, and felt sorry for the Dutch. Each time an English port welcomed a Dutch ship, England drew a little bit closer to war with Spain.

The Dutch Revolt wasn't the only problem between England and Spain. There were also those English privateers we met in Chapter 33, like Sir Francis Drake. We've read how Elizabeth lied to the Spaniards, pretending that her privateers were only pirates. But the Spaniards soon stopped believing Elizabeth, if they ever believed her in the first place.

Queen Elizabeth I of England

King Philip II of Spain

There was also a third problem: the fact that Philip II wanted to make England Catholic again. It wouldn't be the first time he'd tried. Remember that Philip had been married to Bloody Mary, which meant that he had been King of England through his wife. The two of them had done all they could to make England Catholic again. But then Mary died, leaving her Protestant sister in charge. Much to Philip's dismay, Elizabeth undid everything he and Mary had done— turning England Protestant again.

With that many problems between them, England and Spain were almost sure to go to war someday. That day came in 1585, when the **Anglo-Spanish War** broke out.

The main event of the Anglo-Spanish War came three years later. In May 1588, Philip launched a terrifying weapon called the **Spanish Armada** against England. Its mission was to invade the country, tear down the government and make every Englishman Catholic again!

Part of what made the Spanish Armada so terrifying was the size of it. Philip sent about 130 ships against England, including 20 or more brand-new ones built for the occasion. He loaded his armada with about 8,000 sailors, plus another 18,000 marines— sea soldiers who specialized in boarding enemy ships and killing their crews.

An **armada** is a fleet of warships.

As terrifying as all that sounded, it was just for starters. Another 30,000 troops stood waiting for the armada in the Spanish Netherlands— a part of the Low Countries that didn't join the Dutch Revolt. Those troops were the real key to Philip's invasion plan. All the Spanish Armada had to do was hold off the English navy long enough for those troops to cross the North Sea. Once they landed in England, they would crush Elizabeth's army and take over the whole country— or so Philip hoped.

"The Spanish Armada Leaving the Port of Ferrol" by Oswald Brierly

Thanks to all her spies, Queen Elizabeth was ready and waiting for the Spanish Armada. Just before it came, Elizabeth closed all her ports— which is why Governor John White couldn't make it back to Roanoke Colony in 1588 (Chapter 33). The queen wanted all English ships to defend their homeland, whether they belonged to the navy or not!

Elizabeth also built a chain of signal towers along the English Channel, each within sight of the next. The first signalman lit his tower the moment he spotted the Spanish Armada. Then the next tower lit, and the next— until all England knew that the Spaniards had arrived.

After that, all Elizabeth had to do was fight off the Spanish Armada. It all came down to one famous sea battle: the **Battle of Gravelines**, fought in late July 1588.

Gravelines was a port in the Spanish Netherlands, just across the North Sea from England. Since the launch back in May, the ships of the armada had been separated by storms. The Spanish admiral was waiting near Gravelines for the slower ships to catch up. While the Spanish waited, the English attacked— by launching several **fire ships** against the Spanish Armada.

A fire ship was an old ship that was loaded with dry wood, set on fire and then aimed at an enemy fleet. Some fire ships were also splashed with flammable liquids like tar and pitch, to make them burn hotter. Any ship that got rammed by a fire ship was in terrible danger of catching fire itself.

England's fire ships didn't burn many Spanish ships that night. But they did do something just as important: they scattered the Spanish Armada.

The next morning, the English navy attacked the scattered armada with everything it had. Once again, the English didn't destroy many ships. But they did do enough damage to win the Battle of Gravelines. Just as importantly, the battle drove the Spanish Armada north— beyond the Spanish Netherlands.

The army that awaited the Spanish Armada in the Spanish Netherlands was divided into powerful units called *tercios.* Each tercio held up to 3,000 soldiers, including pikemen, swordsmen and musketeers.

The Spanish tercio was the terror of its day, crushing enemy armies from one end of Europe to the other. The English shuddered to think of ten Spanish tercios on the loose in their homeland.

After the Battle of Gravelines, the Spanish admiral had a tough choice to make. He had been at sea for months now, long enough to run low on fresh water and food. Ordinarily, he would have stopped at some friendly port for supplies. But now he couldn't; for the English had driven him north of the Spanish Netherlands, where there were no friendly ports. With the English navy blocking his way south, he was down to two options: either attack the English navy again, or head home. The admiral chose home.

"Defeat of the Spanish Armada" by artist Philip James de Loutherbourg

For the moment, though, the English didn't know the admiral's choice. As far as the English knew, the Spanish Armada might still attack at any moment. That idea was running through Queen Elizabeth's mind after the Battle of Gravelines, when she delivered the best-known speech of her reign.

It happened at Tilbury, a port near the mouth of the Thames River. Thousands of English troops stood waiting at Tilbury, still thinking that the Spanish might attack any time. Elizabeth rode out to talk to her troops in person, saying:

> "I am come amongst you… being resolved, in the midst and heat of battle, to live or die amongst you all— to lay down for my God, and for my kingdoms, and for my people, my honor and my blood, even in the dust. I know I have the body of a weak and feeble woman; but I have the heart and stomach of a king— and of a King of England, too!— and think foul scorn that… any prince of Europe should dare to invade the borders of my realm."

Meanwhile, the Spanish Armada was facing a far stronger enemy than the English navy. Since the armada couldn't sail south without tackling the English navy, it sailed north— planning to sail around the British Isles. Only after sailing around Scotland would it turn south, back toward Spain. The plan was to pass down the west coast of Ireland, far from the English navy.

It might have worked, if not for all the storms. It so happened that 1588 was one of the stormiest years ever around the British Isles. As the Spanish Armada sailed down the west coast of Ireland, high winds and waves blew up— sending ship after ship crashing into the rocks.

A Spanish warship being torn to pieces off the west coast of Ireland

Stormy weather wrecked far more Spanish ships than the English navy had done, and drowned far more sailors and marines. The outcome was devastating. In the end, only about half of the Spanish Armada ever made it back to Spain!

The end of the Spanish Armada didn't mean the end of the Anglo-Spanish War. The Spanish still had the biggest, richest, most powerful empire in the world. No one loss could change that, not even one as big as the armada.

Even so, it was a huge win for the English. In fighting off the Spanish Armada, England proved that it could stand up to anyone— even the mighty Spanish Empire. English power was starting to grow, while Spanish power was starting to shrink.

The end of the Spanish Armada was also a huge win for Protestants. In Catholic eyes, the invasion of England was another crusade— another holy war against the enemies of the Catholic Church. The pope himself had blessed this crusade, promising that all who died fighting it would go straight to heaven. Pope Urban II had made that same promise way back in 1095, just before the First Crusade.

With a promise like that, Catholics felt sure that God would take their side. Instead, God seemed to take the Protestant side— by turning his winds and waves against the Spaniards! King Philip II admitted his disappointment when he said:

After the defeat of the Spanish Armada, the English struck medals in honor of the "Protestant Wind" that had helped them so much. One Armada medal read *FLAVIT YAHWEH ET DISSIPATI SUNT*— Latin for "God blew with His wind, and they were scattered." "They," of course, were the ships of the Spanish Armada.

"I sent the Armada against men, not God's winds and waves."

The Virgin Queen

By the time England fought off the Spanish Armada, Elizabeth had been queen for thirty years— ever since her sister Mary died back in 1558. In all that time, many nobles had lined up for their chance to marry Elizabeth. So why had she never married?

One reason was her family history. After all, Elizabeth's own father had beheaded her own mother— which gave her an excellent reason not to trust marriage.

Portrait of Queen Elizabeth by Nicholas Hilliard

Even so, Parliament pushed Elizabeth to marry— mainly so that she could have children. If Elizabeth had children, then all would know who the next king or queen would be. If she didn't have children, then there might be wars and rebellions to decide— like the Wars of the Roses back in the 1400s. No one wanted that! For Parliament's sake, and for England's, Elizabeth spent a long time trying to find a husband.

Alas, Elizabeth could never seem to find the right man. One problem was that too many of the nobles she might have chosen were Catholic. For example, she might have chosen some French nobleman; for both France and England were enemies to Spain. But most French noblemen were Catholic; and English Protestants would have been furious if Elizabeth married a Catholic.

Another problem was that whoever married Elizabeth would automatically become King of England, at least in name. That had already happened to Elizabeth's sister Mary, with terrible results. Few Englishmen wanted another bossy foreign king like Philip of Spain!

All these problems explain why Elizabeth decided the way she did. After toying with the idea of marriage for twenty-five years, Elizabeth finally decided that she would never marry. In a way, Elizabeth said, she was already married— to England and its people! All the love and service that other women gave to their husbands, Elizabeth gave to her beloved country. The best way for England to stay strong and independent was for its queen to go unmarried all her life.

Since Elizabeth never married, she left no children to take her place. But she did leave a cousin: James Stuart, a.k.a. King James VI of Scotland. James was the son of Elizabeth's cousin Mary, Queen of Scots (Chapter 32). When Elizabeth died in 1603, cousin James became King of England too. Starting then, he was James VI & I: King James VI of Scotland, and King James I of England. See Year Three for more on James VI & I.

An English knot garden is a formal garden with hedges that are carefully planted, trimmed and colored to look like knotted strands of rope.

Elizabeth's friend Sir Walter Raleigh honored her decision to go unmarried all her life. When the east coast of North America needed a name, Raleigh called it "Virginia"— after Elizabeth, England's unwed Virgin Queen.

The Counter-reformation

Ever since Chapter 27, we've read a lot about the Protestant Reformation. It started in 1517, when Martin Luther complained that the Catholic Church had gotten away from the Bible. At first, Luther tried to <u>reform</u> the Catholic Church— which is how the <u>Reformation</u> got its name. The name "Protestant" came later, after the Second Diet of Speyer (Chapter 29).

This chapter tells how the Catholic Church answered the Protestant Reformation. The Church's answer came in two parts: the Catholic Reformation and the Counter-reformation. Since both happened at the same time, most people just use one word for both: Counter-reformation.

Oddly enough, one of the heroes of the Counter-reformation was an author who helped start the Protestant Reformation: Desiderius Erasmus. In Chapter 27, we read how Erasmus criticized the Catholic Church in two of his works (probably): "Julius Excluded from Heaven" and "In Praise of Folly." The first made a mockery of the Renaissance popes, calling them greedy thugs. The second mocked every kind of churchman from top to bottom.

Desiderius Erasmus (1466 – 1536)

Even so, Erasmus never gave up on the Catholic Church. After Luther decided to leave, he wrote letter after letter to Erasmus— trying to win the great author over to the Protestant side. But Erasmus wrote back:

"Would a stable mind depart from the [Sacred Tradition] handed down by so many men famous for holiness and miracles, depart from the decisions of the Church, and commit our souls to the faith of someone like you who has sprung up just now with a few followers— even though the leading men of your flock do not agree, either with you or among themselves?"

In other words, Erasmus thought Luther was crazy for leaving the Catholic Church! No loyal Catholic could ever set aside Sacred Tradition as Luther had. To do so would be to mock the whole history of the Church— as if the old saints were all liars, and none of their miracles ever really happened. No one who believed in Sacred Tradition could ever leave the Catholic Church, no matter how bad it got.

Instead of leaving, people like Erasmus worked to make the Catholic Church better. That was the goal of the **Catholic Reformation**: to fix problems that had crept into the Catholic Church over the years.

Some reformers worked to fix the schools that trained Catholic priests. Before the Catholic Reformation, a lot of priests knew very little about the Bible. The preaching of some priests sounded more like superstition than Christian faith. Reformers wanted better Bible training for priests.

Other reformers worked to fix the way the Church handed out important jobs. The Renaissance popes had a bad habit of handing out all the best Church jobs to their nephews, or to the highest bidder. Reformers wanted Church jobs to go to the people who were best for those jobs.

Still other reformers worked to fix monasteries. A lot of monks had grown just as greedy as the Renaissance popes. Reformers wanted monks to live like Anthony of Thebes, sacrificing themselves for their faith (Chapter 3).

The **Counter-reformation** was something else again. There were some Catholics who felt that the Church's problems had nothing to do with the Church. The real problem, they believed, was Protestant heretics like Martin Luther! Loyal Catholics refused to believe that Sacred Tradition went against the Bible. When Luther criticized Sacred Tradition, loyal Catholics only believed in it all the more. That was the thinking at the biggest church council of the Counter-reformation: the famous **Council of Trent**.

The Council of Trent started in 1545, when Catholic leaders set out to answer all the questions that came up in the Protestant Reformation. Some Protestants had high hopes for the Council of Trent. After all they had said and written about the Bible, they thought the council might admit that at least some Sacred Tradition might be wrong.

A meeting of the Council of Trent (1545 – 1563)

Ignatius of Loyola, founder of the Jesuits

Instead, the Council of Trent said that Sacred Tradition was never wrong! In Catholic eyes, Sacred Tradition was just as inspired as the Bible— just as much a part of what God wanted all Christians to believe. The council also said that Protestants had no right to use the Bible against the Catholic Church. As the one true Church of God, the Catholic Church alone had the right to decide what the Bible meant!

A Spanish priest called **Ignatius of Loyola** felt the same way. In 1534, Ignatius set up a brotherhood of priests called the **Society of Jesus**, a.k.a. the **Jesuits**. The Jesuits were the Catholic knights of the Counter-reformation. Their job was to preserve the Catholic faith and spread it all around the world.

Emblem of the Society of Jesus

With colonial times starting up, the Jesuits became the leading Catholic missionaries. Whenever a Catholic empire moved into a new country, the Jesuits were some of the first ones there. They built missions wherever Catholics went, from India and the Far East to the Americas, Africa and more.

Catholic Bibles contain a section that Protestant Bibles do not. It is called the **Apocrypha**, and it falls between the Old Testament and the New. Some books of the Apocrypha add to Old Testament stories; while other books tell different stories all their own.

One reason Protestant Bibles don't include the Apocrypha is because its books come from different sources than the Old Testament. Some of them seem to have been added to the Old Testament books by later writers.

A scene from the Book of Maccabees, part of the Apocrypha

The little round cap that so many Catholic clergymen wear is called a **zucchetto**. Medieval monks often wore their hair in the tonsure, which meant shaving the tops of their heads. For tonsured monks who spent their days in cold monasteries, the zucchetto added a welcome bit of warmth.

Map Helps

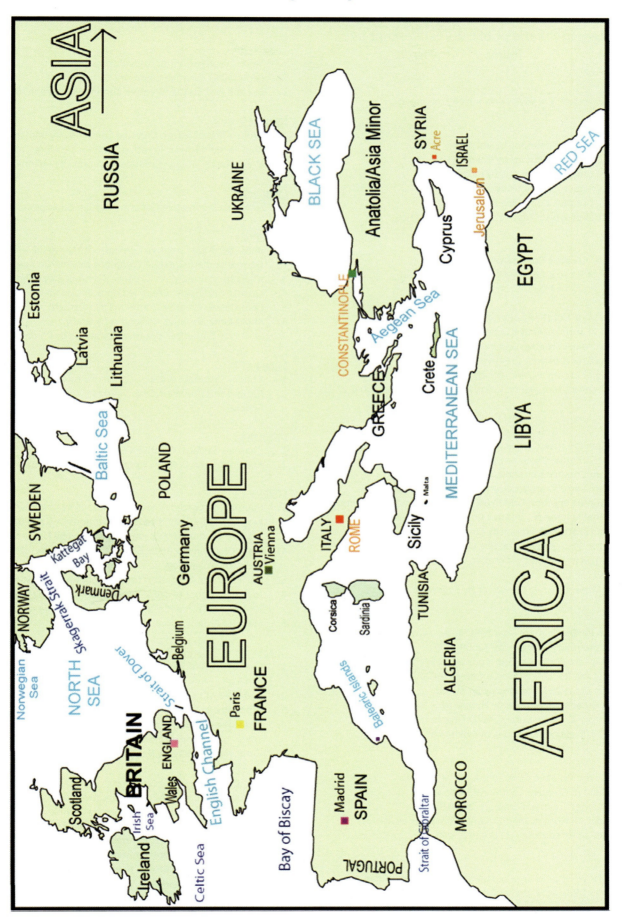

Image Credits

All images are in the public domain except as follows:

Prologue
1. Medieval scene: Creative Commons by unknown

Chapter 1
1. Galea: Creative Commons by unknown
2. Pugio: Creative Commons by unknown
3. Gladius: Creative Commons by unknown
4. Pilum: Creative Commons by unknown
5. Scutum: Creative Commons by unknown
6. Papal coat of arms: Creative Commons by Odejea

Chapter 2
1. Hauberk: Creative Commons by Urban
2. Council of Nicaea: Creative Commons by Jjensen

Chapter 3
1. Europe Map: Creative Commons by unknown
2. Shroud of Turin: Creative Commons by unknown
3. Peter's chains: Creative Commons by Raja Patnaik
4. Thomas Becket casket: Creative Commons by unknown
5. Catacomb: Creative Commons by Dnalor 01
6. St. Catherine's Monastery: Creative Commons by Berthold Werner

Chapter 4
1. Black Sea: Creative Commons by NormanEinstein
2. Balkans: Creative Commons by ArnoldPlaton
3. Justinian: Creative Commons by Petar Milosevic
4. Justinian Coin: Creative Commons by Uploadalt
5. Hagia Sophia exterior: Creative Commons by Andrey Nikolaev
6. Hagia Sophia interior: Creative Commons by Steve Evans
7. Mosaic: Creative Commons by Casalmaggiore Provincia
8. Byzantine Empire map: Creative Commons by unknown
9. Iron Crown of Lombardy: Creative Commons by James Steakley
10. Coptic Cross: Creative Commons by Sagredo

Chapter 5
1. Arabian Peninsula map: Creative Commons by unknown
2. Kaaba: Creative Commons by Tab59
3. Quba Mosque: Creative Commons by Abdelrhman 1990
4. Dome of the Rock: Creative Commons by David Baum
5. Khamsa: Creative Commons by Bluewind
6. Quran: Creative Commons by Hooperag
7. Iconostasis: Creative Commons by Fingalo
8. Icon wall: Creative Commons by unknown

Chapter 6
1. Rhine River: Creative Commons by Felix Koenig
2. King Chlodio: Creative Commons by Rinaldum
3. Notre Dame: Creative Commons by DXR
4. Gargoyles on Notre Dame: Creative Commons by Milvus
5. Gargoyle atop Notre Dame: Creative Commons by Cornellier

Chapter 7
1. Map Islamic Empire: Creative Commons by Mohammad adil
2. Umayyad Mosque: Creative Commons by Roberta F.

3. Strait of Gibraltar: Creative Commons by Xemenendura
4. Rock of Gibraltar: Creative Commons by Joe Vinent
5. Clothar coin: Creative Commons by unknown
6. Chocolate fish: Creative Commons by D. O'Neil

Chapter 8
1. Seax: Creative Commons by Bullenwachter
2. Longhouse: Creative Commons by unknown
3. Eric the Red Statue: Creative Commons by Aleph78

Chapter 9
1. White Cliffs of Dover: Creative Commons by Immanuel Giel
2. King Alfred's Tower: Creative Commons by Jurgen Matern
3. Westminster Abbey: Creative Commons by unknown

Chapter 10
1. New Forest: Creative Commons by Jim Champion

Chapter 11
1. Baltic Sea Map: Creative Commons by NormanEinstein
2. Germania map: Creative Commons by Jani Niemenmaa
3. Adelaide stained glass: Creative Commons by Kaho Mitsuki
4. Otto and Adelaide: Creative Commons by Kolossos
5. Otto statue: Creative Commons by Ajepbah
6. Khokhloma: Creative Commons by Dmfff
7. St. Basil's Cathedral: Creative Commons by Paramecium

Chapter 12
1. Middle East map: Creative Commons by Cacahuate
2. Richard the Lionheart Coat of Arms: Creative Commons by Sodacan

Chapter 13
1. Chateau Gaillard: Creative Commons by Urban
2. King John seal: Creative Commons by W.C. Prime

Chapter 14
1. Caernarvon Castle: Creative Commons by unknown
2. King Edward's Chair: Creative Commons by Kjetil Bjornsrud
3. Wallace Monument: Creative Commons by Finlay McWalter
4. Black Death in Florence: Creative Commons by wellcomeimages.org
5. Royal arms of Lancaster: Creative Commons by Sodacan
6. Joan of Arc coat of arms: Creative Commons by Darkbob
7. Joan of Arc statue: Creative Commons by Intersofia
8. Solstice: Creative Commons by Blueshade

Chapter 15
1. Coat of arms of Richard of York: Creative Commons by Sodacan
2. Red Rose of Lancaster: Creative Commons by Sodacan
3. White Rose of York: Creative Commons by Sodacan
4. Tudor Rose: Creative Commons by Sodacan
5. Tower of London: Creative Commons by Bernard Gagnon
6. Gargoyle: Art Libre by Raminagrobis

Chapter 16
1. Indo-Gangetic Plain Map: Art Creative Commons by Jeroen
2. Hindu trinity: Creative Commons by Calvinkrishy
3. Snakes and Ladders: Creative Commons by Nomu420
4. Gupta coin: Creative Commons by PHGCOM
5. Ajanta Caves: Creative Commons by Soman
6. Buddha and bodhisattvas: Creative Commons by Karthikeyan.pandian
7. Matchlock: Creative Commons by Rainer Halama

Index